How to Get *Free* Software

"An absolutely super book! A must for any computer owner on a limited budget—and who isn't? This book ought to be included with every computer sold."

—Bill Munich
Public Domain, Inc.
(Commodore software supplier)

"An incredibly well researched book. It'll easily pay for itself dozens of times over."

—Jim Button, author of PC-FILE

"Outstanding! Glossbrenner's done it again. This clearly written, in-depth study of free software is a *MUST*. Every personal computer owner will want one."

—Sheryl Nutting, President
American Software Publishing Company

"The definitive encyclopedia of public domain software sources."

—Don Wiss
President
New York Amateur Computer Club, Inc.

"I'm amazed at Mr. Glossbrenner's productivity—both the quantity and the quality! *How to Get FREE Software* is solid gold. The money saved could easily pay for a second computer (or justify the first one). This book would have saved me at least a year of my life."

—Tom Beeston
co-author, *Hooking In*

Praise for Alfred Glossbrenner's previous books,
How to Buy Software . . .

"I wouldn't consider, for a moment, buying a piece of computer software until I read this book."

—Peter A. McWilliams

"A tour de force of software and all its possibilities."

—*The New York Times*

"Glossbrenner has written the most comprehensive software guide in print today."

—Martin B. Schneiderman,
Director, Computer Education Programs
Educational Testing Service (ETS)

"This book, like the last one, is crammed with information—very solid, sensible information. Recommended."

—*The Philadelphia Inquirer*

"Glossbrenner's style and organization invariably result in bible-like compendiums of relevant information. His latest masterpiece is no exception: digestible; concise; clear; and most important, very, very useful. *How to Buy Software* is the most important contribution to a most under-represented field. Brilliant!"

—Phil Raymond,
Peripheral Vision (software evaluation firm)

. . . and for *The Complete Handbook of Personal Computer Communications*

"The first truly complete book on 'connecting your computer to the world.'"

—*Esquire*

"An invaluable guide. Highly recommended."

—Peter A. McWilliams

"This is one of the most useful books I've run across in a long time, destined to become a classic. Definitely required reading for anyone interested in getting started in personal computer communications."

—*Microcomputing*

"Extremely informative. The definitions and explanations are the clearest I've ever seen."

—*New York Times* Information Service

"Glossbrenner tells how to do it, how much it costs, and gives tips clear and detailed enough for the reader to make choices."

—*Publishers Weekly*

"I'm mightily impressed by this book. It's comprehensive and accessible to anybody at any level of computer experience, from beginner to expert. I can't imagine a better book about communications."

—*PC World*

HOW TO GET FREE SOFTWARE

THE MASTER GUIDE TO FREE PROGRAMS FOR EVERY BRAND OF PERSONAL OR HOME COMPUTER

Alfred Glossbrenner

ST. MARTIN'S PRESS · NEW YORK

The author has made every effort to check information such as shipping charges, addresses, telephone numbers, and availability of updated products, but cautions the reader that these are subject to change. Readers should verify costs and product descriptions with sources before ordering.

Library of Congress Cataloging in Publication Data

Glossbrenner, Alfred.
How to get free software.

Bibliography: p.
Includes index.
1. Computer programs. 2. Microcomputers–Programming.
3. Free material. I. Title.
QA76.6.G584 1984 001.64'25 84-13284
ISBN 0-312-39563-9 (pbk.)

Copies of this book are available in quantity for promotional or premium use. Please see page 440 for details.

To the countless men and women who have given of their time, effort, and creativity that millions of computer owners everywhere may benefit from their labor. . . .

And to the users group organizers, officers, and members who regularly and selflessly contribute their energy and knowledge to make personal computing better for all of us. By their works shall ye know them.

Contents

INTRODUCTION

Picture this. You come home from work and check the mail lying on the kitchen counter or hall table. Among the utility bills, life insurance, and free home appraisal offers—possibly buried beneath a stack of oppressively heavy, ad-stuffed computer magazines—is a floppy disk in a stiff cardboard mailer. The return address reads "The ABC Computer Users Group" of Anytown, North America.

Thoughtfully, you finger the disk mailer. Is there time before dinner? Certainly not for one of your computer marathon sessions—the ones where you blink and suddenly it's four in the morning. But . . . it wouldn't hurt to take a peek. Maybe you'll just print out a directory of the programs on the disk. Just a quick look to see what the users group has sent you.

You head for the computer room, power up, and put the disk into a drive. Moments later, a file directory is scrolling up your screen. There's some neat stuff here. There are programs in BASIC, progams in machine language, and what's this? Oh, an assembly language program. Always been meaning to learn more about that.

Eventually, as you secretly knew you would, you pick a program and run it. There is a pause while it loads in. And then the room comes alive with the sounds of music. Color graphics gyre and gimble on your screen. You press a key, and the pattern changes, as a new song begins to play.

They find you the next morning, asleep at your keyboard. The bright yellow "happy face" graphic produced by the last program still smiles at you from the screen, its expression matching the one on your face. It's been quite a session. During the night, you did the following:

- Used a FREE program to customize the layout of your keyboard, assigning characters to whatever keys you chose, regardless of the letters or numbers printed on their surface.

- Used a FREE home budget "template" with your commercial electronic spreadsheet program to finally get a handle on your household expenses.

- Displayed your expenses as a series of overlaid lines on a graph. Since that didn't look quite right, you used the same FREE program to generate a bar graph, with a solid column of color for each major category.

- Used a FREE "screen dump" program to generate a hard copy of the graph on your printer. But since graphics take a long time to print, you first activated the FREE "spooler" program on the disk that lets you continue to use your computer while the printout is taking place.

- Your work done, you decided it was time for a musical interlude. So you loaded and ran a FREE program that turned your computer keyboard into an electronic synthesizer keyboard. Once you got the hang of it, you found yourself writing short tunes and saving them to disk, then bringing them back in again to add more notes. You found you could play the same song in different tempos by pressing a few keys.

- Your last adventure of the evening was to explore a colossal cave with a FREE game program. But that may have been a mistake. Dwarves kept appearing and hurling little axes at you, and every time you assembled your diamonds, gold coins, or other treasure, the pirate would sneak up on you and swipe them. Irritated by his mocking laugh ("Har! Har! Har!"), you typed an expletive on your screen. "Watch it!" the computer shot back, and then prompted you for your next command.

Your total cost for this evening of work, fun, and games? About $6 for the floppy disk, disk mailer, and postage and handling. The programs themselves are *free*. They are yours to keep, use, copy, pass around to friends, or customize as you see fit.

FREE Programs for Every Computer—In Quantity

This brief scenario doesn't even touch, let alone scratch, the surface. There are literally *thousands* of free programs available from hundreds of sources for nearly every brand of personal or home computer. For example, there are over 3,000 programs for computers that can use or be equipped to use the the CP/M operating system—and that includes Apples, IBMs, Ataris, Commodore 64s, the Coleco Adam, and many others. And more free programs are being added every month.

There are thousands of free Apple programs, and at least 4,000 free programs for Commodore computers. A source in San Diego can supply over 2,500 programs for the IBM/PC and PCjr. There are special collections for the Atari, customized CP/M programs for the Kaypro, and a growing collection for TRS-80 models and the Radio Shack Color Computer. If you own a Texas Instruments, Osborne, or Timex/Sinclair, free software could be the best news you've heard since the manufacturers of those machines left the personal computer business. The users groups and computer clubs that support those brands are stronger and more determined than ever, and the flow of free software continues unabated.

Practically every computer on the market has a well-established or rapidly growing library of free software associated with it. The Macintosh and its technology are new, but Apple users groups are among the strongest and most numerous in the country, and there is no question but that the Mac will soon be well supplied with free programs. There are indications that Coleco has great plans for its new Adam system, including a CP/M option, a floppy disk drive, a Coleco modem, and the possibility of running MS-DOS, the generic version of the IBM/PC operating system. As other computers are announced and shipped, they too will attract users groups and become the stimulus for free programs.

Something for Everyone

The world of personal computing is so varied that few statements apply equally to all computer owners. Free software is an exception. Whatever your interests, whatever the reason you purchased your computer, you will find something of value in the libraries of free programs available for your machine.

Games, graphics, music, voice synthesis, puzzles, educational software—it's all here. You will also find crucial convenience programs and "utilities" that are not available anyplace else. And you'll find free programs that will make your commercial software more powerful and easier to use.

Of special note are the "productivity" programs available for nearly every brand of machine. These include word processing software, communications programs, database management, VisiCalc-like spreadsheets, accounting, billing, mailing lists, and inventory control. There are checkbook balancers, home budget programs, stock and investment portfolio managers—the list of useful free programs goes on and on.

Not all of the available free programs are exceptional, of course, and you cannot always count on finding a free program to meet your every need. But some of the free software available for nearly every machine is unquestionably of professional quality and can more than hold its own with any commercial product in the same catagory.

Admittedly, this runs contrary to everything one would assume about a high quality product: "If the stuff's so good, why didn't the author try to sell it?" In point of fact, some of them have. More than a few free programs started out as commercial products. But many more of them were written by computer professionals or skilled hobbyists in their spare time. For philosophical reasons, or simply because they did not want the hassle of "going commercial," many of these individuals have contributed their work to the public domain instead.

If you are a new computer owner, this is especially important. At the very least, good free software can reduce the total cost of entering the microworld. But it may also enable you to equip your system with more memory, more power, and more peripherals than you could afford if you had to sink hundreds of dollars into commercial programs. If you have yet to buy a computer, the availablity of free programs can be an important factor both in your budget considerations and in your decision about which brand to buy.

Where to Get It

Free software is available to everyone, but you have to know where to look for it. If you're on your own, that can be something of a challenge. For example, the quickest, easiest way to obtain free programs is to join a local computer users group or club. Many of these all-volunteer organizations maintain large libraries of public domain software that can be easily copied onto a disk or tape cassette. But while there are hundreds, perhaps even thousands, of users groups in North America, there may not be one in your area.

Fortunately, many of the larger users groups will accept "remote members" who join and obtain free software by mail. But, although you may be able to find a list of users group addresses, there is usually no way to tell a large group from a small one from address information alone. What's more, computer users groups tend to come and go with such frequency that a significant percentage of the addresses on any list are guaranteed to be out of date.

Free software is also available from commercial firms, often as a public service adjunct to their regular business. Most of these companies do not advertise, and those that do quite understandably spend their alloted space promoting profit-making products or services instead of featuring their free software collections.

Free software is also available "online," and if your computer is equipped to talk on the telephone, you can instantly obtain just about any program you want. But again, you have to know where to look. There are thousands of free programs on the CompuServe system, for example, but there is virtually no way for most people to learn of their existence other than to stumble upon them by accident. Nor are there any instruction manuals to step you through the process of obtaining free software from the hundreds of free computer bulletin board (BBS) or remote CP/M (RCPM) systems in North America. And, like some users groups, BBS and RCPM systems tend to come and go.

So what can you do? Short of writing to every users group and dialing every bulletin board phone number, how can you find the best sources of free programs for your machine? The answer is simpler than you might imagine. It lies in the realization that the world of free software is a *network* made up of many diverse elements. If you know how to plug into this network, the appearance and disappearance of individual users groups, bulletin boards, and other sources makes little difference. You will always know about the latest and best free software for your computer, and you will always know how and where to get the programs you want.

How to Get Free Software: Points of Access

This book will show you how to plug in. Chapter 1 will bring you up to speed on the network itself, the kinds of programs that are available, the conventions that are followed, and the techniques that will help you obtain programs as easily as possible. Chapter 2 will introduce you to what is probably the largest single free software collection in the microworld, the vast public domain of free CP/M programs. To help you get a handle on this embarrassment of riches, the CP/M Gems List highlights what many experts feel are the key programs that every CP/M user should have.

Chapter 3 offers an introduction to computer users groups, the natural focal points for free software. You'll find tips on how to locate a group in your area, but you'll also find profiles of what we have called Super Groups. These are large, thriving organizations that are important sources of free software for every brand of computer. They offer ideal points of access to the rest of the free software network, and can lead you to other groups, whether small, large, or "super."

If you use a commercial spreadsheet or database management program, such as VisiCalc®, dBASE II®, Multiplan™, or Lotus 1-2-3™, you'll find valuable information on how to get free templates and command files in Chapter 4. There are also points of access for CBASIC users, MS-DOS users, "Forth fanatics," and others interested in free programs designed to be used with commercial products. Chapter 5 will put you in touch with what might be called machine-specific Super Groups. Some of these organizations have tens of thousands of national and international members, and all have extensive free software collections.

The companies and other non-user group sources profiled in Chapter 6 are another important part of the free software network. In fact, some of them serve as "libraries of record" where no single users group has emerged to fill that role. Some have even prepared instruction manuals or otherwise improved the public domain programs they offer. Other services are available as well.

Chapters 7 through 10 will show you how to plug into the online free software network through telecommunications. You'll learn how to equip your computer to talk on the telephone and how to explore the nooks and crannies of CompuServe and The Source. If you know where to look, you can find more than enough free software on these systems to justify the cost of a subscription many times over. In Chapter 10 you'll learn how to get the most up-to-date bulletin board phone numbers and how to use the often challenging (but exceedingly rich) RCPM systems.

Chapter 11 focuses on the remarkable number of top quality free programs available for the IBM/PC, PCjr, and IBM-compatible computers. The chapter also explains Freeware™ and Shareware, two distribution methods that are largely unique to the IBM world. Chapter 12 uncovers a number of important but somewhat obscure sources that even long-time users group members may never have heard of.

Appendix A concentrates on what may be the most significant program to come out of the public domain—the XMODEM binary file transfer protocol. First embodied in a CP/M program, it has since become an important feature for any communicating computer, whether it's an Atari, an Apple, or an IBM. It is not essential to know how XMODEM works, but it is increasingly important to have XMODEM capabilities if you want to obtain free software over the phone. Appendix A explains the protocol and provides a list of commercial and free software programs that offer XMODEM support for nearly every brand of computer.

Although you will probably have your hands full running all of the free software that is available for your machine, it can be important to be aware of the growing trend toward cross-machine compatibility. With the add-on products described in Appendix B, Apple owners can use a large percentage of the free CP/M and free IBM/PC programs described in this book. Owners of IBM machines and compatibles can run Apple programs as well as those in the CP/M library. The same is true of Commodore 64 owners. Kaypro owners can have access to IBM software, and Atari and TRS-80 owners can run CP/M. Many other "switcheroos" for other machines are considered as well. The Appendix concludes with a Quick Guide to CP/M. This is for new and prospective CP/M users and is intended to make it easier to take advantage of the CP/M Gems List presented in Chapter 2.

Whether you are interested in one of these options right now or not, we strongly recommend that you review Appendix B before purchasing additional hardware of any sort. This is especially important for Commodore 64 owners interested in acquiring a floppy disk drive. The drives Commodore supplies are unusual to say the least. The more conventional Commodore-compatible disk drives described in Appendix B may cost slightly more than Commodore equipment, but they can improve the performance of your computer *and* make it much easier to obtain and use free software.

Appendix C presents the names and addresses of the SIG/M distribution points. As you'll see, SIG/M (Special Interest Group/Microcomputers) is the library of record for the thousands of free CP/M programs. All of this software is available directly from SIG/M's New Jersey headquarters. But in most cases, you will be able to obtain it faster if you contact one of the distribution points listed here. There are distribution points in 24 states and 9 foreign countries.

Finally, throughout the book you will find numerous "FreeTip" boxes. Some of them contain suggestions and ideas or nonvital elaborations on the subject at hand. Others provide brief explorations of side issues or numbers and names of people to contact for more information. Some are addressed to more experienced computer users or individuals interested in certain technical information. And some offer hands-on information designed to make it as easy as possible to obtain, use, and enjoy the many free programs that will be available to you once you plug into the free software network.

FreeTip: At some point you're probably going to need to mail cassette tapes or floppy disks, and it probably goes without saying that they must be protected. Cassettes don't pose much of a problem, but a kink or a crumple in a floppy disk can spell disaster. Although "two-packs" of floppy disks have recently begun to appear in discount, drug, and department stores, you may have difficulty obtaining the stiff cardboard envelopes designed to accommodate a floppy disk.

The easiest solution is to make one of your own. Cut a piece out of a cardboard box that is slightly more than double the size of the disk. Fold it in half and sandwich the disk in between. To prevent the disk from slipping out, tape the three open sides of the cardboard folder shut, then put it in a manila envelope of the appropriate size.

If you find yourself mailing a lot of disks, it may be worthwhile to buy a box of disk mailers. Here are four places that can supply them. Most accept Visa and MasterCard, and will send you a free catalogue of computer supplies.

FreeTip continued

Misco
404 Timber Land
Marlboro, NJ 07746
(800) 631-2227
Package of 10:
$12.95 (8-inch)
$11.95 (5¼-inch)

Inmac
2465 Augustine Drive
Santa Clara, CA 95051
(213) 852-0973
Package of 10:
$15 (both sizes)

NCR
P.O. Box 550
Centerville Station
Dayton, OH 45459-9900
(800) 543-4833
(800) 762-6517 (in Ohio)
Package of 50:
$67.50 (8-inch)
$47.50 (5¼-inch)

Calumet Carton Company
16920 State Street
South Holland, IL 60473
(312) 333–6521
Package of 100 (minimum order):
$19.10 (5¼-inch)

How to Get *Free* Software

...1...

Free Software!
Background and Basics

The affordable microcomputer is only a few years old, but already the term "personal computer revolution" sounds like yesterday's news, not tomorrow's. As well-worn as the phrase may be, however, we have yet to feel the full effects of the phenomenon it describes. In years to come, when these machines are as common as color television sets—and just as easy to operate—the personal computer revolution may be seen to be as consequential as the invention of movable type.

That probably seems like an odd way to begin a book about free software. But the comparison is not as far-fetched as you might imagine. In reality, the disk drive is nothing less than the new printing press, and floppy disks are the new media. This fact has implications for all of us, since it means that anyone with between $500 and $1,000 to spend on a system can write, "publish," and distribute *anything*. Whether you're a poet or a polemicist, you don't need a multimillion-dollar printing press to put your works into an easily distributable form.

And if you're a programmer, you don't need the backing of a major software house to produce and distribute your creations. You can write whatever you want. If you're happy with what you've created or think it is something other computer owners will find useful, you can copyright and sell the program as a commercial product. It may not make you rich, but then again, it very well may.

In more than one instance an independently written program has been responsible for putting a child through college or putting a new car in a part-time programmer's garage. As with any small business, selling the software you have written from your home can be tremendously exciting. But it is not for everyone.

"In the Public Domain"

Many individuals who write personal computer programs have no interest in trying to sell their software, whether directly to the end user or to a software publishing house. Most have full-time jobs and do their programming at night and on the weekends as a hobby. A significant percentage are computer professionals who spend their days wrestling with giant mainframes and find it refreshing to deal with a self-contained system like a microcomputer. But there are also college students and kids, bankers, store clerks, and businessmen, writers, doctors, lawyers, stock brokers, and educators—the personal computer revolution has touched them all, and all of them have written programs.

Most important, rather than let their software sit on the shelf, thousands—even tens of thousands—of them have relinquished their copyrights and contributed their works to the "public domain"—whereupon anyone may copy or distribute that software to anyone else. The one thing you may not do is sell the program at a profit. As with commercial software, programs are provided "as is." But unlike commercial software, the user does not pay a fee, and the author does not supply printed documentation or support. In other words, when you are considering free software, "What you see is what you get."

This is not meant as a negative statement, either. Some free programs are as good as or even better than software you would pay hundreds of dollars for at a computer store. And the on-disk documentation (text that you can print out on your printer) supplied with some programs puts many commercial products to shame. It is simply important to emphasize that public domain software is not a commercial product and you should not expect all of the "extras" that you find (and pay for) when buying software at a store.

The Question of Support

Having said that, it is also important to point out that a considerable amount of support *is* available to users of many public domain programs. Many authors include their addresses and phone numbers at the beginning of a program, and most will be happy to answer your questions. Naturally it is important not to abuse this privilege. You should always read the documentation thoroughly and make a good faith effort to solve a problem on your own. But if you're really stuck, you may very well be able to ask the person who wrote the program for help.

Users groups and computer clubs are another important source of support, as we'll see in Chapter 3. You can also use your computer to seek help in using your computer. The electronic "information utilities" described in Chapters 8 and 9 are marvelous resources and contact points for computer owners of every persuasion.

You will certainly encounter programs that are indecipherable to all but the most dedicated computerists. These tend to be very specialized, however, and unless you're a computerist yourself, it is not likely that you'll have much need of them. In many cases, even if you're a brand new computer owner, you won't need support or outside help in running free programs. Many free games include introductory instructions. And even the more complex "serious" programs like the free word processors and filing programs can be used with very little effort. This is partially because some of them do not contain all of the whistles and bells found in some commercial programs, and partially because they may have been written by people like yourself who may be somewhat more aware of how the average user approaches a program.

The Importance of "Plugging In"

This book will give you the specific information you need to plug into the world of free software. We'll show you where to look for free programs, how to obtain them, and how to contribute something of your own. If you're a new user, you'll be glad to know that many of the best sources of free software are also the best sources of information, help, and assistance in using your machine. If you're an experienced user and you're only vaguely aware of free software, you're in good company. Many of the people we've spoken to report that they are frequently contacted by computer owners with years of experience but virtually no familiarity with the public domain.

FreeTip: Writing in the March 5, 1984 issue of *InfoWorld*, columnist Doug Clapp says:

"It's amazing how many people haven't heard of public domain software. But then I'm sure ComputerLand employees don't go out of their way to tell customers: 'That package is $700, but you can get one just as good (for free) through a users' group.'

In many cases you can get good software for virtually nothing. To find a users' group, ask somebody at a computer store (even the salespeople will usually 'fess up) or look through your stacks of computer magazines."

Regardless of your level of experience, once you plug into the network, an endless stream of tips and tricks will flow your way. You'll also be privy to information that for one reason or another your computer manufacturer has not made available. Commodore, Apple, IBM, TRS-80—every machine has its secrets, and often many hours of hard work and experimentation are required to pry them loose. As a member of the computer community, you'll have access to all of them as they are discovered.

FreeTip: The following example is IBM-specific, but discoveries of a similar nature have been made for almost every machine. The Phoenix, Arizona, IBM/PC users group reports that members have discovered at least three undocumented commands in IBM BASIC 2.0. You won't find it in your BASIC manual, but if you use SHELL "DOS Command" in a program, the system will go out to DOS to execute the command and then return to BASIC. Used by itself, with no specified command, SHELL will take you to the DOS shell. To return to BASIC, type *EXIT*. [The other commands are *ENVRION "name=(parameter)"* and *IOCTL channel #, "argument."*]

What Kinds of Programs Are Available?

The short answer is that virtually every category of commercial program has a free software equivalent. The two best-represented categories for all brands of computers are utilities and games. Utilities are short, limited-focus programs designed to make working with your computer easier and more productive. The CP/M collections are particularly strong in this area. For example, there are an untold number of "expanded disk directory" utilities that will give you more information about what's stored on your disk than the DIR command supplied by the operating system itself. Similar programs exist for many non-CP/M computers. Other utilities, like the CP/M programs known as WASH or SWEEP, make it especially easy to deal with disk files. These programs will present each file on a disk one at a time and allow you to enter a command to erase, print out, copy, rename, or work some other bit of magic. Again, similar programs exist for many non-CP/M machines.

There is another class of utility program likely to interest serious programmers. A typical example is a program capable of displaying the contents of a disk on the screen one sector at a time. (If you don't know yet what a sector is, you're not ready for one of these babies.) A person with the proper knowledge can then directly alter the contents of a disk by changing individual bytes of information.

Just about every free software collection for every machine has its share of utility programs. Utilities are usually written to make up for some feature not offered by a computer's operating system or hardware. As IBM/PC users know, for example, there is no way to tell when the keyboard's SHIFT-LOCK has been engaged. The first you learn that you've accidently turned it on is when you are typing and nothing but capital letters appear on your screen. Consequently, someone has written a utility program to display a little indicator arrow on the upper left corner of the screen.

There are programs that improve upon or replace WEDGE for the Commodore 64, and at least one program that creates a keyboard "type-ahead" buffer for Apple computers. Similar machine-specific utilities exist to "correct" problems with most other machines.

> **FreeTip:** Utility programs are particularly valuable because they are often available *only* as free software. Usually it does not pay for a commercial software house to expend its resources on simple little programs of this sort. But such a program can be like a rubber band: It may be relatively insignificant, but when you need one, you need one, and nothing else will do.

Game programs, like utilities, tend to be machine-specific. Atari and Commodore computers, for example, are particularly well suited to producing the color displays and sound that make for an exciting game. Many public domain programs take advantage of these features. Other games are text-based—the action takes place mainly in your head as the computer responds to the commands you enter. Versions of these games and games that use a very simple display are available for many brands of computers.

On the more serious side, we will show you word processing programs that range from simple text editors to sophisticated commercial-quality programs loaded with extra features. Database management or filing programs to help you keep track of everything from your record or recipe collection to the employees at your firm are also popular. The same is true of mailing list progams and mailing label generators. Communications programs to enable your computer to talk to another computer on the telephone are major items in most free software libraries.

Graphics, accounting, home budget, personal checkbook, stock portfolio analysis, music composition—programs like these are available for nearly every brand of computer. In some instances you will find complete computer languages. There is a Logo program for IBM computers, a PILOT language for CP/M machines, an implementation of Forth for the Atari and many other computers, and a wide selection of other languages for these and other machines. The cornucopia is pointed in your direction.

> **FreeTip:** Of particular note are the growing number of spreadsheet templates, dBASE II command files, and Lotus worksheets. These are explained in Chapter 4, but you should know that if you use a spreadsheet program, dBASE, or Lotus 1-2-3, you're in luck. As more managers and professionals use these programs, more

FreeTip continued.

and more templates and command files have begun to show up in the public domain.

You don't have to know any computer languages to create a SuperCalc or VisiCalc spreadsheet. You simply have to know how to use the program. Once created, the same spreadsheet template can often be used by owners of otherwise incompatible computers. Since a template or a command file consists of simple text, it can be used by anyone who owns the master program. This can greatly expand the number of free programs available to you. The only trick is getting the template or command file recorded on a disk that your machine can read. This can almost always be done through telecommunications. (See Chapters 7 through 10.)

Is There Free Software for Every Machine?

Yes, unless the model of computer you own is very new. Generally, the number of free programs available for any computer depends directly on the number of people who own and use it or the operating system that it runs.

The IBM PCjr, the Apple Macintosh, and Coleco's Adam are three examples of new computers. Since virtually all of the free software available for the IBM/PC will run on the Junior, people who buy this machine have a ready library of free programs available to them. The same relationship does not exist between the Macintosh and its predecessors in the Apple line. The Mac is built around a different microprocessor chip, uses a different operating system, and requires a different kind of disk. As free programs become available, you will be able to use many of the same access points suggested for other free Apple software. But some time will be required before the number of Mac owners reaches the free software "critical mass."

FreeTip: That critical mass has already started to form in the Washington Apple Pi (WAP) users group. In March of 1984, WAP announced the formation of a Macintosh Special Interest Group, a Mac newsletter, and a Mac telephone hotline. As an interesting side note, when Steve Wozniak, the man who designed the Apple computer, introduced the Mac at WAP's January 1984 meeting, 2,500 people showed up to look at the new machine. Membership in WAP is $25 a year and is open to anyone. Contact:

Washington Apple Pi
8227 Woodmont Avenue, Suite 201
Bethesda, MD 20814
(301) 654-8069

As the first computer of its kind, the Adam starts from ground zero on the free software scene. Built around a Z80 microprocessor, it has the basic capability of running the CP/M operating system, and there are indications that this option will be made available. A floppy disk drive to augment the Adam's built-in tape system is also a virtual certainty. When available, these two options will give Adam owners access to the CP/M software collection, undoubtedly the largest library of free programs in the microworld. We understand that an online, electronic special interest group devoted to the Adam is planned for the CompuServe system (see Chapter 8), and this is sure to be an excellent source of free Adam software.

FreeTip: Taylor Barcroft, a man whose experiences with the Coleco Adam were featured in the *Wall Street Journal*, has formed the First Southern California Adam Users' Group. The group's newsletter is called "The Garden of Adam," and a sample issue is available for $1.50. This is certain to be an excellent contact point for free Adam software as it is written. For more information, write to:

Mr. Taylor Barcroft
Adam Users of America
P.O. Box 599
Venice, CA 90294

How Good is the Free Stuff?

Some of it is very, very good. Some of it is fair to midlin', and some of it is not likely to be of use. One could say the same about the current crop of movies, record albums, and books. The difference is that no one is asking you to pay money for public domain software.

You must be the judge. Without question, everyone will find something of value in the public domain. But as one software librarian commented, "One man's chaff is another man's kernel. I've had people ask for programs that are known to be faulty. A lot of them say, 'I've always wanted to get in there and fix something.'" And many people do just that.

Indeed, if you are interested in programming, free software can provide a wonderful learning experience. Unlike most commercial software, the vast majority of public domain programs are "listable." That means you can print out and review the program itself and see how its author accomplished (or failed to accomplish) a particular goal. This can alert you to interesting techniques or save you from making similar mistakes. And in some cases it can teach you more about BASIC, Pascal, assembler, and other languages than many textbooks can.

It can also provide you with an opportunity to make your own contribution. Even the best programs can be improved, or endowed with more features and power. One famous example of this is the well-known CP/M communications program called MODEM7. This program started out as MODEM several years ago, but because it is in the public domain and because it was a good program to begin with, dozens of people have incorporated new features and produced new versions that are also in the public domain. Can you imagine dozens of artists, writers, or musicians collaborating in a similar manner over time, each of them producing a version of a work that is generally agreed to be better than the one that preceded it? This kind of cooperative effort is something quite special and unique to personal computers and the public domain.

When you read about free software elsewhere, you are liable to hear the lesser programs described as "trash" or "garbage." Less polite words are used as well. Certainly everyone is entitled to an opinion, but it is our feeling that few, if any, free programs deserve this description. Even the most bug-ridden program is of value to someone, and all of them represent hours of somebody's labor, however unskilled.

Besides, this outlook does not match what we've experienced in the course of running many different free programs on many machines. There are game programs that you might run once to see what they're like and then never run again. There are utilities that you are not likely to use. And there are programs of such narrow focus that they would be of interest only to left-handed steam fitters. But we have yet to find a program that can legitimately be called garbage. And we have found (and noted in the appropriate chapters) many real gems.

What Are the Most Frequent Problems?

In many cases you won't have any trouble at all. You will be able to run a free program as easily as you run a commercial one. Although there are some exceptions, users groups and other sources of free software usually check every submission they receive at least once before adding it to a collection. There may not be time for a thorough test, but at least the program will run.

The problem you will encounter most often, regardless of the machine you own, is a lack of good "error-trapping" and "error-recovery." These are software industry terms that refer to how the program responds when you do something that the program is not prepared to handle. If the author has forgotten to disable all but a limited selection of keys, for example, hitting a key outside of the available choices can cause the program to "lock up"—stop dead in its tracks. Sometimes a program will fail to work properly if the disk is not in drive A (or 0 or 1).

These are just a nuisance, not major problems. Good error-trapping can require a great deal of extra work, since it means that the programmer must anticipate almost every eventuality and include programming to deal with it. Because many public domain authors do not take this step, you will probably have to be more careful about following the supplied instructions than you would with a thoroughly error-trapped commercial product. If you do this, a large percentage of the time the program will run with no problems.

> **FreeTip:** If the program you are using fails to respond when you enter a menu selection or command, try entering it again in upper case. Many authors fail to include the necessary instructions that will allow their program to accept either capital or lower case letters. This is true even on machines that can produce both types of letters. If you like, you can usually correct the problem yourself by adding the necessary code to the program.

All computer programs have bugs—little quirks or twists that can cause them to malfunction or otherwise fail to perform as they should. (This is as true of commercial products as it is of the public domain.) Sometimes a bug will be quite serious. At other times a bug can be so obscure that only an unusual combination of events will bring it to light. If you never chance upon that combination, you'll never have that problem. A bug in a game program does little serious harm. A bug in a word processing or file management program will usually be fairly easy to spot.

But with relatively complex accounting, budgeting, financial and mathematical programs, it is only prudent to proceed with an extra measure of caution. Give the software a thorough workout using test data and verify the results by some other means before you completely trust the answers it gives you.

There is another problem that is not so much a problem as it is a restriction. The majority of public domain programs will run on whatever is considered the basic or "standard" configuration for your brand of computer. But some require special peripherals. A program designed for use with the Texas Instruments voice synthesizer is an obvious example. Less obvious are programs that have been "configured" to run with an Epson printer, a Hayes modem, the "old" version of the Apple serial card, or the color graphics adapter on the IBM. Some of these programs can be "reconfigured" to work with different equipment, but many cannot. Fortunately, the catalogue abstracts that describe this kind of software will usually alert you to any special requirements.

The least obvious restrictions of all concern the program's relationship to the computer's operating system. For example, a program that incorporates features found only in IBM/PC DOS 2.0 may or may not work with the previous, less feature-filled versions of that operating system. Some CP/M programs require CP/M 2.2 or 3.0 and will not work with Version 1.4. The reverse may also be true.

Other programs "go outside the operating system" to perform certain tasks. An operating system like MS-DOS or CP/M is designed to insulate a program from the quirks and special requirements of a computer's hardware. As long as a program tells your operating system to turn on the disk drive, scroll the screen, send a file to the printer, or perform some other chore, there will be few problems. The version of the operating system that runs on your computer has been customized to match your hardware. Every program must be written to run under the control of a particular operating system, and as long as the program lets the operating system handle the hardware, it can usually be run on many different machines.

To make their programs run faster or perform better, however, some authors write software that bypasses the operating system and takes direct control of the hardware. The result is a program that is highly machine-specific. These programs will not run on a different computer or computer model even if the operating system is the same. Here again, the catalogue abstracts and descriptions will usually alert you.

"Talking" directly to the hardware can be a very difficult programming task. Consequently, most public domain programmers stay within the operating system and produce software that is very "transportable." This is particularly good news if you own a "clone"—like the IBM-compatible Compaq, the Apple-compatible Franklin, the TRS-80 Color Computer-compatible Dragon, or some other machine. A large percentage of the free software for the "parent" machine will run on your equipment as well.

Finally, there is the problem of "media compatibility." Some programs are available only on cassette tape, and some exist only on disk. If you have a disk drive, a cassette tape is usually just a minor inconvenience. Since most machines are equipped to accept tape input, often you need add only a cable and a tape recorder.

FreeTip: To encourage you to "keep it in the family," many manufacturers make it all but impossible for you to use anything other than their own brand of tape recorder with their computers. But if there's one thing most families don't need, it's yet another tape recorder around the house. Particularly one that's incapable of playing the Police, Bowie, or the Beatles.

This is where a little investigation (and a third party manufacturer) can help. For example, instead of purchasing the Commodore Datasette (list price, about $75) for your VIC-20 or C-64, you might want to buy an adaptor cable and "interface" that will let you use your own tape recorder. These sell for about $40. With the money you save, you'll be able to get a clutch of cassette tapes containing free software.

One such third party manufacturer for Commodore equipment is Cardco, Inc. Similar products exist for most other machines; you just have to look for them. For more information on the Cardco product, contact:

Cardco, Inc.
313 Mathewson Avenue
Wichita, KA 67214

FreeTip: If you do not have a disk drive, you will not be able to take advantage of disk-based programs—unless you have a friend with a drive who can "dump" the contents of a disk into your tape recorder. Since this can be a time-consuming process, it is often better to make contact with someone at a users group meeting and arrange to meet privately than it is to do it at the meeting itself.

An even easier alternative is to look for the program from a different source. You may find that one of the access points in this book can supply software on tape that others make available only on disk. You may also find the program you seek on a computer bulletin board (Chapter 10) or in a Special Interest Group database on the CompuServe system (Chapter 8). In either case, you will be able to download (capture) it directly into your tape-based machine.

The other media compatiblity problem concerns floppy disk formats. This is usually not much of a factor with free software written to run on a particular brand of machine. Perhaps the most important exception to this is the matter of single- and double-sided disks in the IBM world. The original PCs were equipped with single-sided drives, but the PCjr and most other IBMs today have double-siders. A double-sided drive can read a single-sided disk, but this does not work in reverse. Most IBM free software is made available in a single-sided format, but there are some exceptions, so be sure to check.

Disk formats are much more of a factor when you are dealing with operating system-specific software. The prime example here is the vast

CP/M library. These programs will run on the literally hundreds of brands of personal computers that use CP/M as their "native operating system" (the operating system supplied by the computer manufacturer). As you will see in Appendix B, they will run on many more machines—like the Apple, the IBM, or the Commodore 64—that have been equipped to run CP/M. The problem is that there are 95 to 100 different ways to store these programs on a floppy disk, and it sometimes seems that every computer manufacturer uses a different format.

There are many ways to get around this problem. There are "downloading" firms that specialize in transferring programs and data to disks in many different formats. Many of them can supply free CP/M software on a disk that can be read by your machine. These and other solutions are explored in Chapter 2.

FreeTip: Some sources supply software on "flippy" disks. You should be aware that *all* disks are double-sided, regardless of what the label on the box says. The difference is that only one side of a "single-sided" disk has been subjected to a quality control inspection by the manufacturer. A flippy disk contains the equivalent of one single-sided disk on each side. As its name implies, you can use one side of such a disk, remove it and flip it over, put it back in the drive, and use the other side.

To transform a standard disk into a flippy, use a quarter-inch paper punch or an X-ACTO® knife to cut a duplicate write-protect notch opposite the one found near the top of the disk. With some machines you may have to punch a matching "index" hole as well.

Because they provide two disk sides' worth of programming for the price of one, flippies are an inexpensive way to distribute free software. However, it is always best to transfer the contents of the flip side to a regular disk as soon as possible. Most disks have built-in dirt filters that work well as long as the disk always spins in the same direction. Flipping a disk over causes it to spin in the opposite direction and that can sometimes shake loose dirt and particles trapped by the filter.

Techniques for Obtaining Free Software

As mentioned earlier, every source of free software has its own way of doing things. One may ask you to send a disk, for example, while others prefer a check to cover expenses. In some instances, you can even place your order over the phone and charge the cost to a major credit card. We've presented the specific procedures to follow in each case. But there are some general things to keep in mind.

The most important thing to remember is that a large percentage of free software sources are volunteer organizations. Although many of them will surprise you with how quickly they fill your request, you can not necessarily expect the same rapid response a commercial firm may provide. Some sources *are* commercial firms, however, and are thus better equipped to mail out the software you request (see Chapter 6).

Because so many organizations are staffed by dedicated people who donate their time, anything you can do to make things as easy as possible for them will be greatly appreciated. A self-addressed, stamped envelope should accompany all of your correspondence, even if it isn't required.

If you are asked to send a disk, be certain to take a moment to format it first, and enclose a slip of paper or a note indicating that you have done so. This requires very little effort on your part, but it can save someone responsible for filling scores of free software orders hours of time. When you mail your disk, make sure that it is adequately protected either in a disk mailer or in a cardboard folder like the one described in the Introduction.

A 5¼-inch floppy disk, disk jacket, and a typical cardboard disk mailer weigh about two and a half ounces. At the postal rates current at this writing, that means you'll need 54¢ in postage to send it via First Class mail. The Post Office will gladly accept three 20¢ stamps, of course. Some disk mailers are heavier than others, however, so it can pay to check. If you think the package might weigh more than this, live a little: add an extra stamp.

Whenever a source requests a disk, you will always be asked to include a self-addressed, stamped disk mailer as well. If you are using a manila envelope and a piece of cardboard, enclose a second envelope with the correct address and return postage. If you are using a disk mailer, enclose several stamps and your address on a pressure-sensitive label. In most cases it is not necessary to pay the freight on two separate disk mailers.

Some non-user group sources ship by United Parcel Service (UPS), so you will want to make sure you use a UPS-acceptable address. PO, APO, and FPO box numbers are not acceptable.

If you are requesting shipment abroad, air mail delivery is recommended. Be sure to include instructions to that effect, along with proper postage. If you live in a non-English speaking country, you should definitely type (or take *extra* care when hand printing) all addresses and correspondence. In addition, almost without exception, sources that ship abroad require payment in United States funds, drawn on a United States bank. If MasterCard, Visa, or American Express credit cards are accepted, we have indicated as much in the descriptions of free software sources.

The First Step: Send for a Catalogue

In some cases, software is available only by the "volume." A "volume" in computer terms is a "standard" floppy disk formatted to hold a certain number of kilobytes of data and programming. Except in the CP/M world, the actual standard usually depends on what most of the people who own a particular brand of computer use. There is usually no need to get technical; you can think of a volume as a diskfull of programs. The important thing to know is the number given to the volume that contains the program you want. Other sources make free software available by the program. Here you will be able to order programs by name or by the number the source has assigned to each one.

Most sources offer some form of catalogue that lists the free programs in the their libraries and tells you what you need to do to obtain them. As you might expect, the catalogues vary widely in quality and depth of coverage. At the low end of the spectrum are the single sheets of paper containing nothing but volume or disk numbers and program names.

At the high end are the wonderful 100-page "books" of CP/M software published by the New York Amateur Computer Club (NYACC). These sell for $10 and provide elaborate descriptions, reviews, and printed documentation for virtually every available free CP/M program. (See Chapter 2 for information on how to order.)

Most catalogues fall somewhere in between. The most common practice is to supply a table of contents for each disk volume in the collection. This will include the name and number of the disk and the filename of each program on the disk followed by a one-sentence description or "abstract." Sometimes there will be a small ($1 to $3) charge for a catalogue.

The first thing you should do is order whatever catalogue your chosen source offers. This will not only tell you what is available from that source, in many cases it will give you valuable information about specific public domain programs. Although there are few "governing bodies" to oversee such things, many programs have unique names. And because public domain software circulates freely, these names will show up in more than one catalogue. However, different software librarians may emphasize different program features. For example, one description of a program called, say, BLACKJACK.BAS might read: "Standard blackjack game. Good color graphics." Another description of the identical program, available from a different source, might read: "Fast play. Many features—double down, buy insurance, etc." You may end up obtaining BLACKJACK.BAS from a third source, but these two descriptions can help you decide whether you want the program.

To help you get started right away, we have highlighted specific programs throughout the book and supplied the relevant volume number, program number, and program name. If one of these programs is of interest, you can use this information to place your order immediately. Be sure to request a catalogue, however, when you place your first order.

A Word about Pricing . . .

Although it has not stopped some disreputable companies from doing so, public domain software is not to be sold. At the same time, there are legitimate expenses associated with distributing free programs. And, as the saying goes, thereby hangs a tale. Anyone can charge whatever they want to cover the costs of distribution. Consequently, prices for a given item of software can vary depending on the source. Wherever possible, we have noted these discrepancies and provided information on the lowest cost alternative. Prices are current as of this writing, but all prices are subject to change, of course.

There is no official governing body to enforce uniform pricing policies. But in most cases, prices vary within a relatively narrow range. A typical 5¼-inch disk filled with free programs will usually cost between $6 and $10. This includes the disk, the disk mailer, and postage and handling. The same range applies to 8-inch disks. Cassette tapes may be slightly higher.

These prices apply to fixed volumes of programs, for which a distributor simply duplicates a master disk and mails it out. If the software is made available by the program, the price will usually be higher. The International 99/4A Users Group (Texas Instruments computers), for example, charges $3 per program and requires a minimum order of four programs. The International PC Owners (IBM computers) charges $3 per program plus $6 for the disk. Despite their names, both of these organizations are profit-making concerns. But by assembling customized disks of free software, they provide a service not available from most volunteer users groups.

Some sources offer "best of" collections as fixed volumes. Others offer public domain programs that they have improved somehow—by adding color, sound, and other features, by locating and fixing bugs, or by preparing additional documentation to make a program easier to use. As a general rule, any time someone puts extra effort into preparing or distributing free software, the cost will be slightly higher.

FreeTip: Why do many users groups charge $6 for a 5¼-inch disk of free software? Here's a rough breakdown to show you where your money goes:

FreeTip continued

$1.50—for the disk
.25—for the disk mailer
.05—for the label
.40—for postage
$2.20

This is probably on the low side. To obtain a good-quality floppy disk at that price, a group must order 800 to 1,000 at a time. That's a considerable investment, so many groups buy in much smaller quantities—and pay more per disk.

Some portion of the remaining $3.80 will go to repair and maintain the disk drives used in the distribution process. Some of it will be earmarked to help build and maintain the program library and to finance software exchange programs with other groups. And some of it will be used to support the users group's other activities. There is at least one IBM group that uses the money generated by software distribution to support the free computer courses it offers at local colleges and schools.

How Can You Contribute a Program?

There isn't a users group in existence that isn't interested in obtaining more public domain software for its library, and many people are interested in contributing. A number of amateur programmers have successfully used the public domain as a springboard to a full-time job with a commercial software house. As one authority we spoke to said, "A lot of times a guy will write a couple of quick little programs just to get his name known and then use that recognition to get a job with a major firm." Another authority said, "The smart software companies keep a sharp eye on the public domain. They are sort of like Hollywood talent scouts. I know of at least two programmers who were 'noticed' as a result of their public domain work and invited to go to work full time."

Reports in the *Wall Street Journal* and other publications have indicated that the demand for professional computer programmers will far exceed the supply for many years to come. If this is of interest to you, the public domain could be your entrée. In any case, it is a good reason to sign your program and to consider providing an address or a phone number where you can be reached.

You'll find specific suggestions on the kind of program you might want to write, and information on how to submit it to various groups, elsewhere in this book. As a rule, though, you should really wait until you have spent some time poking around in the public domain and become familiar with its conventions. Whether you're writing science fiction, romance novels, or computer programs, you can't expect to be successful if you don't know the territory. Some users groups will take anything that comes their way, but many are becoming more selective.

Free Software, Fun, and the Future

The public domain can be an awful lot of fun. Your fellow programmers have created everything from posters of nudes in repose to complete billing systems suitable for a small business. Others have produced programs that will play tunes, draw pictures, or turn the cursor into a tiny twirling baton. Literally anything goes.

To a computer owner and user, entering the public domain is like a stroll through New York's Central Park on a warm Sunday afternoon. There are guitar players and jugglers, singers, acrobats, dancers and mimes. Over here someone is doing magic tricks with a piece of string. Over there someone is standing on a plastic milk crate holding forth on some serious issue. As Sheryl Nutting, an eloquent lady you will meet in Chapter 6, commented, "The public domain is a collection of literally tens of thousands of hours of experimentation with the computer. Taken as a whole, it is a database of computer technique. The programs may or may not solve your problem, but by golly they will show you what that computer can do. It is a bubbling, burgeoning cauldron of uncontrolled experimentation, and it is absolutely marvelous.

"I've been involved with computers since the time when they were vacuum tubes, when you had to plug in wires on the front panel to enter a program. And I have never seen anything so exciting. People do things with these machines—older people, children, office workers in their spare time—that you just don't see anywhere else. *I* never knew a computer could do some of these things. But I have learned from the creativity and free expression of others."

Many of the programs already available are quite good. Many can save you time and money, while others will provide hours of enjoyment. And the thousands of free programs available today represent only a fraction of what will be available in years to come. There has never been a better time to "plug in." The remainder of this book will give you the points of access you need to do exactly that.

...2...

The Vast Public Domain of CP/M®: *Thousands of FREE Programs for Hundreds of Computers*

CP/M® is the monarch of the public domain. The duchies and earldoms ruled by others are quite large, but none is as vast and as rich as the territory presided over by this operating system from Digital Research, Incorporated (DRI). Best of all, nearly every computer can run these programs, even if CP/M is not the machine's native operating system. Indeed, according to some authorities, there are more CP/M-running Apples than any other single brand of computer. An IBM/PC, an Atari, a Commodore 64, and many other computers can also be equipped for CP/M. (See Appendix B.)

There are today over 3,000 free, public domain CP/M programs. Or there are 5,000 . . . or there are 10,000. No one knows the exact number. All anyone can say for certain is that the existing libraries are huge and that they are growing every day.

Actually, once the number of programs in a public domain library passes the 1,000 mark, it doesn't much matter what the real total is. The opportunities and the challenges presented are of the same order of magnitude, namely, How in the world can you wade through so much software to find the free word processors, the free database management and mailing list programs, the dBASE II™ command files and other accounting packages, the free communications programs, and the ocean of free games, music, and educational programs that will suit your needs? And once you've identified them, how can you obtain them most conveniently and for the lowest possible cost?

These are the questions we'll consider in this chapter. With the help of some leading experts in the field, we have put together the CP/M Gems List to give you the names and descriptions of what are considered to be among the very best free CP/M programs. If you're curious, you might jump ahead and take a quick look at it right now. At the very least, you'll find one or more programs that are "must haves."

Depending upon your needs, you may even discover that you can build a powerful personal software library using only public domain CP/M programs.

Although not as convenient as buying a program from a computer store, obtaining free CP/M software is much easier than you might imagine. There are *many* sources other than the SIG/M (Special Interest Group/Microcomputers) and CPMUG (CP/M Users Group) libraries that are inevitably (and usually exclusively) cited in most books and magazines. Indeed, while CPMUG will sell you its programs, the software is available only in a limited number of disk formats. And the volunteers at SIG/M confirm that they view their role as a "repository of record" and would really rather you obtained the actual software from someone else. As we'll see, there are some excellent reasons for doing so.

Any Computer Can!

If you're a new computer owner or someone who is just considering buying a system, you probably have your hands full assimilating a large amount of new information. You may have heard about operating systems, for example, and the incompatibility that exists among them and the computers that use them. You may even view this fact as the single piece of solid ground on which you can stand as you confront the flood of buzz words and technotalk that swirls around you. Well, at the risk of ripping away your foundation and casting you headlong into the flood, it isn't true.

As we said a moment ago, virtually every computer on the market today can be equipped to run CP/M, or any other operating system for that matter. Only two things are required: a microprocessor chip on a plug-in card or cartridge, and a disk containing the operating system itself. If your computer already has the necessary chip, as is the case with a machine like the TRS-80 Model 4, then you need only the CP/M disk. If you own a Commodore 64, running CP/M will cost you $50 to $70 and a trip to your local K-Mart for the Commodore CP/M cartridge and disk package. If you own an Apple, an Atari, an IBM/PC, a TRS-80 Model III, or virtually any other machine, boards and disks are available to convert your computer to CP/M. (You'll find important tips and guidelines for making the conversion in Appendix B.)

The Bad News/Good News About Public Domain CP/M Programs

CP/M was the original microcomputer operating system, and it dates back to the days when a puny 8K of memory cost 400 pre-inflation dollars and floppy disk drives were the stuff of dreams. That was "way back" in 1975. If you owned a computer then, not only was it not enough to simply know where the on/off switch was located, more than likely you had to solder it into place yourself. If you wanted to write programs, you had to have an intricate knowledge of how the hardware was wired up and what effect your software would have upon it.

This is no longer true, of course. But there is still a very strong "hobbyist" orientation to the CP/M public domain, much more so than with almost every other collection of free software. There is also a strong programmer's influence. Many items, for example, were written by programmers *for* programmers, often as an exercise or tour de force. In short, when you enter the CP/M public domain, you are expected to bring with you a certain amount of knowledge about computers and programming. If you don't happen to be so equipped, the folks you meet here will be more than happy to answer your questions. But you can not assume that every program you obtain will be extensively documented (though some are) or that it will run without some programming customization on your part (though many will).

That's the "bad news" about public domain CP/M software. The good news is that the result will be worth every ounce of effort you put into it. For, as one famous computer game might write on your screen: "There are diamonds here." In return for your effort, you will find software that will save you money, save you time, and make using your computer more fun (and productive) than you ever thought it could be. You may even become so skilled that you decide to contribute a program or two yourself.

In the meantime, you may have a little work to do to bring yourself up to speed. Perhaps the most effective step you can take is to immediately join a local users group. Some groups focus exclusively on CP/M and many more have subgroups called SIGs (Special Interest Groups) for that purpose. Here you are likely to find not only the knowledge you need but all of the available software as well. Equally important, you will find individuals who will be happy to guide you and give you a hand when you run into trouble. To locate your nearest group, you might contact the appropriate individual on the "SIG/M Distribution Points" list in Appendix C. Or you might get in touch with one of the "super groups," local organizations, or other "points of access" cited elsewhere in this book.

There are also books that can help. *How to Buy Software* by Alfred Glossbrenner (St. Martin's Press, 1984), for example, was written because the author could find no other book that "put everything together" in a convenient form. Like a certain breath mint (or is it a candy mint?) *How to Buy Software* is really two books in one. Its Foundation section is designed to present the background information a computer owner needs to *understand* a personal computer and to confidently evaluate the software that makes it run. By providing a large chunk of computerdom's common body of knowledge—information many people acquire only in scraps and pieces over a period of years—*How to Buy Software* can help you start life in the microworld much higher on what professional educators like to call "the learning curve." Other chapters offer the specifics of what to look for when buying a commercial package—which may also be of value when you must choose among several similar free programs.

FreeTip: If you are new to CP/M, or if you own an Apple, Commodore, Atari, IBM/PC, or some other computer and are considering equipping your machine to run CP/M, please look at the "Quick Guide to CP/M" section of Appendix B. This section is designed to give you the information you need to have in order to understand and appreciate the free programs on the Gems List later in this chapter.

Here are three more books to look for:

CP/M Primer
by Stephen Murtha and Mitchell Waite
Howard W. Sams & Co., Inc.
4300 West 62nd Street
Indianapolis, IN 46268
(150 pages; $16.95)

This book starts you right at the beginning, as any primer should. In what can only be seen as a humorous touch, the first illustration on the first page presents a rounded square of blue and is titled: "Fig. 1-1. Blank crt screen." Chapters progress in a logical manner from hardware and software concepts, to starting up CP/M, through the use of the system's various modules. The CRT illustrations are frequent and informative, and there are just the right number of cartoons for visual relief.

The CP/M Handbook
by Rodnay Zaks
Sybex
2344 Sixth Street
Berkeley, CA 94710
(320 pages; $14.95)

Written by Zaks, with the aid of Tony Bove and others, this book is the classic work in the field. It is considered a "must have" by nearly all CP/M users. There are CRT screen and other illustrations, and rather more command examples than in the *CP/M Primer*. The book also goes into more detail about the various parameters one can attach to a CP/M command and generally covers the operating system in greater depth. Only major complaint: The index is too perfunctory to be of much help.

Osborne CP/M User Guide
by Thom Hogan
Osborne/McGraw-Hill
2600 Tenth Street
Berkeley, CA 94710
(286 pages)

This is the most technically oriented of the three. Mr. Hogan offers many examples of the use of CP/M commands and parameters. But he also discusses computer languages and provides welcome clarifications and examples on the use of assembly language, including routines for modifying the BIOS (Basic Input/Output System) portion of CP/M. This is not the book to start out with, but as you progress through the world of CP/M, you will find yourself turning to it again and again. The book has an excellent bibliography citing relevant articles through 1980.

The CP/M Libraries of Record

Over the years, two central collection points for public domain CP/M software have emerged. One is called SIG/M (Special Interest Group/ Microcomputers) and the other is called CPMUG (CP/M Users Group). Both are on the East Coast. In the West, groups like PICONET (P.O. Box 391566, Mountain View, CA 94039-1566) and the CP/M Users Group Northwest (1346 NE 28th Street, Portland, OR 97322) serve as major collection points. Other large groups in the U.S. and Canada are also involved, as is the network of RCPM systems (see Chapter 10) that spans the continent. One way or another, though, virtually all public domain programs eventually find their way to SIG/M and CPMUG.

This is fortunate, because both organizations place the programs on standard 8-inch, single-sided, single-density floppy disks called "volumes." Both periodically publish lists indicating which programs are on which volumes. By early 1984, for example, CPMUG had issued 93 volumes, while SIG/M had no fewer than 172 volumes in its library.

FreeTip: Unlike 5¼-inch disks, there *is* a standard 8-inch disk format. It was developed by IBM for the firm's 3740 key-to-disk data-entry system, and thus is known as the "IBM 3740" standard. Eight-inch disks meeting this standard are single-sided, single-density and are formatted into 77 tracks, each of which consists of 26 sectors. When formatted and filled to capacity, these disks hold 241 kilobytes of information. This quantity of information is what constitutes a "volume" in the CP/M public domain, regardless of how many 5¼-inch disks of different formats are required to hold it.

The good thing about this system is that the CPMUG and SIG/M volume numbers are used as master references throughout the CP/M public domain. The bad thing is that there is little correspondence between these two lists. Things are complicated by the fact that at least 20 CPMUG volumes (Volumes 55 through 77) are *re-issues* of selected SIG/M volumes. Interviews with officials at both SIG/M and CPMUG indicate that little communication takes place between the two organizations. To add to the confusion, there is a third organization that anyone interested in public domain software must know about. This is the New York Amateur Computer Club (NYACC).

Let's see if we can't sort all this out with a brief explanation of each organization and how it fits in. Then we'll give you the steps to follow to obtain free CP/M software most efficiently.

CPMUG

The CP/M Users Group (CPMUG) was founded in New York in 1977 by Tony Gold, with the cooperation of CACHE (Chicago Area Computer Hobbyist Exchange). CPMUG never held meetings for users, but it served as a collection/distribution point for public domain software. Digital Research and other companies assisted in establishing the group's initial library. *InfoWorld* quotes Mr. Gold as saying, "People would send in diskettes, and we would copy the software onto them. In the end, it began to take up a large piece of free time."

In 1978, Mr. Gold brought CPMUG under the umbrella of his software firm, Lifeboat Associates. And that is where it is located today. Due to a long hiatus between the issuing of CPMUG Volumes 90 and 91, many CP/Mers elsewhere in the country have gained the impression that CPMUG is either defunct or will no longer issue new volumes. But Ms. Anna Ramos, the individual responsible for CPMUG inquiries at Lifeboat, confirms that CPMUG is still very much alive and intends to continue its traditional role. Ms. Ramos points out that Volumes 91 through 93 were issued without long delays. The hiatus was due to a shortage of personnel and other, more pressing demands.

A catalogue containing the filenames and a one-line description or "abstract" of each program in the CPMUG collection is available for $10, postage included. For overseas orders, the cost is $15. All orders must be prepaid and in U.S. funds. To get a sense of what you can expect to find in the CPMUG catalogue, please see Figure 2.1.

Figure 2.1. Excerpts from the CPMUG Catalogue

This is a typical listing, in this case for Volume 35. It is intended as an example only, since we have edited out many of the other filenames on the disk. The single sentence descriptions are called "abstracts."

CP/MUG VOLUME 35

FELIX—GRAPHICS ANIMATION SYSTEM—with pseudo assembler, etc.
See ABSTRACT.35

NUMBER SIZE NAME COMMENTS

-CATALOG.035 CONTENTS OF CP/M VOL. 35

ABSTRACT.035 Abstract of disk contents

35.1 2K BEE.FAS Source code for a cartoon about a bee and a bird.
35.2 10K BEE#.FEX Executable bee story, with background and objects.
35.4 4K CHECKOUT.FAS FELIX pseudo-machine diagnostic program.
35.5 8K CLEAR.ASM Start of FELIX source code.
35.6 1K CREATE.ASM FELIX source code.
35.7 1K DISPONOF.ASM FELIX source code.
35.8 1K DISTEST.FAS Demo of distance operator, joystick rescaling.
35.9 5K DISTEST&.FEX Executable DISTANCE TEST.
35.10 11K DISTPLUS.ASM FELIX source code.
35.11 14K DOODLE.ASM FELIX source code.
35.12 1K DOODLE.COM OBJECT DRAWING UTILITY.
35.14 1K EXEC.COM PSEUDO-MACHINE INTERPRETER.
35.15 2K EXEC.OBJ The pseudo-machine (loaded by EXEC.COM, TRACE.COM).
35.16 9K EXECPLUS.ASM FELIX source code.
35.18 10K FANCY#.FEX Same as 'PAINTER&' but with a pretty background.
35.20 1K FCBMOV.ASM FELIX source code.
35.23 1K FELIX.COM INITIAL SETUP ROUTINE.
35.24 7K FELIX.DOC SOME DETAILS ABOUT THE SYSTEM.
35.25 3K FELIX.OBJ The 'actual' base routines (loaded by FELIX.COM).
35.26 3K FELIXV1.CAT Author's original volume catalog.
35.27 2K GETF.ASM FELIX source code.
35.30 2K LOADBACK.COM Utility for getting backgrounds from disk.
35.31 2K LOADOB.COM Utility for getting objects from disk.
35.34 2K MUSTANG.FAS Cowboy jumps on a horse as it rides by.
35.35 6K MUSTANG&.FEX Executable cowboy story.
35.39 1K PAINT.FAS Source code for a simple painter. Needs joysticks.
35.40 1K PAINT.FEX PAINTER for use with your own objects.
35.53 2K SAVEBACK.COM Utility for saving backgrounds to disk.
35.57 1K SPIN.ASM FELIX source code.

Ms. Ramos says that CPMUG can supply its software on disks in five different formats. In addition to the standard 8-inch format, disks are available for the Apple II, the Kaypro II, the Epson QX-10, and the North Star. The software is priced by volume. A single volume on an 8-inch disk costs $13. A single volume on 5¼-inch disks costs $18, regardless of how many actual disks are required to accommodate it.

Asked about the most popular disks in the collection, Ms. Ramos indicated that Volumes 47 and 84 are quite popular because they contain MODEM7 software (explained in Appendix A). Volume 57 is also frequently requested because it contains *Adventure* and several similar games. (Note that CPMUG Volume 57 is the same as SIG/M Volume 11. This was one of the re-issued volumes mentioned earlier.)

For more informaton, contact:

CPMUG
1651 Third Avenue
New York, NY 10128

SIG/M

The first personal computer, the MITS Altair 8800, came out in 1975. In April of that same year Sol Libes, a professor of electronics at Union County College in New Jersey, founded the Amateur Computer Group of New Jersey (ACGNJ). The ACGNJ, Inc., is a non-profit organization that is and always has been a real users group. It is a strong and active club that, among other things, founded the country's first computer festival. Held each April at Trenton State College, the Trenton Computer Faire is still one of the largest, best-attended regular get-togethers in the country.

SIG/M is one of the special interest groups that exists under the ACGNJ umbrella. As its literature points out, it is "devoted to the gathering of public domain software, editing and compiling the volumes and distributing them via the SIG/M distribution network. Although volumes may be ordered directly from SIG/M, we strongly recommend that users obtain copies from the distribution point nearest them. SIG/M volumes may be copied at meetings of these groups. The usual donation is $1/volume (recipient supplies disk). . . . We welcome additional distribution points."

You'll find a summary of the SIG/M distribution points in Appendix C of this book. There are very good reasons for obtaining your software from these places instead of directly from SIG/M. First, as an all-volunteer organization, SIG/M cannot be expected to provide a rapid turnaround on orders it receives. Thc individuals responsible do their best, but you may have to wait a month or more to receive the disk you want.

Second, SIG/M makes its software available *only* on standard 8-inch disks. But many of the distribution points may be able to supply the same material on 5¼-inch disks formatted for your machine. (There are other ways to obtain SIG/M software in the disk format you need, and we'll tell you about them in a moment.) The cost per volume is $5 if you do not supply your own disk. If you order by mail, add $1 shipping and handling for the first disk and 50¢ for each additional disk. For foreign shipment, add $4 for the first disk and $1 for each additional disk. (U.S. funds drawn on a U.S. bank, only.)

Like CPMUG, SIG/M periodically publishes catalogues containing filenames and one-line descriptions of the programs in its various volumes. These, too, are available from your nearest distribution point. The cost is $1.50, $2 if mailed in the United States, and $2.50 for foreign shipment.

Again, we have been asked to emphasize that if at all possible you should obtain SIG/M software through one of the distribution points. If this is not possible, follow the prices and shipping charges cited above. You can contact the group at:

SIG/M
Box 97
Iselin, NJ 08830

The New York Amateur Computer Club (NYACC)

The NYACC is a large group that maintains a very close relationship with SIG/M and the ACGNJ. Often the actual volumes distributed by SIG/M are edited and produced by the New York group. The NYACC's most visible role in this field, however, is the publication of "books" that more fully describe the programs in SIG/M volumes. By early 1984, there were seven such books, each more than 200 pages long, and each reproducing all of the documentation files found on a range of both SIG/M and CPMUG disks.

The NYACC books free you from the bother of printing out the documentation yourself. But, more importantly, they offer an excellent way to identify the free programs you want. With an average of several pages of documentation per program, they are much more informative than the simple one-line descriptive abstracts shown in Figure 2.1. Of special value are the chatty paragraphs describing many of the programs. These are written by someone known only as ZOSO, and they can give you the real "inside scoop" on which programs to order (or search for on an RCPM system) and which are probably not worth bothering with. (Book 2 also contains an alphabetical index of all programs in the CPMUG library up to Volume 52 and those in the SIG/M library up to Volume 42.) In short, the NYACC books are essential reading for anyone with a serious interest in the CP/M public domain.

Here is a summary of the software volumes covered by each book:

	SIG/M	*CPMUG*
Book 1	1–18	1–49
Book 2	19–42	50–54, 78, 79
Book 3	43–60	—
Book 4	61–76	80–84
Book 5	77–104	—
Book 6	104–106	—
Book 7	106–107	—
Book 8	108–136	85–92 (Coming soon.)

(Note: The reason for the strange CPMUG numbering in Book 2 is that CPMUG Volumes 55 to 77 are re-issues of SIG/M's 1, 2, 11, 4–10, and 13–25 and thus are included in Book 1 under their SIG/M headings. Books 6 and 7 have as many pages as the others, but they focus on Richard Conn's briliant ZCPR2 replacement module for CP/M's Console Command Processor. This program begins with Volume 98. The documentation for Volumes 104 and 106 is split between two books.)

Each of these books is available by mail from the NYACC. The cost is $10, shipping in North America included. (Allow six to eight weeks for delivery.) For overseas orders, the cost is $15, airmail shipping included. All orders must be prepaid in U.S. funds. The club also offers special volume discounts (no pun) to organizations wishing to sell its books at the same price. The club makes available the disks at meetings to its members only.

The place to contact is:

New York Amateur Computer Club
P.O. Box 106
Church Street Station
New York, NY 10008

FreeTip: If you want to stay on top of what's happening in the CP/M public domain, the newsletter published by the NYACC is "must" reading. As Don Wiss, the club's president, points out, "Our newsletter contains some other articles, but its main focus is public domain software. Each month we announce and describe the

FreeTip continued

new additions to the SIG/M library, as well as programs contributed to PC/Blue, our growing IBM/PC collection."

The newsletter is sent to all NYACC members, and membership is $15 a year. Contact the club at the address given above.

Steps to Follow to Get Public Domain CP/M Software

There are three major problems that anyone who wants to tap the CP/M public domain must solve. The first is finding out what's available. The second is deciding what you want. And the third is obtaining it in a disk format that is compatible with your particular machine. In most cases you can solve all three problems at once by joining a local users group with a CP/M library. In many cases, the listings and abstracts and the NYACC books, as well as the complete SIG/M library, will all be there for you. In addition, you will be able to ask more experienced users for their recommendations on what you should have and for their help in transferring the software to a disk for your machine. If you do not know of a group near you, you'll find lots of names and addresses in Chapters 3 and 4. You might even want to start with one of the SIG/M distribution points listed in Appendix C.

If you do not live near a group, Appendix C is the first place to turn. All of the individuals and organizations listed there as distribution points will have the SIG/M catalog with its program abstracts. They will also have the complete SIG/M library and may be able to advise you on which programs to choose. Though not official distribution points, some of the other individuals on the list will have both the library and the catalogues as well.

Look over the catalogues to determine which SIG/M volumes seem most interesting. Pay particular attention to the newer volumes, as these often have upgraded and improved versions of programs issued on earlier volumes. SIG/M is a true library of record. Programs are rarely removed, even if newer software supersedes them.

At this point, there are several roads open to you. If your machine can run standard IBM 3740-format 8-inch disks, you can simply order the volumes you want from one of the distribution points. If you are in doubt or need more information, you can order the appropriate book of documentaion and descriptions from the NYACC. If you cannot use 8-inch disks, however, there are some other approaches you must take. Indeed, you may find these avenues attractive, even if you have no disk compatibility problems.

FreeTip: If you are a new owner you may not yet have experienced the exquisite (some would say "damnable") complexity of incompatible floppy disks. After all, they all look alike, right? Well, yes. But while a floppy disk for an IBM/PC and one for a Kaypro II may be physically identical, once they have been formatted they are as different as Apples and Otronas. Unfortunately, all too often there is a simple reason for this: It is a deliberate attempt on the part of computer manufacturers to lock you into their format, making it impossible for you to use a disk not formatted on one of their machines. There is even at least one major computer manufacturer that deliberately does not provide a formatting program with its version of CP/M or MS-DOS, forcing you to buy blank disks from them at about $10 apiece.

You'll find more information on how a disk is actually formatted and how this influences compatibility in Chapter 5, "The Media and the Message," of *How to Buy Software.* For now it is enough to know that nearly every computer formats its disks differently and that obtaining free software in the format your machine can read can be something of a challenge.

Dealing with Disk Formats

As you will learn in Chapter 7, one way to transfer programs to the disks you need is through telecommunications. Many of the best programs in the public domain are available either in the database section of the CP/M SIG on CompuServe or on RCPMs (Remote CP/M systems). These alternatives are fine when you are going after programs of relatively modest length, but "downloading" major pieces of software and all their associated files and documentation does not make sound economic sense in most cases. For what you would pay in long distance or CompuServe connect-time charges, you could probably buy a complete SIG/M volume containing many more programs.

FreeTip: If you have a friend with the programs you want and both of your machines are equipped for communications (see Chapter 7), then the two can be cabled together and the transfer can take place that way. Remember, though, if you have added a CP/M board to your Apple or other computer, the communications software you run to download CP/M software must be CP/M-based. Otherwise the file created when you record the download to disk will probably be in a format that your CP/M cannot read.

FreeTip continued

Connecting two communicating computers together also requires a "null modem" cable to fool the two machines into thinking that they are talking to a modem. You may be able to find such a cable at a computer store, but you can also order it through the mail. One especially good source of all kinds of communications-related cables, plugs, and other devices is the Black Box Corporation. A free 100-page catalogue is available, and the firm accepts all major credit cards for phone orders. A null modem cable sells for about $20, plus 25¢ a foot. Or you can buy single null modem adaptor plugs for about $27. Contact:

Black Box Corporation
P.O. Box 12800
Pittsburgh, PA 15241
(412) 746-5530
8 AM to 8 PM (EST)

Disk format incompatibilities are so prevalent in the microworld that a number of firms have been established to offer conversion services. In the trade, as it were, this is known as "downloading." Originally such companies had to own a separate computer for each format that they offered. But new machines and software have been developed that give a single computer the power to read a disk formatted for one computer in one drive and transfer the information to a second disk formatted for a different computer in a second drive. Thus, you could purchase a SIG/M 8-inch disk and send it in to have it copied onto a disk in your format. (Check the classified ads and the back pages of computer magazines for names and addresses.)

Usually there's a better way, however. A number of these companies have obtained the complete SIG/M library, and for a modest fee they will download the volume of your choice onto a disk in your format. In some cases, these companies can offer a faster response time than a users group. But there may be an added benefit as well. Some of the SIG/M volumes contain only one genre of software, but most are decidedly mixed. Thus if you want to obtain all of the available games, utilities, or communications-related programs you would have to buy several SIG/M volumes in each case. In recognition of this problem, a number of downloading firms have assembled collections containing the most important SIG/M programs in a given category on a single disk.

FreeTip: This is a special note to Commodore 64 owners. At a discounted price of about $50 you can give your machine the ability to run many of the same CP/M programs that any other computer can run. At this writing only a few sources offer CP/M software in the Commodore disk format, however. This may change, of course. In the meantime, telecommunications may be your best alternative. With a CP/M-based communications program you can dump CP/M files directly into your C-64 from another computer, from an RCPM, or from the CP/M SIG on the CompuServe system.

One program worth considering is BUFTERM, a terminal program for CP/M-running C-64s. Written in assembly language by John Teloh, this program was announced in February of 1984. Ask for "Release 2," the version of the program that offers XMODEM support. (For more details, see Appendix A.) The cost is $45, plus $2 shipping and handling. MasterCard and Visa, accepted. To order, contact Mr. Teloh by CompuServe E-mail (74275,1154) or at this address:

Quantum Software
Suite 31-B
5252 NE 6 Avenue
Ft. Lauderdale, FL 33334
(305) 776-7421
6 PM to 10 PM (EST)

Seven Firms to Consider

We've located seven firms that provide these kinds of services. The following list is by no means comprehensive, but each of the companies has something unique to offer, and all are worth considering.

Elliam Associates
24000 Bessemer Street
Woodland Hills, CA 91367
(213) 348-4278

Bill Roch, Elliam's founder and president, has done an impressive job of assembling program collections and interesting little bits of business to aid the CP/M user. The firm also offers most major commercial CP/M applications packages as well as many interesting programs you've probably never heard of. If there is a complaint to be made, it is that the placement of text wherever it will fit in the catalogue often results in a lack of separation between the two categories. So read carefully.

It will be worth the effort, though, since there are some good things here. (See the Gems List later in this chapter for more information on the programs cited.) There are collections of directory, catalogue, and disk utility programs. There are two disks of financial software, including the complete Osborne accounting collection. There are disks containing all the master and related files for some 14 languages (ALGOL, the complete JRT Pascal, FELIX, EBASIC, and more). All of the math-teaching programs are on one disk. There are six disks of games and one with 15 versions of *Star Trek*. BusinessMaster II is available in a five-disk package. The complete 10-volume ZCPR collection is available, as is a smaller 2-volume set. And more.

If you like, Elliam will even build you a customized disk containing just the SIG/M and CPMUG programs you want. The cost is $1 per 10K, plus $4 per disk. Many of the public domain programs that are available only in the C (formerly BDS C) and Pascal-Z users group libraries are here as well.

We have not mentioned the cost yet because the prices require a bit of explaining. The catalogue listings for each item or collection quote the price for a standard 8-inch disk. A single 8-inch volume with data on one side is $10. If both sides are required to accommodate the collection, the cost for the disk is $12. Prices for 5¼-inch disks are based on the number of kilobytes each format will accommodate.

To take but one example to give you an idea of the range of prices, the disk utility collection (FINDBAD, DU, CRC, and more) is 230K and sells for $12 in the 8-inch format. If your disks can hold over 250K, the price is the same. If they hold between 125K and 249K, the price is $14. And if they hold less than 125K, the price is $20.

Over 35 different formats are available, including IBM, DEC Rainbow, Sanyo, and Zentec. The only major computer formats Elliam does not supply at this writing are Apple and TRS-80. The formatting is handled by Mr. Roch's special software, so if your format is not on the Elliam list, Elliam may be able to duplicate it if you send him a blank, formatted disk. Call first, of course. And be sure to send for the free catalogue. MasterCard and Visa are accepted.

MICOM Software
304 North 17th Street
(206) 428-0475

In addition to offering the complete SIG/M and CPMUG libraries, Lee Hillard of MICOM also has the complete PICONET and Pascal-Z library. And thanks to his DISCON computer, he can provide volumes from each of these collections in over 100 different formats. The only major exception is Apple. (But if you own an Apple, don't despair. See the MICROCOMP listing below.) Although the prices may change, the cost per volume is $10 on orders of fewer than five volumes, plus $2 for shipping and handling. There is no shipping and handling on orders of five or more, and the price drops to $9 per volume. The lowest price is $7 for twenty or more volumes in the same format. Lower prices may be available: "Please order by volume number. And please contact us if you desire other options such as furnishing your own formatted disks or formatting our disks (which saves us time and you money.)" (The entire SIG/M library through Volume 144 is available in toto for $950, a cost of $6.60 a disk.)

Mr. Hillard has also prepared a disk containing the catalogue directories and abstracts of the CPMUG and SIG/M libraries. The cost is $10 each, plus $2 shipping per order. These disks include the public domain program FIND to let you search the entire disk for keywords. Entering *MODEM*.**, for example, will generate a list of all the MODEM programs and their volume numbers. This can save you from poring over the closely printed abstracts in the paper catalogues. Really a nifty idea.

MICOM has another unique feature. With your approval, the firm will automatically send you the latest public domain volumes as they are released by their respective users groups. The cost is $7.50, billable to your major credit card. As an important side note, Mr. Hillard is an expert dBASE II programmer. His firm offers a number of reasonably priced products, including a dBASE II RunTime™ disassembler, that will be of interest to anyone who uses that database management program.

MICROCOMP
Toronto RCP/M Systems
4691 Dundas Street West
Islington, Ontario M9A 1A7
(416) 239-2835

Jud and Colleen Newell's organization has quite a bit to offer. As the Canadian distributor for all major users groups, MICROCOMP has more than 500 volumes of software available, including not only CP/M, but MS-DOS (IBM/PC DOS) and programs from the C Users Group as well. As the firm's brochure points out, "There are now over 9,000 programs and files in the various user group libraries. Similar programs are scattered on many different disks. . . . With this in mind, we have put together the following collections of programs. The contents of these disks are constantly updated to ensure that you have the best!"

Space does not permit a complete summary of the collections, but here are some highlights. There are at least 15 language disks, including Tarbell BASIC, Forth (two versions), and LISP (two versions). There are nine volumes of games, a collection of 6502 Simulator/Disassembler programs that allow a Z80 or 8080 machine to simulate an Apple ("For serious programmers only . . ."), a volume entitled TRS-80 Model I Omnikron Mapper Programs, collections of programs specifically prepared for Osborne users and one for Kaypro users, and a full range of business and word processing collections.

Over 50 different disk formats are supported, including Apple CP/M (yeah!), DEC Rainbow, TI Professional, and British Mini Micro. ("We're constantly adding more formats. . . . If your machine isn't listed, please call us for current information.") Prices for 8-inch volumes range from $10 to $15; prices for most 5-inch formats range from $15.00 to $22.50. (Remember, a volume is a volume is a volume, regardless of how many physical disks are required to hold it.) Shipping and handling are included.

Perhaps the most unique feature of all is MICROCOMP's "membership" RCPM system. This is more on the order of a "software-of-the-moment" club than it is a traditional bulletin board system, though it does include messaging functions. There are four boards, and the payment of a $30 annual membership fee gives you access to all of them. Both 300 and 1200 baud are supported, and all systems are available 24 hours a day. Membership is limited to a total of 800 individuals. You may access the system "for up to one hour per day and download as much software as you like within this time period."

At any given time, the systems carry well over 40 megabytes of CP/M and MS-DOS public domain software. That's the equivalent of 250 single-sided IBM/PC disks (160K). The software on the boards is the most up-to-date available. Subscribers tend to upload so many new programs that the Newells contribute an average of nearly a volume a month to SIG/M. You do not have to have a membership to obtain the RCPM software, however. On request, the software in the various "hard disk areas" of the boards can be transferred to floppy disk. Prices range from $10 to $20 per disk, depending on the format. Visa, MasterCard, and American Express are accepted.

Note: Jud Newell reports that there is rarely a need to be concerned with customs when ordering software from the United States. "We ship by regular mail, and usually it goes right through." There is no duty on public domain software in any case. Asked to describe the worst possible scenario, Mr. Newell said that the worst that could happen would be a delay. "The customs office nearest to you would simply send you a card asking you to describe what's in the package." You would mail the card back and the package would be forwarded to you. "That's the worst case," Mr. Newell says, "but there's really never been a problem."

Workman & Associates
112 Marion Avenue
Pasadena, CA 91106
(213) 796-4401
9:00 AM to 4:00 PM (PST)

Marcia Workman has an approach that may be just the ticket for the new CP/M user interested in acquiring the most helpful and important public domain utility programs. To quote her brochure describing the Workman Software Anthology Series, "We find the useful programs, test them, write or rewrite instructions for them, and sell them at a low profit. This task is complicated by the fact that we may have to review a hundred programs to find one useful one." There are at least four disks in the series. Prices range from $32.50 to $42.50 per disk, depending on the format. Available formats include Apple CP/M, Kaypro, TRS-80 Model II (Pickles and Trout), TRS-80 Model III (Shuffleboard or Memory Merchant; see Appendix B), Osborne, and others. This is not an extensive collection, but it may be what a new user needs to get started. A free catalogue is available. MasterCard and Visa may be available.

Sheepshead Software
P.O. Box 486
Boonville, CA 95415
(707) 463-1833 (ask for Aunt Juanita!)
9:00 AM to 9:00 PM, (PST)

John Palmer of Sheepshead Software can provide SIG/M and CPMUG software by volume number in over 15 formats, including TRS-80 Models I and III, TI Professional, and DEC VT180. The firm cannot provide Apple, North Star, or Victor 9000, however. The cost for double density formats is $12 per volume; $16 for single density. The firm's unique strength is in supplying customized versions of selected public domain programs for the Kaypro. Mr. Palmer uses a Kaypro himself and makes available the versions of programs he has patched and customized for his own use, particularly MODEM7 (see Chapter 7 and Appendix A). As he points out, with MODEM7 on the Kaypro, "many files can be sent at one time without operator attention. I have used it at 9600 baud to transfer the whole CPMUG library from 8-inch to 5-inch disks." He also indicates that pins 5, 6, and 8 may have to be tied together at the Kaypro's RS-232 connector and that the modem might require pins 4 and 5 to be tied together at its end in order to use the MODEM7 program. A short free catalogue is available. MasterCard and Visa are accepted.

"Computerist News"
P.O. Box 2250
Santa Clara, CA 95055
(408) 252-8873
7:00 PM to 9:00 PM, (PST)

Donn Fisher has a unique combination of abilities. Steeped in technical knowledge and the ins and outs of Silicon Valley, he is an engineer with a strong awareness of the need for good marketing and communications. He is thus well-suited to helping would-be computer entrepreneurs bridge the gap between the workbench and the marketplace, and his publication is designed to do just that. Donn is also dedicated to the concept of public domain and "user-supported" software, and he offers not only the complete SIG/M and CPMUG libraries, but also extensive collections IBM/PC public domain software, and the complete C Users Group (formerly the BDS C group) library.

As part of this effort, he has prepared "The Computerist Micro Directory of Public Domain Software." This is a well-organized list of all the programs in all of the libraries cited above. What makes it special are the comments and tips Mr. Fisher has added to many of the descriptions. Often these are several sentences long and thus more helpful than the single-line abstracts provided in the catalogues supplied by the various users groups. Pages from the directory have begun to appear in "Computerist News," but at this writing, the price for the complete publication has not been set.

Users group volumes are available on standard 8-inch disks for $7.00. ("I supply the disk, label, mailer & postage.") According to the brochure, Mr. Fisher "has the ability to provide format transfer to and from 8-inch/5.25 diskettes, most formats INCLUDING PCDOS/MSDOS. If you need any of the user group library diskettes in 5.25-inch formats, please inquire."

The standard subscription rate for "The Computerist News" is $18 per year (12 issues), but there is a special new-subscriber price of $15. The newsletter is aimed at computer professionals and, while many people will find information of interest within its pages, it is clearly not for everyone. However, subscribers receive a substantial discount on public domain orders of 20 8-inch volumes or more. If you add the cost of a subscription to the discounted price of the disks, the cost per disk is

$4.79. A free sample of the newsletter and a public domain flyer are available. A self-addressed, stamped envelope or return postage and an address label would be appreciated.

P. J.'s Company
The National Public Domain Software Center
1082 Taylor
Vista, CA 92083
(619) 727-1015

Paul Jones of "P.J.'s Company" offers something unique. He will *rent* you the entire SIG/M, CPMUG, PICONET, C Users Group, and Pascal/Z Group libraries for about $40. (Virtually all of the IBM/PC-MS-DOS public domain is available on similar terms.) "One of the factors that motivated me to get into this," Paul says, "is that some companies were putting their names on public domain software and selling it. I know people who have paid $50 for *Adventure*, and I myself paid $25 for MODEM7. That's not fair.

"You would be surprised how many experienced CP/M users don't know about the public domain. We get calls all the time from people who say they've heard about it but don't know what it is or what's available or how to get it." Mr. Jones goes on to cite the three-week to three-month delay one can experience when ordering the software from an all-volunteer users group. "I thought it would be nice if all the programs could be easily, and speedily, available to anyone who wants them."

The service is quite impressive. The company has a DiskMaster machine that lets it produce virtually any disk format. "We currently have about 108 formats, and the rental libraries are available on all of them. We can do more, but we usually wait until we get a request for a format before we transfer the libraries to it. After that, it's available the next time we get the same request." P.J.'s can even supply the CP/M collections in *Apple* and *Commodore* formats. Prices are always subject to change, but the following will give you a sense of what it will cost:

CPMUG Library, Vols. 1-92	$45.00
SIG/M Library, Vols. 1-90	$40.00
SIG/M Library, Vols. 91-150	$40.00
PICONET Library, Vols. 1-34	$24.95

These prices are for 8-inch disks in the standard IBM format. Additional volumes will also be available. P.J.'s uses "flippy" disks, disks that have been notched to permit recording on both sides. The number of disks rented will thus be half the number of volumes. There is a $7.50 charge per library for shipping, handling, and insurance. The rental period is seven consecutive days, with a three day-grace period to allow for return shipment. You can purchase blank 8-inch flippy disks at $3 apiece with your order.

If you would like to purchase any given library, the average price works out to about $2.50 per volume. If you do not want the entire library, you can buy any two volumes of software on an 8-inch flippy or one volume on a 5¼-inch flippy for $6. Visa and MasterCard are accepted. Send a self-addressed, stamped envelope for the most up-to-date information.

There's more. A directory disk is included with each rental order to make it easy to locate the software you want to transfer to your own disks. The directory disk contains the CPMUG and Pascal/Z library listings on one side and SIG/M and San Francisco's PICONET group listing on the other. [Mr. Jones indicates that the PICONET library is particularly strong in programs dealing with I/O (input/output) and communications, though there are some excellent games and utilities. The group's communications program is known as YAM—"Yet Another Modem" program.]

The catalogue disk also contains the FIND program (see the Gems List, below) to enable you to pinpoint the volume number of virtually any program. Many of the abstracts describing each program have been added by P.J.'s. "We've spent quite a lot of time adding comments to help people identify the programs they want." You can buy the catalogue disk in an 8-inch or any other format for $5.

Finally, to make it easier for CP/M users to locate programs of a particular type without being overwhelmed, Mr. Jones has prepared at least four specialized rental collections. These include Business, Modem, Utilities, and Games. Each contains 20 volumes of free software. The rental is $20 to $25. "We've rented these collections and the other libraries to individuals as far away as Europe and Japan and we've never had any problems."

How to Contribute Your Own Programs to the Public Domain

Making It Official

There is always a need for good public domain software, and most major groups will be happy to consider your submissions. The legal formalities are simple. You must submit a letter with your program clearly stating that the program is your own creation and that you are officially releasing it to the public domain. You may also want to include a sentence or two explaining why you are releasing it ("For the greater personal computer enjoyment of mankind . . ."). Some authors incorporate language explicitly granting permission to anyone to copy the program, as long as they do not sell it for a profit. Others reserve the copyright but provide for free copying and distribution. Most of the disks you receive from users groups will include a donation release form you can print out and use when making your submission, and these should be your guides. Naturally, you will want to save a copy of your letter in case a disreputable firm should attempt to profit from your donation.

FreeTip: This cannot be emphasized strongly enough. Do not under any circumstances "borrow" code from a commercial program. Some bulletin board SysOps and users group librarians we've spoken with report receiving "donations" of commercially available programs from enthusiastic contributors. No doubt this is often done with the best of intentions. But it is piracy nonetheless, and not only is it severely frowned upon by nearly everyone associated with the public domain, it exposes the violator to financial damage awards for copyright infringement.

The public domain is to a large extent self-policing. On the one hand, most BBS operators and club librarians spend a great deal of time making sure that the programs submitted do not belong to someone else. "The first thing I do when I receive public domain contributions," says one librarian, "is list the program and look at the code. I can't always tell, but lots of times if it's a commercial program I can spot it."

On the flip side of the coin, woe to the company that puts its name on a public domain program and tries to sell it as its own. "They may get away with it for a while," one club president says, "but sooner or later, the word will spread among the country's users groups. And many people will stop buying any of the firm's products."

What To Contribute

It is probably fair to say that the CP/M world does not need another new modem program, and it has floppy disks full of directory and other utility programs. If you want your program to be accepted, study the SIG/M list to see if you can think of a useful or enjoyable program that may be missing. Then consider filling the gap.

Interestingly, if you view the list as a chronological record, you can see the types of programs changing over time. The early volumes contain material written by hobbyists and others acquainted with computers at the bits-and-bytes level. Then there are the utilities, written by early computer users who needed them to make using their machines more convenient. Today, as the demographics of computer owners changes, you will find more applications-oriented material. As Jud Newell of MICROCOMP and others in the field point out, "Today we're seeing many more SuperCalc templates, dBASE II command files, ProKey files, and other programs submitted by business and professional users."

For someone who has just discovered public domain software, this means that you do not have to be fluent in a major computer language to make a contribution. You can create a model with SuperCalc just as you normally would, for example, and then contribute *that* instead of a piece of sophisticated assembly language programming.

Where to Send Your Programs

Most public domain authors are very interested in seeing that their software is distributed as widely as possible. And there are many routes open to you. You could upload it to an RCPM system, give it to your local users group's software librarian, upload it to CompuServe or the CP/M SIG on The Source if you are a member of that board (see Chapter 9). You could post notices on The Source and CompuServe main bulletin boards and on various BBS and RCPM systems offering to supply the program on disk to people who contacted you. You could submit the source code and an explanation of the program to *Dr. Dobb's Journal* or *Microsystems* or some other magazine. You should also consider sending it to the appropriate "super group" for your machine (see Chapters 3 and 5 for addresses and information.)

As mentioned earlier, if people find the program of value, it will eventually make its way to SIG/M (or possibly, CPMUG). But there is no reason why you cannot submit it to that group from the start. Use the address provided earlier. Due to the close relationship between the NYACC and SIG/M, if you submit to the NYACC CP/M software librarian it will be considered by SIG/M as well. When submitting to SIG/M, be sure to put your program on a standard 8-inch IBM 3740 formatted disk. If this is a problem, consult your local users group or local RCPM SysOp. You may have to "telecommunicate" it from your format to the 8-inch format.

FreeTip: The software librarians of the various organizations are busy men and women. Anything you can do to make their jobs easier will be greatly appreciated.

The first and most important consideration is to make sure that the program really works. Any information you can include on how you have tested the program, the equipment you have used, the machines you have successfully run it on, etc., is important. If you know of any limitations or feel that users of a particular kind of equipment may have difficulty, mention that as well. There is nothing wrong with submitting a program that has been customized for, say, a Kaypro or a Zenith. Owners of those machines will appreciate and use it. Just make certain to say so when you send in your program.

Document Your Program

Lastly, don't forget the documentation! In the early days, contributors could rely on users to be quite computer-wise, and many did not feel the need for extensive documentation. But this is less and less true today. Anything you can do—any instructions, explanations, or other material that will aid people in using your program—is important. Put the files right on the disk with the program and label them with the same filename and a ".DOC" extension. The phrase "Do unto others" was never more appropriate than with public domain software documentation. Put yourself in the shoes of the end user who is trying to figure out and benefit from your creation. Then prepare a document that will guide the person every step of the way. One can never be too rich or too thin, and there can never be too much documentation for a computer program.

Should you sign your name? Definitely. When contributing BASIC or other listable software, most authors place their names in REMark statements in the first lines of the program. Should you provide your address, telephone number, and Source or CompuServe ID? It depends. By tradition, public domain software is not supported. Submitting a program, in itself, does not obligate you to answer user questions; the programs are offered on an "as is, take-it-or-leave-it, fix-it-or-adapt-it" basis. If you include contact information, however, be prepared to have people call on you for help.

There is an interesting contradiction here. Possibly even a misunderstanding. While one can usually count on hearing from a certain number of users, the percentage is often small. Many people wouldn't dream of calling the author of a public domain program for help, even if they have the necessary information. Public domain authors, on the other hand, often say, "Gee, you know, I wish someone would call me. I wonder if anyone is actually using my program."

Ultimately, only you as the author of a public domain program can decide whether to include contact information. If you do, and if you want to hear from users, you might insert a sentence to that effect in your program or documentation file.

FreeTip: There are at least two publications every CP/M user should know about, particularly those who are interested in the public domain. Neither is intended for the beginning user, but both offer an excellent way to "plug-in" to the CP/M world. And both carry articles discussing public domain software. Look for them on your newsstand, or contact:

Microsystems
CN 1987
Morristown, NJ 07960
New-subscriber rate: $21.97 (12 issues)

Dr. Dobb's Journal of Computer Calisthenics & Orthodontia
People's Computer Company
Box E
Menlo Park, CA 94025
Annual subscription: $21 (12 issues)

The Gems List of Free CP/M Public Domain Software

The following list contains many of what are generally agreed to be the best programs in the CP/M public domain. It is designed to help you get a handle on the thousands of programs that are available and, by serving as a shopping list, to help you begin using and enjoying free CP/M software as quickly as possible. As you become more familiar with the SIG/M and other users group lists, you will find many more programs to serve your special needs.

We've divided the list into seven sections: Productivity Software, Critical Programs, Games, Disk Utilities, Communications Software, Others Worth Considering, and Languages. Because specific programs tend to be known by unique filenames, we have not used the various filename extensions. As you will see when you read the SIG/M lists, the same disk will often hold programs in their assembly language form (.ASM) and in their ready-to-run machine language form (.COM). There will often be a file containing the program's documentation (.DOC) as well. Other extensions are also used.

We have focused on filenames instead of volume numbers for two reasons. The filename is the most important identifier. If you see "FIND," "MODEM7," or "DU" on an RCPM, in the CompuServe CP/M SIG, or in a collection of programs offered by a non-user group source, the volume number is irrelevant. More importantly, since new versions of many programs are constantly being added to the libraries, the best version for you may be on a newer volume.

Indeed, the technique to use when trying to locate a version of a specific program is to read the SIG/M list from the bottom up. In most cases, this is the best way to make sure that you locate and obtain the version with the most recent improvements. Look for variations on the main filename. If you know that the RBBS program is a remote bulletin board system program, for example, it should not be too difficult to figure out that MINIRBBS and possibly CONVRBB are in some way associated with remote bulletin boards.

We would like to thank the many software librarians and RCPM SysOps for their help in assembling the raw material for this list. And we are grateful to Donn Fisher, Lee Hillard, Paul Jones, Jud Newell, Bill Roch, and especially Chris Terry of *Microsystems* magazine for their many suggestions. Some selection had to be made, however, and that responsiblity, as well as any blame for missing programs, is solely the author's.

Productivity Software

BIZMASTER. Written by Bud Aaron, this is a complete business software package that formerly sold for $160 but is now in the public domain. It occupies six 8-inch disks and requires CBASIC2 (a commercial product), as well as some knowledge of the BASIC language. (Some may find it a bit difficult to install.) Package contains over 170 files (1025K). Documentation (200K) is on disk. Here's what you get:

- Accounts Receivable
- Accounts Payable
- Accounts Receivable
- General Ledger
- Payroll
- Sample data files
- Purchase Order
- Inventory
- Mailing List
- Order Entry
- Purchase Order

BLOCKxx. A program to generate large block letters. Uses the letter itself as a design motif to create the block. Or you may specify some other character. Similar to "banner" programs.

dBASE II Command Files. Public domain support for Ashton-Tate's best-selling dBASE II relational database program is just getting started. There are dBASE command files and SuperCalc templates on SIG/M Volume 110. But there is a complete dBASE order entry and inventory program on SIG/M Volume 129. Donn Fisher of the "Computerist News" says that "when an order is entered the program advises if it is in stock or back-ordered and makes any appropriate adjustments to inventory." It also prints invoices, shipping labels, floppy disk labels, an assortment of reports, and it includes a utility to search and locate any string in any field in all the records in your database. Important Note: dBASE II command files are text files. They can be used by anyone who owns the dBASE II program, regardless of whether the individual runs the CP/M or MS-DOS version.

DIMS. "Dan's Information Management System," by Dan Dugan of Dugan Sound Design in San Francisco, is a file manager, not a relational DBMS (see *How to Buy Software*, Chapter 16), but quite powerful. Records may have up to 15 fields if records are 128 bytes long; 30 fields, if 256 bytes long. Written in MBASIC V. 5.2 but can be modified to be run by V. 4.x. Cannot be compiled due to use of dynamic array dimensioning. Add, delete, change, list, or print. Sort entire file or by range of records on any combination of fields. Very important: DIMS, unlike some commercial products, allows you to change the structure of your database (add more variable fields) without having to re-key existing data. Can also be used as a mailing label generator.

Chris Terry says: "You know, here at the magazine (*Microsystems*) we use this program to keep track of articles, authors, and to manage other information. Dan Dugan should be congratulated on producing a really fine system. If you can't afford dBASEII, use DIMS!"

Note: There is at least one less capable database-type program called "NAD." This stands for "Names and Addresses," not "National Accounts Division."

ED. Contributed by the Software Tools of Australia, this is a full-screen editor (as opposed to a line editor) written in C for compilation with Ron Cain's Small C. Another program, RED by Edward K. Ream, is considered even more powerful. RED must be compiled with the BDS C Compiler. This program is not in the public domain, but Mr. Ream hopes users "will do anything with this editor except distribute it for profit." It is available from the C Users Group and other sources. See the July and August 1983 issues of *Dr. Dobb's Journal* for Mr. Ream's articles and more details.

Other word processors and text formatters worth considering include ZPTEX, SECRETARY, and POW (Power of Words). ROFF4 by Professor E. Bergmann of Lehigh University does a great job with footnotes and is able to print chemical and mathematical equations with the correct partial line feeds. Also permits use of user-defined special character sets for printing Greek letters and other special symbols. (Special symbols appear on your screen as some character in your machine's ROM character set, but they print as you intended.)

FIND. Program will search through one or an unlimited number of ASCII text files for the string of characters (word or sentences) you specify. Displays all lines containing target string, their filenames, and line numbers. You may also use "wildcards" to specify "any combination of characters."

INDEXER and *GENINDEX*. Both of these programs are written in Pascal and both are designed to generate an index from a WordStar file.

MAGE. This program will preserve your time and effort should you get a "BDOS Error" or "Disk Full" message when trying to save what you have written to disk in WordStar. You can recover changes that are still in the machine's memory even though they cannot be written to the disk currently in the logged disk drive.

MAINT.BAS. A mailing list program developed by CACHE (Chicago Area Computer Hobbyists' Exchange) to handle their membership roster. Written in and requiring EBASIC. You will also need REPORT.BAS on the same disk.

Osborne/McGraw Hill Financial Package. The complete Osborne A/R, A/P, G/L, Payroll, and Cost Accounting package is also available. Some familiarity with BASIC required. These programs are the ones published in the McGraw-Hill books, which you will need to use them effectively. Programs occupy three disk volumes.

SPELL. The version of this program on CPMUG Volume 80 requires Cromemco Structured BASIC in order to run. Since it is written in BASIC it is said to be slow. You may be able to find other spelling checkers on other volumes, however.

TABPRINT. Prints ASCII textfiles with an indentation sufficient to let you use a three-hole punch on the paper for insertion in a notebook.

Critical Programs

/.COM. An online "SUBMIT" program (also known as "DO") written by Ward Christensen, this program is activated by entering a slash at the DOS prompt and following it with a string of commands separated by semicolons. The system will then execute each command just as it would if you had prepared a SUBMIT (batch command) file with your editor.

For example: *A> / ASM filename.bbz; LOAD B:filename* would cause the system to run ASM.COM to assemble filename and, when finished, run LOAD.COM and load the assembled file.

CATALOG. A Ward Christensen program providing comprehensive management of your disk files. Creates an alphabetical list of all files on all of your disks and stores the list as a master file. To update this file, you run the UCAT (or QCAT for single drive systems) module. This reads all disks currently online and automatically updates the master file. Using the CAT module, you can then specify any filename or range of files and have the system instantly tell you where they are located.

MAKE. Written by Terry Lewis. This program changes the directory user number of a file, making it available to different users without the need to copy the whole program to another user area on the same disk.

READ. This program can save you from using a Control-S to alternately stop and start the display of a file. It will display 24 lines of a file and stop; then 24 more, and so on. Another program (VLST.COM) permits you to select one of four speeds of display.

RECOVERx. Written by F. Roland Bjorklund, this program will "unerase" erased files, as long as you have not recorded something on top of them in the meantime. When a disk operating system erases a file, what it normally does is fiddle around with the disk directory—the master list of "what's where" on a given disk. It sets flags indicating that the physical space occupied by the file you have erased is now available for recording. By resetting the flags, and once again reserving the space under the name of the file you want, RECOVER and similar programs "restore" the file. It can then be read or word-processed as if nothing had happened. The DU (or DUU) program described in the Disk section of this chapter can be used to do the same thing, but RECOVER is considered to be easier for most people to use. UNERA ("Un-Erase") is a similar program.

SCRAMBLE. A data encryption/decryption program. Author Ward Christensen cautions that he is not a cryptography expert and makes no claim to SCRAMBLE's effectiveness. On the other hand, he knows of no way of unscrambling a file if you lose the password. CPMUG Volume 36.

SD-xx. A real "goodie" capable of searching all drives and user areas for either unambiguous (exact) or ambiguous (wildcards) filenames. You can start on any drive you specify and tell the program to output the results either to the printer, a disk file, or the screen. "SD" means "super directory."

SPOOL or *UNSPOOL.* Anything with the word "spool" in its filename is probably a print spooler. A print spooler allows you to print a file and move on to something else. Without it, you would be forced to wait until the printout was finished before continuing to use your computer.

SQUEEZE and *UNSQUEEZE.* Written in C by Richard Greenlaw. Data compress/uncompress programs are essential when downloading from most RCPM systems. See Chapter 10.

TYPSQ. Lets you read a squeezed file without creating and recording an unsqueezed version. File remains squeezed after you have run TYPSQ. Good for taking a quick look at squeezed RCPM textfiles before deciding whether you want to download them.

WASH or *SWEEPxx.* These programs will present a list of a disk's files in columnar form one at a time. As each filename appears, you may enter commands to erase, view, copy, or rename. The program takes care of the rest, freeing you from using CP/M DOS commands. SWEEP incorporates the features of WASH but makes it possible to copy files to different disks in the same manner. Essential.

XDIR. "Extended" (X) directory. Written by Bruce Ratoff. Presents the files on your disk in three columns, alphabetized by filename and accompanied by file size. The CP/M public domain is filled with directory programs, each with its own whistles and bells. You may find that you will eventually want several of them, but this is a good one to start with.

Games

*ADVEN***.* Any time you see a filename similar to that above (the *'s represent any other characters) you know you have encountered some version of *the* classic computer game, *Adventure.* To misquote Dr. Johnson, "When a man is tired of *Adventure,* he is tired of life." Joysticks need not apply. A "B" usually signifies "Beginner Level," (350 possible points) while an "X" (550 points) is for experts and is considered by some to be impossible to win.

If you need help with *Adventure,* John Palmer of Sheepshead Software suggests sending $2 for "Original Adventure Tips" to:

Steven Tippett
P.O. Box 6907
Stockton, CA 95206

If you think a map of the Colossal Cave would be helpful (it would be), check the FEEdback online ordering section of CompuServe for two maps. The $4.98 version covers the entire cave. You might also consider the map from Sterling Software ($3.95). It is less artistic but more directional. The firm also sells *Adventure* for Apple owners (not CP/M) at $9.95. Contact:

Sterling Software
120 Pepperidge Place
Sterling, VA 22170

CHESS. Several versions of this one are available. But be warned, most do not provide on-screen graphics. If you can play chess over the telephone ("Queen's knight to heaven knows where . . ."), you'll be fine. Sometimes called ZCHESS or Z80CHESS.

Educational Games. There are over 50 math drills and other teaching games for CBASIC and MBASIC. Most are considered fair. Games on CPMUG Volume 54 are said to have errors. Same volume has a TYPING TUTOR program that appears to work.

Disk Utilities
COPYFST3. Copies complete disk to another drive making an exact duplicate. Pours as many tracks as possible into available memory (buffer). Uses read skewing and track-to-track skewing for additional speed. Versions higher than V.3, if and when created, may contain error-checking and a check for CP/M version number. (FAST and SPEED are older, but similar programs.)

DU-Vxx. The "DU" stands for "Disk Utility." Original version by Ward Christensen. Gives you direct access to data stored on disk as an aid in reconstructing damaged files or simply looking at how data is stored. Access any file, block, or sector on a specified track as your starting point. Move forward or backward, patch the memory image and rewrite it, look at the allocation bit map, etc. Versions DU-V65 and later run under CP/M 2.2 as well as 1.4. With some you may be able to customize I/O for various disk controllers.

FINDBAD. Non-destructive testing program (does not overwrite recorded data) that attempts to read all disk sectors. If it finds a bad sector, the block containing that sector is locked out by being isolated in a file called UNUSED.BAD. Makes sure you will always be able to retrieve information you've recorded. Versions up to 3.8 are for 8-inch

SSSD disks only. Later versions handle both 8 and 5¼. (DISKTES1 is a destructive test for 8-inch SSSD. DTST.Z80, contributed by Laboratory Systems of Los Angeles, allows read-only, write-only, and read/write testing of any range of tracks/sectors.)

LU. The "library utility." This program lets you store more files on disk than CP/M ordinarily permits. Several files can be stored in a "library," but since the library is seen by CP/M as a single filename, the system considers it a single file.

Communications Software
APMODMxx. MODEM7 for CP/M-running Apple computers. May lack MODEM7 menu and batch facility. Includes Help. For use with 56K Apple and Hayes Micromodem or CCS 7710A serial card and external modem.

COMM723. Enhanced communications program (Oct. 1983) based on MODEM7. Gives you access to DOS without leaving the communications program itself. Can erase or copy single or multiple files, rename, log new drives and user areas, view files on the screen or print them, and more. Also includes a "Softkey" or "macro" feature allowing you to load frequently used strings into the number keys. To generate string, hit <ESCAPE> followed by number key. Written by Frank Gaude; 16- and 32-bit versions are planned.

CONVER and *UNLOAD*. CONVER and programs with similar names are "hexadecimal converters" (see Chapter 6). UNLOAD-type programs will take a .COM (machine language) file created with LOAD.COM or DDT.COM and convert it into Intel hexadecimal format. Both are used for transmitting and receiving machine language files in the absence of the XMODEM (or some other) protocol.

CRCK. "Cyclic Redundancy Check." This is a program for checking the accuracy of a file that you have downloaded from an RCPM or other online source. Many programs in hex format will include a CRC "checksum" in their last lines. If you download a file and run CRCK (or a similar program) against it and obtain the identical checksum, you can be certain that the file was downloaded without errors. The checksum is in hexadecimal format. (See Appendix A for more information on cyclic redundancy checking.)

FILTER. This is one of several programs designed to remove eight-bit control codes from files such as those created by WordStar. WordStar embeds codes in its textfiles that have a special meaning to the program. Unfortunately, these same codes have meanings entirely unrelated to communications software. Thus they must be removed to be sent under standard communications conditions. It is also necesary to remove control codes if you want to prepare a BASIC program in WordStar and then LOAD it into BASIC. Some versions of FILTER may require the Digital Research MAC assember.

KERMIT. Developed at Columbia University, KERMIT is a program designed to make it easier for a personal computer to communicate with a mainframe. Available on SIG/M Volume 113.

LINK or *PLINKxx*. Written and contributed by Larry Hughes, author of the MITE communications program (Mycroft Labs; see Appendix A). A transient program designed to let a TRS-80 Model I or II or Heath H8 or any S-100 computer using a PMMI or Hayes board modem communicate with a remote computer not running a special communications program. Latest version may be PLINK65.

MODEM7xx. See Appendix A—The XMODEM File for more information on this classic program. Also see Chapter 8 for information concerning the online support, overlays, and patches available for scores of machines through the CP/M SIG on CompuServe.

RBBSxx. RBBS stands for Remote Bulletin Board System. See Chapter 10 for more information on BBS (RBBS) and RCPM systems. If you want to set up one of your own, you might look for a series of related programs in the RBBS category on SIG/M Volumes 7 and 8. The software is available elsewhere, of course. You will also need BYExx (SIG/M Volume 16; PMMI modem users only) or a similar program to let your computer answer the phone. And XMODEMxx to allow callers to download files error-free with their MODEM7 or other program. (They will run XMODEM remotely on your system.) Note: MBASIC is required for the RBBS series mentioned above, though other versions may be available. Priceless advice: Contact an active SysOp for tips before trying to bring up a board of your own.

SMODEMxx. Version of MODEM7 written to support the D. C. Hayes Smartmodem, both 300- and 1200-baud units.

Others Worth Considering
The FED. Written by Decision Sciences and Software of Irvine, Califor-

nia, this is a CBASIC version of the financial model used by the St. Louis Federal Reserve District to test alternate money supply policies. If you're an M1 watcher, perhaps this will help your predictions. No source code. Available only in semicompiled CBASIC.

LINKASM. Christensen enhancement of the standard ASM.COM module. Runs faster, allows unlimited number of source code files to be assembled into a single .HEX file. Said to have been written specifically to assemble the modules of MODEM. Other public domain assemblers include:

> *ASMX*. Recognizes Zilog mnemonics. Make sure you restrict output to drive A.
>
> *MACASM*. Similar to Intel's macro assembler. Recognizes Zilog mnemonics while running on an 8080. Nesting of macros sometimes clobbers locations 5, 6, and 7. No fix known.
>
> *Z80ASM*. Recognizes Zilog mnemonics. Can run on an 8080. Said to be hardware sensitive. Check with a fellow user.

MBREM. One of a genre of programs for removing "REMark" statements from BASIC programs. Saves storage space. "MB" stands for MBASIC. Be sure to keep a backup of your original program, REM's and all.

POWER. The early release version of the commercially available POWER CP/M enhancement package. Contains about 50 utilities similar to those cited in this chapter. Commercial version sells for about $150 and comes with complete documentation. Call COMPUTING! (800) 227-3800; in California (800) 792-0990.

RESOURCE. The 8080 disassembler of choice, by Ward Christensen. It is well documented and considered extremely powerful. RESOURCE is for 8080 chips, ZESOURCE is for Z-80s. (Workman Associates, cited at the end of this chapter, offers both programs, plus science fiction author and programmer Jerry Pournelle's BLACKART.DOC on the mysteries of disassembly.)

Yale Star Series. The Yale series of Bright Stars by the National Space Science Data center contains information on every star in the sky. And it takes eight volumes to do it.

ZCPRx. Written by Richard Conn, the complete set of programs and documentation for this item occupy ten volumes of the SIG/M library (volumes 98 through 107; 2.3 megabytes); but a smaller, two-volume set is available. This is nothing less than a replacement for the CCP (Console Command Processor) module of the standard CP/M package. Considered to be a truly superb piece of programming. Offers more powerful and friendly versions of standard resident commands, plus a number of additional ones. Also includes utilities such as online documentation and help files and the capability of searching for .COM files on any disk in the system. Full implementation requires BIOS modification and reduces the TPA by 3K to 4K. Check with your users group if you are not skilled in assembly language programming.

Complete printed documentation is available in Books 5 through 7 from the NYACC. Book 7 contains the author's rationale and the documentation for the SYSLIB, a SYStem LIBrary of assembly language subroutines designed to be used with the Microsoft M80 Assembler. Important note: Runs only on Z80 systems.

Languages

BDS C compiler programs. The C compiler from BD Software is not in the public domain, but there are many programs written to be run with it. To obtain this software ($150), contact:

Leor Zolman
BD Software
P.O. Box 9
Brighton, MA 02135
(617) 782-0836

You might check CPMUG Volume 50, the "BDS C Sampler Disk," for a manual to give you the flavor of the compiler as well as some interesting programming examples. Assembled by Leor Zolman, the sampler disk includes both source code and compiled versions of games like Othello, Polish Pong, Stones, and Bugs (makes things crawl around your screen). You will not need the BDS C compiler to run the precompiled .COM versions.

Although there are many C programs in the SIG/M and CPMUG collections, the BDS C Users Group (also known as the C Users Group, due to a recent name change) also maintains its own library. For more information:

C Users Group
Box 287
112 North Main
Yates Center, KS 66783

EBASIC. A semicompiler with run time interpreter written by Gordon Eubanks. Antecedent of CBASIC, CBASIC2, and CB-80. Chris Terry of *Microsystems* says, "This is more powerful than other public domain BASICs, in that it has higher precision, requires no line numbers except in statements that are targets of GOTOs or GOSUBs, and has better control structures." You'll find related files on various CPMUG and SIG/M volumes.

FIG-FORTH 1.1. This is the Forth Interest Group (FIG) Forth language, version 1.1 (CPMUG Volume 65). You should get the FIG model manual and FIG Assembly Source Listing before trying to use this.

Pascal compiler. Written in Pascal and considered very good for advanced users. Not a complete Pascal, however. CPMUG Volume 50. On SIG/M Volume 82 there is JRT Pascal and this is said to be a complete language; related material is on Volume 129. For more information on Pascal/Z, contact:

Pascal/Z Users Group
7962 Center Parkway
Sacramento, CA 95823

PILOT. Programmed Inquiry and Learning. A version of a language that is becomming increasingly popular among computer-using school teachers. Well suited for easy pattern-matching of responses from students. CPMUG Volume 12 has source code patched for correct interface with CP/M.

RATFOR. Rational Fortran. A preprocessor for FORTRAN source code. RATFOR output must be compiled with the Microsoft FORTRAN-80 compiler.

TINIDISK. A version of Wang Palo Alto BASIC. Occupies only 3K. Comes with a 6K version of *Star Trek*.

FreeTip: Languages are popular and diverse among CP/Mers. The following list will help you decipher many of the listings in the SIG/M and other catalogues:

ACTOR—Chris Terry: "A TRAC-like string-processing language that comes with a comprehensive manual and some sample programs." CPMUG Vol. 4.
CASUAL—See *Dr. Dobb's Journal*, December 1976.
FELIX—Graphics animation system with pseudo assembler.

FreeTip continued

FOCAL—Language similar to the BASIC supplied by DEC for PDP/8 computers.

PIDGIN and TINCMP—PIDGIN is a systems progamming language; TINCMP is a compiler for special purpose programs written in PIDGIN.

PISTOL—Portably Implemented Stack Oriented Language; said to have evolved from Forth and STOIC.

SAM76—Macro and string processing language. Said to be good for controlling a mobile robot (?).

STOIC—Similar to FORTH.

Taking the First Step

To avoid being overwhelmed by the riches of the CP/M public domain, it is probably best to start slowly. Choose a program or two from the Gems List and contact one of the organizations or individuals cited in this chapter to obtain a copy. If all of this is new to you, you will probably be best off selecting several of the simpler programs like SWEEP, WASH, XDIR, FIND, or SD-xx. These can be used immediately, without the need to read lengthy instructions, and they provide a dramatic illustration of how useful free CP/M software can be.

If there is a computer users group in your area, you should definitely plan to join. (See Chapters 3 and 5 for tips and information.) And if your computer is equipped for communications, you should also strongly consider a CompuServe subscription. This is probably the fastest way to begin sampling free CP/M software. Hundreds of free CP/M programs—many of them Gems—are available on CompuServe at almost any hour of the day. Chapter 8 will show you how to get them. One way or another, you clearly have a lot to look forward to once you plug into the CP/M public domain.

...3...

Users Groups: *Firstline Sources of Free Software*

Almost every machine on the market today has attracted libraries of free software similar to those discussed in Chapter 2. Similarly, many computer languages, such as Forth, Pascal, and C, have served as focal points for growing collections of public domain programs. In both cases (machine-specific, and language- or software-specific), you face the same two challenges—discovering what is available and finding out how to get it. Unfortunately, things are not quite as simple here as in the CP/M public domain. As we saw in Chapter 2, the collection and distribution of CP/M software is relatively well-organized. It may take a while, but most of the "good stuff" eventually finds its way into the SIG/M library and is distributed from there. Although there is a major Apple group, and at least one organization that appears to be on its way to becoming the "library of record" for free IBM/PC software, neither of these is quite comparable to SIG/M. The public domain for other machines is even less well-organized.

But there are techniques you can use to overcome these problems, and in this and succeeding chapters we'll show you what they are. Here we'll be talking about local and "super" users groups. In the following chapter we'll look at software- and language-specific groups and the public domain libraries available through them. In Chapter 5 we'll show you how to get in touch with some outstanding local and national machine-specific groups with libraries to offer. And in Chapter 6, we'll discuss the large collections of public domain software available through non-user group sources.

What Is a Local Users Group?

In most cases, the best way to obtain free software for your machine is to join your local users group. Users groups are mutual help societies that are usually staffed and run by volunteers and dedicated to the general promotion of computer knowledge.

According to Sol Libes, professor of electronics at Union County College in New Jersey, "The first computer club was founded in 1965. It was a national organization called the American Computer Society, and it had as many as 250 members. [Professor Libes should know, since he was one of them.] The first local group was the Homebrew Computer Club of Palo Alto, California, which was established in April 1975."

The Homebrewers were hobbyists. They had to be. The only microcomputer available at that time had to be soldered together by hand. The technology was new. Information was scarce. And users groups were a natural development. Today, exactly the reverse is true—there is more technology and more information than ever before. But on at least one level, the fundamental situation hasn't changed. New computer users still need help in making sense of it all.

FreeTip: That first computer was the MITS Altair 8800, and it appeared on the cover of *Popular Electronics* in January of 1975. The enthusiasm that greeted this do-it-yourself kit took everyone by surprise. Created by retired Air Force engineer Ed Roberts, the Altair was a watershed machine. It was the catalyst for many of the things you will encounter as you move through the world of users groups. For example:

- The S-100 bus (essentially a "standard" wiring diagram for a computer's main circuit board) was introduced by the Altair and is still in use today. As you will see later, there are even special interest groups devoted to S-100 machines.

- Bill Gates and Paul Allen created Altair BASIC, the predecessor to Microsoft BASIC, now the de facto standard in the industry and the most widely used computer language in the world. The two went on to found Microsoft, Inc., one of the largest, most successful software firms in the country.

- David Bunnell, Vice President of MITS, Inc., was the founding publisher of *Personal Computing*, *PC* Magazine, and *PC World*.

- The Homebrew Computer Club spawned by the Altair was the site chosen by Steven Jobs and Steven Wozniak to present the Apple I, a machine they designed and built in the Jobs family garage.

Finally, the success of the Altair encouraged other companies to bring out their own machines. Among the early ones were the Polymorphic, Processor Technology, and Vector. The now defunct IMSAI, the computer used by the "hero" of the movie *WarGames,* was another early machine that is significant because it was the first to offer CP/M as its standard operating system.

Given the millions of people who now own computers, the need for assistance has grown far beyond what even the most prescient Hombrewer could have imagined. Thus it is little wonder that by some estimates there are between 2,000 and 2,500 computer users groups in North America. What is surprising is how few computer owners are aware of them and of the many things they have to offer.

On the other hand, perhaps it isn't so surprising after all. The store you buy your system from may or may not have a users group bulletin board to aid you in making contact. Your salesperson may be aware of local groups, but if you don't know to ask, he or she may forget to tell you. Most users groups do little or no advertising, so you may not discover them that way. In short, you as a new computer owner must frequently take the initiative.

Once you get "plugged in," you'll discover that there is an informal network of users groups across the continent. Many groups regularly exchange newsletters and information, and many share their member-contributed free software.

In almost all users groups there will be a "software librarian" who has taken the responsibility for organizing, building, and maintaining the group's free software collection. Frequently, the librarian and assisting members will bring the entire library to the group's monthly meeting. And either before, after, or during the meeting, members will be free to pick up any programs they want. If you bring your own blank disks, there will usually be a copying charge of about $1 to help maintain the library. But often a club will be able to provide you with a disk at a discounted price. (If you do bring your own floppies, try to format them beforehand.)

Many clubs produce newsletters, and a subscription will almost always be included as part of your membership fee. When new public domain disks are received or prepared, they will often be announced, and their programs described, in the newsletter. Membership fees range from about $10 a year to about $25. Family memberships may also be available, usually for an extra charge of about $5 per person. The larger clubs have begun to incorporate as nonprofit, educational organizations, and in some states this makes your membership fee tax-deductible.

FreeTip: If you are an attorney, your professional expertise would undoubtedly be appreciated by your local club since the complexities of the legal system are often as foreign to programmers as the complexities of an operating system may be to you. We'll look at how other nonprogramming computer owners can contribute in a moment.

Organization and Activities

Although some computer manufacturers may offer assistance in setting up users groups, many do not. Thus there is often no national source to which a prospective organizer can turn for guidance in structuring an organization. Consequently, a users group can take many forms. It can range from a monthly get-together at someone's house to a large organization with elected officers, bylaws, and a full schedule of planned activities. Almost all active groups hold some form of monthly meeting, usually on a Saturday and usually at a local college, high school, company, or other facility.

There are usually presentations by members on how to use some commercial software package or how to solve some problem. Demonstrations of both new software and new hardware are also popular features, as are presentations by local computer retailers, businesspeople, and professionals, and others with information to share. A question-and-answer period may follow, but if the discussion of a question becomes too involved, you may hear, "See me in that corner after the meeting." Indeed, the small discussions that take place before and after the meetings can be among the most beneficial aspects of user group membership.

Many times, the informal discussions after the meetings lead to the formation of a more structured subgroup, usually called a "SIG" (Special Interest Group), and more often than not it is the SIGs that have the free software. Educators contribute instructional and grade-book management programs to their SIG; dBASE II users, Apple owners, and people who are interested in music and graphics do the same to theirs.

Making a Contribution

We'll give you some tips on the best way to locate and "plug into" a users group in your area, but first you should be aware of the need to make a contribution. As with so many things, the more you give of yourself, the more you will get out of it, and a users group can pay handsome rewards for even a small investment. On the other hand, if the members do not contribute, a group will simply cease to be. We've corresponded with or spoken to the officers of literally hundreds of users groups across the continent. It is sad to report, but after years of devoting nearly all of their spare time to operating and maintaining their clubs, more than a few of them are burned out.

So what can you give? You're a new computer owner. You don't know how to program and may see no good reason to learn. You've got your hands full just trying to use your system. How can you contribute anything of value? Many of the groups we contacted said that new users can contribute by asking questions. A new computer owner often has a different perspective than someone who has been involved for several years, and simply asking a question often enlightens everyone. Many experienced users *want* you to ask because they enjoy answering.

There are many other, more substantive things you can do. As one users group newsletter editor writes: "I joined the group in 1979 as a novice. I am still a novice, but I put out a good magazine. Non-programmers can contribute, as I do, by assuming responsibility for some segment of the club's activities. I get the bulletin out, and others contribute articles. Some members take charge of the raffle, others assist the membership chairman in enrolling new members. And with 50 to 60 new ones every month, that's a real job."

You could offer to help the club librarian organize and maintain the disk collecton. You could volunteer to establish contact with other clubs across the country (a good use for the free word processing and mailing list programs we'll show you how to get in this and other chapters!) and serve as liaison. You could help organize the monthly meeting, perhaps using contacts in your own business or profession to bring in interesting speakers. You might work at persuading local retailers to give club members a discount or organize a bulk purchase program to provide members with floppy disks, printer paper, and supplies at significantly reduced prices.

Some larger groups are even able to buy commercial software in sufficient volume to qualify for a wholesale price. But someone has to take the orders from members, handle the money, and oversee the distribution. Perhaps you could run the project. Clearly, there are many things a non-programmer can give. And each of them, however small, will be appreciated.

How to Find a Local Users Group

Start with the computer store where you purchased your machine. If you bought your system at K-Mart, Toys-Я-Us, Kiddie City, or a department store, call the Computerland, Byteshop, Software City, or other computer retailers in your area.

What you're looking for is a name and a phone number. You need some point of access to the users group world, and it often does not matter whether the specific group is dedicated to your machine or not. Call the individual (at a reasonable hour), explain that you are interested in locating a local users group for your brand of equipment, and ask about others you might contact. At that point, you will be tapped into the network. By making a few more calls and asking the appropriate questions, if the group you seek exists, you'll soon find it.

It can also be a good idea to ask friends or business associates who own computers for their suggestions. You might also contact someone at your local school system to see if any groups use the school's facilities for meetings. If there is a college in your area, check with the secretary of the engineering or computer science department to see if the college hosts a users group of some sort. Attending a local computer fair or swapmeet is another good way to make contact. Some groups also set up tables and booths as part of hobbyist and crafts exibitions at local shopping malls.

FreeTip: Radio and electronics stores can also be good sources of computer contacts. Amateur and ham radio operators have been heavily involved in personal computers from the beginning. With an interface box or two, for example, even the lowly Commodore VIC-20 can be used to access radio-based computer bulletin boards halfway around the world. (Look Ma, no telephone bill!) There is thus a good chance that a member of a ham radio club will know of computer clubs in your area. It might be worth checking with an electronics store for the name of a local ham radio club.

Computer magazines are another source of users group addresses, and you may find computer source books with a users group section. These are generally not the most reliable lists, however. In the three- to four-month lead time required for the publication of most magazine issues and the six months to a year typically required to produce a book, many of the user group addresses will have changed. Sometimes a group will fade out completely, and sometimes the person you are supposed to contact will have moved.

The most accurate magazine-based lists are usually to be found in publications devoted to your brand of computer, as opposed to those that address the computer world as a whole. Machine-specific magazines tend to keep in contact with related users groups, and many members of those groups are subscribers. There is at least one notable exception to this rule, however, and that is *The Computer Shopper*, a newspaper tabloid-style publication now available on many magazine racks. *The Computer Shopper* has a regular "users group" column in every issue featuring machine-specific tips gleaned from club newsletters and an extensive list of addresses contributed by the clubs themselves.

> **FreeTip:** Even the most accurate list will not be completely reliable. In the course of preparing this book we assembled a list from many sources and sent out hundreds of letters. Slightly over 14.15% of them were returned stamped "Return to sender. Address unknown." All of which underlines the benefits of locating a group by personally contacting people in your area.

Super Groups and Software-Specific Organizations

Virtually everyone interested in free software can benefit from membership in a local organization, but if you happen to live in a less populated area, there may not *be* a local group for you to join. Or you may find that the library available for your machine is not as extensive as you would like. Or you may be interested in free programs for which there is no local library. In addition, some people don't have the time to participate in a local group. Others simply are not "joiners."

This is why it is important to know about "super groups," a term we have coined to refer to especially large users groups. For example, where a local group may have 60 to 80 members, a super group will have hundreds, and in some cases thousands. A local group may have five or six SIGs, while a super group will have dozens or even scores of special subgroups, each with its own free software collection. Most importantly, a super group will usually accept memberships from people all over the continent and sometimes around the world.

The super groups did not start out as national or regional entities. They still function as local "umbrella" organizations and view serving local members as their primary goal. But due to their location, the nature and size of the surrounding population, and sometimes the dynamism of their leaders, they have grown beyond their local area. (Many of the software- and language-specific groups discussed in the next chapter, in contrast, have always been national groups and can only be joined on that level.)

Membership in a super group is worth considering for at least three reasons. First, since they are so large, they are likely to have more members contributing to their free software collections. They are also more likely than many local groups to have a regular free software exchange program with other large groups. With more workers at its disposal, a super group or one of its SIGs may be able to respond more quickly to your request than some other organizations. Finally, if you have either a very new computer model or a very old one, you are much more likely to find a SIG devoted to its support under the umbrella of a super group than anywhere else. The same is true if you have a special area of interest (legal, medical, marketing, robotics, artificial intelligence, etc.) that is not supported by your local group.

There are other benefits that may or may not be important to you. Large groups, for example, can often attract a greater variety of speakers for their monthly meetings. You may not be able to attend, but the newsletter you receive with your membership will cover the presentations of significant speakers in detail. There may be discount buying plans for members, enabling you to order supplies and commercial software through the group at reduced prices. And the information and publications you receive may be of a somewhat higher quality and present a broader view of computers and personal computing than local group newsletters can be expected to provide.

How to Locate and Join a Super Group

The techniques for locating a super group are similar to those used to find local organizations. More persistence may be required, however. From an organizational standpoint, the personal computer field is so new that at this writing group-to-group communication can be spotty. Some large organizations maintain active correspondence programs, some simply exchange newsletters, and some are largely unaware of what's going on outside of their states or regions. A national association of computer users groups has yet to emerge, though it seems like a logical development some time in the future.

Until this happens, the best course is to look at the users group list in *The Computer Shopper* or some other magazine, pick several addresses that look promising, and send them a letter requesting a sample copy of their newsletter. Groups with words like "Area," "Regional," "Society," or other non–machine-specific words in their names are the most likely candidates. Write each one a letter expressing your interest in becoming a remote member and ask whether this is possible. (At least one super group we know of, the North Orange County Computer Club in California, requires members to apply in person as a way of encouraging participation.) You might suggest that the recipient jot a reply right on your letter and mail it back with the newsletter.

Be sure to send two or three first class stamps and an address label to eliminate the possibility that your stamped envelope may be too small for the newsletter. As a thoughtful gesture, you might include about two dollars to cover the cost of the newsletter itself. If the group exists and the address is correct, nine times out of ten you will get a response.

> **FreeTip:** Even if you are not a CP/M user, it may be a good idea to look at the list of SIG/M distribution points in Appendix C. Each of the individuals on this list—both in North America and abroad—has agreed to distribute the SIG/M public domain CP/M library. Since most of them are active or in some way involved in users groups in their areas, they may be the perfect people to contact for information you need, regardless of whether you use CP/M or not.

When the newsletter arrives, look to see if it includes lists of SIGs and perhaps even reports from the SIG leaders. (New additions to the SIG free software library and descriptions of the programs are a favorite topic.) Often the names, addresses, and telephone numbers of the various SIG leaders will be printed on the newsletter masthead. After you have collected several newsletters, you will be in a good position to decide which, if any, groups you want to join.

You must join the group and pay your membership fee if you want to receive its free software. However, you will not encounter any uniform policy on free software distribution. Generally, there will be a $1 to $2 copying charge per disk, plus the cost of the media (the disks) and postage. You may be able to supply your own formatted disk. But unless you are sending software to the librarian (always appreciated), it may make more sense to simply buy the disk from the users group instead of sending in one of your own. The price is usually whatever the club or individual had to pay.

A copying charge is more than fair. Disk drives, like printers, are electromechanical devices and as such represent the weak link in the computer equipment chain. They wear out and must be serviced and maintained. There are also disk mailers to buy, library catalogues to print, and the cost to the librarian of obtaining software from other groups.

> **FreeTip:** Whether you obtain your free software from a super group or not, sometimes the newsletters themselves are worth the membership fee. An article by Bill Lee in "The I/O Port," the newsletter of the Tulsa Computer Society (profiled below), demonstrated a technique for increasing the Atari 400's memory from 16K to 64K for about $60. Users group newsletters frequently con-

FreeTip continued

tain programming tips, short pieces of code you can type in yourself, and other pieces of information that can save time and money. If tips like these are of interest, however, you will probably be better off obtaining the newsletters published by the appropriate machine-specific group cited in Chapter 5.

Super Group Profiles

We have prepared four profiles of super groups in different parts of the country. These are intended both as examples of what you can expect when contacting a super group and as suggestions of groups you may want to join. Each is unique, and we think you'll find each of them fascinating.

The Boston Computer Society, Inc. (BCS)
One Center Plaza
Boston, MA 02108
(617) 367-8080
9:30 AM to 5:30 PM (EST)

Membership: 12,000.
Cost of Membership: $24/year.

Youth: $15/year	Sustaining: $120
Family: $36/year	Corporate: $200
Overseas: $48/year	Life: $2,000

Publications: Computer Update; 6 issues/year; 60 pages; "slick" magazine format.
"Calendar"; monthly summary of meetings and events.
Various sub-groups publish their own newsletters as well.

BCS Information Line: (617) 227-9178 (24 hours; 7 days a week; updated by noon every Monday).

BCS Computer Bulletin Board: (617) 969-9669 (300 baud; 8/N/1; see Chapter 7 for an explanation of these communications settings.)

User and Interest Groups:

Apple
Artificial Intelligence
Atari
Kaypro
Legal
Logo

Business
Commodore
Consultants & Entrepreneurs
CP/M
Database
Digital Equipment
Displaywriter
Educational Resource Exchange
80/Boston
Family HUG
Graphics
Hewlett Packard
IBM/PC
Investment
Medical/Dental
Osborne
Ohio Scientific (OSI)
Otrona
Pascal
Real Estate
Research
Robotics
Sinclair/Timex
Social Impact
Telecommunications
Texas Instruments
Training & Documentation
UNIX/C
Victor

Comments: The Boston Computer Society (BCS) is a phenomenal organization. There's simply nothing else like it anywhere in the world. Founded by Jonathan Rotenberg ("Wrote-en-berg") in 1976 when he was 13, the BCS now has has more than 12,000 members, a figure that officials report *doubles* every year. Part of the group's success is its location. Route 128, the "beltway" (also known as Interstate 95) that girds Boston, is the home of so many computer hardware and software companies that it is often called "Silicon Valley—East." The Boston area also has more colleges and universities than any other city. But most important of all, Boston has Jonathan Roberg, a man whose energy, ideas, and enthusiasm are responsible for what the BCS is today—and what it is likely to become in the future.

Mr. Rotenberg is exceptional for another reason as well. His interests have never been "computers for the sake of computers." From the beginning, Mr. Rotenberg has been dedicated to aiding the nontechnical, noncomputerist computer owner in really benefiting and using the technology at his disposal. The Boston group reflects this orientation in nearly all of its many activities.

The BCS itself serves as a master super group umbrella organization that is responsible for all major events and activities. Beneath that umbrella are more than 30 User and Interest groups, and some of these are quite large. Over 4,300 BCS members are also members of the IBM group, for example. The Consultants & Entrepreneurs group has 3,500 members.

All of these groups have separate meetings, and many publish their own newsletter. Within the U&Is there may be any number of Special Interest Groups (SIGs) dedicated to some aspect of the main group's interest. For example, within the Consultants group there are SIGs or subgroups focusing on marketing software, getting venture capital, accounting, business planning, and more. The Commodore group has SIGs for most Commodore models (PET, VIC, C-64, etc.). These subgroups also have separate meetings, usually just prior to the main group get-together.

"PC Report," the 44-page magazine-style newsletter published by the IBM/PC SIG, offers an excellent example of the free software possibilities open to BCS members. "PC Report" carries a regular column devoted to free IBM software. A recent issue, for example, reported on HOST-III and HOSTCALL (Disks 37 and 38), two automatic communications programs. HOSTCALL is especially interesting because it allows you to tell your system to call any number of databases or BBSs at the times you specify and automatically exchange specified files. The same issue described Charles Bicking's PAYBYFON ("Pay-By-Phone"). If your bank offers a pay-by-phone service, this program can help you automate that monthly chore.

EPSLIST (Disk 40; prints text files in newspaper-style columns), RV-EDIT (Disk 14; a full-screen word processor), and a program that will phone the Dow Jones News/Retrieval service and automatically update your stock portfolio, were also described. All of these disks (single-sided) are available to members by mail at a cost of $6 each. Double-sided disks containing two volumes of free programs are $7.

FreeTip: HOST-III and HOSTCALL are available under the Freeware concept explained in Chapter 11. The suggested contribution is $35. Contact the author of this software at:

Mr. William H. T. Bailey
P.O. Box 29723
Elkins Park, PA 19117-0923
CompuServe: 74145,1046

It's good to remember that the Boston society is the original core group, as opposed to a loose confederacy created after the fact. Virtually all of the U&Is were spawned by various BCS members, so the main BCS group is still where much of the action is. There is no better example of this than the BCS monthly meeting, sometimes attended by as many as 2,000 people. This meeting is often a major event in the industry. The January 1984 meeting, for example, featured Apple Chairman Steven Jobs and served as the "world premier" of that firm's new Macintosh computer. When the portable IBM-compatible Compaq computer was introduced, Rod Canion, the firm's president, flew up from Houston to present it at a similar BCS meeting. Though not always such a major event, the BCS monthly meeting almost always features either a new product introduction or a presentation by a well-known industry figure.

This doesn't do you much good, of course, if you are a member living in Nevada or western Canada or are otherwise unable to attend. But you can read about it in the society's slick *Computer Update* magazine that all members receive. Edited by Stewart Alsop II, the magazine has a different flavor than most computer publications do. It aims to keep readers informed about what is going on in the microworld with straight talk, a minimum of jargon, and technical details on an "as necessary" basis.

FreeTip: For anyone seriously interested in the details of microcomputer market developments, a subscription to *InfoWorld* is a sine qua non. However, if you're into computers but not *that* into computers, *Computer Update* may be a good alternative. It will keep you abreast of major developments in hardware and software and what they mean without going into the kind of detail professionals need. Interestingly, Stewart Alsop II is the editor of *InfoWorld* and the editorial director of *Computer Update*.

In addition to receiving the magazine and a single-sheet calendar that announces meetings and activities taking place during the coming month, each BCS member is entitled to join two User and Interest groups free of charge. You may join an unlimited number of other groups, as well, but there is a $5 charge per group. Membership in a U&I entitles you to attend the group's meetings and receive any publications that it issues. It also provides you with access the the group's free software library. As with many other users groups, public domain software is normally exchanged before or after the group's regular meeting. However, Ms. Kathi Kuehn, director of member programs, reports that many groups are willing to mail library disks to distant members. At this writing there is no uniform policy on software distribution or pricing among the various groups, though the question is being actively considered. Consequently your best approach would be to join the BCS and then plug into the User and Interest groups that are most important to you.

FreeTip: According to the February 1984 issue of *Computer Update,* the following groups produce regular newsletters: Atari, Commodore, Consultants, TRS-80/Boston, IBM/PC, Investment,

FreeTip continued

Logo, OSI, Osborne, Sinclair/Timex, Training/Documentation. Other newsletters—and other groups—may be added in the future, so be sure to check with the BCS for the latest information.

If you happen to live near Boston—or if you are ever passing through—you'll be able to take advantage of other BCS facilities as well. The Resource Center in the group's main office, for example, serves as a central information clearinghouse, offering a library of computer books and magazines, collections of personal computers, and information files on computers, software, applications, consultants, and courses. The center is open Monday through Friday, 9:30 AM to 5:30 PM.

Every Saturday between 10:00 AM and 2:00 PM, the BCS holds one of its Saturday Clinics. These are small, informal, hands-on workshops, and you must phone ahead to make a reservation. The cost is $4 for BCS members, $8 for nonmembers. If you can, you'll want to check the "Calendar" to find out which clinic is being held on which Saturday. Clinic topics include Beginners, Hardware, Word Processing and Software, Financial Software, and more.

BCS membership entitles you to discounts of 5% to 10% at many computer stores in the Boston area. And whether you are a member or not, you will be interested in the new Computer Discovery Center scheduled to open sometime in 1984. It is hoped that this will be "the only comprehensive, public computer-education facility of its kind in the United States," according to BCS planning director Jim Zien. It will be open seven days a week and will offer access to hands-on exhibits of computer applications in many fields, a public computer laboratory with perhaps 50 personal computers and associated software and peripherals, a retail store, regular seminars and lectures, and more. (If you are a computer or software manufacturer, Mr. Zien would be interested in hearing from you about donating your products for use at the center.)

At this writing, it is planned to offer memberships in the center. But a nonmember admission fee policy will also be established. If you're ever in Boston, "check it out," as the saying goes.

The San Diego Computer Society
P.O. Box 81444
San Diego, CA 92138

Cost of Membership: $15 for the first year and $10 per year thereafter, if renewal is received before first year's membership expires. For family membership, add an additional $5 per person. Foreign membership: $25/year. Life membership: $100.

Publication: "Personal Systems"; monthly; 44 pages.

SIGs:

Atari
BUG (Beginning Users Group)
Commodore (PET)
Commodore 64 (South Bay)
CTUG (Cal-Trans employees)
dBASE (North County)
dBUG—dBASE II, beginners
dBUG2—dBASE II, advanced
DIG (Disabled Interest Group)
EDIG (Educators Interest Group)
Epson QX-10
Forth Systems
Heath/Zenith
IBM/PC
Kaypro
68xx
Kaypro (Solana Beach/Encinitas)
Kaypro (Southbay)
Microcomputer Innovators—Z-80, CP/M, Pascal, S-100, etc.
Morrow
NEC-6100 1-A
Osborne
Otrona
Personal Investment
Robotics
Sorcerer (formerly Exidy SIG)
Texas Instruments
TRS-80
UNIX/C
Wang
Xerox

Comments: As its information sheet points out, "the San Diego Computer Society (SDCS) is a non-profit corporation chartered in the State of California in 1976 for the advancement of personal computing. SDCS is a general interest collection of both diverse and specialized activities." The group's main activities are producing its monthly newsletter, holding an annual Computer Fair (begun in 1980, the Fair has become a major computer event in the San Diego area), and conducting monthly SDCS meetings.

The monthly meetings usually feature a speaker and a demonstration of some hardware or software product, or a tutorial on some subject of special interest. During the meetings, a computer "swapmeet" is held in adjoining rooms. Here members of the various SIGs meet to exchange public domain software and to buy and sell equipment. "Members can attend as many Special Interest Groups as they desire. There is no fee or extra charge except as it may apply within the particular group for certain services, such as copying disks, etc."

In addition to the software libraries maintained by most SIGs, the Microcomputer Innovators SIG (CP/M, Z-80, Pascal, etc.) has several major series of floppy disks available. These include UCSD Pascal Version 1.4, JRT Pascal, the entire CPMUG and SIG/M users group libraries, and a library of disks contributed by SDCS SIG members. The cost is $2 per disk when you supply the disk, but the SIG has blanks available at a reduced price. The Heath/Zenith has the complete CPMUG library available for downloading to Heath format.

For remote members, the group advises joining the SDCS and then getting in touch with the appropriate SIG leader for details about ordering SIG library disks by mail. Names and addresses of SIG leaders are published in "Personal Systems." And speaking of the club's newsletter, if you have an article, a tip, or other information you feel may be of interest, the SDCS would love to hear from you. No payment is made for contributions, but wouldn't you like to see your name in print?

The group also maintains several bulletin board systems. These run at 300 baud 8/N/1 and are available to members 24 hours. Hit your <ENTER> key once when the phone is answered. Here are the numbers:

SDCS CBBS: (619) 236-0742
SDCS IBM SIG: (619) 268-0437
SDCS RC-HEATH SIG: (619) 461-5117
SDCS CP/M Exchange: (619) 273-4354

The Tulsa Computer Society
P.O. Box 1133
Tulsa, OK 74101

Membership: 600.

Cost of Membership: $10/year.

Publication: "The I/O Port"; monthly; 24 pages.

SIGs:

Apple	dBASE II
Atari	Engineering
Audio-Video	Handicapped
COCO and MICRO COLOR	IBM/PC
Computer BBS	Texas Instruments
Commodore	Youth Users' Group
CP/M	Other regional groups

Comments: This is one of the largest, most active groups in its region, and it offers remote members an excellent way to "plug in." A major event is the group's annual Woodland Hills Computer Show. When the first one was held in 1982, the group had only 65 members, but by the end of the two-day event, more than 100 new members had signed up. The society now has in excess of 500 members, and its shows get bigger and bigger each year.

Si Hawk, editor of "The I/O Port," says that "A big problem in the past was that people would join, learn everything we had, then go their merry way. Now they learn about the machines, then help others learn about them, as well as sharing information with other members." All of the society's SIGs either have or are actively building public domain software libraries. The newsletter carries the names of the individuals to contact in each case. It also carries machine-specific tutorials and Annette Hinshaw's excellent "Generic BASIC" column.

The Connecticut Computer Society
180 Bloomfield Avenue
Hartford, CT 06105
(203) 233-3373

Cost of Membership: $20/year
Family: $30
Student: $15 (up to 12th grade)
Institutional: $55 (nonprofit; may send five individuals to society meetings; receive three copies of newsletter).
Corporate: $150 (same privileges as nonprofit institutions but also receive listing in each newsletter issue).

Publication: "CCS News"; monthly; tabloid-style newspaper; 12 pages.

Comments: The Boston Computer Society has Jonathan Rotenberg, and Connecticut has Bruce Brown. The two men have created two very different organizations, but the spirit, intent, and dedication are the same. The Connecticut Computer Society (CCS) is an umbrella organization established by Mr. Brown at least in part to provide a common meeting point and forum for all the users and users groups in the state and surrounding areas. Other users groups are completely independent of CCS, but CCS actively encourages its members to join. Each issue of the "CCS News," for example, lists more than 50 users groups, their meeting schedules, contact person, and phone number.

As quoted in *InfoWorld*, Mr. Brown says, "I was concerned those groups might think we wanted to take them over, but we're only interested in supporting them. My fantasy is to have people join the CCS and then move on to specific groups. We'll still be here as a central clearinghouse of information, and they can still attend whatever meetings interest them."

Meetings and seminars are at the heart of CCS activities and offerings. Mr. Brown, a former teacher and counselor at the Watkinson School, feels quite strongly that people have a need for computer information that is not being adequately met through other sources. Thus, for new or prosepctive owners, the CCS holds the Computer Literacy/Survival seminar; for more experienced users, there is a Z-80 Assembly

Language seminar; other meeting and seminar topics include buying your first computer, word processing, an introduction to Lotus 1-2-3, and educational uses of computers.

If you are interested *strictly* in free software, the Connecticut Computer Society is not for you. At least not yet, since at this writing a library of programs has yet to be created. However, if you live in Connecticut or any of its contiguous states, a CCS membership is worthy of your consideration for a number of reasons. First, the newsletter can make it easy to get in touch with nearby users groups that *do* have extensive free software libraries. These are organizations you might not discover any other way. And if you did, you might find only a possibly unreliable address in an out-of-date users group listing. If a group is listed in the monthly "CCS News," it is a going concern.

Second, if you are interested in purchasing computer hardware and software at a discount, Mr. Brown has arranged for all CCS members to join the National Computer Club at a net cost of $14.95 (regular price: $29.95). Mr. Brown has investigated the firm, and he reports that it makes its money solely on membership fees. All products are sold at cost, plus shipping.

Third, if you own a Coleco Adam computer, this may very well turn out to be one of the major clearinghouses for information on that system. Coleco is based in West Hartford, and CCS members have on a number of occasions been enlisted to aid in testing and providing their reactions to prototypes. Though CCS is not associated with Coleco in any way, the lines of communication between the former Connecticut Leather Company and the Connecticut Computer Society appear to be quite good.

Finally, there is an undefinable "good feeling" to the organization that leads one to conclude that they may have something here. There are small touches and details, like the low admission charge for nonmembers ($1 for kids under 12, $2 for everyone else, for a four-hour, five-presentation meeting); like the fact that driving directions are provided in the newsletter following all meeting and seminar announcements; like the tone of the (largely original) articles and the prohibition against computer jargon, and the nature of the seminars that are offered.

There is also the fact that like many users groups, the CCS depends on volunteer labor but somehow manages a more professional approach. Members know their newsletters are going to arrive on time and that they will contain something of value. They know that the meetings will be well-organized, start reasonably on schedule, and that events will take place as announced. For all of the wonderful, selfless work put in by volunteers in other organizations, these things can only happen when at least one person devotes his full time and energies to making them happen. And at CCS, that person is Mr. Bruce Brown.

FreeTip: Here's a tip for Apple users taken from the December 1983 issue of "CCS News." Two teenagers in the Bolton, Connecticut, area have begun a unique service. Send them a disk with a single well-written, original program (DOS 3.2 or 3.3 in Applesoft, Integer, machine, or assember), and they will mail back five programs on disk. There is a $3 charge for shipping and handling.

You will want to send for a list of the programs you have to choose from. But at this writing there is one to alter all DOS 3.3 command names, one to handle your checking account, a hi-res graphics demo, *Starcross* (a pinball game written using Bill Budge's famous pinball program), a program that makes musical sounds as game paddles are moved around, and more. The gentlemen to contact are Ken Reiss and Dan Costello (Please make all checks out to Dan Costello) at:

Apple Program Exchange (A.P.E.)
150 South Road
Bolton, CT 06040

Recommendations

Although no recommendation will apply to every computer owner, it is probably fair to say that almost everyone interested in free software should join a local users group. These organizations provide the fastest, easiest access to the the programs you want. For a wider perspective and a greater selection of programs, it is also a good idea to consider joining one or more super groups.

The super groups profiled in this chapter are good places to start, but remember, they are not the only super groups in existence. The New York Amateur Computer Club and the Amateur Computer Group of New Jersey (see Chapter 2) are large organizations with multiple machine-specific SIGs. On the opposite coast there is the Northwest Computer Society (P.O. Box 4193, Seattle, WA 98104) and the Silicon Valley Computer Society (P.O. Box 60506, Sunnyvale, CA 94088). You may want to consider contacting all of these organizations as well as the others that you discover.

Then again, you may not. It all depends on how deeply involved you wish to become. And, at $15 or more per membership, you may find that joining many groups is not financially feasible. Consequently, we suggest joining a local group immediately (if there is one in your area). There's more good stuff coming up, so you may want to wait until you have read the rest of this book before deciding which nonlocal organizations to join.

...4...

VisiCalc®, dBASE II®, and Other Software-Specific Collections: *Templates, Worksheets, Command Files, and More*

None of the super groups in the previous chapter started as national organizations. They began as local users groups and achieved their present stature either through growth or, as is the case with SIG/M, by filling the need for a central clearinghouse for public domain CP/M programs. The points of access we'll look at in this chapter are different. Instead of being organized along geographical lines, they are organized on the basis of software ownership, in the same way that an association of Ford owners might be formed without regard to where its members happened to live.

These national sources divide naturally into a number of categories. There are sources of spreadsheet templates, such as those used with VisiCalc; sources of dBASE II and other database management program command files; and sources of software written for use with specific computer lanugages or operating systems like the the p-System™, Forth, CBASIC, or MS-DOS. (We will explain all of these terms in a moment.)

The reason these points of access exist lies in the nature of the software they were created to support. For example, although various public domain collections have programs that will let you customize your copy of WordStar™ or remove control characters from its files, there is not much opportunity to create software for use with a word processing program. But spreadsheets and database management systems like dBASE II are an entirely different matter.

These programs can serve as "software engines" to drive an all but infinite number of applications—if you feed them the right template or command file. Since these are among the best-selling kinds of applications software, national support organizations are a natural development. Local support is growing as well, though not quite as fast.

Nationally based language-specific groups are also a natural, though for a different reason. You may know many people who program in BASIC, but how many do you know who use the computer language called "Forth"? If you live in a large city, you may know quite a few. But more than likely, there will not be a Forth SIG in your local interest group. Consequently, a Forth programmer must often turn elsewhere for support. Many are members of FIG, the national "Forth Interest Group" profiled later.

If you are interested in VisiCalc, SuperCalc, dBASE II, or other free, product-specific software, this chapter will help you "plug in" at the appropriate point. If you already use one of the languages, you are probably aware of its national support group and its free software collections. But if you are interested in learning more about a different language, you'll find that the groups discussed here are excellent places to contact.

Free Spreadsheet Software

A Word About Spreadsheets . . .

There is a growing amount of spreadsheet template software in the public domain, but if you have never used a spreadsheet program like VisiCalc, SuperCalc, or Multiplan, you probably don't have any idea what a template is or why it's important. The relationship between templates and spreadsheet software is not difficult to understand. Spreadsheets consist of columns and rows (lines across), and where the two intersect, they form a "cell." When you lay out a personal computer spreadsheet, you assign labels to various rows and columns, and you assign "formulas" (operations to be performed) to many of the cells. All this makes it possible for you to enter information, such as your most recent stock sale or purchase, and let the program automatically figure your net profit (or loss).

Once the "model" has been created, it can be recorded on disk as a file. That file is the template. The next time you want to update your stock portfolio, you have only to load your main spreadsheet program and then load the file or template that reproduces all the labels and formulas in your stock-portfolio worksheet. As long as the template is of the type that the spreadsheet software can accept, it doesn't matter whether you created the template yourself or obtained it from someone else.

FreeTip: Here are several lines from a VisiCalc breakeven model template. As you can see, this is a simple textfile:

```
>L46:/FR
>D21:+C21*B6*(.01*(100-B19))-(B11+(B18*C21
>A21:"  UNITS
>A19:"%DISCOUNT
>D18:+C18*B6*(.01*(100-B19))-(B11+(B18*C18
>A16:"PACKAGE:
>A15:"LABOR:
>A5:" WIDGETS
```

Although some of the words that will be used as labels are obvious, the other symbols have a special meaning only to the VisiCalc program. VisiCalc, SuperCalc, Multiplan, and similar programs use this same technique to record and then reconstruct the spreadsheets created by their users. (For more information on spreadsheets, how they work, and what to look for when buying one, see *How to Buy Software*, Chapter 15.

Spreadsheets can be used for many things. So many, in fact, that a growing number of people are using VisiCalc and similar spreadsheet programs as "software engines" to drive applications that include everything from home accounting, budgeting, and checkbook balancing to inventory accounting, payroll, and internal rate of return calculations. For many, buying a spreadsheet program and then using an inexpensive (or free) template for these applications makes more sense than purchasing commercial programs dedicated to each of these tasks.

Predictions are always hazardous, but as more and more businesspeople and professionals equip their offices with personal computers, the number of free spreadsheet templates in the public domain is bound to grow dramatically. Relatively few computer owners can (or care to) write an assembly language routine or a Pascal procedure, but almost anyone can create a spreadsheet.

Because templates exist as textfiles, it's generally true that if you can find a way to get the file onto a disk your machine can read, you can use that template with the appropriate commercial program. The best way to do this is often to download the file into your computer from a bulletin board, or from a CompuServe SIG or a group on The Source. (See Chapters 8 and 9.)

FreeTip: The fact that spreadsheet templates are non–machine-specific greatly increases the number of places you can look for them. If you own an Apple, for instance, you would not normally look for free software on an IBM bulletin board or in the IBM SIG on CompuServe. But since both machines can run VisiCalc, a template from an IBM source could be as useful to you as one from your normal Apple sources. The same thing applies to all brands of machines. And, as we'll see in the next section, it applies to dBASE II command files as well.

Now let's look at some sources of free worksheet and template software for Lotus 1-2-3™, Multiplan™, SuperCalc®, and VisiCalc®. If you have just purchased one of these programs, you may be amazed at what the following files will enable you to do. For example, here's a good free program that will help you with your investments:

"Keeping Track of Your Stocks"

Mr. Andrew T. Williams
915 Contra Costa Avenue
Berkeley, CA 94707

Form: Spreadsheet template.

Cost: $10 (Be sure to specify which of the above commercial programs you plan to use; IBM/PC DOS only.)

Among other things, the "Keeping Track of Your Stocks" template will tell you how much you've made or lost since you bought your stocks each time you enter their current prices, how much commission will be subtracted from the gross sale price when you sell, the percentage change on an annualized basis so you can see how stocks you've owned for different periods of time are performing, whether you have held a stock long enough to qualify for captital gains tax treatment, and more.

Mr. Williams plans to do more templates in the future. He is particularly interested in combining this one with a dividend payments table. In the meantime, you might want to take a look at his book. Mr. Williams is a skilled writer with a special knack for explaining things clearly. The title to look for is:

> *WHAT IF . . . : A Guide to Using Electronic Spreadsheets on the IBM Personal Computer*
> by Andrew T. Williams
> John Wiley & Sons

FreeTip: The "Keeping Track of Your Stocks" template was originally published and described in *PC World* magazine (vol. 1, no. 4). Mr. Williams provided all of the information needed to create the identical template on your machine, but at the end of the article he offered to send the template on disk to readers who requested it. (It was originally available in VisiCalc and SuperCalc formats only, but Mr. Williams tells us that versions for Lotus and Multiplan are now available as well.) All of which goes to show that it pays to read computer magazines.

Computer magazines have always published type-it-yourself program listings. But every now and then, you will encounter someone like Mr. Williams who is willing to supply a disk that will save you hours of work. Increasingly, you will also find computer magazines themselves offering to supply the programs they print on disk or cassette tape.

Management Information Source, Inc.
3543 N.W. Broadway
Portland, OR 97232
(503) 287-1462

Publications: The Power of Multiplan and other books with similar titles devoted to specific commercial programs.

Price: $14.95 for each book; $28.95 for book with MS-DOS/PC-DOS disk.

This is not a source of public domain software, but one must admit that at a cost as low as $1.31 per spreadsheet template on disk and a tutorial manual that will show you how to use your program, the book/disk products published by this firm may be the next best thing. There are book/disk combinations available for Multiplan, Lotus 1-2-3, financial calculations for Lotus 1-2-3, and financial calculations for Multiplan. Each book contains between 10 and 22 templates, and to save you the trouble of typing, the same templates have been recorded on disk. Other titles are available without disks, including one for Commodore 64 owners who use Calc Result. In these cases, you will have to type things in yourself.

We asked the company if they knew of any spreadsheet-based users groups who might have libraries of free templates, but they did not. However, a spokesperson wanted to be sure that Commodore owners were aware that the HESWARE package available for their computers is that firm's version of Microsoft's Multiplan, and the Multiplan books (but not the disks) can be used by them. Also, the Altos Financial Planner program is that firm's version of Multiplan, and Altos owners can use the same books as well.

The books are being distributed by Prentice-Hall, so they should be widely available. If they are not in your local book or computer store, you may order them directly from the above address. There is a $1 charge for shipping. Visa, MasterCard, and American Express accepted.

FreeTip: There is a new publication that may be of interest to users of spreadsheets and other programs, called *Business Software Magazine*. This is a reincarnation and significant expansion of *The Power of Electronic Spreadsheets*, formerly published by MIS, the firm cited above. Conversations with editor Jeff Brown indicate that the magazine, which "premiered" at the SOFTCON '84 software convention held in New Orleans in February of that year, will focus on the use of spreadsheets, database management programs, word processing, and other types of software used by business managers to increase productivity and profitability.

The magazine is scheduled to average approximately 130 pages an issue, with a controlled circulation of 200,000. There will be a business-at-home section, a business solutions section, tutorial material, and more. Most important of all to a free software hunter, Mr. Brown indicates that the magazine will present in-depth solutions and problem-solving examples. Consequently, you may discover that you can find useful additions to your spreadsheet templates, dBASE command files, and similar software.

For more information, contact:

Business Software Magazine
2464 Embarcardaro Way
Palo Alto, CA 94303
(415) 424-0600

Subscription: $25/year (12 issues)

dBASE II Command File Software

A Word About dBASE II . . .

Available for both CP/M and MS-DOS (IBM/PC DOS) machines, Ashton-Tate's dBASE II is one of the best-selling database management systems (DBMS) on the market. This program, often called simply dBASE, is a relational database with the power to do everything from handling a simple mailing list to serving as the basis for a completely integrated accounting package. You'll find more information on dBASE II, as well as an explanation of the crucial differences between a "relational database" and a "file management" program, in Chapter 16 of *How to Buy Software*. For now it is enough to know that "command files" are the key to unlocking dBASE power.

Just as you can build a financial model by laying out a VisiCalc or other spreadsheet, you can build a dBASE II program by entering a series of unique commands to tell the program what to do. As with spreadsheet templates, these commands are stored in a textfile. Whenever you want to use dBASE to, say, print a list of names on your mailing list, you first load the main program and then tell it to load the appropriate "command file." From then on, the dBASE program follows your prerecorded commands, just as BASIC follows a prerecorded program.

FreeTip: Here's the beginning of a command file written to print address labels taken from a dBASE file called CONTACT.

```
USE CONTACT
SET PRINT ON
STORE 0 TO COUNT
DO WHILE FIRST < LAST + 1
GO FIRST
IF MR:S:FNAME <> "  "
? TRIM (MR:S:FNAME), LAST:TITLE
ENDIF
```

As with VisiCalc and other spreadsheet templates, this is a simple textfile. Each of the words has a special meaning to dBASE and, as with a spreadsheet, the program itself doesn't care where the words came from, as long as they are in its vocabulary and arranged in the proper order.

The specific commands and syntax required by dBASE really constitute a unique programming language. And as with any programming language, some applications can be quite complex. You can create menus, for example, and have the program branch to a particular subroutine based on the item the user selects. Entire office management systems can be created using dBASE, as can accounting, inventory control, invoicing, and many other applications. This is not necessarily easy to do, but most people will find that the dBASE language allows them to produce sophisticated results with far less effort and far less programming knowledge than would be required using BASIC or some other traditional computer language.

This is wonderful news if you are interested in obtaining and writing free software. With a little experience, individuals who would never attempt a major BASIC program can feel comfortable writing worthwhile applications in the dBASE II language. Equally important, since those applications exist as simple text in a command file, they can be shared among all dBASE II users, regardless of their operating system or brand of computer. (Please see the previous section on spreadsheet templates for information on how to get such files into your machine.)

> **FreeTip:** dBASE II was originally issued for CP/M systems and later for the IBM/PC. However, as long as the program you are using is Version 2.4 or higher, you will have no command file compatibility problems. There is one cosmetic difference you should be aware of, however. In the CP/M version, command files end with .CMD, but in the IBM/PC version, those identical files must end with .PRG (for "program"). If you download a .PRG file into a CP/M-running Apple, you must rename the file with the .CMD extension to make it acceptable to your CP/M version of dBASE II.

Ashton-Tate's dBASE II is such a popular program that it is not surprising that users groups dedicated to sharing information about this software have recently begun to form. Some of these are free-standing groups, and some are SIGs formed under the umbrella of a super group (see Chapter 3). All are prime sources of free dBASE command files and applications software.

"dNEWS"™
10150 West Jefferson Boulevard
Culver City, CA 90230
(213) 207-1472
9 AM to 5 PM (PST)—Subscription inquiries only.

Subscription: $18 (12 issues) to U.S., Canada, and Mexico; $24 overseas. Check in U.S. dollars drawn on U.S. bank, only. Visa or MasterCard accepted. 40–50 pages.

Comments: The Ashton-Tate publication "dNEWS" is a good place to find the names of the users groups nearest you. A recent edition listed 18 of them in 10 states. (If you are forming a database users group,

Ashton-Tate would be happy to include you on their list. Contact them at the address above.) You'll also find a questions-and-answers column, "how-to" articles by dBASE II users, and handy short dBASE programs you can type in yourself.

"dNEWS" may be available in your computer store's magazine rack at a single copy price of $3. It is certainly worth a look, and if you are seriously interested in using dBASE II, it is worth a subscription.

"dNOTES"™
P.O. Box 86
Woodvale
Deerfield, IL 60015
(312) 940-1010

Subscription: $24/year (6 issues); $37/year outside of the United States; 20–30 pages.

Comments: This is a publication offered by Jim Graham, a professional dBASE II programmer and consultant. Mr. Graham is involved with the dBASE users group movement and seems to have good lines of communication to Ashton-Tate. His articles on using dBASE and related products have appeared in a number of publications, including *PC* magazine. "dNOTES" was started because Mr. Graham sensed a genuine need among the growing number of dBASE users for support, information, tips, and help. One of his first projects, published in "dNOTES," was to show users how to create and use "macros" in dBASE by using one of its commands to assign strings to various user-selected keys.

The publication offers at least six "dPARTMENTS," including sections covering commands and features that are not in the Ashton-Tate manuals, reviews and previews, editorial comment, applications, users groups lists and other "dSOURCEs," and "dWORKS," a section devoted to command files. Mr. Graham has had a very encouraging response to his efforts and, noting that dBASE will soon be available for the PCjr and Apple Macintosh, he expects interest in dSUPPORT to grow.

FreeTip: We are grateful to Mr. Graham for suggesting the following source of free dBASE command files. ADBUS, the Atlanta Database Users Group, is said to have quite a respectable collection. For membership information, contact:

Atlanta Database User's Group (ADBUS)
Mr. Kieth Plossl
c/o George Plossl Educational Service
P.O. Box 19817
Atlanta, GA 30325

The dBASE Bulletin Board

Mr. Roger D. Brown
Computer Systems Design
131 East Hamilton Avenue
Campbell, CA 95008

Cost of Membership: $5/month; $12.50/quarter; $40/year.

BBS Phone Number: (408) 378-8733

Baud Rate: System will accept either 300 or 1200 baud.

Comments: Established in 1983, this board specializes in the exchange of tips, information, and free command files for dBASE II users. There are close to 40 free programs on the system, and more are being added every day. Roger Brown, the SysOp, reports a large amount of upload activity on the part of users who have created command files they wish to share. Among the best programs are a file that will make certain a computer operator has entered the correct ZIP code for each address on a mailing list, a complete personal income tax calculation program (requires 20 minutes to download at 1200 baud), and a command file/database catalogue of BBS and RCPM telephone numbers.

Mr. Brown's firm began the board as an outgrowth of its commercial, custom dBASE applications activities. Originally the board was open to all callers, many of whom turned out to be unfamiliar with dBASE II and the board's purpose. Expenses were also considerable, and that, combined with Mr. Brown's determination to maintain a quality board, made a membership fee a necessity. Asked whether people might not join for one month, download the complete library, and not renew their memberships, Mr. Brown says, "That's fine. Our purpose is to share information and aid the dBASE user." But he pointed out that since so many new programs are uploaded by board members each month, those people would miss out on the latest material.

dBASE II Users Association

Tradenet
Suite C-110
1930 South Alma School Road
Mesa, AZ 85202
(800) 321-9004

Product: An electronic dBASE II interest group.

Cost of Membership: $25 one-time start up fee.

Connect Time Charges:

	8 AM–6 PM	*6 PM–Midnight*	*Midnight–6 AM*
300 baud	$16/hr.	$7/hr.	$5/hr.
1200 baud	$20/hr.	$10/hr.	$8/hr.

Access via Tymnet, Uninet, or WATS line. No monthly minimum. Visa or MasterCard.

Comments: Tradenet's primary business is offering private networks, electronic mail, and other special communications services to business and industry. However, as Cheryl Repp, a company spokesperson, points out, the dBASE II Users Association is one of the company's most popular offerings. The Association is in effect based inside a Prime mainframe computer. There is an electronic service for member-to-member communication. There is a bulletin board open message exchange offering a form of computerized conferencing over time. And there is a Questions-and-Answers section that provides members with direct access to Ashton-Tate technical support. Tradenet is not a part of Ashton-Tate, but according to Ms. Repp, the Association and the creators of dBASE II work closely to support the product. Thus, the Q&A section in effect serves as Ashton-Tate's online support facility.

There is also a library section that facilitates the exchange of dBASE command files and related information. Examples of free software include a complete mailing list program that includes code for tracking magazine or other types of subscriptions. There's a personal checkbook balancing program, and there are helpful utilities like the one that automatically converts Gregorian dates to their Julian form, something that must be done when you want to calculate elapsed time or add or subtract dates.

In addition to the free software, members will find dBASE applications available for sale. There is a complete accounting package at $100 per module, for example. And there is an inexpensive application for running a plant nursery (created and uploaded by a Florida nurseryman).

In the future, many experts believe that a large percentage of commercial software will be delivered electronically, directly to the computer of the purchaser. This eliminates the need for software vendors and retailers to deal with many different disk versions of the same product, and presumably means lower prices for the consumer. Ms. Repp would like both end users and producers of dBASE applications to know that Tradenet is already serving as an important delivery mechanism for a number of software houses, at considerable savings to both parties. Interested vendors or prospective Association members should get in touch with Tradenet at the address given above.

Languages and Operating Systems

CBASIC

CBASIC Users Group
Alastair Dallas
Software Magic
11669 Valerio Street #213
North Hollywood, CA 91605
(213) 765-3957

Membership: $12/year.

Newsletter: “CB News”; 12 issues/year; 7–10 pages.

Comments: Mr. Dallas writes: “My particular interest is Compiled CBASIC, and my company, Software Magic, supports its use several ways. Our users group publishes a newsletter . . . which typically mentions the CB-80 support products that Software Magic sells, but describes competitive products as well . . . . Non-programmers (or non-professionals) can easily contribute articles, and users with a CBASIC product to sell are invited to use ‘CB News’ as a house organ. . . . Our group shares information, but not software.”

This newsletter is for serious users of Digital Research’s CBASIC product only (see Chapter 11 for an explanation of CBASIC). And while the newsletter is brief, readers will find many tips, short routines, and valuable technical discussions of CBASIC and related products. Although scrupulously independent, Mr. Dallas appears to have good contacts at Digital Research and is thus able to convey information sure to be of interest to CBASIC applications developers.

Another "rival" group that appears to maintain friendly relations with "CB News" is CBUG (C BASIC User's Group). Contact Joe Butler, editor of "CBUG," 6101 Birdcage #47, Citrus Heights, CA 95610.

MS-DOS

SIG/86
The International MS-DOS Users Group
Joseph Boykin, President
47-4 Sheridan Drive
Shrewsbury, MA 01545
(617) 845-1074 (Home)
(617) 366-8911, Ext. 3216 (Office)

Cost of Membership: $18/year; for users groups of five or more individuals joining together, the rate is $15/year.

Newsletter: "SIG/86 Newsletter"; 4–6 issues a year; 28–30 pages.

Comments: This group concentrates on MS-DOS, the Microsoft "generic" version of IBM/PC DOS designed to run on any 8088/8086 system. Mr. Boykin wants to emphasize first that the group is international in scope and thus works closely with many local MS-DOS users groups, and second that it supports *all* MS-DOS based systems. Consequently, "we require that the software we distribute run on a generic MS-DOS system and not use poor coding practices which makes that software non-portable."

The group actively pursues volume purchases of disks and other supplies to offer them at substantial discounts to members. A printed list of the SIG/86 software collection is available for $2. Or you can download it from one of the SIG/86 bulletin boards (see below). Software is available only to members.

"One of my basic philosophies," Mr. Boykin writes, "is to not take the attitude of some clubs of shipping anything they can get their hands on. I want our software to be good quality software, relatively bug free, and come with documentation. No, the software we distribute is not useful for everyone, but what piece of software is?

"In particular, our disks include the following: a text output processor (TOP) which supports over 50 commands including underlining, centering, right-margin justification, paragraphs, chapter and appendix handling, table of contents, revision bars, etc.; a UNIX-compatible spelling checker; a two-disk FIG-Forth distribution; Columbia University's KERMIT mainframe file transfer program; MODEM7; and many others."

Disks are $10 each (standard 8-inch or 5-inch double-sided/double-density). Programs occupying two 5-inch disks are $15 for the set. (The spelling checker occupies four 5-inch disks and thus costs $30.)

The newsletter is written at a computer-wise but not excessively technical level. It contains helpful articles and tips, plus a number of complete assembly language programs. Mr. Boykin would be interested in publishing articles by members on software they have used, problems encountered, and other topics of interest to the group. Individuals are also needed to serve as liaisons with local users groups around the world.

The SIG/86 bulletin boards are other good sources of information. There are two of them, one for 300-baud users and one for 1200-baud users. Please note that the systems are available from 11 PM until 6 AM, Eastern Time. Here are the two numbers:

300 baud: (617) 842-1435
1200 baud: (617) 842-1712

This is an impressive organization that is bound to be helpful to anyone using either IBM/PC DOS or MS-DOS, the dominant operating system in the 16-bit world. It is undoubtedly no accident that the group's name is patterned after SIG/M, the best-known group for users of the 8-bit standard, CP/M.

Oasis

Oasis Users' Group
Fred Bellomy
P.O. Box 2400
Santa Barbara, CA 93120
(805) 965-0265

Membership: 500.

Cost of Membership: $35/year.

Newsletter: Yes.

Comments: Oasis is a UNIX-like operating system that has been optimized for use in business applications. Fred Bellomy indicates that about 70% of OUG members are computer professionals, 15% are noncomputer professionals (doctors, attorneys, CPAs, etc.), and the balance are other end users, including "some very sophisticated hobbyists."

The group releases approximately ten volumes of member-contributed software per year. It now has over 1200 files containing utilities, tutorials, applications, games, and help files. There is a "service fee" of $35 per volume for the software on standard 8-inch disks. Tape and 5-inch disks for ONYX, Altos, Northstar, Vector Graphics, and Billings computers are slightly higher. The collection consists of about 20% utilities, 20% business and finance, 25% engineering and math, 25% games, and 10% education and miscellaneous.

Free software highlights include *Adventure*, home budget, modem, spelling checker/dictionary, typing drills, *Star Trek*, and many of the Osborne Accounting Series. (See the Gems List in Chapter 2.)

There is a members-only bulletin board called CARAVAN, for use in keeping up-to-date on Oasis developments and for ordering volumes of free software. Nonmembers may use the system to enroll in the OUG and to review reports of recent activities. The board is available 24 hours a day at 300 baud only. The phone number to dial is: (805) 965-5415.

Pascal/MT+

MTPUG
Pascal/MT+ Users Group
P.O. Box 192
Westmont, IL 60559
(312) 986-1550

Membership: 800.

Cost of Membership: $7/year; $8 in Canada or Mexico; International memberships are priced somewhat differently. (U.S. funds drawn on a U.S. bank, or add $5 for U.S. bank charges. There are discounts for 2-year and 3-year memberships.)

Newsletter: "MTPUG Newsletter"; quarterly; about 20 pages.

Comments: This is a nonprofit corporation for the support of Digital Research's Pascal/MT+ family of compilers, software that runs on most major operating systems. Founded in 1981 by Henry Lucas, the group is in no way associated with Digital Research, but information flows freely between the two organizations. The group was formed to encourage "the use of Pascal and provide the users of this rather special program product with the opportunity to communicate with others who speak their language."

The newsletter is impressive, but since most articles are written by professional and semiprofessional programmers, it is not for the new user. "The MTPUG Newsletter only publishes Pascal programs if they are short, since we have never found anyone who was willing to type long ones from printed material. Therefore, the exchange of programs between members of MTPUG will be on 'MTPUG Program Disks.'"

An index of each new disk is published in the newsletter, and an index of the entire 11-disk collection (January 1, 1984) is available. Send $2 and a self-addressed, stamped envelope. A single volume on 8-inch disk is $10. Prices for 5-inch disks range from $10 to $16. If you supply your own disk, the 8-inch cost is $2. There is a list of members who have volunteered to provide library disks in various 5-inch formats. Air mail and overseas shipping is extra. The group's European address is:

MTPUG
Pascal/MT Users Group
Guenter Musstoph
Schimmelmannstr. 37A
D-2070 Ahrensburg
West Germany
Phone: 04102/56629

UCSD Pascal and p-System

USUS
P.O. Box 1148
La Jolla, CA 92038

Cost of Membership: $25/year; surcharges for air mail delivery of newsletter to locations outside of North America.

Newsletter: "USUS News and Report"; quarterly; 100 pages; typeset.

SIGs:

Advanced System Editor	IBM/PC
Apple	NEC

Application Developer's	Publications
Communications	Sage
DEC	Software Exchange Library
File Access	Technical Issues
Graphics	Texas Instruments
IBM Displaywriter	USCD Pascal Compatibility
	. . . and more.

Comments: This is without a doubt one of the most impressive and well-organized users groups anywhere. "USUS" stands for "UCSD (Pascal) System User's Group." The p-System™ was developed by Kenneth Bowles at the University of California, San Diego (UCSD), and the trademark is held by the Regents of the University of California. (SofTech is the primary licensed vendor.) This is a computer language/operating system pairing that makes it possible for identical applications programs to be used on the Apple, IBM/PC, Texas Instruments, or any other computer, regardless of the microprocessor it is built around. (See Chapter 3 of *How to Buy Software* for more information.)

The USUS Software Exchange Library is available only to members. According to the group, it "is *not* in the public domain, but can be *used* by our members." The library consists of more than 30 volumes and includes simple and complex games, software tools, disk utilities, communications programs, business applications, LISP implementations, and more. (When you join, ask for the software library order form, which contains summaries of the volumes and all ordering information.)

If you attend one of the group's semi-annual meetings, you can copy the software for a cost of $1 per volume. However, most people will want to contact the various members who can make the library available on disks in many different formats. Prices range from $10 to about $20 a volume. Contributions to the library are always welcome. (Please try to supply programs on a standard 8-inch disk; contact the chairman of Software SIG if this is not possible.)

If you have a CompuServe subscription, you can plug into USUS immediately. The group maintains an active and growing SIG called MUSUS (MicroNET USUS) on that system. Type *GO PCS-1* at the CompuServe exclamation prompt and select MUSUS from the menu of computer groups and clubs that will appear. (See Chapter 6 for tips on using CompuServe SIGs.) If you don't have a CompuServe account—wait!—USUS can get it for you at a discount. (Typical savings: $7 off the CompuServe Starter Kit.)

"Non-programmers and new users can contribute by asking questions on MUSUS. Both the questions and the answers enlighten everybody. Also, some non-programmers help through their own specialty areas—lawyers, publishers, printers, etc."

Clearly, if you're into or interested in UCSD Pascal and the p-System, this is the group to join.

Forth

FORTH Interest Group (FIG)
P.O. Box 1105
San Carlos, CA 94070
(415) 962-8653

Membership: Over 40 chapters and over 4,000 members.

Cost of Membership: $15/year; $27/year (foreign air).

Newsletter: "FORTH Dimensions"; quarterly; 40–50 pages; typeset.

Comments: Whether you view Forth as a programming language or, like many, as something of a religion, your local FIG chapter is *the* group to belong to. The newsletter, "FORTH Dimensions," is quite impressive, though quite technical. You will find short pieces of code, discussions of various programming problems, and important advertisements for Forth products. Forth can be used on the Commodore 64, Atari computers, Apples, Northstar, and many, many more.

The newsletter includes lists of FIG chapters both in North America and worldwide; Taiwan, Belgium, Colombia, and many other countries are represented. We were not supplied with a catalogue of FIG public domain software; however, one is available for a self-addressed, stamped envelope. This is clearly a strong and vibrant users group—a real "must" for serious Forth users.

If you are interested in more information about Forth, you might contact Dick Miller of Miller Microcomputer Services. Dick and Jill Miller are responsible for MMSFORTH, an implementation available for TRS-80 and IBM personal computers. The product has been well-reviewed, though it is far from the only implementation available for those machines. But whether you are interested in MMSFORTH or not, you will find this firm a superb resource for information and publications on the Forth language. Contact:

A. Richard Miller
Miller Microcomputer Services
61 Lake Shore Road
Natick, MA 01760
(617) 653-6136
9 AM to 9 PM

Nevada COBOL

Nevada COBOL Users Group
5536 Colbert Trail
Norcross, GA 30092
(404) 449-8948

Cost of Membership: $18/year.

Newsletter: "NCUG News"

Comments: The Nevada COBOL Compiler from Ellis Computing is a subset of ANSI-74 COBOL that runs on Z80 and 8080/8085 machines. It sells for $30. As Robert Blum of the NCUG points out, the low cost has led to extensive use "in the university environment; although this is not where most of the group's support originates. The professional programmers, hackers for lack of a better term, are largely responsible for most of the contributed programs."

"Our public domain library officially began operation in December 1983. The volumes are kept small, around 120K bytes each, to insure that even the lowest density 5-inch disks can hold one volume from the library." The cost of each volume is $10, and you must be a member to obtain the software. All announcements about new volumes and updates appear in the "NCUG News," which every member receives.

"Because of our diversity of members, there is no reason why the person with no experience, as well as the professional, cannot join in and learn while sharing." The masthead of the "NCUG News" carries the following legend: "Enjoy your journey into the hearts and souls of those who believe that to share the fruits of their labor is reward enough.

If you are interested in learning more about COBOL (Common Business Oriented Language), the Ellis Computing product would appear to be an excellent—and inexpensive—way to start. You need only 16K of memory, CP/M-80 or PTDOS, and either a 5- or 8-inch disk drive. Contact:

Ellis Computing
3917 Noriega Street
San Francisco, CA 94122
(415) 753-0186

Janus/Ada

Janus/Ada Users Group
Douglas J. Wagner
R.R. Software, Inc.
P.O. Box 1512
Madison, WI 53701
(608) 244-6436

Newsletter: Yes.

Comments: Mr. Wagner writes: "Right now the 'user group' is just a newsletter that is our R.R. Software, Inc., house organ." This publication is read by the firm's base of licensed Janus/Ada compiler owners. The firm is not a supplier of public domain software, but it does have the Janus/Ada Software Exchange. "Basically, the Exchange is a collection of low-cost Ada software that any licensed user can participate in. We do charge for programs ($2) and libraries ($1)." For more information, please call Mr. Wagner at the number given above.

Making the Most of It

As you can see, there are many sources of software-specific free programs. We've tried to highlight all of the commercial products with significant users groups and libraries in this chapter. But you may be able to find other sources for different products. Much depends on how many computer owners have bought the product or, in software industry terms, the size of "the installed base."

A good first step would be to contact the firm that offers the product, but plugging in to the users group network can be essential as well. The most important point to be aware of is that sources devoted to supporting specific commercial products do exist. Using the techniques and points of access presented in this book, if there is a source for the product you use, you will almost certainly be able to find it.

Software-specific sources of free software can help you get much more out of a commercial product than you may ever have imagined. In the next chapter, we'll look at the giant free software libraries and other sources that can help you get the most out of your particular machine, regardless of the applications you have in mind.

...5...

Machine-Specific Groups and Sources: *Free Programs from A (Apple) to Z (Zenith)*

You don't have to spend more than five minutes in the microworld to realize that every machine is different. Similarly, the machine-specific users groups that support them vary widely in organization, services, vigor, and in the kinds, quality, and quantity of the free software found in their libraries.

There are a number of reasons for this. Clearly the total units of each brand of computer that have been sold is a major factor. The general health of the machine's manufacturer can be crucial, as is the amount of support the firm provides. Over the years, different companies have taken distinctly different approaches. The Apple Computer Company, for example, has from the beginning encouraged and aided user group support of its machines. On the other hand, we have heard from many sources that user group support has not been a high priority at Tandy Radio Shack. As you will see in a moment, there are huge collections of programs for Apple computers. The TRS-80 public domain, in contrast, is not nearly as rich or as well organized. (The Fairfield County TRS-80 users group profiled below is one of the best sources we have discovered.)

FreeTip: The availability of technical information makes a difference, too. If you are new to computing, you should know that just about everything a computer does is determined by what numbers have been placed in what locations inside the machine's memory. This is what computerists call "poking memory." If you as a writer of public domain software want to make a letter on the screen blink, for example, you may have to place a particular number in a particular memory location. The problem is that there are literally hundreds of thousands of possibilities. If the manufacturer does not tell you which locations and numbers control which computer features, you will be left to discover the correct information by yourself.

Needless to say, this lack of information can make it much more difficult to write good public domain programs. But if the manufacturer will not give you the information—and some won't—your only alternative is trial and error. This is a laborious process, to say the least. Fortunately, the memory locations and pokes that other users have discovered are frequently published in user group newsletters. If that's an interest of yours, this kind of information may be reason enough to subscribe.

How to Use this Chapter

Many of the machine-specific groups profiled below have large free software collections. All offer you a way to plug into the universe of users groups and free software that surrounds your particular machine. If there is no local group in your area, you may want to become a remote member of one of the groups profiled here. If you already belong to a local organization, you may still want to join one of these groups, since many may offer better free software selections and a wider perspective than you may have locally.

Here are some things that apply to all of the groups in this section:

- A subscription to the newsletter or magazine listed as the group's publication is included with your membership. Interestingly, postage and production costs often account for the largest percentage of your membership fee. For example, Alan Abrahamson, editor of "The Voice of the 80" for the Fairfield County, Connecticut, TRS-80 group, estimates that each copy costs about $1 to produce. If you add 40¢ postage per copy per month, the cost for a year's worth of newsletters comes to $16.80. Since individual and family memberships are $24 and student memberships are $12, there is not much left over to pay for other group expenses.

  Whenever the information was provided by the group, we have reproduced the rates for non–U.S. members. Again, newsletter postage is often a major factor in the cost.

- Unless otherwise specified, you *must* be a member of a given group in order to obtain free software from its library.

- All foreign memberships must be prepaid in U.S. funds drawn on a U.S. bank, except in the few instances where an organization accepts major credit cards.

• You will usually get a much faster response from these largely all-volunteer organizations if you enclose a mailing label bearing your address and two or three first class stamps.

Finally, the following list of groups, while extensive, is not intended to be comprehensive. The list was developed with two goals in mind. First, to identify as nearly as possible the major machine-specific groups with the largest collections of free software. And second, to provide computer owners with initial points of access to information, free software, tips, and *other* users groups, regardless of their brand of machine.

In most cases, you won't have to reach beyond the appropriate group profiled here. But if you need or want more information about the network of users groups and the free programs that exist for your machine, the groups cited here can be the ideal place to turn. We know because we have either corresponded with or spoken to the officers or other active members of each group profiled. We've read many of their publications, gone over their free software catalogues, and tried to present the kind of information you need to decide whether to join and how to do it. Needless to say, the assistance of the group officers and members was invaluable in this effort. Without exception, they were simply superb, and we are in their debt.

FreeTip: A firm called Business Applications Systems has recently begun to publish a series of users group directories. These are provided in 5½-by-8½-inch three-ring binders and sell for between $5 and $35. At this writing there are 40 directories, classified in three main categories. The "Hardware" category focuses on machine-specific groups; "Software" lists VisiCalc, Pascal, and similar groups; "Special Interest" lists groups with SIGs for medical applications, word processing, robotics, and similar topics. According to Pierre A. Dungee, the president of the firm, updated pages to be inserted in each binder will be available annually at a cost of $3 to $4.

The 1984 IBM Users Group Directory ($20) contains 31 groups and about 59 pages of text. The descriptions of the groups vary from a single page containing little more than an address, to about three pages citing meeting information and available resources. (All information is supplied by the group itself.) We also looked at the Business User Group Directory ($20) and found a number of the same pages used in the IBM book. According to Mr. Dungee, if a group has indicated that it has a SIG devoted to a particular topic, its listing may appear in a number of directories.

Groups are charged a one-time fee of $15 to be included in the directory, a policy Mr. Dungee says is designed to make sure that the directories include only legitimate and active groups. (Each group paying the fee and filling out the listing form receives a copy of a directory.) For more information, contact:

Business Application Systems
1734 Barry Avenue
Los Angeles, CA 90025

Apple, Franklin, and Compatibles

International Apple Core
908 George Street
Santa Clara, CA 95050
(408) 727-7652

Membership: 450 user groups, worldwide, serving over 75,000 individual members.

Cost of Membership: Annually, in U.S., Canada, and Mexico: $30 per individual; $90 per user group package. International: $72 per individual; $152 per user group package.

Publication: Apple Orchard; monthly; 100 pages; slick. Subscriptions available separately ($24 in the U.S.; more elsewhere), but you are better off paying for a full membership since membership includes the magazine and other privileges as well.

All *Apple Orchard* correspondence should be sent to:

Apple Orchard
P.O. Box 6502
Cupertino, CA 95015
(408) 727-7652

SIGs:

Agriculture	Handicapped
Apple ///	Health Services
Calc Applications	Investments
Data Management	Laboratory Applications
Dental	Languages

Education	Lisa
Family	Medical Office Management
Games	Telecommunications

Regional Directors:

Region / Director	No.	Phone
CA ZIPs 94100 & up, WA, OR, NV, HI, AK, & American Samoa		
Stephen Lloyd	1	(415) 571-7370
Southern CA, ZIPs 93999 & lower		
Jim Simpson	2	(805) 492-3391
AZ, MN, TX, OK, AR, MO, LA, MS, TN		
Mike Kramer	3	(713) 358-6687
ID, UT, MT, WY, CO, ND, SD, NE, KS, MN, IA		
Bob Sander-Cederlof	4	(214) 324-2050
WI, IL, MI, IN, KY		
Barry Bayer	5	(312) 798-6496
PA, NJ, FL		
Neil Lipson	6	(215) 356-6183
ME, CT, MA, NH, RI, VT, NY, DC		
Robert Ramsdell	7	(617) 546-3104
OH, WV, MD, DE, VA, NC, SC, GA, AL		
Tom Wysocki	8	(216) 942-7086

Australia	*Canada*	*Japan*
Roger Keating	Auby Mandell	Dr. Steve Bellamy
P.O. Box 448	409 Queen Street West	#402, 5-7-13 Tajiri
Double Bay 2048	Toronto, Ontario	Ichikawa, Chiba
N S W	Canada M5V2A5	Japan
Australia	(416) 593-9862	0473-79-3610
(612) 389-2994		

Comments: This is an absolutely super organization, both in terms of its size and in terms of its attitude, approach, and overall goals. And as far as free software is concerned, how does a library of 1,200 *disks* filled with the stuff strike you? How about a regular DOM ("Disk of the Month") subscription to easily obtain the best public domain programs on various themes (education, hi-res graphics, Bill Budge's *Pinball* games, and more)? If this sounds enticing, read on.

The International Apple Core was created by the Apple Computer Company several years ago to serve as a bridge between the firm and users of its equipment. But unlike many corporate-created organizations, the IAC conducts its relationship with the firm at arm's length. You have only to speak with IAC officials or, better yet, review the group's *Apple Orchard* magazine, to realize that the Core is not a puppet organization and its publication is not a house organ. Competitive products are advertised and discussed in feature articles ("Diagnosing and Repairing Your Apple II or Franklin," for example), and criticism or praise is doled out on an as-deserved basis, regardless of the software, peripheral, or computer.

IAC membership is open to individuals and users groups alike. The users group package includes a subscription to the magazine, a DOM subscription, lists of other Apple Core groups, and, if you need it, assistance from the Core in organizing the group. Sample constitutions are available, for example, as is help in legally establishing nonprofit status. As reported by *A+* magazine, IAC Executive Director Ken Silverman estimates that the group delivered $482 worth of educational and other materials to each member club in 1982, all for the cost of a club membership.

Individual membership includes a subscription to the magazine and makes you eligible to take advantage of other IAC services. These include up to $15,000 of insurance for your computer and software for about $50 a year, no deductible; discounts on IAC copyrighted software (The IACalc™ spreadsheet program, for example, is $85 to nonmembers; $65 to members); and discounts on free software disks.

The best and most economical way to obtain free IAC software is through your local IAC Apple users group. If you can't find a group in your area, either contact the IAC directly or phone one of the regional directors cited at the beginning of this section. By March of 1984, there were 34 separate DOMs, with a new one being issued every month. More than likely, your local group will have all of them in its library and be able to make them available to you for a small copying charge ($1 to $2), if you supply your own disk.

The range of subjects covered by IAC free software is broad indeed. Here is just a brief sample of some of the filenames to be found on various IAC disks:

Disk 3
LUNAR-LANDER
DEATH STAR
HI-RES DRAGON MAZE
SPACE WAR

Disk 9
TRANSISTOR PARAMETERS
SIN PLOT
METRICS KITCHEN
PRIME FACTORS INTEGERS
FAST FOURIER TRANSFORM
LOOP ANTENNA
HEX-DEC CONVERTER

Disk 14
HAYES MENU
STORE & FORWARD
PICKUP
AUTO DIAL
DIAL A HUMAN
ANSWER ON NTH RING
SOURCEON
MICROMODEM FLAGS

Disk 18
UP & DOWN THE SCALE
JOYSTICK/PADDLE TESTER
SOMEWHERE OVER THE RAINBOW
PLAY THAT TONE AGAIN SAM!
TWIRLING CURSOR
HI-RES SOLAR SYSTEM SIMULATOR
SOUND BY WAGNER

Disk 21
BASICALC (spreadsheet)
BASICALC.DOC
VISICALC (several files)
BASICALC.COMPILED
BASICALC SAMPLE DATA

If you would like to receive the DOM directly from the IAC, you can do so with a DOM subscription. The cost is $30 for six months ($5 per disk), and it makes no difference whether you are an IAC member or not. If you want previously issued DOMs, however, your membership entitles you to a discount. The cost for back issues is $10 per disk for nonmembers; $7.95 per disk for members. Add $2.50 per order for shipping. California residents, add 6½% sales tax. In an effort to encourage people to obtain disks through their local users groups, the IAC formerly charged what it called an "outrageous" price ($25 per disk) for direct DOM orders. The new policy was instituted in December 1983. Phone orders (MasterCard or Visa) are also accepted, but there is a minimum order requirement of $20.

So what's on a DOM? The best way to find out is through *Apple Orchard* since it carries a regular full-page feature describing each DOM as it is released. The education disk (DOM 24), for example, contains nine programs including BOXES (test for single digit addition and subtraction skills, aimed at first and second graders), DRILL (math for eight and nine year olds), FRED FRACTION (animated graphics; fraction-related problems), and MAKING CHANGE (hi-res graphics teach you how to break a dollar bill).

DOM 25 was contributed by L.O.G.I.C. (Loyal Ontario Group Interested in Computers) and as Barry Bayer said in his *Apple Orchard* review, it "gives the answers to 90 percent of what you ever wanted to know about machine language, but were afraid to ask." The disk includes MASM, a "mini-assembler," that can be used with the programs it teaches you to write, and a number of tutorial programs. Other IAC disks offer Pascal Attach-BIOS, Applesoft Tutorial, IEEE Pascal Attach Disk, the aforementioned *Pinball* games collection, and much more.

The $30 you pay to join the IAC could be the smartest investment you make after buying your Apple. Indeed, the IAC does all of its jobs so well that, if you are on the fence about buying an Apple, a membership may be just the thing to help you decide.

Call-A.P.P.L.E.
21246 68th Avenue, S.
Kent, WA 98032
(206) 872-2245
Weekdays; 9 AM to 4 PM (PST)
Orders and membership application only: (800) 426-3667; 24 hours

Membership: 25,000.

Cost of U.S. Membership: $51 ($25 initial sign-up; $26 dues); $26/year after initial sign-up.

Cost of Foreign Membership: Non-U.S. rates are higher due to postage costs associated with mailing the magazine. U.S. funds drawn on a U.S. bank required. International money orders, Visa, and MasterCard accepted. In Canada, West Indies, Central America, Colombia, Venezuela: $66 (includes $15 postage). In South America (except above), Europe, North Africa: $72 (includes $21 postage). In South Africa, Australia, Asia, elsewhere: $78 (includes $27 postage).

Publication: Call-A.P.P.L.E.; monthly; 100 pages; slick.

Comments: We spoke with Mr. Val Golding, editor of the group's magazine, and learned that Call A.P.P.L.E. was founded in February of

1978, and there were about 13 members at its initial meeting. Today this nonprofit corporation is the largest single Apple users group in the world, with members in many foreign countries. On the local level, the group holds regular monthly meetings and offers classes in various aspects of personal computing. But somewhere along the way, it grew to have an international scope, and it is well-prepared to accept remote members, either as individuals or as users groups.

You can call the toll-free 800 number above and charge your membership to your Visa or MasterCard. Or write for a membership application. If free software is your primary interest, you might ask the group to send you its catalogue of over 200 public domain disks. Disks are available to members only. The cost is $4 apiece, including postage and handling.

The collection can be divided into several major sections. There are over 110 disks from the Apple Avocation Alliance (see the next chapter for details on the "AAA"), over 20 disks produced by the International Apple Core, over 12 Pascal disks, and over 14 public domain CP/M disks (including APMODEM, the Apple CP/M version of MODEM7). The balance are disks submitted by various users groups and clubs.

A simple CATALOG listing providing only the names and types of files (A, T, I, B, etc.) on disks in the Call-A.P.P.L.E. library occupies more than 12 pages of small type. But here are a few filenames of programs from the users group disks. (There are many more files on each of these disks.)

Volume 200

BUZZ CLOCK
CHECKBOOK
DISK CLEANER
EPSON DRIVER
MUSIC ORGAN
SMURF

Volume 201

APPLESPEAKER
CLOCKFACE
EPSON LABEL
JOHN'S DRAGON MAZE
MAGIC STORY
SUPER SYNTHSIZER [*sic*]

Volume 005

HIGHER TEXT UTILITIES
HEBREW.SF
RUSSIAN.SF
GREEK.SF
THREE-D.SF

Free software is only part of what Call-A.P.P.L.E. has to offer. ("Call" comes from a programming instruction; the other part of the name stands for Apple Puget Sound Program Library Exchange.) For one thing, members can subscribe to The Source for $60, a savings of $40 off the normal subscription price. Once online with The Source, members will discover a special Call-A.P.P.L.E. "Private Sector" containing summaries of articles and listings of the programs that have appeared in the magazine. (If you have a Source subscription already, and are interested in more information about Call-A.P.P.L.E., you can use SourceMail to send an information request to ST1570.) There is also a special Washington state–based Apple Crate BBS for members to use.

There is discounted name-brand hardware as well. "We do not carry a complete line of hardware," Mr. Golding says, "but whatever we carry has gone through our testing and evaluation process, so members know it will work. I'm happy to say that some people have equated us with the Good Housekeeping Seal of Approval.

"We also have a line of software products, many of them exclusive, created by our members. And we have a reputation for having some of the finest documentation anywhere. In many cases, it's better than most commercial products.

"The typical price range is $15 to $35 per program, though of course there will usually be several files related to the program on the disk. For example, probably one of the finest program editors ever written for the Apple originated with us. One of our members wrote the Big MAC Assembler. This is a full-featured assembler very similar to its commercial version, a product known as Merlin, that we offer for $28.50. We think it puts the DOS Toolkit Assembler produced by Apple Computer to shame.

"We have a program called V-Spreadsheet which sells for $75 and out-performs VisiCalc. It offers variable column width and recognizes any of the standard 80-column cards. It has a 70-column mode. And it reads VisiCalc files." Mr. Golding reports that the group is currently looking into adding a communications program to its offerings.

Of course, the group does not support its public domain programs, but Call-A.P.P.L.E. fully supports all of the products it sells. For example, all members have access to a special hotline that can be used not only for product support but also as a source of answers for your programming and other generic questions. If the hotline cannot answer your question, Call-A.P.P.L.E. has a list of consultants who can.

FreeTip: The Big Red Apple Club in Norfolk, Nebraska, offers over 100 public domain disks to its members. Annual membership is $12. Contact:

The Big Red Apple Club
1301 N. 19th
Norfolk, NE 68701

FreeTip: Apple-Dayton, Inc.,is one of the major Apple groups in the country. Its members frequently contribute programs to the I.A.C. and write articles for *Apple Orchard*. If you would like to contact the group directly about its public domain library ($5 per disk) write to:

Apple-Dayton, Inc.
P.O. Box 1666
Fairborn, OH 45324

Atari

Computer Users' Support Program
Atari, Inc.
1265 Borregas
P.O. Box 3427
Sunnyvale, CA 94088
(800) 538-8543
(800) 672-1404 (in California)
(800) 538-5282 (from Alaska or Hawaii)
(408) 745-2000 (main non–toll-free number)

Comments: Anyone interested in obtaining free software from Atari users groups should look at the following book:

Free Software for Your Atari
by David and Dorothy Heller
ENRICH/OHAUS
2325 Paragon Drive
San Jose, CA 95131
$8.95; 208 pages

This book, available at most major bookstores, will give you a good idea of the kinds of free programs that are available and some tips on where to get them. You may find that the book is a bit thin on substance. But the authors indicate that an update is planned. Perhaps it will use less white space. It should also be added that we contacted six of the eight groups profiled in the book. None of the letters was returned, but we received only one, rather irate, reply. On the other hand, at $8.95, how can you lose?

Digging a bit deeper, we contacted the man who has been in charge of Atari's user group support program for the past two years. He indicated that the best way to proceed is to contact Atari at the address and numbers provided above and request the most recent list of official Atari users groups. (The list is updated approximately once a month and you can phone the appropriate toll free number to get it. Please allow two to three weeks for a reply.) Then contact the group nearest you, and plug in that way.

The Atari spokesman was not aware of any "master source" of free Atari software but suggested that groups located in large cities would be most likely to have the largest selection. Formerly Atari made a communications program available to "official" users groups, but that practice has been discontinued. At this writing, Atari does not provide groups with any kind of "seed" library to get them started.

Commodore 64 and VIC-20

The Compucats
Compucats Software Development Company
680 West Bel Air Avenue
Aberdeen, MD 21002
(301) 372-4195 or (301) 272-0472

Membership: 200.

Cost of Membership: Maryland residents, $15/year, individual or family; out-of-state residents, $20/year, individual or family.

Publication: "Compucats Chronicle"; monthly; 40 pages; designed and offset.

Comments: Commodore users generally agreed that they have suffered from a lack of company support and, in some locations, a lack of a strong user group organization. If you're a C-64 owner and you need help, free software, and information from people who really "know," you could do far worse than to invest $15 or $20 in a Compucats membership. The club was formed on January 1, 1983, by Betty Jane and Gerry Schueler as a means of sharing information and discoveries about how to use the 64. As programmers and machine language Commodore game creators, they found that it was extremely difficult to get the kind of technical information they needed from any source, but especially from the manufacturer. They discovered that others had similar needs and faced similar problems, and in classic user group fashion, formed a club.

We have spoken to both Betty Jane and Gerry and they, like so many in the users group community, are *good* people. They have built up a library containing more than $5,000 worth of books, magazines, hardware, and software for local members to borrow for a month at a time. (They spend over $70 a month on magazines alone.) All of the software is copy-protected by some of the most sophisticated locking mechanisms available. But the Schuelers know from personal experience that not everything works for every user and that often the only way to find out is to actually invest in the product. The loaner library offers members an opportunity to try before they buy.

The Compucats have members located all over the world, but while these individuals cannot avail themselves of the loaner library, there is a "disk of the month" containing public domain Commodore software. Actually it's a disk or tape of the month. The disk costs $6 and the same programs on tape cost $5. There is at least the possibility that in the future those prices will go down, since as more members join it will be possible to obtain greater bulk discounts on disks and tapes.

FreeTip: Betty Jane Schueler brings up an interesting point regarding other "users groups." She says she has tried to contact other groups and that people call her from all over the country saying that they can't contact their local clubs. "A lot of 'groups' have just post office boxes for addresses and don't make their phone numbers available," she says. "Because, as I understand it, a lot of so-called 'user groups' are fronts. They consist of individuals who simply want to get free demo disks and other material from manufacturers interested in promoting their products. Apparently there are at least three of them here in Maryland that have definitely been verified as fronts.

"It irritates me to no end because people are wasting their money on stamps and sending letters, and they sit around waiting and waiting to hear back from one of these 'groups' and there's no real group."

Asked how people could tell the difference, Ms. Schueler said that things will probably come to the point where users groups will have to be required to include a phone number in any listing. She also says that close to 100 people have called her and said what a pleasant surprise it was to find that the Compucats is a legitimate group. There are evidently a significant number of "groups" that are essentially marketing organizations. "They get you in," Ms. Schueler says, "and then try to sell you all kinds of products."

The software in the Compucats public domain library comes from a variety of sources. Some of it is written by Gerry Schueler, some has been typed in by users from public domain programs published in magazines, and some has been converted from VIC-20 code. The Commodore public domain education series is also represented, and because Compucats is a member of TPUG, the world's largest Commodore club, that group's programs are there as well. (TPUG is based in Toronto; see next section.) Highlights of the Compucats library include:

- STARTREK—Improved and documented by Gerry Schueler

- DOS 5.1 WEDGE—Loads Wedge onto disks so that you can use disk commands without disturbing a BASIC program in memory.

- SIMULATION—Commodore Public Domain Series. Simulation of how a computer follows a flow chart.

- WACHET AUF—Adaptation of the Bach chorale prelude designed to show off the capabilities of the C-64's sound chip. A Compucats original.

- GOBLINS—Game from July 1983 *Compute!* magazine.

Other titles include: DOCTOR DEMENTIA, TELEPHONE LIST, WORD HUNT, PIO, METRIC MASS, BALANCE SHEET, COPYALL, BIORHYTHM, CHRISTMAS CARDS (graphics and music), DEFENSE OUTPOST, DOWN OUR WAY (musical program for barber shop quartet lovers), and more. All programs on the disk of the month are described in the monthly "Compucats Chronicle."

FreeTip: Betty Jane and Gerry Schueler pass along the following tips for Commodore owners who want to plug into the users group/public domain software world. One of the largest Commodore-supporting groups is the San Diego PET Users Group (PUG). Contact the group at:

San Diego PUG
c/o D. Costarakis
3562 Union Street
San Diego, CA 92103
(714) 235-7626
7 AM - 4 PM (PST)

The same group has spawned a sprightly, informative, and tutorial newsletter called "The Comm'putoy Cult." They can be reached at P.O. Box 7776, San Diego, CA 92107. Articles welcome, but send for sample issue first.

The man who "keeps everyone in touch with everyone else in the Commodore world," according to Ms. Schueler, is Colin F. Thompson, technical editor of *Commander* magazine, a member of the Compucats and a regular contributor to the "Chronicle." Mr. Thompson also publishes "The VIC LIST," a comprehensive list of VIC-20 and C-64 hardware and software suppliers that is updated every two weeks. It is free. But you must send a 9 × 12 envelope, addressed to yourself, and bearing 37¢ postage. Send it to:

Mr. Colin F. Thompson
BASF Systems Corporation
1307 Colorado Avenue
Santa Monica, CA 90404

FreeTip: Interested in making contact with C-64 and VIC-20 owners over the air? If you are a ham radio operator (or know someone who is), Bruce Cameron of Temple Terrace, Florida, holds a weekly confab each Saturday starting at 3:00 PM, Eastern time. Dial or punch up: 7228 Khz.

FreeTip: The magazine *Software Supermarket* reports that there is a club in Illinois with over 200 public domain educational programs for the Commodore in its library. We have not checked but would guess that the core of this collection is probably made up of the educational software originally sold by Commodore but released into the public domain several years ago. For information, contact:

Illinois Commodore Users
c/o Community H.S. District #94
326 Joliet Street
West Chicago, IL 60185

Toronto PET Users Group (TPUG), Inc.
Chris Bennett, Business Manager
1912A Avenue Road, Suite 1
Toronto, Ontario
Canada M5M 4A1
(416) 782-8900 or (416) 782-9252

Membership: 14,000.

Cost of Membership: $30 local; $20 associate (North America); $30 associate (overseas).

Publicaton: TPUG Magazine; 10 issues; 96 pages; typeset.

SIGs: Commodore 64, VIC-20, PET/CBM, and SuperPET.

Comments: This club, started in 1978, may be the largest Commodore users group in the world. It is the home of Jim Butterfield, a programmer of some renown in Commodore public domain circles, and it boasts more than 4,000 free public domain programs in its library, "with more coming in each week," according to Chris Bennett, the club's business manager.

Writing in *Commodore* magazine (vol. 4, no. 5, issue 26), Mr. Bennett says, "Someone asked if we could have a special membership classification for out-of-town members who could rarely attend meetings. For this type of person we created the 'associate' membership. This person receives our newsletter and can order tapes and disks from our library through the mail. Our disks are $10 each ($12 for 8050) and our tapes are $6 each. Each tape or disk contains from 15 to 62 programs. This has been very popular for people in out-of-the-way places where there is no local club and often no local Commodore dealer. . . . We are now in the process of getting other clubs to affiliate with us. Members of these clubs may join TPUG at a reduced rate by signing up 15 or more members at a time. Depending upon the number of members signed up, we then send to that club from one to three of our monthly disks for the VIC 20, Commodore 64, and PET/CBM. In this way we hope to circulate the many excellent public domain programs available for the Commodore machines."

We spoke with Ms. Doris Bradley, a club staffer, and learned that new associate members receive a 24-page catalogue listing the club's public domain software for the member's model of machine. At this writing, there are approximately 700 public domain programs for the C-64, about 400 for the VIC-20, about 100 for the SuperPET (a collection started in the fall of 1983), and over 1,000 for the PET computer. In addition, Ms. Bradley says, the club has available the entire series of 800 or more programs that Commodore Business Machines released into the public domain. These are for the C-64 and the PET. Ms. Bradley says that a new subgroup and library is forming to focus on COMAL, a computer language that is evidently quite popular among European Commodore owners.

Here's a brief sampling of just a few of the files on two recent disks, one for the PET and one for the Commodore 64. Both disks were issued in December 1983.

Disk PET T4

PENCIL   A word processor, complete with a printer formatting utility, and a file for converting PENCIL output to other word processor formats.

BRAILLE.Z   An educational program that produces braille characters on your printer.

CALENDAR.Z   Prints a calendar for any year.

THE VALLEY.Z   Dungeons & Dragons with graphics.

PHONE BOOK.Z   Phone directory utility.

Disk C-64 T4

GLACTIC EMPIR.C   Space game for up to ten people.

COPY SOME.C   Utility program to copy any selection of program from one disk to another.

BLACKJACK.Z   "Twenty-one" on the 64.

BIRTHDAY2.C   Sound and music. Tune is played, words appear, then a cake with candles. Blow them out with the <F1> key. Can change name on cake by altering two lines of the program.

SQUAREROOT.C Enter any positive number, computer does the rest.

BANKER.C A game program that can be used to act as the banker in *Monopoly*.

PERSONALACCNT.C Business program to keep track of money inflow and outflow.

DBASE.C A disk-based database management program.

WORD PRO64.C A tape-based word processor for the C-64.

BACH INVENTN#8.C Music and sound; plays Bach's Invention no. 8 in F.

Folklife Terminal Club
Box 2222-FC
Mt. Vernon, NY 10551

Membership: 500.

Cost of Membership: $15; includes the library "Catalog Disk."

Comments: Intrigued by a report in *Ahoy!* magazine that this group had more than 5,000 programs, we contacted them to find out if perhaps a zero hadn't been inadvertently added to the number. John Krebs, the group's software librarian sent this reply:

"Yes we do indeed have more than 5,000 programs for COMMODORE computers. . . . Our library grew because of a small local group of dedicated 'givers.' [Now] we have opened our membership ranks to people in other areas. We now have more than 500 members in 12 countries."

Mr. Krebs enclosed a press release indicating that public domain programs are available in "the areas of Education, Science, Business, Games, Utilities, and more than 25 other categories. The programs are stored on diskettes and are usable on various configurations of PET, CBM, 64, and VIC computers. The software itself is free. The first diskette that should be ordered is the 'CATALOG DISK' which contains an Automatic Disk Cataloging Program, a listing of all the available programs, complete instructions, and associate membership in the club. There is a copying and mailing fee of $15 per diskette. Specify which COMMODORE disk drive you have."

The membership application also requests that you specify the model of Commodore computer you have and how many kilobytes of memory it is equipped with.

Dynabyte

Dynabyte Users Group
c/o Random Factors, Ltd.
P.O. Box 2875
Durango, CO 81301

Comments: This is not a users group, per se. It is more of a last outpost fighting a holding action. Mr. William Borsum writes:

"DYNABYTE did not have a booth at Comdex or Wescon, and with their recent losses of key people, it appears that the handwriting is on the wall. . . . I still see the need for a central clearing point for information, parts, software, and the like for the Dynabyte systems in the files—particularly if factory support disappears. For us, this will have to be on a profit basis to cover our time and material. As long as Dynabyte exists, we will re-sell their hardware and software on a cost plus 15% basis. We will also maintain a "Wanted/For Sale/Trade" list of parts, systems, and peripherals. The listing charge will be $5. Send us a legible 3-by-5 card with your wants or offers on it. We will periodically put together a "card pak" and mail them to the 250 or so individuals and companies on our list. . . . If you are looking for a new system, we are Master Distributors for MicroStandard Technologies. Please call Dick Burke at (303) 247-9306 for more information."

Note: The MicroStandard is not a machine we are familiar with. However, an impressive four-color brochure indicates that it is a transportable with a 9-inch 80-character-by-24-line screen, 64K, and lots of built-in standard features. It runs CP/M Plus (CP/M 3.0) and may be worth a look.

EPSON QX-10, HX-20, and VALDOCS™

Rising Star Industries
24050 Madison, Suite 113
Torrance, CA 90505
(213) 378-9861

Publication: "The Rising Star"; 16 pages; slick.

Cost of Membership: Free.

Comments: The Epson QX-10 is a relatively new computer, and at this writing we know of no large libraries that have been developed for it. Such libraries are inevitable, however. The above address is a prime point of access for Epson computer users and those interested in the VALDOCS™ operating system. (VALDOCS™, HASCI™, and TELOS X™ are all registered trademarks of Rising Star Industries.)

At this writing, "The Rising Star" is free and scheduled for monthly publication. A recent issue included the following users group addresses:

Epson's Users' Group
P.O. Box 14027
Detroit, MI 48214
(313) 822-0090
Contact: Carolyn McCarthy, president

Publishes a bi-monthly newsletter ("The Epson Connection").

Epson Computing Group
400-2 DeYoung
Marion, IL 62959
(618) 993-3600
BBS: (618) 997-3220
Contact: George Vensel, president

Publishes a monthly newsletter ("QHX"). An advertisement in a recent *InfoWorld* classified section indicated that charter membership was $25. "We invite your letters, questions, and tips."

QX-10 Special Interest Group
San Diego Computer Society
3612 Lotus Drive
San Diego, CA 92106
(619) 223-9311
Contact: Doug Dickerson, coordinator

QX-10 Group
Long Island, NY
24-hour electronic mail BBS: (516) 567-8267
BBS (7 PM–9 AM): (516) 567-8267
Pittsburgh, PA
Sponsored by Computer Brokers
(412) 642-7750
Contact: Jack Friedman

Heath/Zenith

Heath/Zenith Users' Group (HUG)
Hilltop Road
St. Joseph, MI 49085
(616) 982-3463

Membership: 14,000.

Cost of Membership: Initial membership $20 (U.S.), $22 (Canada and Mexico), $30 (International); renewal $17, $19, and $24, respectively.
Note: Non–U.S. memberships must be in U.S. funds. Membership in England, France, Germany, Belgium, Holland, Sweden, and Switzerland is acquired through the local distributor at the prevailing rate.

Publication: REMark; monthly; 100 pages; typeset.

Comments: This is *the* contact point for new Heath/Zenith users, and it is without a doubt one of the most impressive users groups we have encountered. One reason for this may be that, as *InfoWorld* points out, the group was founded and nurtured by the manufacturer, though it is at least partially independent. Membership includes the following:

- Subscription to *REMark*
- A HUG magazine binder
- A personal identification card
- HUG software catalog
- Access to the HUG software library
- Access to the databases and program collections in the HUG SIG on CompuServe
- Discounts on a variety of Heath/Zenith products

FreeTip: *REMark* magazine subscriptions are available only to members. But if you are interested in more information about the group, you may be able to purchase a single copy for $2.50, plus 10% shipping and handling. The issue to ask for is the most recent January issue since this always contains a complete summary for new members, a cross index of previous issues, and, usually, lists of the software available and the addresses of HUG users group chapters.

The discounts range from 10% to 20% and include complete computer systems. Purchases can be made at any dealer, but they must be made in person and your ID card must be presented. (If you are interested in a Heath/Zenith, it might be worthwhile to consider joining HUG *before* you buy to take advantage of the discount. There is a ceiling of $5,000 per year and you may purchase only one of any given product under the discount plan.)

The nearly 1,000 programs offered by HUG fall into two categories. The public domain group, available for the cost of a disk, consists primarily of utility programs to interface various disk drives, printers, modems, and other peripherals. According to Bob Ellerton, HUG's manager, lately "users have been writing a lot of neat stuff." These newer programs include text editors, small business programs, and games.

The second category is the HUG software library. This consists of hundreds of programs that have been contributed by members on a royalty basis. HUG tests, reviews, and, if necessary, brings them up to HUG standards. The programs are then offered to members at an average cost of about $20. Sample titles include: *Adventure* ($10), PILOT ($19), Inventory ($30), Mailing List ($30), Home Financial Package ($18), *Seabattle* ($20), and CheapCalc, a CP/M spreadsheet for $20.

FreeTip: If you have a CompuServe subscription and would like more information on HUG, see Chapter 8 for information on accessing the HUG SIG on that system. You will not be able to get into the databases, but you can send and receive messages to HUG members via the SIG's bulletin board function.

IBM/PC, XT, and PCjr

Capital PC User Group
P.O. Box 3189
Gaithersburg, MD 20878
(301) 978-1530

Membership: 2500.

Cost of Membership: $25 ($40, for international members).

Publication: Capital PC Monitor; monthly (except August); 60 pages; typeset.

SIGs:

Advanced
APL
Artificial Intelligence
BASIC
C/UNIX
CEAM (Construction, Engineering, Architecture, and Management)
COBOL
Communications
DataBase
Educational
Financial/Accounting
Forth
FORTRAN
Games
Government Operations
Novice
Pascal
PC Compatibles
PC/XT
Software
Statistics
University Personal Computing
Word Processing

Comments: If you own an IBM/PC, a PCjr, an XT, or any other IBM computer or compatible, you should give strong consideraton to joining this group, regardless of where you live. Find the $25 or the $40 somewhere and send it straight to Gaithersburg, for this is one of the best-managed, best-organized, most active users organizations in the IBM/PC world.

Since we want to focus on the hundreds of free software programs that will become available to you once you join, we have space only for a few highlights concerning the group itself. These include:

- Sponsorship of over 20 Capital PC bulletin board systems.

- Group discounts on name brand hardware, software, and supplies.

- A hotline for beginners.

- Reprints of *User Updates* in the magazine. These are published by IBM and available at authorized retailers, but if you do not visit your retailer frequently, it is invaluable to have them in the magazine.

- Hands-on articles ("Using Random Files in BASIC," for example). Product reviews ("My Experience with the Howardsoft Tax Preparer"). SIG reports. And more. Published in each issue of the magazine.

This is an all-volunteer club run by a group of exceptionally selfless people. For example, in order to accommodate all members in the area, the club holds two meetings a month, presenting the identical program at each. The officers attend both. Each SIG holds its own monthly meeting, so if you're a club officer and a member of a SIG, you attend at least three meetings a month. More, if you belong to more than one SIG, as many officers and SIG chairmen do.

To find out about the free software, we spoke with Rich Schinnell, the chairman of the Software SIG. (Rich also runs one of the premier IBM/PC bulletin boards in the country. This is an excellent source of all the latest public domain IBM/PC software. Call: 301-949-8848; 8/N/1; 300 or 1200; 24 hours; password: IBMPC.) From the beginning, public domain software has been a major interest of the Capital PC group. As Rich says, "We had a disk of public domain programs by the second meeting of the group. At the first meeting, in March of 1982, we simply told everyone that we wanted them to go home and write a program and bring it on disk to the next meeting. That was our 'seed' disk and it was the beginning of our software library."

Software SIG meets regularly, and each member is assigned a certain number of disks to copy and orders to fill. At this writing, there are more than 25 single-sided IBM/PC disks filled with public domain software in the collection. The disks are available only to group members, and the cost is $8 per disk, including media, postage, disk mailer, and handling.

FreeTip: One disk in the collection is double-sided. This is Disk 18, the one containing the complete remote bulletin board package, RBBS/PC. The club feeling was that if you do not have double-sided disk drives, you have no business running a BBS in the first place. There are over 30 related files, including a patch to PC-

FreeTip continued

TALK III to permit you to communicate at 450 baud with a Hayes Smartmodem 300. Everything you need, in short, to set up your own BBS with an IBM/PC. If you want to be able to offer free software to callers, you can easily obtain programs by ordering other Capital PC disks.

FreeTip: Want a free dedicated phone line for your BBS? In the February 1984 issue of the club magazine, Tom Mack, one of the authors of RBBS-PC, says, "I know of one SysOp who already has succeeded in persuading his local telephone company to give him a free telephone line because of the revenue his RBBS-PC was generating for them. All the Bell Operating Companies have a business practice of providing no-cost telephone lines to places that generate revenue for them." Mr. Mack points out that the revenue level required to qualify for a "free phone" is set by the local company.

The reason this is relevant is that the RBBS-PC program is constantly being expanded and improved. The most recent version at this writing is RBBS-PC Version CPC12.1 and it contains a feature that records the duration of each call in the CALLERS file. The date, start time, and city and state of origin are also recorded. Mr. Mack says that all that is required to determine the revenue your board is generating for the phone company is to "write a little utility program that reads the CALLERS file, matches each caller with a rate record, and tallies the totals." The telephone company evidently is required by law to provide you with rate information.

We ordered and ran the entire Capital PC collection, and the quality is exceptional. When you run the AUTOEXEC.BAT file on each disk, a screen-filling logo appears showing the dome of the Capitol atop an IBM/PC. On most disks, a file that briefly describes the various programs will be displayed, along with information about the group. At that point, you're on your own.

Disk O contains descriptions of every program in the collection. Available for $5, it is continually updated as new programs are added, so this is clearly the first disk you should order. The other disks are priced at $8 each, and the group requests that you enclose a self-addressed mailing label for each disk you order. (All profit generated by the Software SIG are used to support the club's educational efforts).

Highlights of the collection include PC-FILE and PC-WRITE, two of the "PC Big Three" described in Chapter 11. There is also "One-Ringy-Dingy," also known as PC-DIAL, (300 to 9600 baud; XMODEM support), a PC-TALK III rival from Jim Button, author of PC-FILE.

CHASM—the "CHeap ASseMbler" described in Chapter 11—is on Disk 15 ("Assembler II"). Disk 13 is called "Assembler I." Both disks contain assembly language programs for you to assemble into .COM files with CHASM. If you are interested in assembly language, these disks are a good place to start.

There are too many games to mention. But as an example, the BLKJACK.BAS game on Disk 4 is particularly good. (This should not be confused with a similar game called BLAKJAK.BAS on Disk 5.) After you enter your wager, the program deals two cards to itself and two to you. You may then hit, stand, double down, split a pair, or buy insurance. (Hours of fun. "Guaranteed to break the ice at parties.") Like many of the games in the collection, this one is not in color. However, if the tradition of rewriting and improving public domain programs holds true, one can expect to see greater use of color graphics and sound in the future, particularly since the design of the PCjr places an even greater emphasis on these capabilities than is the case with the PC.

FreeTip: There is a particularly good program on Disk 5 called MORSECOD.BAS. This software is designed to teach Morse code, and so may be of limited interest. But it is an excellent example of the imaginative gems you can find if you look for them. There are two main options. You can type in a letter or word and hear the corresponding "dits and das" as the program performs the translation. Or you can prepare text beforehand and have it played back as it is displayed. Both the speed and the pitch of the tones can be adjusted at will.

There are many helpful utility programs as well, though the need for some of them has been eliminated by DOS 2.0 and 2.1 since this software incorporates many similar features. Of particular interest in this collection are the many VisiCalc templates contributed by IBM users. Disk 12 (May 10, 1983), for example, contains over ten templates. Topics include weekly payroll, break-even analysis, checkbook balancing, income statement, computation of return on investment resulting from covered option writing, and more. There is also a program for sorting VisiCalc spreadsheet data and one that will show you how to do a bar chart in VisiCalc. Disk 17 (July 18, 1983) contains templates for doing your federal income tax, plotting points with VisiCalc, and doing your home budget.

FreeTip: If you need a word processing program for your PC or PCjr, wait—we can get it for you wholesale. Well, not quite. But if you're interested in an excellent word processor *and* membership in the Capital PC group, there's a special deal you should know about. As explained in Chapter 11, PC-WRITE author Bob Wallace offers this program under his "Shareware" concept. (We spoke to Bob, and PC-WRITE's latest version *does* run on the PCjr.) Normally, to receive printed documentation and full telephone support, as well as updated versions, one must send in $75 to become a registered user. If you pass the program to somebody else and they too send in $75, you receive a $25 Shareware commission.

Under a special arrangement with Capital PC, the copies of PC-WRITE available from the group ($8) do not contain this provision. Capital PC members can register their program and receive full support (but no commission) for $50. Though it was not done for this purpose, that savings of $25 means that in effect your first year's membership in Capital PC is free.

FreeTip: Though we strongly recommend that owners of IBM and IBM-compatible computers join this group, you should know that many of its public domain programs are available elsewhere. The PC Software Interest Group (PC/SIG) featured in Chapter 6 is an excellent source. The cost is $6 per disk, plus $4 shipping and handling per order. (California residents, add 6.5% tax.) There are more than 135 disks in the collection. For more information, send $5.95 for a complete directory to:

PC Software Interest Group
1556 Halford Avenue, Suite #130
Santa Clara, CA 95051
(408) 730-9291

FreeTip: If you belong to a users group that is interested in establishing tax-exempt status with the Internal Revenue Service, you may be interested in the experiences of the Capital PC group in this regard. As reported in *PC* magazine (February 21, 1984), Ms. Jimmie Faris, the group's volunteer treasurer and a professional accountant, fought a long (and ultimately successful) battle to win tax-exempt status for Capital PC. A disk containing copies of relevant letters and documents generated by the case is available from the Software SIG for $6. You do not have to be a member of the group to obtain this disk, but obviously you have to have a PC or compatible or an MS-DOS–based machine to be able to read it.

The PC/BLUE Collection

If you are a frequent reader of IBM/PC-related publications, the chances are that at some point you've come across a reference to something known as the "PC/BLUE" collection assembled by the New York Amateur Computer Club (NYACC). And quite naturally, you may be curious ("blue," "yellow," or some other shade). We spoke to Don Wiss, the club's president, and learned that the reason why this may be the best-known collection of IBM software is that the club sent out press releases announcing its formation. We are indebted to Don for the following information.

The PC/BLUE collection consists of at least 53 disks. Following the tradition established with SIG/M and CP/M public domain software (see Chapter 2), the club has published a "book" that presents the tables of contents and abstracts of the files, and printouts of all document files contained on the disk. Book 1 is 215 pages long and covers the first 26 volumes. Book 2 has not been produced at this writing, but it will cover volumes 27 through 50.

Book 1 is available by mail from the NYACC, at a cost of $10 for addresses in North America and $15 for overseas airmail. All orders must be prepaid in U.S. funds, and one should allow six to eight weeks for delivery. ("Resellers, write for details.")

You do not have to be a member of the club to order disks. The cost is $6 per disk postpaid (UPS) to North America. (Note: Please be sure to use a proper UPS address; no "P.O. Boxes," "APO," or "FPO" addresses.) For overseas shipment, add $3 per order. Prepayment in U.S. funds required. The group wishes everyone to know that the volumes may be freely redistributed and "it is expected that they will be available from most local IBM PC groups for a nominal copying charge." Membership in the NYACC is $15 a year and $10 for students. Contact:

New York Amateur Computer Club
P.O. Box 106
Church Street Station
New York, NY 10008

So what's in the collection? A catalogue is available for $1.50 (mailed in the U.S.A.) or $2 (foreign shipment) from PC/BLUE, Box 97, Iselin, NJ, 08830. But since it will save you time and make it possible for many people to order directly, we have provided an edited version of the information sheet you would receive from the NYACC regarding the collection. As the info sheet points out, volumes 2 through 17 were extracted from the CPMUG and SIG/M libraries and some programs may require an 8080 co-processor and CP/M support. (These volumes are marked with an asterisk.) "Other disks contain programs which will run, or can be modified to run under PC/DOS. Modifications include adding spaces in the MBASIC programs and line numbers in the EBASIC programs."

PC/BLUE

Volume	*Description*
1	Misc. utilities: SDIR, IBM Asynch. Comm. support extension, other display utilities.
2–4	MicroSoft BASIC programs
5	MicroSoft Monstrous *Star Trek* programs
6	General Ledger; Monstrous *Star Trek*
7*	RATFOR
8*	Misc. FORTRAN programs; portraits
9*	EBASIC Compiler/Interpreter and programs
10	Monstrous EBASIC *Star Treks*
11–12	EBASIC programs
13*	Original *Adventure* (350 points)
14*	Bob Van Valzah's "Pascal Compiler"
15*	ALGOL-M
16*–17*	Misc. utilities from SIG/M
18	PC-TALK (Author's note: This is not the latest version, PC-TALK III. See Chapter 11 and Volume 31.)
19	PC-FILE (Author's note: This is not the latest version. See Chapter 11 regarding Jim Button's enhancements to his program.)
20	Remote Bulletin Board System; miscellaneous utilities
21	Cross reference utility, front-end interface utility (monitor)
22	Expanding the Lister Utility for BASIC programs
23	RATBAS, Warm System Restarts, Strip-Off Word*, High Bits, Graphtrax utility
24–25	BASIC games

26	8087 Sampler programs
27–28	KERMIT PC-to-mainframe communications package (Columbia University)
29	Miscellaneous BASIC programs
30	Miscellaneous application systems: cryptography, filing, inventory, mail list, regression
31–32	PC-TALK III (XMODEM support and other enhancements), miscellaneous communication systems
33	Miscellaneous applications: compression, music, dates, sunrise, plotting, etc.
34	dBASE II & SuperCalc templates
35	Miscellaneous BASIC utilities
36	IBM Keyboard Drill system
37	MODEM7 for IBM/PC, program control system, WordStar mods, miscellaneous utilities
38	Disk directory utilities, Squish REMarks, Lotus 1-2-3 mods
39	Screen editor, primitive word processor, Memo Minder, history and multiplication drills
40	EPISTAT statistical package (Author's note: See Chapter 11), IBM modem programs
41	*Galaxy Trek* with color graphics (also works on monochrome)
42	CHASM (Cheap Assembler, see Chapter 11), RAM-disk, miscellaneous utilities.
43	Inventory order control system in dBASE II
44	PC Graphics, by Eugene Ying
45	Bulletin Board system
46	One-Ringy-Dingy communications program, PC-FILE III
47	Software Encipherment, miscellaneous utilities from the Capital PC Users Group
48	Portfolio Evaluation system, Graphic Draw, Hi-Res Screen Print, Print Spooler
49	Remote Bulletin Board system: RBBS-CPC Version 12.1 from the Capital PC Users Group
50	FreeCalc—user supported electronic spreadsheet program
51	Tax456—Lotus 1-2-3 worksheet for 1983 federal income taxes
52	New Key; miscellaneous utilities and games by Vincent Bly
53	PC-Dial (a.k.a. One-Ringy-Dingy); PC-Write; PC-Compare (file management)

FreeTip: The PC/BLUE collection has spread as its authors intended, and it is now available from many different sources, though it may not always be available as a unified collection. One additional source we found that can make the entire collection available is the Long Island Computer Association, Inc., in Hicksville, New York. This is a strong, active super group with at least eight SIGs, including groups for Commodore, FRAN/APPLE, PolyMorphic, S-100, CP/M, and TRS-80. Membership is $12 and includes a subscription to "The Stack," the group's monthly newsletter. The disks are available to members attending local meetings at a cost of $3 each. But you should contact them for details if you plan to order by mail. The address is:

L.I.C.A.
P.O. Box 71
Hicksville, NY 11802

FreeTip: Since the following information will be of interest to owners of IBMs and several of the machines that serve as focal points for the users groups we are about to profile, it seems appropriate to include it here. At long last there is help for the disk format dilemma. This is the UNIFORM program from Micro Solutions. Briefly, UNIFORM runs on the Kaypro (all models, even the new MS-DOS–compatible Model 4-88), the Osborne, the SuperBrain, and many other computers. Depending on the machine, the program allows you to read from 23 to 25 formats (single sided) or from 37 to 41 formats (double sided). You merely tell the software that drive B is to emulate a particular format, while drive A remains in its normal mode. As a spokesperson for Micro Solutions says, this means for example that you can put an Epson QX-10 disk in drive B of your Kaypro and copy its contents to a Kaypro disk in drive A.

Available from the firm and from many dealers at a list price of $69.95, it would be hard to imagine a commercial program with a greater potential impact on the distribution of public domain software than UNIFORM. To give you an idea of its capabilities, we have reprinted information supplied by FOG (First Osborne Group, see below; also, note that FOG members may be able to purchase the program for $49.95). These are only a *few* of the formats UNIFORM can read:

Computer	*Format*
Access Matrix	DD
Cromemco	CDOS
DEC VT-180	DD
Heath/Zenith	Magnolia Board
IBM/PC	CP/M-86, DD
Kaypro 2	(from Kaypro)
Micro Decision	DD
NEC PC-8001	DD
Osborne SS/DD	(from Osborne)
SuperBrain	junior format
Texas Instruments Professional	CP/M-86, DD
TRS-80 Model I	Omikron CP/M
TRS-80 Model III	Memory Merchant CP/M
Xerox 820	SS/DD
Zenith Z-100	DD

Again, this is not a complete list, but it will give you the general idea. This program should greatly facilitate the distribution of public domain software. It also helps with typesetting: the manuscript for this book was prepared on a CPT word processor and communicated to the author's IBM/PC. The SS/DD DOS 1.1 format IBM disks were sent to the typesetter, who used his Kaypro computer and WordStar to add any typesetting codes the author forgot to include. From there it was a straight shoot to the compositor's typesetting interface.

For more information on UNIFORM, contact:

Micro Solutions, Inc.
125 South Fourth Street
DeKalb, IL 60115
(815) 756-3421

Kaypro

North West Kaypro Users' Group
P.O. Box 11
Portland, OR 97207

Cost of Membership: $15.

Publication: "NWKUG Newsletter"; monthly; 10 pages; typeset.

Comments: The January 2, 1984 issue, of *InfoWorld* reports that "Kaypro is now fourth in the market for desktop computers." (The top three being IBM, Apple, and TRS-80.) This adds up to a huge and growing installed base, and bodes well for the Kaypro users group movement and free Kaypro-compatible software. The Kaypro is a CP/M-based machine and so can run most of the CP/M programs described in Chapter 2. The trick, as always, is to get the software onto a disk in a format that the target computer can read. Then too, there are a few public domain programs, like MODEM7, that must be patched to customize port addresses. (See the information on Sheepshead Software in Chapter 2 and Appendix A.)

The UNIFORM program available for the Kaypro allows it to read many different disk formats. (See previous section.) And co-processor boards (containing an Intel 8088 microprocessor) that permit the Kaypro to run MS-DOS are also available. The company itself is said to be developing a board that will make its machines IBM/PC-compatible. All in all, a very versatile machine.

This group offers a Kaypro owner an ideal way to plug into the world of Kaypro users groups and free software. A recent edition of their newsletter, for example, summarized the "bundled" software offered with each Kaypro model. The article cited the fact that the contents of the bundle had been modified several times by the firm and that earlier purchasers who received fewer programs were understandably miffed. The group contacted Kaypro and published a reply indicating that those group members who were dissatisfied could receive 20% discount coupons from the firm to buy the missing packages. The group handled the transaction.

FreeTip: Here's a tip that exemplifies the advantages of belonging to a users group. This is a direct quote from the "North West KUG Newsletter":

> If anyone is using SELECT with an 8510A Prowriter printer, the Houston Kaypro Users Group has published a fix to make the printer do bi-directional printing. Let your Newsletter Editor know, and I'll send you a copy of the fix.

The group has at least ten disks of public domain software in its library. Most of the CP/M Gems are available, including SQUEEZE/UNSQUEEZE, MODEM7, SMODEM (for the Hayes), SWEEP, DU, LU, WASH, and ADVENTURE. There is a spelling checker, a word counter, *Star Trek,* and lots of other games. There is also a character graphics disk containing files like PINUP, TWEETY, SNOOPY, DRAGON, and something called NUDES, whatever that is. The cost of the first disk ordered is $5. Each additional disk in the same order is $4. Postage is included. All disks are SS/DD brand name disks (3M, BASF, or other). Finally, the club is interested in any public domain contribution, but as the newsletter points out, "There is a need for good Perfect Calc programs."

NorthStar

North Star Computer Society (NSCS)
P.O. Box 311
Seattle, WA 98111

Membership: 200.

Cost of Membership: $18.

Publication: "Polaris"; monthly; 10 pages.

Comments: This group has members all over the world and appears to be developing into a major contact point for owners of NorthStar computers, both in the U.S. and abroad. Neil Smith, the 1984 president of the group, writes that anyone who wants information on "our public domain library can just send a request for a catalogue to our address. (The catalogue is free. Individual disks are $6.)

"Besides the usual collection of CP/M utilities and games, our library includes PC-FILE, a very friendly and fairly powerful data manager, and a mailing list manager in NorthStar BASIC. . . . Included in the utilities are MODEM795, configured for both the Advantage and Horizon computers, ZCPR, SWEEP, and several programs written by club members to set baud rates, parity, ports, and other parameters from a menu, rather than patches. The library includes disks in both CP/M and NorthStar DOS operating systems." (See Chapter 11 for more information on PC-FILE and Chapter 2 for more information on the CP/M utilities Mr. Smith cites.)

Mr. Smith kindly sent us several copies of "Polaris." It is a useful publication with software, book, and hardware reviews, and lots of tips, answers to technical questions, and up-to-the-minute reports on what's going on in the NorthStar world. It is also one of the best written users group newsletters we have seen, thanks no doubt to Barry E. Abrahamsen, its editor. When asked about what group members could contribute, Mr. Smith responded that "I think what most user groups need (I know ours does) is contributions to the newsletter. Either reviews, short stories, technical advice, public information (such as laws affecting computer owners/users), or editorials."

The NSCS has a very good "feel" about it, and if you own a NorthStar it may be the ideal way to "plug in."

Osborne

First Osborne Group (FOG)
P.O. Box 3474
Daly City, CA 94015-0474
(415) 755-4140

Membership: 6500.

Cost of Membership: $24; for foreign membership, add the following amounts (for additional postal charges) to the annual dues:

Canada and Mexico (first class airmail)	$6
U.S. Members preferring first class	$6
Central and South America, Caribbean and Europe (first class airmail)	$12
Asia, Africa, and Far East (first class airmail)	$15
Out of North America preferring surface mail (delivery not guaranteed)	$6

Publication: FOGHORN; monthly; 50 pages; typeset.

SIGs: dBASE II, Ham radio operators, Personal Pearl.

Comments: This is the largest, strongest Osborne group we know of, and it offers an ideal way for Osborne owners to "plug in." According to the group's membership information, "In September of 1983, there were over 5400 members from around the world. Most attend local group meetings at over 300 locations. . . . Computer systems owned or used by members include the Osborne 1, the Osborne Executive I, all models of the Morrow MicroDecision, the Zorba, all models of the Kaypro, several MicroMates, and many more."

This group was formed in October of 1981 "by a small band of early buyers of the Osborne 1. The primary purpose was to organize a library of public domain software to run on the Osborne 1. . . . While the meetings are organized on a local basis, many of these local groups are joining the FOG network, thus increasing the sharing of information, tips, problems, and so on. Those local groups which opt to formally join the FOG network receive a portion of local member dues to assist with the cost of maintaining a local copy of the disk library."

Ms. Gale Rhoades, the group's executive director, writes that "FOG currently has 128 disks in the library . . ." Disks are maintained on the Osborne 1 single-density format, but separate libraries are being established for other computer formats. "Library files are carefully screened and divided into category types (utilities, games, applications, and computer languages are the four major categories). Programs that contain run or other errors are put into the hacker section so interested members can fix them and resubmit for inclusion in the correct section. Items that do not fit into one of these categories are in the miscellaneous section. A catalog and descriptions of all the disks is maintained in the library section. . . . The FOG library contains only public domain software. Piracy (the copying of proprietary software) is strongly condemned."

FOG is a nonprofit, tax-exempt corporation, and copies of *FOGHORN* are normally mailed by nonprofit bulk mail. If you want first class delivery, see the chart above for the additional postal charges. Membership applications are processed within a week of the receipt of your dues, and applications received before the fifteenth of the month generally are entered in time to receive the next issue. The group cautions, however, that you should allow at least two months for the arrival of your first issue since bulk mail can take as long as nine weeks. "The Post Office says that it should only take about three weeks for nonprofit bulk mail but some members on the East Coast have experienced longer delays."

There is more to say about FOG than there is space to say it. The newsletter is excellent. Perhaps first and foremost one should say that it offers one of the best ways to stay on top of the situation brought about by the failure of the Osborne computer company. The people at FOG *know*, and they dig for the details. Upon reviewing several issues of the newsletter, it is our feeling that FOG and its members are stronger and more determined than ever. As FOG points out, one of Adam Osborne's greatest accomplishments was to build his computer out of standard, off-the-shelf parts, making it relatively easy to get service and replacements.

The newsletter contains hardware and software reviews. But it also has a regular "Tips for Tyros" feature. Recent articles have included "SuperCalc—A Spreadsheet Shortcut," and "Just Starting dBASE II." There are also regular articles on how to use public domain utilities and software, something you are not likely to encounter in many other publications. Recent articles have discussed DU-V77.COM, FILTER, SQ.COM and UNSQ.COM (the "squeeze" and "unsqueeze" twins on the

CP/M Gems List in Chapter 2). You'll also find tips and patches for using commercial products like WordStar, dBASE II, SmartKey, and more.

The FOG library contains a great deal of the SIG/M and CPMUG public domain CP/M software. Here is what Ms. Rhoades says regarding the FOG library and obtaining disks:

"FOG members may purchase copies of the library disks from the FOG offices if copies cannot be obtained through their local group. Individual disks are $5 each. Bulk orders of ten or more disks earn a discount of $1 per disk.

"Shipping and handling charges are $5 per order or address. This charge must be included with every order. Please be sure to include your account-membership number. . . .

"For a listing of the programs and files in the library, consult the library column in each issue. . . . In response to the many requests, we have published a typeset guide to the library. This has the descriptions of every disk in the library, as well as the guidelines for library use. It is a loose leaf binder, punched volume. This format was selected to facilitate updates. Each copy will be in a portfolio. The price is $5, which includes shipping by third class (surface mail). Update pages will be offered on a quarterly basis. . . .

"Affiliated Member Organizations (AMO) may participate in a monthly update service. Only the librarian of an Affiliated Member Organization may make arrangements to participate in this plan." Contact Ms. Rhoades at the address given above.

This is a truly impressive group. And if you belong to a local organization, you might want to contact them regarding their special AMO plan that provides a rebate of 25% of the membership rate. "To be eligible for the rebate, the name of the group MUST be on the membership form (or check) when the yearly dues (new or renewal) are paid. No rebates will be made until the Affiliated Member Organization is formally approved by the Board of Directors."

FreeTip: We're not real certain about the T-shirts the group sells with the FOG logo, but the commercial software products are sure to prove interesting. Here is a price list from the November 1983 issue. All prices include third class (surface mail) shipping, but please remember that prices are subject to change and that other products may be available:

SMARTKEY	$60.00
SMARTPRINT	$35.00
(both)	$85.00
UNIFORM	$49.95

SORCERER and smart-ALEC

International SORCERER and smart-ALEC Users
P. O. Box 33
Madison Heights, MI 48071

CBBS: (313) 535-9186

Comments: SORCERER users apparently need all the help they can get. The newsletter published for the last four or five years by this group ("Sorcerer's Apprentice") appears to have met its demise with volume 5, number 2. The editor indicates that he has transferred the publication to another users group and suggests that interested parties contact Mr. Tommy Stokes, Route 1, Box 121, Everton, AR 72633, for details.

According to information supplied by the group, the public domain CP/M collections of CPMUG and SIG/M are available for SORCERER owners at this address:

Mr. Bruce Blakeslee
906 Crestwood Road
Westfield, NJ 07090

The software is available on Micropolis Mod II format only. You may send a formatted disk and $3 plus $1.50 for postage, or send $8 and $1.50 for postage for any disk. Make checks payable to Bruce Blakeslee.

Another access point you might try is a commercial firm whose advertisement appeared in an issue of the newsletter. The firm services Exidy SORCERER computers and looks like it might be a good source of equipment and additional information. Contact:

Mr. Jack MacGrath
Tercentennial Technical
73 Jordan Road
North Chelmsford, MA 01863
(617) 251-4776

SuperBrain, CompuStar, and Headstart

"Superletter"
Abrams Creative Services
P.O. Box 3121
Beverly Hills, CA 90212
(213) 277-2410

Subscription: $25/year; bi-monthly; 8–10 pages; typeset.

The above rate applies to subscribers in the U.S., Canada, and Mexico. All other foreign subscriptions are $35, airmail delivery only.

Comments: This is not a users group and, according to publisher Albert Abrams, there is no collection of public domain software. The newsletter is quite good, however. Mr. Abrams takes a personal interest in digging out and reporting the latest information of interest to owners of Intertec Data Systems equipment (the computers cited above). There are also letters, ads of interest, software reviews, and a significant number of assembly language programs and routines. Definitely worth a look if you own the above computers. (You may discover an address or an individual in the "Superletter" to whom you can write for the public domain stuff.)

Texas Instruments

International TI 99/4 Users Group
P.O. Box 67
Bethany, OK 73008
(405) 948-1023

Members: 80,000.

Cost of Membership: $12

Publication: Enthusiast '99; newsletter; bi-monthly.

Comments: This organization evolved from what is generally acknowledged to be the first TI users group in the country. We spoke with Charles La Fara, the founder and president of this organization, and learned that the group has the largest collection of public domain programs for TI computers in North America. At this writing, there are more than 1200 of them for the 99/4, 99/2, and the CC40. The programs have come from users groups, individuals, and through the group's TEXNET section on The Source (see Chapter 9). Today, I.U.G. programs form the core of many local users group libraries. So check with the group in your area.

If you wish to obtain your software from the I.U.G., you must be a member. The cost is $3 per program, on disk or on cassette. There is a minimum order of at least four programs ($12). If you have written a program you would like to donate to the collection, the group will send you three free programs in exchange.

The I.U.G. started out as a regular users group in August of 1980, but for a variety of reasons changed its status to that of a profit-making business. It is important to point out that a cost of $3 per program is not out of line in the TI world. Local users groups that are set up to fulfill mail orders typically charge between $2 and $3 per program, plus shipping.

Although the I.U.G. would appear to be the "master" TI group, Marshall Gordon of the TI Atlanta group (see next profile) sent us the following list of other names you might want to contact. Like the I.U.G., they are businesses, not users groups:

International Home Computer User's Association
P.O. Box 371
Rancho Santa Fe, CA 92067

The 99/4 Program Exchange
P.O. Box 3242
Torrance, CA 90510

New York 99/4 Users' Group
34 Maple Avenue, Box 8
Armonk, NY 10504

FreeTip: David and Dorothy Heller have prepared a book containing addresses, contact points, and other useful information of interest to TI owners. The book is called *Free Software for Your TI-99/4A* and is available at local bookstores or from the publisher. The cost is $8.95. Contact:

ENRICH/OHAUS
2325 Paragon Drive
San Jose, CA 95131

This book is particularly strong on educational contacts and resources and on software to aid the handicapped. TI is one of the few computers offering a voice synthesizer module, for example. Among other things, this makes it possible for a blind person to sign on to a database and have the text that appears on the screen read aloud.

Atlanta 99/4A Computer Users Group
P. O. Box 19841
Atlanta, GA 30325

Membership: 300.

Cost of Membership: $15.

Publication: "Call Newsletter"; monthly; 10 pages.

Comments: TI owners should be feeling pretty good, despite the exit of their computer manufacturer from the market. Not only do they have numbers on their side—2.5 to 3 million owners is a formidable installed base—but they've got people like Marshall Gordon on their side. Mr. Gordon, his wife, Elise, and several other TI owners founded this group in October of 1982. And thanks to the 20 hours or more a week its officers often devote to club activities, it has become one of the strongest TI groups anywhere.

This group has a library of more than 800 TI public domain programs, and it will make them available to members and nonmembers alike. However, and this is very important, Mr. Gordon emphasizes that most users will be much better off obtaining free software through their local groups. This is not because the Atlanta group objects to supplying it. It is because a local group is the best place to turn should you have problems with a program.

For example, Marshall Gordon cites an instance of a program that did not present the correct display on a user's TV screen. It turned out that the software was written to be used with a monitor and that a few lines of code had to be changed to shift the display to the right for proper viewing on a television. "This isn't difficult to do," Mr. Gordon says, "but a new owner might not be aware of the cause of the problem or how to fix it. That's what local users groups are for. You'll always find people to ask about such problems, and almost always someone will have a solution."

On the other hand, as Mr. Gordon points out, some owners do not live near a users group, or prefer not to join. And the Atlanta club is happy to help by making its library available. For members, the price is $2 per program, plus $1 for shipping per order. For nonmembers, the cost is $2.50 per program, plus $1.50 for shipping per order. Programs are stacked on a cassette tape and mailed to you. A catalogue that lists the program number, name, and a one- to two-sentence description is available.

We asked Marshall Gordon if he had any recommendations. He said that TEX SCRIBE, a public domain word processor, is pretty good, if a bit slow. He also confessed a fondness for a program that plays Beethoven's *Moonlight Sonata* while doing some interesting things with boats on the screen. Other titles in the library include:

DEPRECIATE
MAIL LIST
ROCKY ROBOT (speech synthesizer; recites nursery rhymes)
STATES AND NATIONS (education)
HOMEWORK HELPER (education; fractions; division)
ROBOT JOKES (speech synthesizer tells "hilarous jokes")
SPRITE DEMO
TYPING TUTOR
WORLD FLAGS
CHECKERS ("well-written program")
TAROT CARDS
CHECKBOOK
LISTS (stores appointments, birthdays, etc.)
DATABASE
MAIL PREP (used to create messages for easy sending via Sourcemail)
RECORDS (many search features; can be used as an accounts receivable program)
AUTOLOGON (for automatically logging onto TEXNET)

The group built up its library by actively trading and swapping programs with other users groups across the continent. And it still continues to do so today. Thus, if you have an original program to submit, the Atlanta club will be happy to look at it. If it is accepted into the library, you will be able to select any three programs in exchange. The program must be in the public domain, of course. Mr. Gordon reports that a considerable amount of time is spent reviewing programs to make sure that they have not been pirated.

If you are not a programmer, you can still lend a hand. Mr. Gordon indicates that the group really needs individuals who can type in public domain programs published in users group newsletters and other sources. In addition, if you have discovered something about your TI, you might want to share it by submitting a brief article or letter to the newsletter. The newsletter, incidentally, is an excellent source of TI information. Combined with the discount group members get on library programs, this is a good reason to consider joining the Atlanta group instead of ordering programs as a nonmember.

FreeTip: Here are three tips for TI owners, provided courtesy of Marshall Gordon. "Many places sell disk drives, but for both the best prices and the most knowledgeable assistance for TI machines, I think Software Support, Inc. is one of the best." Contact:

FreeTip continued

Software Support, Inc.
1 Edgell Road
Framingham, MA 01701
(617) 872-9090

There's even a hard disk available for the TI. "But at $2,600 for 5 megs and $3,000 for 10 megs, it may be a bit much. At present there is only about one place to contact." That is:

Myarc Inc.
P.O. Box 140
Basking Ridge, NJ 07920
(201) 766-1700

Finally, due to the unavailability of necessary technical details from Texas Instruments, TI owners have only recently been able to figure out how to set up a bulletin board. "The software our group plans to use for its BBS is from Sam Pincus in Illinois." The cost is about $100. Contact:

Mr. Sam Pincus
10 South 671 Ivy Lane—B
Hinsdale, IL 60521

Timex/Sinclair

Tampa and Suncoast Bay Area Microcomputers (TAS BAM)
P.O. Box 644
Safety Harbor, FL 33572

Membership: 200.

Cost of Membership: $15, individual; $25, family.

Publication: "Keyboards"; bi-monthly; 10 legal-size pages.

Comments: We spoke with Mel Routt, editor of "Keyboards" and one of the principle organizers of the club. TAS BAM exists as a discrete group, but it is also in the process of establishing or affiliating with autonomous chapters. Another important goal is to broaden the group's original Timex/Sinclair focus to include owners of many different kinds of inexpensive computers.

TAS BAM does not have a library of free T/S software, which is not unusual since we have not been able to locate one either. However, the group is actively trying to establish one. And after talking to Mr. Routt and after reading a year's worth of newsletters, one senses that if anyone can do it, TAS BAM can. In a word, these folks are serious. At this writing, TAS BAM is seeking nonprofit, tax-exempt status. Since the officers have elected to place all club dues in a bank account that cannot be touched until that status is granted, they are funding the club largely out of their own pockets.

Our newsletter review indicates that TAS BAM is an excellent way for T/S owners to plug into the T/S world. There are hardware and software reviews and summaries of important articles on the Timex computer appearing in magazines you may not have seen. Most important of all, Mr. Routt and other group officers closely follow Timex developments and seem dedicated to digging out hard-to-find information.

The Tampa/St. Pete area is no small shakes, either. As one newsletter article points out, it is the third-fastest-growing market in the U.S. The same article quotes International Data Estimates as saying that "the Sinclair microcomputer had 35% of the 1,775,000 microsystems shipped last year (1982). Commodore was second with 22%," and TI was third with 17%. "These figures are not mine. They come from the May 16, 1983, issue of *Fortune* magazine."

TRS-80

Fairfield County TRS-80 Users Group (FCUG)
c/o Alan Abrahamson
10 Richlee Road
Norwalk, CT 06851

Membership: 150.

Cost of Membership: $24, individual and family; $12, student.

Publication: "The Voice Of The 80"; monthly; 10 pages.

Comments: According to Alan Abrahamson, a professional computer consultant and editor of "The Voice of the 80," this group has approximately 1,000 public domain programs in its library for TRS-80 machines. At this writing, however, a list is not available. "Our president felt that the former lists did not include enough decscriptive material about the programs," Mr. Abrahamson says. "So all of our club librarians were asked to prepare new catalogues. That process is still [as of January 1984] going on." The group is also attempting to prepare documentation for many of its programs to make them easier for new owners to use.

Mr. Abrahamson indicated that the group has recently begun to actively build its libraries by swapping public domain software with other groups around the country. "We're trying to encourage greater use of the library at our local meetings. And while in the past there has not been a great demand for us to send disks through the mail, we would be happy to do so." You must be a member of the group to take advantage of its library, of course. Since a mail-order policy has yet to be established, it is not possible to report exact prices. However, Mr. Abrahamson said that the price would be the cost of the disk, the disk mailer, postage, and a small copying charge. Be sure to write for details.

We found the newsletter to be filled with useful hands-on information. Typical articles include: "Function Cures Memory Address Problem in BASIC," "Line Edit Function & DEF FN," and a collection of tips, routines, and hex memory addresses for the Model 4. You are also likely to find both short and medium-length BASIC routines in most issues.

FreeTip: Here's some information that will be of interest to owners of the Radio Shack Color Computer. According to a recent classified ad in *The Computer Shopper,* the International Color Computer Club has over 140 programs in its library. "All are public domain. If you have some that you would like to exchange, please write." Contact:

International Color Computer Club
119 County Fair
Houston, TX 77060

Software Supermarket reports that this group will sell nonmembers "120 cassette programs" for $30.

...6...

Non-User Group Distributors of Free Software: *Convenience, "Collections," and Cost*

As we've seen, users groups are the primary collection points for public domain software, but they are not the only distributors. In almost every case, as the free software written for a machine has grown, companies or sole proprietorships have been established to help make it available to the increasing numbers of computer owners who want it. Typically, these firms will charge a fee to cover the cost of the disk or tape, the mailing envelope, postage, and other expenses, including the labor of preparing the tape or disk and the cost of preparing and mailing a catalogue of free programs. They do not sell the programs themselves.

Other firms are less scrupulous. We have heard numerous stories, for example, of individuals who have been "burned" by companies that charge $25 to $40 for a single program that is available elsewhere for free. Needless to say, such firms do not inform their customers that the products they are selling are in the public domain. Unfortunately, there is virtually nothing to be done about this since there is no one to do it. After all, whose ox has been gored? Who will bring suit?

The only solution is to become an informed consumer. You'll find in this chapter much of the information you need to achieve this stage of enlightenment. You will also find many reputable firms. Their prices are fair, and you will find the services they render to be valuable. Indeed, having spoken to or corresponded with many of the principals involved, it is our feeling that all of these individuals have a genuine interest in spreading the good word about free software and in helping the new user take advantage of his or her machine. The one thing you will not find in this chapter are firms devoted to distributing CP/M software, since these were covered in previous chapters.

Why Buy from a Non-User Group Source?

There are a number of advantages to obtaining your free software from a non-user group distributor. Perhaps the most important of these is the generally faster response time. Users groups are usually a hobby for most members, and although most will do their best to fill your software requests, many of them are not set up for mass distribution. In some cases there can be a delay of from three weeks to three months between the time you send in your check and the time you receive your disk or tape.

Non-user group distributors, in contrast, are usually well prepared to handle your orders. It is relatively easy for a company like the Apple Avocation Alliance to add public domain Apple software to its other mail-order items, while an organization like the American Software Publishing Company exists for no other reason but to distribute public domain programs. Many of these distributors offer catalogues and accept telephone orders, chargeable to your major credit card.

The second major advantage of dealing with one of these organizations concerns the way they package and produce the software. A common approach is to prepare, on a single tape or disk, "collections" of free programs that relate to a particular theme. There are business and finance disks, for example, disks with nothing but games, and disks devoted to utility programs. Many users groups, in contrast, assemble their collections largely on the basis of when a program was received. This can lead to extremely mixed "volumes" and and make it necessary for you to buy several disks or tapes to get all of the programs you want.

Some distributors carry things even further and offer to prepare customized collections of progams you specify. In such cases, your cost per volume will usually be somewhat higher than it would be if you were to purchase a regular collection, and you may end up receiving fewer programs for your money. (Of course the reverse may be true as well. Purchasing a single customized disk containing all of the software you want for $12 may make more sense than buying three disks at $6 to obtain those same programs.)

FreeTip: The distributors discussed in this chapter charge between $1.75 and $3 per program to prepare a customized disk. That really isn't out of line if you consider the work involved in locating the requested program, inserting the master disk containing it into the drive and waiting for the copy to be made, replacing the master disk and locating the next one, and so on. Nor should one forget the wear and tear on the disk drive, the costs of light, heat, and electricity, or the costs associated with obtaining the master disk in the first place.

One can quibble with the nickels and dimes, but when you elect to ask for a customized disk, you are requesting a service. The size, virtue, or desirablility of the specific program has nothing to do with it since the costs and labor involved are essentially the same in every case. Since far less is involved in duplicating an entire master disk, purchasing prepared collections is almost always cheaper than taking the customized approach.

Interestingly, as Sheryl Nutting of American Software Publishing Company points out, you may actually pay less for public domain software when you obtain it through a non-user group source. If a distributor deals in a large enough volume, it can purchase blank disks, tapes, and mailers at a greater discount than may be available to a users group. If, as is the case with Ms. Nutting's firm, the distributor is inclined to pass the savings along to you, then your total cost could be less.

The one real disadvantage to going through a distributor is that you receive none of the benefits of belonging to a users group. With the notable exception of IPCO, the International PC Users Organization, none of the sources cited in this chapter provides anything comparable to a users group newsletter. Nor do they hold meetings or provide any of the other support services that can be so important to new and experienced computer owners alike. Consequently, you may very well want to consider joining a local group or one of the groups discussed in previous chapters, regardless of where you obtain your public domain software.

Random But Important Points

Here are some points that apply to all of the distributors profiled below:

- All payments must be in U.S. funds drawn on a U.S. bank, unless the organization accepts major credit cards.

- When contacting these groups, sending an address label and postage, though not always required, will always be appreciated and may speed your response.

- All prices are subject to change.

- The number of available programs is constantly increasing, so send for the latest catalogue in every case to be sure of getting the most complete selection.

- Virtually all of these organizations will be happy to look at any program you care to contribute, but please do not send them a commercial program. A number of individuals report that an inordinate amount of their time is taken up examining the software they receive to make sure that it is really in the public domain.

  You will have to send a letter or sign a statement indicating that to the best of your knowledge the program you are submitting is in the public domain or formally notifying the recipient that a program you have written may be freely distributed. Most organizations supply a copy of their submission form with their catalogues.

A Master Source of Public Domain Software

American Software Publishing Company
P.O. Box 57221
Washington, D.C. 20037
(202) 887-5834

Public domain programs for:

Apple	Commodore 64
Apple Pascal	IBM/PC and PCjr
Apple CP/M	Texas Instruments 99/4
Atari 400/800/1200	Timex/Sinclair
Commodore VIC-20	TRS-80

Catalogue: Free; includes offerings for all machines.

Comments: Sheryl Nutting, President of American Software Publishing, estimates that her firm has nearly 10,000 public domain programs in the collections it offers for each of the machines cited above. What's more, the specific programs offered usually represent the "best of" nearly everything that is available for any given machine. There is a good reason for this: Although all of the software is available in disk form, it is also available on cassette tape.

If you're a dyed-in-the-Mylar® disk fan, that statement will not exactly send chills coursing up and down your spine. But as Ms. Nutting points out, it can be crucial to many computer owners, and has a direct bearing on the quality of programs the firm makes available. "Almost all of the software we receive comes in on disk," Ms. Nutting says, "but we take the extra step of transferring it to tape because that's what many people use. A lot of people bought their computers at a deep discount or as part of a close-out sale when the computers themselves cost between

$50 and $150. Then they discovered that it costs between $300 and $500 to add a disk drive. For many, that's more than a bit steep. So they either added their own tape recorder or bought the computer manufacturer's tape recorder and now operate via cassette. That's the way many home users have gotten into personal computing. These people are in dire need of software, since the next thing they discover is that commercial programs can cost anywhere from $10 to $50 to several hundred dollars each.

"This is why we made the decision to make sure that everything we offer is available on cassette. But since space on a tape is precious, we decided to make a selection of only the very best public domain programs in each case."

Ms. Nutting is correct. Although tape distribution is not uncommon in some public domains, in our experience, disks are the preferred medium. You will undoubtedly find that some public domain programs are available *only* on disk from users groups and other sources. This does not prevent you from using them, but it does mean that you must locate a friend with a disk drive who is willing to transfer the program to a cassette.

What's Available?

American Software Publishing has assembled a "collection" for each of the machines listed above. With the exception of programs for Apple computers, which we'll explain in a moment, each collection consists of five "volumes." It is important to point out that *volume* has a special meaning here. Whereas in the CP/M world and other public domains, *volume* means a single disk full of programs, here each volume consists of 10 to 12 cassettes or their disk equivalent. Each volume in a collection contains approximately 50 individual programs devoted to a particular subject.

The company did not start supporting non-Apple computers until early in 1984 and, perhaps because of this, the Apple volumes are somewhat more extensive. In addition to these five categories there are also Apple volumes for graphics and sound, adventure games, Apple CP/M, and Apple Pascal. The pricing for all volumes is the same, however. Each is sold separately at $44.95 for the cassette version and at $75 for the disk version (7 to 10 disks, average). Discounts are available to individuals electing to purchase all the volumes in a collection at the same time.

Each volume in a collection comes with a users guide that provides safeguards, tips, and instructions for loading and using the programs with a particular brand of machine. "When we first began offering public domain software several years ago," Ms. Nutting says, "we did not include the guides. But we've found that people don't read their manuals when they get the machine. We rather thought they would. But we discovered that it was terribly important to provide instructions because people simply did not know what to do when they got a binder full of disks or cassettes.

"The manuals that come with many machines are really quite good, so in addition to step-by-step instructions, our users guides include frequent references to specific page numbers in the manuals that come with the computers to encourage people to read them.

"The first section of each volume guide explains what you have in your package and what to do with it. Then you are directed to a reference section that describes the various types of files that exist on the disks or cassettes. This section refers to each program by name and helps you locate it quickly. We also provide some sample runs.

"We regret that we are unable to support public domain software over the phone, but we have not built that into the cost of our distribution. To do so would make the packages cost considerably more. The users guides do go a long way in that direction, however."

Asked how she would respond were someone to suggest that American Software Publishing was profiting from the sale of public domain software, Ms. Nutting said, "The programs we offer are free. We do not charge for the software. Nor do we guarantee it. But we have to charge for the media—the tapes or disks—and for the services, the accompanying material, and the distribution we provide.

"We are a for-profit organization, but many of our products are priced below those of a lot of the nonprofit organizations because we benefit from the economies of scale, and we pass those savings on to our customers."

FreeTip: As Ms. Nutting points out, people who obtain their public domain software from American Software Publishing pay an average of between 20¢ and 95¢ per program, depending on the length of the program and the media it is supplied on. This compares to as much as $3 per program for the *same* software from other sources. On the other hand, one cannot purchase just one program from this company. The minimum unit is one volume at $44.95 (about 50 programs), whereas the minimum purchase from, say, the International 99/4A Users Group (Texas Instruments) profiled in Chapter 5 is $12 (four programs).

Free Catalogue

If American Software Publishing sounds interesting to you, the first thing to do is to send for the company's free catalogue. "This is a single catalogue in newsprint format that lists all of the material we have available for all computers. It also includes ordering information, costs, and information on what's in the various volumes. The catalogue indexes each program in the collection and tells you the volume in which it can be found. This makes it easy for people to pinpoint the programs they want and just order the appropriate volume."

Ms. Nutting says that new volumes will be issued as the software becomes available. There are also plans to translate programs into a form that is usable by newer machines in the same product line. Translations of programs for the Timex/Sinclair 1000 into 2088 form are a high priority. "New computers will be supported as they come along."

FreeTip: In June of 1984, Ms. Nutting began a new venture, the National Software Lending Library. "For an annual membership fee of $75, you may borrow one loose-leaf volume of software at a time. A volume contains several diskettes or cassettes with 30 to more than 500 programs. . . . When you return the borrowed volume to the Library, you may borrow another volume." All of the programs for all of the machines cited above are in the Library, and you may borrow as many volumes for as many machines as you like over the course of a year. Contact:

National Software Lending Library
P. O. Box 360
Damascus, MD 20872
(301) 428-9694

Apple

(Or a Quadlink-equipped IBM/PC, Columbia, Compaq, or other IBM/PC compatible. See "Switcheroos" in Appendix B.)

Apple Avocation Alliance, Inc.
3A Computer Products
2111 Central Avenue
Cheyenne, WY 82001
(307) 632-8561
8 AM to 5 PM (Mountain Time)

Public domain software for:

Apple	Apple CP/M
Apple+	Apple Pascal

Apple //e	Franklin
Apple III	Basis (a German-made Apple-compatible)

Catalogue: $2 in North America; $3.00 overseas. Price is deductible from one order of $25 or more.

Comments: This firm is a mail order house with a difference. It is not the type of firm that places those ads that seem to scream at you from virtually every page of most computer magazines. Instead, 3A has a more personal touch. The first thing you should do is send for the catalogue. Here you will find over 5,000 items (hardware, software, supplies, and peripherals), including many special products for the Apple II and III and //e. Even Commodore, NEC, and the IBM/PC are represented. You will also find conversational explanations of how the firm works ("You send you money and your order to 3A. Then we order what you ordered from a distributor. . . . Eleven to 18 days is the normal turn-around time. . . . Often the time is shorter"). And scattered throughout, you will find random bits of humor/wisdom ("Pascal is Wirthwhile").

FreeTip: Here's a tip that most experienced computerists know about, but it is not the kind of thing one would normally expect to find in a computer mail-order catalogue. The following is a direct quote:

> USE BOTH DISK SIDES
>
> We have seen advertisements for kits . . . to use both sides of your disks. Their prices are ridiculous! Please help spread the word. The minimum you need is a paper punch with a 1/4″ diameter hole . . . available for about $1.20 or less. With the tool, punch a half circle hole on the edge of the disk exactly opposite the half square cutout and you're in business.

The resulting disk is called a "flippy" since it can be flipped over and used on either side. A note of caution is in order here. You should be aware that *all* disks are double-sided. But only one side of a brand name single-sided disk has been tested for errors by the manufacturer. You should also know that most flippy nee floppy disks have a dirt filter that works quite well when the disk always spins in the same direction. When you flip the disk, you cause it to spin in the opposite direction, and there is a chance that the dirt will be dislodged from the filter. Flippies are fine for fun, but we suggest that you avoid using them to store crucial programs or data.

Most important of all, for our purposes, at the back of the catalogue you will find information on how to order any of more than 185 disk volumes of public domain Apple software. "Each disk volume contains from 2 to 40 progams and usually fills up one disk side. Included are 8 CP/M and 29 Pascal volumes."

All volumes are supplied on 3A media disks, described as "excellent quality generic brand SS/SD disks with hub rings and envelopes." Here's the price schedule taken from a recent 3A catalogue:

1 to 9 disks	$3.00 each
10 to 99 disks	$2.55 each
100 or more disks	$2.50 each

> Add $2.00 for packing and handling per order. All orders must be prepaid in U.S. dollars. Read our shipping instructions.

If you order 50 or more public domain volumes at the same time, you may deduct 5% from the cost of the disk order. Depending on whether 3A is conducting a sale when you order, prices may be even lower. The catalogue we looked at offered a 10% discount on orders placed during one month and a 5% discount during the following month. In explaining the 5% volume discount for public domain software, the catalogue said "This discount is in addition to our Fall sale discount."

FreeTip: The 3A library is a collection of contributions from user groups, college students, computer professionals, and others who write programs. The company encourages people to contribute by offering to exchange a disk full of your progams that are not in the catalogue for any volume you select. "Your exchange programs may be long or short, modified or original; in Integer or Applesoft BASIC, Pascal, PILOT, Forth, LISA, Microsoft BASIC, DOS 3.3, CP/M, and so on."

What's Available?

Each disk volume contains programs devoted to a particular subject, and at this writing there are more than 20 subject areas. These include:

Apple Tutor
Art & Graphic
Astronomy
Aviation
Business & Finance
Education & School
Electronic & Radio
Math & Statistics
Music & Sound
Utilities
Pascal
CP/M
Eamon Adventure

There are so many programs that it is impossible to present even a brief overview. But it appears that 3A has collected a large percentage of the programs you will find elsewhere in the Apple public domain. The best approach, of course, is to send for the catalogue and see for yourself. To give you a quick idea of the wide variety of programs available, here are some eclectic highlights:

- The two Aviation disks (034 and 035) contain programs with titles like: AIRCRAFT DATABASE, WW II FIGHTER AIRCRAFT, RNAV GLIDE SLOPE, US BOMBERS, and SILENTYPE HI-RES DUMP.

- In addition to standard calculation programs, the eight Business & Finance disks (042 through 049) contain programs like: STOCK OPTION ANALYSIS, LETTER WRITER, VISICALC FORMULAS, INVENTORY, DISCOUNT COMMERCIAL PAPER, GEN LEDGER, and A DATA BASE MGMT PGM.

- The eight CP/M disks contain many of the programs cited in Chapter 2, including: MODEM7, DU, RESOURCE, STARTREK, UNERA, SQ/UNSQ(ueeze), and APMODEM.

- Disks 066 and 067, the Education & School disks, contain programs like: ALPHABETE & SOUND, CLASS GRADE BOOK, SPELLING, TEST IN WOODWORKING, TYPING PRACTICE, and READING DRILL.

- There are three music disks (182–184) with "and-who-can-forget-these-favorites" tunes like: ALLEY CAT, BACH, ODE TO JOY, SMALL WORLD (ugh!), and STARWARS. You will also find: MUSIC WRITER, HARMONIC ANALYSIS, NAME THAT TUNE, and MUSIC KEYBOARD.

With 14 disks or more, the Art & Graphic collection is especially strong. If you have an Epson printer, you'll want the Epson Hi-Res graphic screen dump program on Disk 228. Interestingly, the 3A catalogue pointed out that there was a bug in the original version of this program. The bug has now been fixed and, as yet another example of what we mean by the "personal touch," 3A says, "If you wish, return your copy of 228 and we will recopy it for you, free."

Whether you have an Epson or not, if you are interested in good color graphics, the one disk you should be sure to order is Disk 020. This is the disk that contains SPARKEE, a wonderfully inventive series of graphics programs created by three independent artists using CEEMAC, a visual composition language from a company called Vagabondo Enterprises. It's easy to describe SPARKEE: The program generates a new swirling, rotating, expanding abstract image on your color television whenever you press any Apple key. Some of the designs are accompanied by music, though most are not. It is not so easy to appreciate SPARKEE—until you've seen it.

FreeTip: Though made available by 3A, SPARKEE is what its authors call "Personal Domain Software." You are encouraged to copy the program and pass it around, but if you like it you are asked to send $9 to the following address. (Note this is in addition to the money sent to 3A for the disk itself.)

Mr. Ken Sherwood
117 N. 25th Street
Reading, PA 19606

The CEEMAC language system itself is available from:

Vagabondo Enterprises
1300 East Algonquin—3G
Schaumburg, IL 60195
(312) 397-8705

The cost for Release 1.1 is $75, though 3A will sell it to you for about $53. Ken Sherwood writes that "Brooke Boering, the author of CEEMAC, is virtually always accessible by telephone as well as by mail, and I've always found Brooke to be willing, in fact eager, to share his time discussing questions about the use of this marvelous language system."

If you are interested in creating your own graphics with your Apple, this could be just the ticket. Though we suggest that you send for 3A Disk 020 (SPARKEE) first to get a better idea of what CEEMAC can do.

There are three other programs that deserve special mention. In the "Personal Domain" (you send the author $9 if you like the program) is "One-Key DOS." Written by Brooke Boering, the author of the CEEMAC language, this program is on Disk 229. It lets you enter 11 different DOS commands with a single key. For example, instead of typing *CATALOG* every time you want a disk directory, you simply enter a colon (:). When you want to "BRUN" a program, you merely hit the <2> key; <9> will UNLOCK a file; the [<CONTROL><I>] combination will reposition the cursor at the end of the text; and so on.

There is also DIVERSI-DOS (Disk 226), an author-supported program that we will discuss in Chapter 12. (This program requests a voluntary licensing fee of $25, and unlike SPARKEE and "One-Key DOS," it is available from the author as well as from 3A.) And there is the AAA Title Library (Disk 250). This disk contains the complete 3A catalogue (every filename) and a program that allows you to sort by title, type (A, I, B, or T), or disk volume number. Disk 250 thus makes it easy for people who have purchased several 3A volumes to quickly locate the programs they want.

Finally, if you are interested in games like *Adventure*, you should definitely step into the world of *Eamon*. There's no other word for it—this is really neat. *Eamon* works just like *Adventure;* that is, it is a text-based game. But unlike *Adventure*, it is infinitely expandable. The EAMON MASTER module (Disk E01) must be loaded in first. After that, you have more than 45 different adventures to choose from, each on a separate disk. Sample titles include: *Lair of the Minotaur*, *Cave of the Mind*, *Death Star*, *Tower of London*, and *Gauntlet*.

We played several of these games (of course!) and found the text both literate and amusing. As you prepare to enter a particular cave, for example, there is a pause while the proper segment of the program loads in from disk. The display says "One moment please . . . (Waking Up Monsters)." The games themselves are a combination of *Adventure* and *Dungeons and Dragons* (you define your characters' attributes), and they are written by many different people with the EAMON *Adventure* Designer modules on Disk ED5. There's even a newsletter and a users group. Contact John Nelson at 1226 East University, Des Moines, IA 50316, for more information.

Eamon, incidently, is the creation of Donald Brown. It turns out that it is the name of a heretofore undiscovered planet at the very center of the Milky Way. Mr. Brown states that Eamon "doesn't orbit any sun—all the stars orbit Eamon, all four billion of them. The shifting pulls of these great bodies bring strange forces to bear upon this planet . . ." Well, enough. You'll just have to see for yourself.

FreeTip: *Eamon* and other programs, including a number of VisiCalc templates, are also available from Micro Co-Op, a "member-based retailer and mail order" firm. Disks are $5 each, and a "lifetime membership" and catalogue is also $5. Contact:

Micro Co-Op
610 E. Brook Drive
Arlington Hts., IL 60005
(312) 228-5115

Atari

ANTIC Publishing
Public Domain Software
600 18th Street
San Francisco, CA 94107
(800) 227-1617, Ext. 133
In California: (800) 772-3545, Ext. 133
MasterCard and Visa accepted.

Catalogue: Free, single page.

Comments: ANTIC is a magazine for Atari owners (one year, $24.), but the publishing company also offers 12 disks of public domain Atari software. The single sheet "catalogue" we received indicates that none of the programs is yet available on cassette. The information sheet goes on to point out that "The potential buyer should note that these programs are sold *as is*. Their usefulness may depend on your experience with the computer. They may contain programming quirks that require some modification. However, all perform reasonably well . . . and represent an excellent value at $10.00 each, plus $1.50 per order for shipping/handling." The information says that you may send a check or money order (payable to ANTIC Publishing) to the above address, but we called the "800" number listed above and learned that you may order that way as well, charging your purchase to your credit card. "Allow four weeks for delivery. All orders are sent by First Class Mail. Please add 6½% sales tax for California residents."

There are five volumes of games, each with six to eight programs. Among other things, Games Disk 1 has *Hangman*, computerized *Monopoly*, *Lunar Lander*, and *Clewso*, a detective adventure with graphics. *Speed Demon*, *Deathstar*, and *Blackjack* are among the programs on Games Disk 2. The three ANTIC utility disks contain programs to execute a bubble sort, home inventory, a modem communications program (Utilities Disk 2), a real time clock, a dissembler, a word processor called "Tiny Text," a printer set-up routine (MX-80) for VisiCalc, and a routine for connecting a parallel printer from jacks 3 and 4.

There is also the ANTIC Graphics Demo 1 with "Spider," "Rainbow," "ATARI Logo," and other programs. And there is Music Disk 1 (Music Composer Cartridge required) with "Prelude," "Joplin," "StarTrek," "Yellow Submarine," and many more.

The information sheet closes by pointing out that "The price of the diskettes is based on the cost of making them available."

Commodore C-64, VIC-20, PET, SX-64

Public Domain, Inc.
5025 S. Rangeline Road
West Milton, OH 45383
Bill Munch: (513) 698-5638
George Ewing: (513) 339-1725
10 AM to 5 PM (EST)
MasterCard and Visa accepted.

Catalogue: Free.

Comments: "When I unboxed my Commodore PET 2000 back in '77," says Bill Munch of Public Domain, Inc., "I dug to the bottom of the box and lo and behold I reached in and I found a grand and glorious twenty-four-page 'Operating Guide' that spent five pages telling me how to plug the computer in and turn it on. The rest of the pages were taken up pointing out the features that it had. But nowhere was there any information to tell me how to use them. Also, it failed to point out a great many of the features that we've found through the years. And I had a heck of a time getting software.

"I saw the same thing happen again when the Commodore VIC first came out. Here we had all these guys, buying these systems, and they were saying 'Oh, gee, that's nice—now what do I do?' They really wanted to get into it, but they didn't know how. There were no published guidelines. And rather than have them have to learn the hard way, I've found that so very many of the hints and things that I've picked up over the years on the PET worked quite nicely with the VIC and the 64.

"I believe that if you can pass that along and get the users of these machines educated a little bit quicker, they'll be able to go a lot farther.

There are a good many of them who have long since surpassed me.

"It gives me a very good feeling to walk into a users group meeting and see a guy sitting there who's 89 years old, learning and playing and tinkering around and doing this and that, and by the same token, to walk in and see some little squirt seven, eight, or nine years old and he's just walking all over me.

"I say, 'Hey, fine. Go for it!' This is the thing they're going to have to learn if they hope to even keep up nowdays. The computer is here, and it's going to stay. There are no ifs, ands, or buts about that."

What's Available?

Bill Munch and his partner George Ewing are doing a great deal to help people get more out of their Commodore computers sooner than would otherwise be the case. Public Domain, Inc., has at least six volumes (available on both disk and cassette) of software for the VIC-20, six for the C-64, and 22 for the PET. The VIC collections contain about 70 programs each, while the C-64 collections average about 25 programs. All in all, it's a lot of software. The cost per collection, regardless of medium, is $10, postage included. Write or call for your free catalogue. Note that the disk format is compatible with Commodore's models 2040, 4040, 2031, 1540, and 1541 drives. No other drives are supported.

The programs in most collections are divided fairly evenly among games, educational software, and utilities. "If someone calls who doesn't know what is on each of the collections and doesn't know what to get," Bill Munch says, "I'll ask them what they're interested in. And if it's all right by them, I'll pick one out for them.

"If you're really into games, fine and dandy, I've got one that has more games than the others. If you like adventures, I've got one disk that is nothing but one monstrous adventure for the 64. This is the classic *Adventure* game that was originally brought up on a DEC PDP11, and it was sent over to us by Jim Butterfield."

The software we tested arrived on SS/DD Centech disks. The disks are packed in a zip-lock plastic bag, and each includes a printed table of contents. This is an especially nice feature because it lets you begin running the software immediately, without first keying in LOAD "$",8 and then LISTing the disk directory.

To give you an idea of what's available, Collection 2 for the Commodore 64 contains a high-resolution ("hi-res") loader and associated files to display five-color pictures on your screen. The program runs through its "slide show" once and stops, but since the loader is listable, you could alter it to make it repeat by inserting a loop in the code. If you wanted to create your own high resolution pictures, you could add the filenames to the same loader to make it display them as well.

The game BABY CARE was written by a man and a woman and it pits you against "baby." Your goal is to feed, diaper, and care for baby, but there are trade-offs for "FREE TIME" and "SANITY." When you go insane, you lose the game. The program NUKE 64 challenges you to run a nuclear power plant without causing a meltdown. (The graphics in this program are especially good.) There are other programs as well.

MONOPOLE 64—One of the Best

But there is one program that we feel is a "must have" for every C-64 owner. This is MONOPOLE 64. As you can surmise from its title, this is *Monopoly*, C-64 style. This program was originally written by John O'Hare in 1978 for the PET 2001 series. In late 1981, Tim Borion and Sal Oeper converted it to the C-64 and added color and sound. In a word, it is one of the best public domain programs we have ever seen—for any machine. When you boot it up, a screen that bears a remarkable resemblance to the *Monopoly* board appears. There is a display for the dice in the center. The game is for two players, each of whom alternately "rolls" the dice by pressing <R>. The computer then advances your token the correct number of squares.

If the property is still for sale, you will be given a chance to buy it, and the computer will deduct the appropriate amount from your game stake. If your opponent already owns the property, the computer will inform you of same and deduct the stipulated rent. The machine also keeps track of how many properties of each "color" you own. You can build houses and hotels, of course.

There are some surprises as well, but we'll let you discover them for youself. This is truly a super program. And like all programs offered by Public Domain, Inc., it is copyable. Indeed, you are encouraged to copy all of the firm's software and pass it around. The only thing you may not do is sell it at a profit.

Other C-64 highlights: Collection 1 contains a checkbook manager, FUGUE (Bach), and ENTERTAINER (Joplin), a music program arranged by Rick Sterling that requires three minutes and 25 seconds to initialize but is definitely worth the wait. On Collection 3 you will find DAM BUSTERS, BOND YIELD, FICA TAX, TYPING TEST, and CHEMICAL DRILL (Periodic Table practice).

FreeTip: Collection 3 also contains LATIN TUTOR, FRENCH VERBS, and MATH DRILL. These programs are excellent examples of one of the benefits of using public domain software. Since they are all listable, you can alter the BASIC code to suit your purposes. If you are a teacher, for example, you might use a program like LATIN TUTOR as a skeleton upon which to hang your own selection of LATIN words. You might add to those that are tested or substitute words of your own choosing. You could even convert the program to test for Spanish, Esperanto, or words in some other language. This is not something one can normally do with copy-protected commercial software.

Building Communications Bridges

We asked Bill Munch about the "Inc." following his firm's name, and about the fact that the company copyrights its collections. "Public Domain started out as a collection area for the original Commodore PET stuff," Mr. Munch said. "Since then we've added programs for the VIC and the 64. We got started because we found that the users groups just wouldn't talk to each other. I don't understand it. I've seen Atari and Apple groups, and they talk back and forth just fine. But the Commodore groups have just never gotten it together and set up good communications.

"We managed to set up something of a clearinghouse to make the stuff that's in the groups' libraries available to everyone. There are also programs that are sent straight to us, often by authors who live in areas where there are no users groups. And we sometimes receive programs from commercial firms who no longer wish to sell them but do not want to let the software just sit on the shelf. They release it to us knowing that everyone will have a fair shot at it.

"We incorporated so that we could do a few other things for our customers. This made it possible for us to copyright the collection—as a collection, we are not copyrighting the individual programs." Mr. Munch explains that this gives both the company and the contributors grounds for legal recourse should a disreputable firm try to sell the programs.

"There are a lot of companies—little fly-by-night outfits—that don't really particularly care about soaking the individual user by reproducing public domain software and selling it for unreal prices. I know of a company out in California, for example, that will sell you 50 public domain programs of your own choosing—for about $96." Mr. Munch's firm does not sell individual programs. The software is available only in collections. But since there are approximately 25 programs on each C-64 disk, and since each disk sells for $10, 50 programs would cost $20 from Public Domain, Inc.

"Now, let's suppose you have a group of individuals or a users group or even a school system that buys a number of collections and they copy it and pass it around among themselves. That's fine. Absolutely no problem. In fact, that's what we're hoping people will do. But no one should sell these programs to make a profit."

Your Name in Lights—How to Contribute Your Programs

If you would like to "publish" your VIC-20 or C-64 software creations by submitting them to Public Domain, Inc., here are the things to keep in mind:

- "Include your name and address and phone number, if you want, within the program itself. And don't just put it in the REMark statements. I think you should write the program so that it displays on the screen."

- The program must be your own. No programs copied from magazines or "from a friend" can be used. "A great deal of our time is spent making sure the program is noncommercial."

- Send the program on tape or disk. "We also need a short letter, nothing fancy, saying 'Here it is, you guys can throw it on the collection.' The person who wrote the program is still the owner, and I'll never have any objections if they ever want it pulled from the collection for any reason whatever." The company needs to retain the original media you submit, but it will send you a blank tape or disk in return.

- Although it is not something you can count on, Mr. Munch indicates that on more than one occasion, a software house has noticed a program in a collection, liked the author's style, and hired him for commercial projects.

FreeTip: The Public Domain, Inc., catalogue has lots of useful and imaginative technical tips for Commodore users. Have you ever thought about installing a small, inexpensive speaker ($1.69) in your cassette-based unit to let you *hear* all LOADs and SAVEs? We hadn't. But that was Helping Hint #4 in a recent edition of the catalogue.

There are also some addresses and publications that Bill Munch and George Ewing feel are likely to be especially helpful to new and experienced Commodore owners alike. Here are the ones you might not have heard of:

NUGGET$ Magazine
P.O. Box 34575
Omaha, NE 68134
(402) 496-4133

COMMANDER Magazine
P.O. Box 98827
Tacoma, WA 98498
(206) 565-6816
(800 426-1830

VIC-NIC NEWS
Box 981
Salem, NH 03079

MIDNIGHT
635 Maple
Mt. Zion, IL 62549
(217) 864-5320

IBM/PC, PCjr, XT, and Compatibles

International PC Owners, Inc. (IPCO)
P.O. Box 10426
Pittsburgh, PA 15234
CompuServe: 71545,467

Publication: "IPCO Info," six issues, 60 pages; offset.

Cost of Membership/Subscription:

U.S. residents (bulk mail)	$20/year
U.S. residents (First Class)	$30/year
Canada & Mexico	$25/year
Other Foreign	$50/year

(Note that all payments must be in U.S. funds.)

Comments: IPCO can best be thought of as a users organization that exists on paper and on disk. People we have spoken to in the IBM users group world frequently point out that IPCO is a profit-making firm, not a genuine users group. That may be, but it certainly performs an important service. It is essentially an international forum for the exchange of information, tips, and public domain software for the IBM/PC and related products. We have watched "IPCO Info" grow from a handful of stapled pages produced in December of 1981 into a saddle-stitched, near-professional-quality magazine. It is truly excellent, and Jim and Cindy Cookinham, the husband and wife team who run IPCO in their spare time, deserve a great deal of credit.

Our only complaint is that there is so much good information that it is nearly impossible to open an issue and go directly to the points that interest you. The best practice is to read "IPCO Info" with a colored felt-tipped pen in hand to circle items you want to return to. At this writing there is no index, cumulative or otherwise.

As an example of what you will find, a recent issue contained comments and tips from users groups all over the continent including Boston; Long Island; Madison, Wisconson; Ft. Wayne, Indiana; St. Louis; Toronto; and Tucson. There were notices of groups forming in Lubbock, Texas; Regina (Saskatchewan), Canada; and Ashfield (N.S.W.) Australia. There was a 14-line BASIC patch to modify PC-TALK for 450 baud communications. There were comments and questions from readers regarding their experiences with various commercial software and hardware products. (Some of these two-paragraph reports are worth more than entire multipage magazine articles and reviews.) In short, IPCO offers anyone who owns an IBM/PC or compatible an excellent way to "plug in."

FreeTip: Here's a tip we've offered in previous books but were glad to see surface in "IPCO News." If you own an IBM or Compaq computer, you've got a free one-year magazine subscription (worth $24) coming to you. The magazine is *Softalk* and you need only mail in your PC or Compaq serial number to qualify. (*Softalk* is a full-blown monthly magazine that thinks of itself as the "third alternative." *PC* magazine and *PC World*, of course, are the other two. Send your name, address, and serial number to:

Softalk
IBM Circulation
P.O. Box 7040
North Hollywood, CA 91605
(800) 821-6231
(818) 980-5074

What's Available?

IPCO also offers public domain, member-contributed software. At this writing there are close to 300 individual programs, and the library appears to be growing at a rate of 25 new programs or more per month. Because IPCO makes its programs available individually—you can order up a customized disk—each program has a four-digit number. The first digit signifies the classification, and these include: Games, Math and Engineering, Graphics and Demos, Educational, Home Applications, and Miscellaneous. A number of "user supported" Freeware™-like programs are also available. The authors of these programs ask you to send a donation if you like their software.

As you would expect, many of the programs in the various categories originated with and are available from other sources. A surprising number, however, are IPCO originals, submitted by IPCO members. For example, to the best of our knowledge, DOCTOR.BAS (IPCO 2025), an artificial intelligence–like program that enables the PC to formulate questions based on your responses, originated in this organization. As did CLERK.BAS (IPCO 1016), a card catalogue program (with search and sort routines) and GROWTH.BAS (IPCO 1017), a program that plots monthly data using color line and bar charts and projects annual growth. Like all public domain programs, these and other IPCO originals eventually appear in other collections, but in many cases they are available from IPCO first.

There is a free catalogue that contains the program names and numbers as well as some very helpful comments and descriptions from Jim and Cindy Cookinham. Be sure to send a stamped, self-addressed envelope. The catalogue measures 5½ by 8½ inches, so an appropriate-size manila envelope (with two stamps) is preferred. New additions to the library are announced in each issue of "IPCO News."

The size (in bytes) of each program is also given, and this is important because of the way IPCO distributes its software. The cost is $3 per program and $6 for the disk, handling, and postage. As the catalogue points out, "If you order enough programs you may need more than one disk. Please include $6.00 for each disk that is required." Both single-sided (160K) and double-sided (320K) disks are available. You are asked to determine how many programs will fit on a disk by adding up the byte size for each. Also, be sure to specify which type of disk you use and which version of DOS you own.

There is an additional $3.00 per order charge for mailing outside the U.S. or Canada. Nonmembers may order the same software by paying a 25% surcharge on the disk and program total. Pennsylvania residents, add 6% sales tax.

In addition to preparing customized disks containing the programs you choose, IPCO has recently begun to offer "Fixed Selections." These are DOS 1.1 single-sided disks containing programs classified by category. There are at least five games disks, two miscellaneous, and one each for the other IPCO categories. The cost for each disk is $15 and it includes everything. This is a much cheaper way to obtain IPCO software. The Business & Professional Fixed Collection, for example, contains 13 programs. If you were to purchase the identical software as a customized disk, your cost would be $45.

Less Expensive Alternative?

A charge of $6 for the media, postage, disk mailer, and handling is right on target compared to other organizations, and if you want customized disks, IPCO clearly deserves your consideration. But if you want the most public domain software for the lowest price, you might want to look elsewhere. For example, IPCO offers JUKEBOX.BAS, a very impressive music-selection program (IPCO 4026) and it offers Rubik's Cube (IPCO 2032). Were you to purchase these programs, your total cost would be $6 for the software and $6 for the disk and postage, or $12.

However, both JUKEBOX.BAS and RUBIC.BAS can be found on Disk 4 of the Capital PC collection described in Chapter 5. In addition to these two programs, that disk has a blackjack game, *Othello*, cribbage, *Yahtzee*, and eight other game programs. Your total cost: $6.

FreeTip: Disks in the Capital PC collection tend to be relatively well organized by category. The libraries of other groups may be less so. Conceivably, to obtain the same or equivalent programs offered on IPCO's Fixed Selection Business & Finance disk ($15), you would have to purchase several disks from another source. Although you would probably obtain a larger number of programs, this might not be convenient.

Which is why you should know about the PC Software Interest Group (PC/SIG) discussed in the next section. PC/SIG software is available in collections that have a much sharper focus than most user group libraries. Disk 29 FINANCE, for example, contains 16 financial and business programs. Disk 25 FINANCIAL contains 30 programs. The cost is $6 per disk, plus $4 per order for shipping and handling, a total of $16 for 46 business and financial programs. (Since everyone's prices are always subject to change, be sure to investigate to obtain the latest information before making your decision.)

How to Get FREE IPCO Programs

There are two ways to obtain free IPCO software. You can either submit a single program of your own creation, or you can submit an article to "IPCO News." To quote from the catalogue, "If you have a program you have developed for the PC, send it to us on a disk and tell us which four (4) free programs you would like in return for your program. We will return your disk to you with the four programs on it. We will add your program to our index."

And to quote from a recent edition of the newsletter, "Four free programs (as long a they fit on one disk) will be sent for each article of one page or more, submitted to IPCO on DISK and PRINTED in IPCO INFO. You MUST send your article in on a disk. This disk will be returned to you with the four programs of your choice on it." Note that any textfile will do, but the Cookinhams are at this writing in the process of switching from Easy Writer™ to Volkswriter™. If you happen to use Volkswriter, that would obviously be ideal.

Discounts on Commercial Programs

If you are planning to buy commercial software for your system and also think you might subscribe to IPCO, you might want to subscribe *before* making your software purchase. IPCO offers discounts to members on a limited selection of high-quality software. Volkswriter was recently available from IPCO for $125; Prokey was available for $55; and a program called "Datacount General Ledger," said to have once retailed for $295, was available for $35. Prices and program availability changes, so use these figures only as an indication of the discounts available from IPCO.

PC Software Interest Group (PC/SIG)
1556 Halford Avenue Suite #130
Santa Clara, CA 95051
(408) 730-9291
Visa and MasterCard accepted

Catalogue: $5.95, including postage; 110 pages.

Comments: Founded and managed by Richard Petersen, PC/SIG is one of the best organized, most comprehensive, lowest priced, free software distribution mechanisms we have encountered anywhere. If things work out as Mr. Petersen plans, PC/SIG may one day become the IBM equivalent of SIG/M, the "master source" of public domain software in the CP/M world. With more than 135 disks full of programs at this writing, one can say that PC/SIG is off to an excellent start.

Mr. Petersen began PC/SIG because he wanted a master source of public domain programs himself and realized that other IBM/PC owners, many of whom are unaware of the public domain, needed the same thing. "Public domain programs are available all over the country," he says, "but you almost had to know somebody to find out what and where they were. There was no central place where you could look and say 'Hey, these are *all* of the things available.'" PC/SIG was started in hopes of establishing a national or possibly even international focal point for free IBM software.

Since no one was offering this service, Mr. Petersen assembled a collection based largely upon the library of the Silicon Valley Computer Society, the users group to which he belongs, and paid for a number of ads in *PC* magazine and other publications. "The only way to let people know about public domain software is to advertise," he says. He prepared a catalogue and began adding disks and programs from other users groups, bulletin boards, and other sources. Now that PC/SIG is becoming better known, people have begun to send the organization any new programs that they encounter, so the collection is constantly growing. "Many of the authors of 'User Supported' software have sent us their programs because they have found that PC/SIG offers them an easy way to get their products distributed." ("User supported" is a relatively new term made necessary by the fact that Freeware™ has been trademarked by its creator, Andrew Fluegelman. See Chapter 11.)

PC/SIG sells its disks for $6 apiece, plus $4 for shipping and handling per order. California residents, add 6.5% tax. For foreign shipment, add 10% or $10, whichever is greater. At this writing, the ads have generated enough interest to pay for themselves, which is exactly what Mr. Petersen hoped would happen. Is PC/SIG a profit-making enterprise? Mr. Petersen says, "It really hasn't gotten that far. We haven't incorporated or spent a lot of money on lawyers' fees. This started as something that we just wanted to try. I'm not looking at it for profit at all. I basically want it to pay its expenses."

FreeTip: If you have or have written a program that you would like to contribute to PC/SIG, the first thing to do is to check the catalogue to make sure that it is not already in the collection. In the catalogue you will find a submission form requesting you to sign a statement indicating your intention to place the work in the public domain. "If somebody sends in programs or a disk," Mr. Petersen says, "I will send back programs or disks on a two-to-one basis." You have only to request the software you would like in exchange.

What's Available?

Your entree to the PC/SIG collection is the catalogue, and it is so impressive that it is worth more than a passing reference. The catalogue itself is a 110-page, 5½-by-8½ inch booklet with a glossy stock cover. The first thing you encounter after the contents and preface is a section titled "Notes About Using Public Domain Programs." This section explains that one must load BASIC or BASICA before trying to run a BASIC program, an elementary point to an experienced computerist, but one which Mr. Petersen reports many new users are not aware of. There is also a list of filename extensions and what they mean and the command one might use to print out the documentation found on many public domain disks.

An explanation of the "user supported" concept comes next. Essentially a user supported program is one which may be freely copied and distributed. If you as the beneficiary of such software like the program, you are asked to send a small donation ($10 to $40, depending on the program) to the author. Next are at least 15 descriptions of user supported programs available through PC/SIG, the names and addresses of the authors, and the requested donation. (Please see Chapters 11 and 12 for more information on this kind of software.)

Next is a summary of the disks in the collection. Each disk has a number and a title ("RATBAS," "DESKTOP," "GAMES 10," etc.). The title is followed by a one-line description highlighting the specific programs to be found on each disk. Individual tables of contents for each disk follow and occupy the bulk of the catalogue. At the very end of the catalogue, you will find an alphabetical index of every program name and the number of the disk it can be found on. This is an important convenience feature that, surprisingly, is little used in the public domain. Mr. Petersen has the entire catalogue on disk, of course, so it is relatively easy to produce a sorted list. Would that other providers followed his lead.

Finally, one of the most important features of the PC/SIG way of doing things concerns the way in which the programs are classified. Instead of producing disks containing programs more or less in the order in which they were submitted, Mr. Petersen prefers a sharper focus. This is not to say that you will not find unrelated programs on the same disk, but by and large programs tend to be grouped by function or subject matter.

Here are a few highlights:

- Disk 18 — I.Q. Builder, including tests for analogies, synonym, antonynms, and more. Menu-driven.
- Disk 31 — Mountain View Press public domain Forth language.
- Disk 39 — Flight Simulator.
- Disk 41 — Complete KERMIT communications System (Famous PC-to-mainframe comm program from Columbia University).

- Disk 42 Documentation for KERMIT
- Disk 90 Genealogy package; 25 related BASIC programs, including one to create a marriages file, print family groups, and list a parent-child index.
- Disk 95 Math Tutor package; 20 related programs and files to teach mathematics; grade selectable (1–6).

FreeTip: If you have some free time, an IBM/PC, and several boxes of floppy disks, you may be interested in the deal offered by P. J. 's Company. P. J. 's will *rent* you the entire 100-volume PC/SIG collection for $99.50, plus $7.50 for UPS shipping, handling, and insurance. You can keep the volumes for up to seven days after you receive them, with three additional "grace" days to allow for mailing them back. You can place you order by phone and charge it to your major credit card.

This approach could be particularly effective if you are starting a new users group or trying to obtain software for a school or other organization. Here's what we suggest. First, order the catalogue from PC/SIG. Then contact Translation Storage Systems, Inc. (TSS). These are the "Expect a miracle" people whose advertisements you've seen in most computer magazines, and we've found them to be a pleasure to deal with:

Transaction Storage Systems, Inc.
22255 Greenfield Road
Southfield, MI 48075
(800) 521-5700
(800) 482-4770 (in Michigan)
(800) 265-4824 (in Canada)
(800) 821-9029 (in Alaska and Hawaii)

Order five or six boxes of Control Data single-sided disks (at about $19.90 per box, plus $4.00 shipping). These come in nifty sliding-drawer plastic storage boxes designed to be snapped together side-by-side, an especially convenient way to hold your public domain collection.

Next, format the disks under DOS 2.x for double-sided use and rent the PC/SIG collection from P. J. 's. Almost all of P. J. 's disks are "flippies" containing a 160K PC/SIG volume on each side. Use the MKDIR command to create directories on your disks labeled with PC/SIG colume numbers and make your copies. This will keep the programs segregated and allow you to take advantage of the index in the PC/SIG catalogue. You'll be able to fit two volumes on each disk.

Your cost for everything will come to about $217, a savings of nearly $400 over the cost of buying 100 disks at $6 each. [P.J.'s will also sell you 100 (or more) PC/SIG volumes on 50 flippy disks for $100.]

For more information, send a self-addressed, stamped envelope to the address below. Note that there are two phone numbers, one for information and one for orders. The "order line" is connected to an answering machine and is operative 24 hours a day. Visa, MasterCard, and American Express are accepted. Contact:

P.J.'s Company
National Public Domain Software Center
1082 Taylor
Vista, CA 92083

For information: (619) 941-0925

To order: (619) 727-1015

Software Distributors Clearinghouse (SDC)
3707 Brangus
Georgetown, TX 78626

Catalogue: Free; seven pages; computer-generated.

Comments: James Ellis of Software Distributors Clearinghouse uses an approach similar to that of IPCO. His firm will prepare customized disks containing the public domain software you choose. While the selection at this writing is not as extensive as IPCO's (there are approximately 60 programs in the SDC collection), the price per program is lower. The cost is $1.75 per program for the first five, $1.50 per program for the next five, and $1.25 per program for any beyond 10. There is also a $1 postage and handling charge. Since a minimum order of five programs is required ($8.75), the least you can spend with postage is $9.75.

Many of the names of the programs will be familiar to anyone who has studied the IBM public domain. You will find IQBUILD, BLACKJAC, TRUCKER, NIM, BACKGAM, and HANGMAN, for example. If you were to purchase these programs from SDC, your total cost with postage would be $11.25. As it happens, however, the same programs (the version of HANGMAN is different) are available on PC/SIG's Disk 18, as well as a math drill, a speed reading program, and the game *Mastermind.* The cost for this PC/SIG disk is $6 plus $4 per order for postage and handling, a total of $10, in other words. Since everyone's prices are subject to change, you will want to investigate thoroughly to obtain the latest information before making your decision.

There may be good reason to place your order with SDC, even if you feel it is slightly more expensive. As James Ellis writes, "I started collecting free software when I got my PC last year and several months ago decided to find out if there is a need for a service to distribute these programs. I have reviewed well over 500 programs and those listed in the catalog seem the most useful and interesting in addition to being almost error free.

"My experience thus far indicates that most buyers are interested in financial, educational, and utility programs. My interest is to search out the best programs in these categories. I believe that many of these programs compete very well with more expensive 'professional' programs."

As the firm's literature points out, the programs themselves are free. The money charged covers the cost of preparing the disk, the disk itself, and other handling and administrative costs. Certainly $1.75 per progam is not unreasonable when you consider the work involved. And there is a liberal money-back guarantee: "If you are not completely satisfied with the programs you have received from SDC, return your diskette and we will refund your money." SDC will also swap programs with you. "For information, write for our Program Submission form."

FreeTip: MICROCOMP Services in Ontario also has public domain software for the IBM. To quote from the firm's catalogue, "The MS/DOS library of over 40 5¼-inch disks of software released by NYACC . . . is the most recent addition to our libraries. The material . . . is outlined and cross-referenced on the catalog disk NYACC.CAT ($10). The user group disks are available at $10 each in single-sided IBM PC format only."

We have not checked, but this sounds like the PC/BLUE collection published by the New York Amateur Computer Club (NYACC) and described earlier. MICROCOMP also offers the Silicon Valley Computer Society library of some 47 IBM/PC disks. The programs are "outlined and cross-referenced on the catalog disk SVCS.CAT ($10)." The format and price per disk is the same as that cited for the NYACC collection.

For more information, contact:

MICROCOMP Services
4691 Dundas Street West
Islington, Ontario M9A 1A7
Canada
(416) 239-2835
Visa, MasterCard, and American Express accepted

TRS-80 and Color Computer

Mr. Jack Decker
c/o The Alternate Source
704 N. Pennsylvania Ave.
Lansing, MI 48906
(517) 482-8270

Comments: Jack Decker bought his TRS-80 Model I in 1979, and he still uses it as his home system. Since that time, however, he has explored Tandy computers as few others have and is as at home with Model I and Model III ROM routines, memory locations, and the like as most people are in their own living rooms. This is significant because, unlike some computer manufacturers, Tandy is said to be rather reticent about providing users with this kind of information. With much labor, and through his long involvement in the user group movement, Mr. Decker has discovered just about everything a programmer needs to know about the Mod I and Mod III and the Model 4 when operating in its Model III emulation mode. He has assembled his knowledge in a book that is sure to be of interest to all serious TRS-80 programmers. Here's the title and ordering information:

TRS-80 ROM Routines Documented
by Jack Decker
Alternate Source; Jan. 1984
126 pages; $19.95

This book is available directly from The Alternate Source. Please include $3 for shipping and handling.

The Alternate Source is a software house, not a users group. Mr. Decker's home users group is Microcomputer Users International in northern Michigan. That group is apparently in flux right now, however, and Mr. Decker has increasingly begun to work with The Alternate Source to establish what may be the first "master" source of public domain software in the TRS-80 world. "What we've been trying to do here," Mr. Decker says, "is to get together some *good* public domain software for TRS-80 Models I, III, and 4. I want to emphasize 'good,' because as many TRS-80 owners know, there's a lot of public domain software floating around out there, but a large percentage of it is what I call 'filler.' We want to assemble disks and make them available to TRS-80 owners the way the CP/M and Apple groups do. Up to now, no one has really organized things."

The Alternate Source will serve as the distribution point. Disks cost $10 each, but they are "flippy" disks, so each has two readable sides. By February of 1984, after reviewing many programs, Mr. Decker had prepared two disks. Disk 1, Side A contains NEWDOS 80 programs; Side B holds miscellaneous Model I and III programs that will also run in the Model III mode of the Mod 4. Disk 2, Side A contains three smart terminal programs, including utilities for using the XMODEM binary file transfer protocol; Side B contains miscellaneous Model 4, MULTI-DOS, DOS PLUS, and several communications programs for cassette users.

If you have written or obtained a program you know to be in the public domain, Mr. Decker would appreciate hearing from you. "A lot of people feel they have to fill up an entire disk before sending it in. But I'd really rather they did not do this since it takes time to separate the wheat from all the chaff. I would much prefer one or two programs the user has selected because they have been found to be really good." If the contributions are acceptable, Mr. Decker will load up your disk with one of the public domain collections and mail it back to you. (Note: If you can, send your contributions on a "flippy" disk. This way you can obtain two sides of the free stuff.)

There is a one-page catalogue listing for each disk, but Mr. Decker expects the number of sheets to grow. For the time being, however, The Alternate Source will mail you copies free of charge, in return for a mailing label and postage. Here is what you should do to plug into this source of public domain software. Perhaps the easiest thing to do is to mail $2 to The Alternate Source. They will put you on their mailing list and send you a copy of "Northern Bytes," a newsletter edited by Mr. Decker and published irregularly. In your letter, be sure to mention that you would like a copy of this publication and that you would like to receive the public domain catalogue sheets. The Alternate Source receives many letters and orders for its products, and specifying what you want is the best way to avoid confusion. Mr. Decker says that for the time being you may save yourself the $2 by sending a mailing label and two twenty-cent stamps. Again, be sure to specify what you want.

FreeTip: Jack Decker has written an assembly language program that may be of interest to Model 4 owners. Called Video4, the program allows you to use the Model 4's 80-column mode when it is running Model III software. The source code is provided and it is "heavily commented," according to Mr. Decker. The cost is $24.95, and it is available through The Alternate Source.

FreeTip: If you own a Radio Shack Color Computer, you may want to contact the International Color Computer Club, Inc. The club maintains a library of books, Radio Shack ROMpaks, and free software that members may borrow for up to three weeks at a time. Tapes are available for $2, and there are six programs per tape "mixed in a variety for your convenience." There is also a bimonthly newsletter averaging 56 to 80 pages an issue. For more information, contact:

International Color Computer Club, Inc.
2101 East Main Street
Henderson, TX 75652
BBS: (214) 657-8147

The address for the Canadian branch is:

International Color Computer Club, Inc.
P. O. Box 7498
Saskatoon, SK S7K-4L4

... 7 ...

Free Software Over the Phone: *Getting Ready to Go Online*

Telecommunications is probably *the* most exciting area of personal computing. As millions of computer owners have discovered, an entire electronic universe of possibilities opens up to you once you connect your machine to the telephone. Among other things, a communicating computer can be used to:

- Send and receive electronic mail—instantly—anywhere in the world.
- "Meet" and converse with people who share your interests, wherever they may be on the globe.
- Participate in online users groups and tap the expertise of its members to answer your hardware, software, and other computer-related questions.
- Obtain every conceivable kind of information, from the latest stock quote to a learned essay on ancient Samaria.
- Send Telex and TWX messages to nearly two million locations around the world or communicate directly with facsimile machines.
- Become a "telecommuter" by working at home and accessing your company's mainframe or minicomputer with your micro.

These and many other possibilities are detailed in *The Complete Handbook of Personal Computer Communications* by Alfred Glossbrenner (St. Martin's Press, New York), a book we can recommend without reservation. In this and succeeding chapters, however, we're going to leave the communications and information aspects of the electronic universe aside and concentrate instead on an equally exciting application—the use of telecommunications to distribute public domain software.

There are three main online sources of free software. There are the two major information utilities, The Source and CompuServe. And there are a host of computer bulletin board systems (BBSs) owned and operated by private individuals across the continent, and even around the world. The BBSs fall into two main categories: "conventional" BBSs, and remote CP/M systems or RCPMs.

> **FreeTip:** Actually, the RCPM systems came first. Ward Christensen and Randy Suess, both members of CACHE (Chicago Area Computer Hobbyist Exchange), created the first one in February of 1978. Known as CBBS #1 (Computer Bulletin Board System™), it is still on the air today [(312) 545-8086; 110, 300, 600, or 1200 baud, 8/N/1; needs several CRs without CFs to sense baud rate at sign-on]. Both the "board" and Christensen's famous XMODEM protocol were from the very start designed to transmit public domain software over the telephone. RCPM systems differ from what we've called "conventional" BBSs in that they tend to concentrate on public domain software instead of messaging facilities and usually don't have much in the way of menus and convenience features. As we'll see in a later chapter, callers are expected to run the remote computer by issuing CP/M operating systems commands from their own console (keyboard).

We'll focus on The Source and CompuServe and show you where to look for the the huge reservoirs of free software on those systems in the next two chapters. Then we'll show you how to get the most out of the nation's bulletin board systems and how to use an RCPM efficiently. By the time you finish those three chapters you will probably want to equip your machine for telecommunications. If you do, you'll open up yet another possibility—direct, computer-to-computer communications.

As we said in earlier chapters, locating the public domain programs you want is often only the first step in building a free software library. A program may be written to run under CP/M, MS-DOS, or some other operating system that is available for your computer. It may be written in a language fully supported by your system. But if it doesn't exist on a disk or a tape that your machine can read, it might as well not exist at all. Though a program hath the power to remove mountains and hath not media compatibility, it is as nothing—unless, of course, the source code is available and you're willing to spend several evenings typing it into your machine.

Telecommunications offers a better way. You and your friend may own computers that use different disk formats. But if both are equipped for communications, the two machines can be coupled together with a specially wired cable and programs can be "dumped" from one to the other. Once the program has been transmitted to your machine, you can record it on one of your own floppy disks and run it as you would any other piece of software. Alternatively, the two of you might establish a phone connection and transfer programs with the same techniques and hardware used for calling an information utility or bulletin board. One way or another, communications offers a neat way to skate around the problem of media incompatibility.

What Software and Hardware Do You Need?

Let's look at the various things you'll need to equip your computer to communicate with commercial databases and bulletin board systems. In addition to a telephone, you'll need four main components:

- A communications card or a card with an RS-232 serial port.
- A telephone interface device called a *modem.*
- A cable to connect the modem to the RS-232 port.
- Communications software to tie everything together.

Naturally there are some exceptions, depending on your particular computer and the type of modem you buy. The thing to keep in mind, though, is that *every* computer can be made to communicate, and most computers need these four things to do it. Fortunately, the cost is not terribly high. A communications or "comm" card might cost about $100. Modems have become considerably cheaper in recent years, and some models are now available at a list price of about $70, including a cable. Add anywhere from $30 to $50 for a basic communications program, and you can be online for around $200.

Please bear in mind that these are general figures. For example, the Radio Shack Color Computer (CoCo) and the TRS-80 Model 4, the DEC Rainbow 100, computers made by Commodore, Kaypro computers and other transportables, and many others come with a built-in communications card. In such cases you can buy a modem and cable for about $70 and a basic communications program for about $40, bringing the total cost to just over $100.

If you own an IBM/PC, on the other hand, and you want to go first class all the way, you might spend as much as $850—or more. Owners of the Radio Shack Model 100 lap-sized portable computer won't have to buy anything, since that unit comes with a built-in communications card and communicatons program *and* a modem. Discounts, special package deals, and promotional offers may be available for both hardware and software, to further reduce the total cost. And in all likelihood there is a serviceable public domain communications program for your machine, available for the cost of a floppy disk or cassette tape.

A Word Processing Program—The Fifth Component

In addition to the items listed above, you'll also need a word processing program to "clean up" the files you download (capture) from databases and bulletin boards. If you happen to capture and record sentence fragments or other stray characters when you are downloading Jack Anderson's "Washington Merry-Go-Round" newspaper column from The Source, you'll still be able to make sense of the text. But if the same thing happens—as it will—when you are downloading a BASIC or other program, your computer will become quite peevish and refuse to run the software until you remove the offending characters.

In a pinch, you may be able to use a line-oriented text editor, if one came with your operating system. But these programs are often challenging to master, and none is as convenient as a genuine word processor. If you don't have a word processing program already, you might want to consult Chapter 13 of *How to Buy Software* by Alfred Glossbrenner (St. Martin's Press, New York) for information on what features to look for in a commercially available program. But you may also find what you need for free in the public domain. Check with the appropriate user groups and other organizations listed in this book. If you have an IBM/PC or PCjr, be sure to read Chapter 11 for its discussion of the full-featured PC-WRITE "Shareware" program.

Getting Ready to Go Online

In the following sections we'll look at each component in more detail, explain what it does and what you need to know about the role it plays in communicating, and offer some suggestions to help you decide what to buy. We'll also explain the difference between ASCII text files and binary program files. And we'll look at the all-important XMODEM protocol. Although it is not necessary for a person to know these things when using the communications and information resources of the electronic universe, to a seeker of free online software this information is as important as knowing how to turn on a computer.

Communications: It's in the Cards

A communications card is a printed circuit board that is designed to be plugged into your computer's internal expansion slots or expansion interface box. Its job is to rearrange the electrical impulses whizzing around inside your machine into a form that is acceptable to a modem. An RS-232 ("R-S-two-thirty-two") port is a 25-pin plug or socket designed to accommodate the cable that links your communications card to your modem.

That's the short answer to the question, What is this thing called a comm card? For a more complete explanation, it is necessary to talk (briefly) about bits and bytes and internal computer communications versus external telephone communications. As you probably know, bits (*bi*nary dig*its*) are the very essence of a digital computer. In physical terms, a bit consists of a particular electrical voltage level, while the computer itself consists of a massive collection of microscopic switches designed to manipulate and respond to these voltages. Nothing can happen inside a computer until the commands you have entered are converted into bits. And you won't see anything on your screen or printer until the results of those commands have been translated from patterns of bits into something human beings can understand.

Bits come in two varieties. You will hear them referred to as "on" and "off" or as "high" and "low" voltage states. But they are most frequently represented as 1 and 0. Whatever you call them, they don't give a computer much to work with. Yet the machines don't seem to mind, for with just two kinds of bits they can symbolize and manipulate any number, thanks to the "base 2" or binary system. If numbers are assigned to each character in the alphabet, a computer can manipulate letters as well.

The catch is that since there are only two kinds of bits, computers must use quite a few of them to represent even relatively small numbers. Indeed, for a variety of reasons, most personal computers deal with bits in eight-bit packages called *bytes*. That means that when you strike a *T* on your keyboard, what actually gets sent into your computer is the following "byte" or bit pattern: 01010100. This happens to be the binary representation of the number that most manufacturers have agreed to assign to a capital T. In human or "decimal" terms, it is an 84 in the ASCII ("as-key") code set.

We'll explore ASCII in a moment. Right now the thing to focus on is the fact that all the bits in the above pattern leave your keyboard and enter the computer at the same time. They travel along eight wires or printed circuit paths in a *parallel* arrangement. Similarly, when many computers need information that is stored on a floppy disk, they will retrieve it in eight-bit chunks, with every bit leaving the disk drive at the same time and traveling in parallel formation. Many printers are designed to operate the same way, receiving the characters they are supposed to print eight bits at a time.

There are some exceptions regarding disk drive and printer connections, but they're not important here. The point is that personal computers, even the 16-bit IBM/PC and similar machines, move information around inside themselves in an 8-bit, parallel arrangement. (The Apple Macintosh is a 32-bit machine that uses a 16-bit data path, but that's another story.) This is their natural way of communicating. The problem is that a telephone has only two information-carrying wires, making it impossible to send and receive information eight bits at a time.

FreeTip: An explanation of 8-bit and 16-bit computers is beyond the scope of this chapter. However, lest these terms prove confusing, you should know that they refer to the number of bits the microprocessor at the heart of a computer can deal with at any one time. This is significant for two reasons. First, by dealing with 16 bits instead of 8, a 16-bit machine can work faster, though it isn't likely you'll notice the difference when using most programs. Second, and more importantly, a computer that can handle 16 bits can deal with memory addresses that are twice as long as an 8-bit machine. Without going into detail, this is the reason most 8-bit microprocessors can address only 64K of memory versus the 1,000K of memory possible with 16-bit machines.

Finally, the fact that 16-bit machines like the IBM/PC and its compatibles move information around internally in 8-bit chunks is a function of their design and not related to their use of 16-bit microprocessors. In plain terms, things were done this way to save money and to keep the price down.

Clearly, if two computers are going to communicate over the telephone, the bits they use will have to be rearranged before they leave the machine. That is the job of the communications card. Or more properly, it is the job of a microchip on the card called a UART (Universal Asynchronous Receiver-Transmitter, pronounced: "you-art"). *UART* is a generic term applied to many specific brands and models of microchips to indicate that they perform certain standardized functions. You might think of a UART as an eight-armed alien capable of simultaneously catching eight baseballs or bits and then turning around and throwing them at a target one at a time. The UART thus converts a computer's internal parallel communications into the one-bit-at-a-time *serial* communications that is acceptable to the telephone line. Of course the chip works in reverse as well, catching incoming serial bits and throwing them into your computer in a parallel formation.

The RS-232 Port

The target the UART throws its serial bits at is the number two pin of the 25-pin RS-232 port provided on all communications cards. It also catches incoming serial bits thrown at it by the number three pin, converts them to parallel, and sends them on their way into the computer. If you have a DTE (Data Terminal Equipment) RS-232 port on your computer, this arrangement is something you can count on, regardless of the brand of machine you own. The reason you can count on it is that RS-232 (or RS-232-C, to give it its full name) is in fact the official designation of a widely accepted standard. The standard dictates the arrangement of the pins or sockets and what kind of information and control signals will be carried on each one. (Usually only about eight of the pins are actually used for "asynchronous communications.")

This standard is what makes it possible for you to connect virtually any kind of modem to your computer. All you need is a cable with properly sexed DB-25 connectors on either end. DB-25 is another name for the physical arrangement of an RS-232 plug or socket. Unlike RS-232, it does not imply anything about what signals will appear on which pins.

A Brief Word About Cables

When it comes to communications cables, appearances can be deceiving. They all consist of either a length of flat ribbon cable or a round multiwire cable sporting a male or female DB-25 connector on either end. However, while there may be 25 pins on the DB-25, this does not mean that there are 25 wires in the cable or that all of the pins on the two plugs are connected to each other. Thus, although you can probably use any standard "communications" cable with your equipment, you should be aware that some exceptions do exist.

The exceptions center around the pins on the RS-232 interface. The RS-232 standard dictates what signals will appear on which pins, but it does not require all modem manufacturers and software houses to use all of the possible signals. If your equipment is designed to use ten different signals, but your cable contains only nine wires, you could have a problem. It's a small problem, since a computer store can easily make up the right cable for you, but it can be a nuisance. When you buy your modem, it is worth taking the time to ask if it requires a special cable, and if so, whether the correct cable is included with the unit.

How to Choose a Communications Card

All communications cards or "serial cards" perform the same functions. But while the UART chip and RS-232 interface they contain may obey widely accepted standards, all of the other chips and circuitry have to be customized for your machine. If your computer does not include an RS-232 serial port as standard equipment, the simplest and sometimes the only solution is to buy whatever card your computer manufacturer offers.

For many computer owners, however, there are a number of additional considerations. The first is whether or not you need a separate card at all. If you own an Apple, for example, you can choose to buy a Super Serial Card for use with either a serial printer or an exterior modem. Or you can choose a Hayes Micromodem™ or similar plug-in card that contains both a UART and a modem, as well as a modular jack designed for direct connection with your telephone. IBM owners have the same kind of choice. As mentioned earlier, Commodore owners have no need for a card at all since they can plug a VIC-Modem directly into the user port on their machines. (We'll look at modems-on-a-board and at an RS-232 interface for Commodore equipment in the next section.)

The second point is of concern to anyone with a machine that offers expansion slots designed to accept special-function plug-in circuit boards. These are usually 16-bit machines like the IBM/PC. With this kind of equipment, once you've filled your expansion slots with printed circuit boards, you face nothing but unappealing alternatives if you want to add something else. You can either purchase an additional "box" with more slots or you can put up with the nuisance of pulling one board out and putting another board in each time you want to take advantage of its features.

Third-party manufacturers have helped to solve this problem by producing "multi-function boards" or "combo cards." A combo card is a printed circuit board that incorporates two or more functions while occupying a single slot. Such a card may offer a minimum of 64K more memory with rows of sockets for even more memory chips. Or it may offer additional memory, plus an on-board, battery-driven clock/calendar and a variety of other functions.

Clearly it pays to plan ahead if you have an IBM-like machine. It is important to be aware, however, that all combo cards offer a UART and an RS-232 port. These have become such standard features that you probably shouldn't even consider such a card if it does not include them.

FreeTip: From the beginning, IBM has offered an "asynchronous communications adapter," a.k.a. a simple communications card, for its machines. The company sold a lot of them, since for a long time they were the only type of comm card available. Virtually no one buys them today, however, because the multi-function boards made by third-party manufacturers offer a better value. Consequently, there are thousands of PC owners who have long since

FreeTip continued

upgraded to a combo card who would love to recoup part of the $150 they paid for IBM's "async adapter." If you want to hold expenses down, you should be able to pick up one of these used cards for about $50. You really shouldn't pay any more than that, and you may be able to get one for less.

Use the information provided in Chapter 3 of this book to contact a nearby users group to locate someone with a card to sell. Ideally, you should be able to see the card in operation before you buy. If that is not possible, make sure that it is clearly understood that you have the option of returning the card if it does not work properly. Don't forget to ask for the booklet with the installation instructions that IBM supplied with the card.

Modems and Cables

By converting parallel bit patterns into a serial arrangement, a communications card solves one of the problems of connecting a computer to the telephone. But telephone lines have another limitation that must be overcome. For a variety of technical reasons, they are not capable of reliably transmitting voltage differences of the sort that comprise a computer's bits. The telephone system is designed to carry *sound*, and if computers are to use the system for communications, that is what their bits must be converted to.

This is why you need a modem. A modem *mo*dulates and *dem*odulates a computer's digital signals. It converts the bits coming out of your RS-232 interface into sound (modulation) and sends the sound out over the phone lines. As with the UART, it also works in reverse (demodulation), taking the sound coming in from your correspondent's modem, converting it into digital pulses, and sending these to the RS-232 port.

If you think about it for a moment, it will be clear that four different tones or other electrical designations are required to bring this off. You need one pair of frequencies to symbolize the 1s and 0s of your machine and a second pair to symbolize the 1s and 0s coming from the database or bulletin board computer. Fortunately, there are widely accepted standards that specify what these frequencies are. One pair is used when the modem is in the "originate" mode and the other pair is used in the "answer" mode.

Although there are "originate only" modems, the vast majority are capable of operating in both originate and answer modes. Broadly speaking, it makes no difference which mode your modem is set for, as long as the modem it is talking to is set to the opposite mode. In the electronic universe, all commercial databases and private bulletin board systems are set to "answer," and all expect you to be set to "originate" when you call. When you and a friend are communicating, however, you will have to agree beforehand which one of you will be "answer" and which one will be "originate."

How to Choose a Modem

As when buying any piece of hardware or software, the first thing to ask yourself when considering a modem is, What am I going to use it for? Clearly, if you are reading this book, you are going to use it to download free software from information utilities and bulletin boards. But at other times you may also find yourself accessing your company's mainframe to obtain information and to transmit messages to co-workers. Or you may decide to use one of the public domain bulletin board programs to set up your own BBS. In each case, some modem features will be more important to you than others.

By the same token, you should be aware that few of the features described below are absolutely essential. The cheapest modem will perform its primary job of converting computer bits into sound just as effectively as the most expensive model. With the exception of an automatic answering capability, the difference is one of convenience and price. In the following section we will concentrate on those features that will be most important to you when downloading free software. Then we will briefly cite the additional features that may be important to you for other applications.

FreeTip: Here's what might be called the "quick and clean" solution to buying a modem. Skip over the pages that follow and don't worry about what the terms mean. Simply make sure that the modem you buy has these characteristics:

- A direct connect, free-standing unit (as opposed to a modem on a card or plug-in board)
- Full duplex, 300/1200-baud capabilities (meets the Bell 212A standard)
- Auto-dial with both tones and pulse (lets you enter phone numbers from your keyboard or under software control, selecting Touch Tone™ or rotary pulse)
- Complete D. C. Hayes Smartmodem® compatibility

These criteria are admittedly a matter of personal opinion, but there are reasons for each of them, the chief of which is a convic-

FreeTip continued

tion that hardware and software should make online communications as easy and convenient as possible. The main drawback is price. It is unlikely that you will find all of these features in a $70 modem. About the least you can expect to spend is $300 for a discounted Anchor Automation Mark 12. The most is about $500 for a discounted Hayes Smartmodem 1200. Modems can usually be safely purchased through the mail, so check your computer magazines for mail order house prices and advertisements.

FreeTip: This is a special note to Commodore owners. As you know, the user port on the front left section of your C-64 or VIC-20 provides something called an IEEE-448 interface. Like RS-232, the IEEE-448 interface is an accepted standard that dictates the specific signals that will be carried on certain portions of the connector. The IEEE-448 has traditionally been used to permit computer control of scientific instruments and other devices, but it can be used for online communications as well.

As a Commodore owner, you have two choices. You can buy a modem designed to plug directly into your IEEE-448 port, or you can buy an adaptor that will convert IEEE-448 signals into an RS-232 arrangement, in addition to a modem and a cable. If you stick with the IEEE-448, your selection of modems will for all practical purposes be limited to those made by Commodore. These include the VIC-MODEM, the VIC 1650 Automatic Modem, and the VIC/64 auto-answer/auto-dial modem. At a discount, these are priced at about $65, $110, and $150 respectively.

The downside is that while all of these units will put you online, they do not offer all of the features available on the more widely used RS-232 modems. For this reason, you may want to consider buying an IEEE-448–to–RS-232 converter (Commodore product number: VIC-1011A RS-232 C Terminal Type). Commodore sells these at a list price of about $50, but you may be able to find one at the discounted price of about $40. Unfortunately, the item may have to be special-ordered, as many dealers do not stock them.

A better alternative may be to buy a product like the Omnitronix VIC-20/CG4 interface. This unit includes both an RS-232 adaptor and a cable and sells for $24.95, postpaid (Add $1.75 for shipping to Canada or Mexico.) It comes with a type-it-yourself BASIC program and will allow you to use any RS-232 modem with your Commodore equipment. Contact:

> Bytesize Micro Technology
> P.O. Box 12309 Dept. HJ12
> Seattle, WA 98111
> (206) 236-2983
> Visa and MasterCard accepted.

Physique—The First Consideration

The first thing you've got to decide is whether you want an "acoustic coupler" type of modem, a modem on a plug-in circuit board, or a free-standing modem in a box. An acoustic coupler uses a pair of rubber cups designed to accept a telephone handset. The handset is placed into the cups and the modem sends and receives its tones through the mouth- and earpieces. Other types of modems are called "direct-connect" or "hard-wired" because they are designed to be plugged directly into a modular telephone jack. This is usually a jack on the wall, though some modems plug into the handset jack on the telephone itself and require you to plug the handset into *them.*

Acoustic modems used to be significantly cheaper than the direct connect variety, but this is no longer true. Today about the only advantage to an acoustic modem is that you can use it with any telephone, whether or not a modular jack is available. If you're in a hotel room where you cannot unplug one of the phones and plug in your modem, perhaps an acoustic coupler still makes sense. But even nonmodular office phones can be converted to modular plugs by phone company service personnel. And if your home phones do not use modular connections, you have only to buy an adapter plug to make the conversion. Radio Shack and other stores sell these adapters for about $5.

There are at least two reasons *not* to buy an acoustic coupler. The first is the possibility of outside noise. If the handset isn't securely mounted in the modem's cups or if for one reason or another the modem picks up some outside sound, that noise will interfere with your communications. The second is the fact that acoustic couplers can't incorporate an automatic dialing feature. This is something you'll appreciate from the very start, and we'll have more to say about it in a moment.

The second major type of modem is one that comes to you with all the necessary chips on a plug-in circuit board. These are available primarily for machines like the Apple and the IBM, but you may find that they are available for other computers as well. You plug them into an expansion slot, put the computer's cover back on, and simply plug the phone into a modular connector on the back of the card.

Board-mounted modems have a number of advantages, particularly for users of transportable computers. They eliminate the need for a comm card and cable. They save space on your desktop. They use the computer's power supply and so do not require a separate electrical outlet. And they reduce the amount of equipment you have to carry around.

However, there are a number of disadvantages that may not occur to you if you are new to computer communications. In addition to taking up one of your expansion slots, they can also add more internal heat to your system than most other expansion boards. And unlike a free-standing modem, they cannot be unplugged and used with another computer. By eliminating the need for a comm card, they may save you money. But since they do not include an RS-232 interface, they also eliminate the possibility of cabling two computers together to dump programs and data back and forth. Nor do they include LED (light emitting diode) indicator lights to let you know what's going on.

Finally, there is no quick and easy way to clear all previous communications settings and return the modem to its default state. With a stand-alone modem this can be done by simply turning the unit off and on. But with a board-mounted modem you must either enter several commands from the keyboard or turn the computer itself off and on.

Most modems on the market today are stand-alone modems in a separate plastic or metal box. They require a comm card with an RS-232 port and a cable. And most of them also require a separate electrical outlet as well. They do take up space on your desk, and they do add yet another strand to the rat's nest of wires that probably surrounds your computer. But as long as you don't have to carry them around, they are really the most convenient to use.

Speed: 300 or 1200 Baud?

The second major consideration is one of speed. The speed with which characters are transmitted and received by modems and computers is measured in units called "bauds," named after J. M. E. Baudot, the inventor of the Baudot telegraph code. In the binary world, baud rate is equal to the number of bits per second (bps). A chip on your communications card that is designed to work with the UART is responsible for generating the baud rate. Available speeds range from a low of 110 baud, the standard mechanical teletype rate, up to 9600 baud. In some cases the top speed may be as high as 19,200 baud or 19.2 kilobaud. Mainframe and minicomputers can send and receive data even faster.

Unfortunately, even though a personal computer can operate at 9600 baud or higher, the quality of the connection provided by standard "dial-up" telephone lines places a limit on the top speed you can use. As long as your software will permit it, you can send information back and forth between two directly coupled computers at 9600 baud. But for all practical purposes, you can go no faster than 1200 baud when communicating on the phone. By convention, the slowest speed most databases and bulletin boards use is 300 baud.

Thus there are 300-baud modems and modems capable of communicating at either 300 or 1200 baud. The reason for the distinction is that different techniques are used to transmit bits at these two speeds. Because a 1200-baud modem must contain all of the circuitry found in a 300-baud unit, plus the circuitry needed for 1200-baud communications, it will always cost more. And the question you must answer is whether it is worth it.

FreeTip: In the past, the price differential between 300- and 300/1200-baud units has usually been at least $200. The additional circuitry required for 1200-baud communications doesn't cost manufacturers anywhere near that amount, so there is considerable room for price-cutting as the modem market becomes more competitive. Although you will miss out on much of the fun of owning a home computer if you wait for prices to fall before going online, it definitely makes sense to wait until you're really ready for a modem before making your purchase. You have nothing to lose and there is at least the possibility that you'll save yourself some money.

This is probably one of the most difficult choices a prospective modem owner must make. After all, how can you tell which speed you want when you don't have any idea what either of them is like? As a suggestion, go to a computer store and ask for a demonstration of both speeds, or contact a member of a local users group to see if you can play with somebody's system.

For technical reasons, 300 baud translates into a speed of 30 characters per second. At this speed one can comfortably read online messages and other text. At 1200 baud (120 characters per second), letters and numbers zip by too fast for anything other than a quick perusal.

If you were going to be doing nothing but reading online messages and features, 300 baud might be satisfactory. But if you are going to be collecting free software, most of your time will be spent downloading programs. Consequently, unless you absolutely cannot afford it, a modem with 1200-baud capabilities is the clear choice.

How a 1200-Baud Modem Can Save You Money

If you're on the fence about whether to spend an extra $200 for a

1200-baud modem, here are a few facts (rationalizations) to help you make up your mind. It isn't likely, but if you later find that you regret your purchase, you can always say that "de Debil made you do it."

A 1200-baud modem may cost more initially, but it can end up saving you money over the long term. The reason is that at 1200 baud you can download programs four times faster than at 300 baud. That means that the length of time you spend on a long distance call to a BBS will be 75% *less* than at 300 baud.

Because the rate structures of the various long distance services vary, that doesn't directly translate into a 75% saving. But it can still represent a considerable amount of money. One can see the savings more clearly when using a service like CompuServe. As you will discover in a later chapter, many of that system's free software riches are stored in files maintained by machine-specific special interest groups (SIGs). We'll use the IBM/PC SIG as an example.

There are two public domain programs in the IBM/PC SIG that every IBM owner is sure to want. They are SQUEEZ.HEX and UNSQUZ.HEX. Like their CP/M counterparts, they are used to compress and uncompress files so that they take up less room on a floppy disk. Together with the documentation file (SQUEEZ.DOC), they occupy 73,815 characters or bytes.

At 300 baud, downloading all three files would require about 41 minutes and cost $4.10 in connect time at CompuServe's lowest 300-baud rate. At 1200 baud, downloading the same files would require 10.25 minutes and cost $2.14 at CompuServe's lowest 1200-baud rate. A savings of $2 may not sound like much, but it doesn't take long to mount up. And of course your time is valuable as well. Why spend nearly three quarters of an hour to do something you can accomplish in ten minutes with a 1200-baud modem? For most people, 1200-baud capability is worth the extra cost.

Full- and Half-Duplex

All commercial databases and almost all BBSs require full-duplex communications. And as long as you make sure to buy a modem that has this capability, that is really all you need to know. An easy way to do this is to make sure that a 300-baud modem meets the Bell 103 standard and that a 300/1200-baud modem meets the Bell 212A standard.

The only time you will need half-duplex is when communicating with some corporate mainframe systems. If you plan to do this, here is a brief explanation of the two terms.

Full-duplex and *half-duplex* refer to whether or not a modem is capable of sending and receiving at the same time. Half-duplex communication is very similar to the way two people communicate on a walkie-talkie or CB radio. One person says, "This is Atom Smasher . . . *Over.*"

The other person says, "You got the Big Biker here, Atom. What's shakin'? . . . *Over.*" And so on. Only one person can talk at any one time. The data communications equivalent of "Over" is a "line turnaround character," and just like its radio counterpart, it causes delays.

Full-duplex communication, on the other hand, is like talking on the telephone. Both parties can send and receive simultaneously. In full-duplex communications, for example, the remote computer is constantly asking your machine "Are you ready?" and your machine is constantly responding, "Yes I'm ready . . ." Without full-duplex, there would be a line turnaround delay between each question and answer.

If you are going to be talking to a corporate mainframe or minicomputer, be sure to check with your firm's data processing supervisor or system manager to find out what form your micro-based communications must take to communicate successfully with the larger system.

FreeTip: The Bell 103 and Bell 212A standards mentioned above dictate the frequencies and techniques a modem will use when translating computer bits into a form suitable for telephone transmission. They also dictate whether the modem offers both "originate" and "answer" modes and whether it can run at both half- and full-duplex. You do not need to know any more details than this. But there are other standards and it might be helpful to know which ones to *avoid*. These include:

- Bell 113 (a 300-baud, originate-*only* modem)
- Racal-Vadic (nothing wrong with the standard itself, but not all remote systems support it; acceptable only if offered in addition to the desired Bell standards)
- Bell 202 (a 1200-baud modem limited to half-duplex communications)

"Smart" or "Dumb"

The less expensive modems provide all of the features we have cited up to this point. But they have no capabilities beyond serving as a simple pass-through circuit, dutifully performing their translation chores once your software has enabled the communicatons port. This means that you must do almost everything else by hand. Specifically, you must:

- Turn the modem on and make sure it is in "originate" mode.
- Make sure that the modem is set to match your baud rate and other communications parameters.

- Dial the target telephone number by hand and wait for the remote modem to issue a high-pitched tone.
- Wait until you hear your modem start to issue a matching tone.
- Hang up the phone and return to your keyboard to begin communicating.

If the target telephone number is busy, as is often the case when phoning computer bulletin board systems, you must switch off the modem to clear it and then repeat the dialing process. This is not much fun, to say the least, and will quickly become a major chore.

Fortunately, modem manufacturers have developed "intelligent" modems that can relieve you of this burden. An intelligent or "smart" modem is often a small, limited-function computer. Hayes Smartmodem® units, for example, contain a Z80 microprocessor with a ROM-based 4K control program and 16 user-setable memory registers. Other intelligent modems have similar circuitry.

Once a modem has been equipped with intelligence, a whole range of convenience features can be incorporated. Not all intelligent modems offer the same collection of features—some are "smarter" than others—but all of them will include an "auto-dial" capability. This is probably the single most important "extra" feature a modem can provide. Indeed, for anyone who plans to regularly access computer bulletin boards, it is a virtual necessity.

Why You Need an Auto-Dial Modem

An auto-dial feature is important for at least two reasons. First, it enables you to enter the target phone number from your keyboard. If you were using a Hayes modem, for example, you might type in the following string of characters: *ATDT 1 800 555 1212*. You never have to turn away from your computer.

The second reason is that an auto-dial modem can be operated under software control. The modem doesn't care whether the phone number you send it was freshly typed at your keyboard or recorded on floppy disk and transmitted from there. That means that with the proper communications software, you can record many phone numbers and tell the modem to dial whichever one you choose at the touch of just a few keys. Programs like these usually include a "dialing directory" menu that lists all of your numbers. To get the program to send the modem the target phone number, you have only to type its single- or double-digit menu number and hit <ENTER>.

Other comm programs allow you to load strings of characters into the special "function keys" found on many computers. Often all of the keystrokes you need can be recorded in on disk and loaded by telling the program to use that file. In some cases you may be able to set things up so that the program automatically loads the desired phone number file as soon as you boot up.

Single-key, automatic dialing is convenient for any type of online communications. But it is especially important when you are "working the boards." You will always be able to connect with The Source or CompuServe, but since most bulletin board systems can only handle one caller at a time, you may find that they are busy when you dial them. If you use an auto-dial modem and a comm program with a dialing directory, you can easily run through a long list of BBS numbers searching for a system that isn't busy.

Other Dialing Features

Auto-dial modems often include other dialing-related features that may or may not be important to you. Here is a summary of the major features in this category and what they mean:

- Manual dial. Commercial databases and BBSs are equipped with auto-answer modems capable of immediately talking to your unit. When you want to communicate with a friend, however, you will probably dial the phone by hand and have a brief chat before you begin communicating. In this case, you need to be able to control your modem manually, flipping a switch or typing a command that will cause it to go online when you tell it to.

- Auto-redial last number. An intelligent modem may be able to remember the last number you asked it to dial. Ordering it to try that same number again may be a simple matter of entering */A* or a similar keyboard command. Although some modems also offer a "repeat dialing" feature that allows you to specify the number of times a number will be tried, this may not be necessary. As long as the modem can remember and redial the last number, your communications software can handle the repetition. Hayes Smartmodems do not include an auto-redial feature, but a program like PC-TALK III for the IBM/PC can be told to keep a Hayes modem dialing and redialing a number until there is an answer.

- Tones, pulses, and pauses. Ideally a modem should be able to use either Touch-Tones™ or rotary pulses when dialing phone numbers. Tone dialing is much faster, but if your local phone company has yet to switch to Touch-Tone, your modem must be able to imitate a rotary dial telephone.

It is also important to be able to make your modem pause between strings of numbers. Although this is scheduled to change over the next several years, if you use MCI™ or Sprint™ or some other non–AT&T long distance service, you must dial a local number, wait for a connection tone, key in your target phone number, wait, and then key in your service account number. Altogether, as many as 24 or more numbers may be involved. If you are dialing out of a PBX system at the office, you face a similar situation.

In the absence of instructions to the contrary, an auto-dial modem will squeeze off all 24 numbers in a single, rapid-fire burst that will do nothing but confuse the telephone system. This is why it is important to be able to insert pause commands between your phone numbers. If you enter a comma between two phone numbers when using Hayes equipment, for example, the modem will pause two seconds before dialing the second number. More commas can be used for longer delays, and it is even possible to set the delay each one causes from 0 to 255 seconds.

Additional Modem Features

Auto-Answer

Most modems offering an auto-dial feature are also capable of automatically answering the telephone and issuing the proper tone to connect a remote computer to your system. This feature is essential for anyone who plans to set up a computer bulletin board, but it has nothing to do with accessing databases or BBSs. Consequently you may be tempted to think of it as an unwanted extra. For many people it may be just that. After all, you'll need special software to enable your computer to respond once the modem has answered the phone, and unless you really want to set up your own BBS it isn't likely that you'll be inclined to write such a program or pay $200 or more for a commercial product.

Free software, however, can make the difference. For example, there are public domain bulletin board or "host" programs for both CP/M and IBM-PC users. The programs are quite capable and are available for the cost of the floppy disk they are recorded on. Thus, while you might not buy a commercial product, a host program for as little as $6 may prove irresistible.

FreeTip: There are quite a few CP/M bulletin board programs in the SIG/M, CP/MUG, and PICONET libraries, so be sure to check the appropriate chapters for more information on the various ways to obtain them. You might also consider buying the Communications Programs #3 disk offered by Elliam Associates. This contains the latest version of the communications program MODEM7, a program for maintaining phone numbers, and several bulletin board programs and help files. The files total 375K and thus will require a different number of disk sides depending on your disk format. The cost will range from $22 to $38, depending on the number of sides required. Contact:

Elliam Associates
24000 Bessemer Street
Woodland Hills, CA 91367
(213) 348-4278

FreeTip: For IBM users, the program to get is RBBS-PC. Like CP/M programs, this too is available from many sources. If there is no IBM users group in your area, though, you might write to the Capital PC Software Users Group in Washington, D.C., the group that created the program. Ask for Disk 18. In addition to RBBS-PC.BAS and RBBS-PC.EXE, this disk contains a 20-page instruction manual that shows you how to use the program, print spooling software, and several utilities. It also contains TALK450, a file designed to be merged with the BASIC version of the PC-TALK Freeware communicatons program. Once merged, you will be able to use PC-TALK and a Hayes Smartmodem 300 to communicate at 450 baud, a speed some BBSs are now offering.

Send your request for Disk 18, along with $8, to the address below. Note that this is a double-sided disk, so if you have single-sided drives, be sure to say so and include an extra $8 for the second disk. Contact:

Capital PC Software Exchange
P.O. Box 6128
Silver Spring, MD 20906

With one of these programs and an auto-answer modem, a business associate or friend could call your system when you were away and upload or download messages, programs, price lists, or any other kind of file. You could do the same thing yourself if you had a second computer. You might load the host program into your desktop computer at work, switch on the auto-answer modem, and leave for the day. Later that evening, you could use your home computer to call up your office system and access its files. With some host software you may even be able to operate your desktop computer as if you were sitting in front of its console instead of sitting in a hot tub or in front of a roaring fire at home. None of this would be possible, of course, without an auto-answer modem.

LED Indicator Lights

You will also find it convenient to have a modem that can sense the baud rate and duplex settings you are using and match them automatically. With some modems, for example, you have to press a button labeled "HS" (high speed") on the front panel whenever you want to use 1200 baud. Other modems may require additional button pushing. Hayes modems and similar equipment, in contrast, are smart enough to sense your settings from the first character you send them.

LED indicator lights on the modem itself are another important feature. If you are new to communications, they may look like something only a factory authorized technician should have to understand. But in reality they can be a big help to even a novice user. The most useful LEDs and their abbreviations include:

OH	(Off Hook)	The modem has control of the phone line.
CD	(Carrier Detect)	Your modem is receiving a valid carrier signal from a remote system.
SD	(Send Data)	This light flashes as each character is transmitted.
RD	(Receive Data)	And this one flashes each time a character is received.

These lights are important because they tell you what's going on when you are online (or trying to get there) and because they help you identify the probable cause of communications problems. For example, if you are communicating with a BBS and that system suddenly fails to respond to your typed commands, the first thing you should do is look at the CD light on your modem. If it is not on, the carrier has been lost, probably because of something that happened at the remote system. If the CD light is on, however, the characters you are typing may not be "getting out the door." You can test for this problem by striking a key and watching to see if the SD light responds with a blink. If it doesn't, you might check your cable to make certain that it is properly connected to both the modem and the computer. If that doesn't work, you know that the cause lies elsewhere, possibly in the program you are running.

FreeTip: A modem's LED indicators can be especially important if you plan to collect public domain communications programs. Because public domain programs are not formally supported by anyone—there is no manufacturer or dealer to call if you run into trouble—you may have to solve any problems you encounter by yourself. In such a situation it is invaluable to be able to identify the cause quickly. The program itself might not be at fault, but without LEDs on your modem there is no easy way to tell.

D. C. Hayes Command Compatiblity

Though at times it may not be obvious, one of the trends that has been developing in the personal computer industry in recent years is a move toward "de facto standards." No official body declared CP/M-80 and MS-DOS the "standard" operating systems for 8-bit and 16-bit computers, but few would deny that that is what they have become. Similarly, no one declared that all hardware and software had to be compatible with the IBM/PC. But they might as well have, because IBM compatibility has become the touchstone of the micro market.

In the electronic universe, the acknowledged "standard" for modems is the best-selling D. C. Hayes Smartmodem. There are many other fine modem manufacturers, some of whom make equipment that will do even more than the Hayes. But for one reason or another, the Smartmodem is the unit most commercial communications software and a large number of public domain programs are written to support. Commercial programs may support other modems as well, and non-Hayes modems may have their own way of doing things, but the best products in both categories will also offer full Smartmodem compatibility.

"Hayes compatibility" in a communications program means that the software is capable of issuing the commands the Smartmodem needs to see to perform a particular function. In a modem it means that the unit will respond just as the Hayes would if your software sends it a Hayes-type command. The Hayes command to get the modem's attention is *AT*, for example. To get it to dial using tones you enter *ATDT*, followed by the phone number. To order it to redial the last number, you enter */A*. And so on.

This really amounts to a unique modem command language. You will not be unable to communicate if your software or modem cannot speak this lingua franca, but things will be much easier for you if both components have this capability. Hayes compatibility in a modem is also the best way to insure the widest selection of both commercial and public domain communications programs.

FreeTip: If the modem you are interested in is Hayes compatible, the manufacturer will be sure to say so in ads and product literature. If Hayes compatibility is not mentioned, proceed with caution. Better yet, ask members of your local users group if anyone has had any experience with the unit. Indeed, you might ask fellow members for their recommendations on which modem to buy. They are likely to be able to tell you more of what you need to know than most computer store personnel.

Where to Buy Your Modem

If you have yet to buy a computer, you may be able to get a good price on your system, comm card, and modem in a package deal from your local retailer. The advantage of doing things this way is that you are entitled to call upon your retailer for support (help) if you have questions or run into problems. The disadvantage is that even the dealer's best price is likely to be higher than that of a mail order firm, due to the latter's lower overhead.

Fortunately, modems—unlike computers—require little in the way of dealer support. Basically, they either work or they don't. And if they don't, you—like most computer stores—have to send them back to the manufacturer for replacement or repair. Consequently you can feel reasonably secure about buying a brand name modem at a discount through the mail. If you do so, you will not be able to call on your computer store for help, but then you won't be paying for that privilege either.

The instructions that come with modems vary from a few typewritten sheets of paper to the 60-page spiral-bound manuals provided with every Hayes modem. The Hayes manuals, written by Barbara Sajor, are superb and should be required reading for anyone interested in learning how computer documentation *should* be written. If the documentation of the modem you buy proves to be less than adequate, *The Complete Handbook of Personal Computer Communications* may be able to help.

FreeTip: You will find ads for mail order firms in all the major computer magazines. But there is one publication you might overlook due to its tabloid newspaper-style format. This is *The Computer Shopper*. Edited by Stan Veit, a highly respected former columnist for *Computers and Electronics* (formerly *Popular Electronics*) magazine, *The Computer Shopper* is stuffed with ads from both commercial firms and private individuals seeking or selling hardware or software. You will also find extensive lists of users groups, tips and advice excerpted from users group newsletters, lists of BBS numbers, and short articles.

Because the magazine has a "fast close"—ads received by the 20th will be published in the next month's issue—prices tend to be more up-to-date than in "slick" computer magazines, most of which have at least a three-month lead time. The publication has recently begun to appear in the magazine racks of major bookstores, so you may be able to find a copy there. Otherwise, contact:

The Computer Shopper
P.O. Box F
Titusville, FL 32780
(305) 269-3211

Six-month subscription: $6; annual subscription (12 issues): $10.

Before You Buy a Communications Program . . .

Perhaps the first thing to remember about buying a communications program is that you may not have to *buy* one at all. Basic communications programs are not terribly difficult to write, and over the years amateur programmers have contributed huge numbers of them to the public domain. Some of them go far beyond the basics and are really on a par with commercial software costing $150 or more. Ask around at your local computer club to find out what others are using, then check with the group's software librarian to see about getting a copy.

You should be aware, though, that communications programs, like modems, can offer a wide range of features. Public domain programs tend to focus on those features required for sending and receiving software. This makes sense; that is why most of them were written in the first place. If this is your only goal, then you probably won't have to look any further than the public domain to find the program you need. However, if you also plan to send and receive large quantities of electronic mail, communicate with corporate mainframes, or want to be able to use many different "file transfer protocols," you may need a commercial product.

FreeTip: Appendix A discusses the relative merits of using a public domain comm program or purchasing a commercial package. It also provides details on where to obtain a version of MODEM7

FreeTip continued

that will run on your machine. And it highlights several particularly good commercial programs for the Commodore 64, machines made by Apple, IBM, Radio Shack, and others, including most CP/M-based systems. These are programs you may not have heard of because they have not been heavily advertised.

For more information on commercial communications programs, what they offer, and which features are likely to have the greatest value, you might consult *How to Buy Software*. In the following section we will be concentrating on those features that are most important for downloading free software over the phone. Before discussing communications programs *per se*, however, there are three pieces of information you must have. You need to know about ASCII text files, binary program files, and the XMODEM file transfer protocol.

ASCII "Text" Files

The American Standard Code for Information Interchange (ASCII) is very easy to understand. As mentioned earlier, everything a computer does ultimately ends up as a series of numbers. Thus the only way for a computer to transmit the letters of the alphabet, punctuation marks, and other characters is to assign a number to each symbol and send the number. As long as the receiving computer knows the code, it can translate those numbers back into readable text. An infinite number of codes is possible, of course. But clearly it is to everyone's advantage to use the same one. And that's why the ASCII standard was created. You may hear of other codes, but all the components of the electronic universe have the ability to "talk ASCII."

The basic ASCII code set that everyone uses contains 128 numbers, from 0 through 127. (These are decimal numbers that human beings can easily use and understand. Don't forget that there is a binary or 1s and 0s eqivalent for each of them and that the binary form is what the computer actually uses.) There is an ASCII number for every capital letter, every lower case letter, every Arabic number, and almost every punctuation mark. But there are also numbers for things called "control codes." These are the codes that are assigned to your <ENTER> (or "carriage return"), <BACKSPACE>, and <TAB> keys, for example. They also include many other codes that are designed to control the devices used in online communications. There's even one that will cause a computer's internal speaker to beep when that code is received.

There are 26 major control codes—one for each letter of the alphabet—and they are normally entered by holding down a special key or combination of keys and striking the target letter. For example, when you are communicating with most databases, if you hold down the <CONTROL> key and hit <S>, the remote computer will temporarily stop sending you information. To tell the remote system to start up again, you have only to send it a Control-Q.

The 128 numbers in the standard ASCII code set cover just about all the bases as far as human and computer communications are concerned. Using these numbers, you can send and receive almost any readable text, whether it's "Hi Mom!" or "400 OPEN 'DATA' FOR OUTPUT AS #1." The point to remember is that any file that exists in readable form is considered an "ASCII" or a "text" file. It does not matter whether the text is actually a BASIC, Pilot, C, or assembly language program. It is still a text file.

Most of the free software on The Source or CompuServe exists as text files. You might, for example, sign on to one of these systems and download a BASIC program. The program will appear on your screen just as would a stock quote, electronic letter, or any other kind of text. When you sign off, you can clean up the file with your word processing program, save it to disk, load BASIC, and load and run the free program.

If the program fails to run, you can list it out and read through it to see if perhaps a character or two was garbled in transmission. If that's the case, you can make the correction, re-save the program in ASCII format, and try it again. You can do these things because the BASIC program text file that you downloaded does not contain anything that cannot be displayed and read. All of the characters fall within the 128-number ASCII code set.

Binary or Program Files

As we've said, a computer cannot act on your instructions or those contained in a program until those instructions have been converted into "machine language." Machine language consists of nothing but the 1 and 0 bits we've spoken of before. While it is possible to write software using only 1s and 0s, record the results in a file, and run the program, it is extremely difficult to do. Consequently, various other computer languages have been created to make things easier. These languages work in different ways, but they all have one thing in common: Every one of them is designed to translate the human words and symbols in its special vocabulary into the 1s and 0s of machine code.

The translation process might be performed each time a program is run, or it might be performed just once. In both cases the program will be recorded as a file. But the contents and structure of those files will be very different. The best example of a program designed to be translated every time you run it is one written in BASIC. The program exists as an ASCII file on disk, and you must have a BASIC language package to translate the text into machine language each time you run it.

The best example of a progam that is translated only once is one that has either been "assembled" or been "compiled." Assemblers and compilers are special programs that go to work on the ASCII version of a program and translate it into machine language. When they are finished, you will have two files. One will be the original text file, and the other will be the machine language translation. Because the machine language version consists of nothing but 1s and 0s, it is called a *binary file*.

Binary files can be run all by themselves. The original program may have been written in Pascal, BASIC, FORTRAN, or C, but if it has been compiled and recorded as a binary or "program" file, you don't have to own any of those language packages. The same is true if the program has been assembled. You may not realize it, but you've probably already worked with many binary files, since that is the form used by your disk or tape operating system. Thus, when you enter a DOS command, what you are really doing is running a short machine language program that will give you a directory of your disk, copy a file, list the contents of a file on your printer or your screen, and so on.

Sending and Receiving Binary Files

As we've said, programs stored as text files can be sent and received as easily as an electronic letter. The only catch is that in order to use such a program you must have an additional piece of software to translate the text into machine code. Since most people have a BASIC interpreter package, it's easy for them to run BASIC programs that have been downloaded as text files. But what do you do if the free program you want is written in assembly language? Unless you happen to own an assembler package for your machine—and know how to use it—you may be out of luck.

This is one of the reasons why many public domain authors make their programs available in a preassembled or binary file form. If you obtain one of these files from a users group, you can run it just as you would a DOS program or a piece of commercial software. But if you want to download the program into your machine from a BBS, some special communications problems have to be overcome.

This gets a bit technical, but stick with it for a moment and it should become clear. There are three main difficulties with sending and receiving binary files. They include the possibility of misinterpretation by your communications software, the inclusion of nonprintable characters, and the need for stringent error-checking.

Let's look at misinterpretation first. Earlier we talked about the control codes that are part of the standard ASCII code set. We also said that the computer translates all ASCII codes into binary or machine language form before sending them. When you are dealing with text, for example, you need to have the remote computer send the unique string of 1s and 0s that symbolizes a carriage return (<ENTER>) in the ASCII code set, at the end of every line. If the remote computer didn't do this, your machine might not know when it should send the cursor zipping back to the far left of the screen to begin a new line.

The problem with sending and receiving a machine language program is that the program may use an identical string of 1s and 0s for some purpose related to the program itself. It doesn't mean the same thing when it is used in a program, but your communications software has no way of knowing the difference. As far as your comm program is concerned, when it sees that unique string, it thinks "carriage return" and responds accordingly. Similarly, when your program sees a unique binary string that in ASCII means "end of file," it is likely to think that the transmission has been completed and close up shop.

These are just two examples of the misinterpretations that can occur when the "text" file that your comm program thinks it is receiving is actually a binary file. There are many other control codes whose unique binary strings can occur any number of times anywhere within a machine language file.

Nonprintable characters are a related problem. The standard ASCII code set that everyone agrees upon contains 128 numbers. But in there is another group of 128 numbers, running from 128 to 255, that computers also use. These are called the "high codes," and they are not standardized at all. Every computer manufacturer is free to assign any special text or graphics character to any of these numbers. Or the manufacturer can leave them blank. Together the two groups make up an "extended" ASCII code set of 256 numbers.

As with control codes, the binary equivalent of any of these 256 numbers can easily appear in a machine language file. But even if there were a way to overcome the control code misinterpretation problem, one could still not receive binary files as if they were text. If your machine receives a high code number to which your computer manufacturer has not assigned a character, your computer will simply throw it away or perform some other mischief.

The solution to both problems is clear. The comm program must be put into a "binary transfer mode" in which it forgets about ASCII for the time being and simply captures everything coming in the door without displaying it or responding to it in any way. *If your communications program does not offer this feature, you will not be able to download binary program files.*

XMODEM—99 44/100% Pure

Personal computer owners everywhere owe a great debt to Chicagoan Ward Christensen for solving the problem of insuring the accuracy of binary file transmission. One of the most prolific of all public domain authors, Mr. Christensen has generously contributed many interesting and useful programs to the body of free CP/M software. But he will always be remembered for creating XMODEM, a file transfer protocol that has become the de facto standard in the microworld.

A transfer protocol is a set of rules dictating how the contents of a file will be sent and received. As such, it is not machine- or operating system–dependent and has been implemented in public domain and other software written for almost every kind of computer. The XMODEM protocol can be used to transfer any kind of file, but it *must* be used when dealing with binary files. The static and other electrical noise on a typical voice-grade phone line can wreak havoc with a machine language program, since if even a single bit is garbled in transmission the program may fail to run. (See Appendix A for more information on how XMODEM performs its magic.)

The XMODEM protocol has been shown to be 99.5 to 99.9% effective in accurately transferring machine language files. There *are* other protocols, however, and if you're not careful they can lead to confusion. The key thing to remember about all protocols is that none of them will work unless both computers are using the same one. For example, Microstuff's Crosstalk™, one of the best-selling communications programs for the IBM/PC, offers its own transfer protocol. But to use it, both your system and the remote system must be running Crosstalk. The Crosstalk protocol is *not* compatible with XMODEM. Fortunately, beginning with version 3.4 (released in January 1984), the Crosstalk program gives users a choice of Microstuff's protocol or XMODEM.

FreeTip: It can be a little confusing, but the term "XMODEM" is used to refer both to the protocol and to some of the programs that offer it. In the CP/M world, the original Christensen communications program that supported this protocol was called MODEM. That program has been improved and expanded many times by other authors, each of whom has given the program a number to indicate a more recent version. (Christensen himself has produced MODEM765; that is, MODEM, Version 7.65.) Although additional "mods" (modifications) have been made to the seventh version, the program has come to be known as MODEM7. Other versions, and versions designed to use certain direct connect modems, are also available.

Generally, any time you see the word MODEM as part of a public domain CP/M filename, you can assume that it is some version of the original program.

What to Look for in a Communications Program

Whether you use a public domain or commercial program, there are certain features your software *must* have if you want to to download free programs. Fortunately, virtually all programs have them, so your decision can usually be based on comparative ease of use. In this section we will discuss only the features essential to obtaining free software online. Please be aware, however, that communications programs can be among the most feature-filled of any software genre. The features we are about to look at barely scratch the surface.

Communications Settings

To communicate successfully, both computers must agree on how fast they will converse and how the 1s and 0s they send and receive will be formatted. They must also agree on whether they will use a particular error-checking procedure, and on whether they will echo characters back to each other. Thus, before you can go online, you must make sure that your software is set to match the communications parameters of the remote system. The most crucial settings are: baud rate, character length, parity, stop bits, and duplex.

All information utilities and a growing number of BBSs can communicate with you at either 300 or 1200 baud. You will, of course, need a 1200-baud modem if you plan to use that speed. Since most software packages support both settings, there's not much to worry about. However, if you plan to cable two computers together to dump programs and data files from one to another, you will appreciate a package that will permit rates of 9600 or even 19,200 baud. Not all comm programs offer this option, so be sure to check, if this is one of the things you want to do.

Character length (or "word length") refers to the number of bits used to transmit an ASCII code number in binary form. They are also called "data bits" to distinguish them from other bits making up the package that gets sent to the remote computer. Because of the way the binary numbering system works, the ASCII character codes from 0 through 127 can be sent using seven 1s and 0s. If you want to send and receive machine language programs, many of which contain "high codes" ranging from 128 through 255, a total of eight 1s and 0s are required. Most programs let you set character length to either seven or eight.

Parity refers to a form of error-checking in which each character is sent with an extra 1 or 0 tacked on the end of the binary string. This is not the same as the file transfer protocols discussed earlier. Stop bits are used to signal the end of a character and the start of the next character. They really aren't "bits" in the conventional sense, but you do not have to be concerned with either stop bits or parity—as long as your settings match those of the remote system. The major settings for parity include odd, even, and none, and for stop bits: 1, 1.5, and 2. All comm programs permit virtually all of these settings.

As you know from our discussion of modems, *full-duplex* refers to simultaneous two-way communications, while *half-duplex* means that only one computer can talk at any given time. With the exception of some corporate mainframe and minicomputers, everyone uses full-duplex. You may not be aware of it, but when you are communicating in full-duplex, the characters that appear on your screen do not come from your keyboard. Instead they are sent straight from the keyboard to the remote computer. The remote computer then echos them back to your system and *that* is how they get onto your screen. This process is called "echo-plex," for obvious reasons.

"Smart" or "Dumb" Terminal and Data Capture

Although full-featured communications packages are sometimes called "terminal programs," this is not a completely accurate description. Technically, a terminal is little more than a box with a keyboard and a CRT screen. These so-called "dumb" terminals have traditionally been used to obtain information from mainframe computers. They may be able to print out what they receive, but they cannot capture and record it on disk. A "smart" terminal, in contrast, can do all of these things and more.

The distinction would not be worth mentioning were it not for the fact that there are still many communications packages on the market designed to turn personal computers into dumb terminals. These programs are next to useless to anyone interested in obtaining free software online. Make certain that the program you plan to use will allow you to capture and record the information you receive online.

There are two main ways that computers can capture and record information. The simplest way is for the software to include a command that will let you open and close a "capture buffer." A buffer is nothing more than a certain amount of computer memory that the program sets aside as a temporary holding tank. When you are ready to receive a program, you open the buffer, the information flows both to your screen and into the buffer, you close the buffer at the end of the transmission, and then you record the buffer's contents on disk or tape. Some programs will automatically close and dump the buffer when it becomes full and will then reopen it to continue the download. With others you must do everything by hand.

The second method does not use a buffer as such. Instead the program automatically records incoming information on disk. Your software opens a disk file, records the information, and closes the file when the transmission has been completed. This is the technique used under XMODEM and other protocols. Both systems must be using the protocol for it to work.

Essential Non-Essentials

With the features described so far, plus XMODEM protocol support, you will be able to do everything you need to do to download free software from the services and bulletin board systems described in the next four chapters. However, some communications programs include a number of other features that are particularly well suited to the free software searcher. They aren't essential, and you may not find a program that offers every one of them. But each will make life online much easier. Here are the essential non-essentials to look for:

- Prerecorded command files. These allow you to record your communications parameters and other information in a file and set your software by simply loading the file. Without them you may have to go through a set-up process each time you boot the program.

- Dialing directory. As explained earlier, this is a recorded list of phone numbers, each of which can be dialed by pressing one or two keys. It's an ideal place to put the local phone numbers you dial to access The Source, CompuServe, or frequently called bulletin board systems. You must have an auto-dial modem to use this feature.

- Auto-redial. Since bulletin board phone numbers are frequently busy, it is nice to be able to tell your software to keep trying until the number answers. To free you to do other things, the software should sound an alarm summoning you back to your machine once a connection has been made.

- Automatic database sign-on. CompuServe and The Source require users to enter their account numbers and passwords before gaining access to the system. Some sophisticated software is capable of taking responsibility for signing you on to one of these services automatically. And some can do this, unattended, at a preselected time.

- String-loadable keys. If the program doesn't offer a dialing directory or auto sign-on, this feature can be a good substitute. The feature allows you to load a string of characters into one or more function keys. Other key combinations may also be supported. The string can be a phone number, a Source account number, a CompuServe password, or a frequently used information utility command. Usually you will be able to record your strings and key assignments in a command file. Sometimes called a "macro" feature, this is similar to Rosesoft's best-selling ProKey™ program for the IBM/PC. Indeed, if you own ProKey, you might be able to use it with your communications program. This is something that should be carefully checked, however, since ProKey will not work with all comm programs.

- X-ON/X-OFF Support. These are two control codes of the type mentioned in the discussion of ASCII. A Control-Q is an X-ON and a Control-S is an X-OFF. If both computers support the X-ON/X-OFF protocol, sending an X-OFF will cause the transmitting computer to stop transmitting until it receives an X-ON. Temporarily stopping the flow of information can be important when the receiving computer must take time out to write a buffer to disk or perform some other chore.

- Character-prompted upload. Because mainframe computer systems are used by many people at the same time ("time sharing"), most cannot give you their undivided attention. If you want to transmit a file or a program to them, you will find that they can only accept a limited number of characters at any given moment. If your computer continues to send characters in an uninterrupted stream, much of the information will be ignored by the receiving computer.

The X-ON/X-OFF protocol offers a partial solution to this problem. But a feature called "character-prompted uploading" works even better. Some mainframes send a single character—like a colon or an exclamation point—each time they are ready to receive a line of text. If your software has a character-prompted upload feature, you can tell the program to look for that character from the mainframe and send a single line each time it appears.

This feature makes it much easier to upload the programs or messages you have written and to do so with greater accuracy. It can be especially useful to CompuServe subscribers wishing to contribute programs to the SIG databases discussed in Chapter 8.

The Next Step

It is not difficult to obtain free software online, and you will be pleasantly surprised at the large numbers of programs that are instantly available once you equip your machine for communications. The next three chapters will give you a much clearer idea of what is available and how to get it. We suggest reading them before you take the plunge and invest in a comm card and modem.

...8...

CompuServe: *The Online Free Software Goldmine*

The CompuServe Information Service (CIS) is an online database owned by the H&R Block Company, though it should probably be renamed "The Goldmine," since to a free software hunter that's exactly what it is. Regardless of the brand of computer you own, regardless of its operating system or your personal interests, the free software you want and need is virtually certain to be on this system. And be there in quantity.

There are games similar to *Centipede*™ or *Dambusters*™; music programs, sprite generators, and software for the Koala Pad™. The entire Commodore educational series is available. There are special effects printer routines, VisiCalc™ templates, Lotus 1-2-3™ worksheets, dBASE II command files, and files for use with Rosesoft's ProKey™. There are also complete database and file manager programs; a variety of quite sophisticated communications programs; some of the best public domain CP/M software; and literally hundreds of helpful utilities. (See the "SIG Software Sampler" section at the end of this chapter for more specific details.) It's all yours for the asking, if you have a communicating personal computer and a subscription to CompuServe, and if you know how to find it. This chapter will show you where to look.

A Quick CompuServe Overview for Newcomers

If you're new to the electronic universe, there is some background information you need in order to fully understand what we're going to be talking about in this chapter. If you already know about CompuServe, you might want to skip ahead to the next section.

Perhaps the most important thing to emphasize is that CompuServe is much more than a repository of huge collections of free software. It is a full-fledged information utility offering everything from electronic mail to online shopping and banking services. There is a bulletin board where you can post an announcement or ask a question, software and hardware reviews from *InfoWorld* magazine, and late-breaking news from the Associated Press. There are stock quotes, the Value Line investment database, and financial analysis programs. And there are real-time games in which you match wits and reflexes with other users, regardless of where they happen to be on the continent, or in the world.

It all adds up to a very appealing package that computer owners everywhere have responded to in great numbers. People have been signing up so fast that in January of 1984 CompuServe raced past the 100,000 mark. And it is still growing, both in subscribers and in additional features.

CompuServe is described in much greater detail in *The Complete Handbook of Personal Computer Communications*. In this chapter, however, we are going to focus on but one aspect of the system, so here are the general things you need to know:

- The CompuServe Information System (CIS) is a time-sharing system that physically consists of many large computers. The service used to be known as MicroNET, and you will still see vestiges of this name around the system. The Apple SIG, for example is known as "MAUG" for "MicroNET Apple Users Group."

- Although the computers themselves are located in Columbus, Ohio, anyone with a communicating personal computer can tap into them as if they were in the next room.

- To access CIS, you dial a *local* phone number that connects you with a "packet-switching" network designed to route your call to Columbus. The major networks are Telenet, Tymnet, Uninet, and the CompuServe Network, but they all have one thing in common: they are much cheaper than regular long distance service.

- Although subscriptions to CompuServe may be available through Radio Shack stores, most individuals purchase the CompuServe Starter Kit. (See Figure 8.1 for more information.) All subscribers receive 128K of storage on the system, plus the slick monthly CIS magazine, *Today*, and "Update," the monthly CompuServe newsletter.

New User's Survival Kit

The Complete Handbook of Personal Computer Communications explains the various ways to move around within the system, how to have your electronic letters delivered to you immediately upon sign-on, and other convenient features and commands. You do not need to know those things to obtain free software, but there are several commands that you *must* know, regardless of how you plan to use this system. They include:

- <BREAK> This is the key to hit when you find yourself in the midst of something you want to get out of. When the system receives this signal, it will return you to a menu and function prompt.

- [<CONTROL><C>] Acts like <BREAK> and can be used if your computer does not have a <BREAK> key.

- [<CONTROL><S>] Causes the onscreen scroll to stop temporarily by sending CIS an X-OFF.

- [<CONTROL><Q>] Restarts an onscreen scroll by sending an X-ON.

- <T> Will take you to the TOP menu that greeted you when you first signed on. It may not be the most efficient way to do things, but should you get lost, this is the easiest way to get right back to where you started from.

- [<G> (Page Number)] CompuServe formats its information and features as "pages," and each page has a number. One way to get to the pages you want is to follow the menus, and this is definitely the approach most new users should take. With more experience, however, you will find that the *G* command offers a better way. This will immediately take you to the CIS page number you specify. The word *Go* may also be used. (See "Downloading the Index" later in this chapter.)

- HEL This will almost always generate a list of the commands that are available to you at any given prompt. The list will include a short explanation of each command.

- OFF One of the most important commands of all since it lets you sign off the system at virtually any point and thus stop the connect-charge meter from running.

The only other thing to watch out for is the *OK* prompt. CompuServe can be thought of as consisting of two large areas. One is called the "Display" area and the other is the "Programming" area. The Display area consists of the menus and "pages" of information most people use to move about the system. In reality, Display is a huge program running on the mainframe computers. When you are in the Programming area, you are in direct contact with those computers. The onscreen prompt in this area is *OK*. You might think of it as a DOS prompt similar to the one your own computer generates when it is not running a program.

You can do everything in Programming that you can do in Display, but you must know which programs to tell the mainframe to run. Until you have more experience, try to stay out of Programming. If you should end up there by accident, type the following:

```
R DISPLAY
```

This will run (*R*) the Display program for you and return you to the menus.

Figure 8.1. CompuServe Subscription Information

CompuServe
5000 Arlington Centre Blvd.
P.O. Box 20212
Columbus, OH 43220
(800) 848-8990
(614) 457-8600

Initial subscripton: $20–$50 (see *Comments*, below).

Availability: Computer stores and bookstores.

Hours of operation: 21 hours a day, your local time.

Costs: Prime Service (8 AM–6 PM); $12.50/hour for 300-baud service, $15/hour for 1200-baud service.

Standard Service (6 PM–5 AM); $6/hour for 300-baud service; $12.50/hour for 1200-baud service.

Access through CompuServe's own ComLink is free. There is a $2/hour surcharge for Telenet, Tymnet (DataPac), and Uninet access. Connect charges for Alaska and Hawaii are higher.

There is a minimum charge of one minute's worth of connect time (10¢–25¢) each time you sign on.

Monthly minimum fee: None.

Comments: To obtain a subscription to CompuServe, you purchase a "CompuServe Starter Kit" that includes everything you need (account number and password) to go online immediately. The kit sells for about $50 and entitles you to five free hours on the system. Subscription packages may also be available from Radio Shack computer stores for $20. Ask for the Universal Sign-Up Kit (catalog number: 26-2224). In the past this has included a free subscription to the Dow Jones News/Retrieval Service as well. These packages usually include one free hour on each system but offer little or no documentation.

Each time you sign on to the system while using your free time, CompuServe will ask whether you want to sign up to continue your account. This is something you should do immediately, since you will not be able to send electronic mail or order manuals until your account and credit information has been validated. Simply follow the prompts, and the system will walk you through the paperwork, but be sure to have your credit card handy. A new password will be mailed to you within 10 days, and you'll be an official CIS subscriber with all the rights and privileges accruing thereunto.

Where the Programs Are

Miles and Miles of Pretty Files

As with all computer-based systems, everything on CompuServe exists as a file of some sort. The files we're interested in exist in a section of the system called ACCESS. ACCESS is the great exchange place for CompuServe subscribers. It enables each individual to upload a file to his or her 128K "personal filing cabinet" and then enter a command that will make that file available to everyone. The file can be a computer program you have written, a collection of poetry, or an essay summarizing your personal view of the world. Whatever it is, you can make it available to other CIS subscribers through ACCESS. [If you want to sample this feature right now, enter *GO PCS-30* at the exclamation prompt (*!*) found at the end of many CIS menus.* The system will tell you when you have entered ACCESS, and at that point, type *HELP* for a list of available commands.]

There's a bit more to ACCESS than this, however. In reality, the feature is like a single large building with a main entrance and *many*

*Page numbers on the CompuServe system are subject to change. Consequently, the ones cited in this chapter may no longer apply. You will always be able to reach a feature by following the menus, however. Once you get to a feature this way, note the page number in the upper right corner of your screen and use it with the GO command the next time.

side doors. If you enter by the main door, you will be able to download a wide assortment of files, including programs for almost every major brand of machine. But you will not be able to probe all of the ACCESS's corridors and storage areas. Indeed, you will not even be aware that they exist.

The only way to find out what's *really* available in ACCESS is to enter by one of the side doors. These side doors in CompuServe parlance are the SIGs or special interest groups. The CompuServe SIGs can be thought of as online users groups, each devoted to a particular topic, computer, or operating system. The SIGs are unique in the electronic universe, and each of the nearly 60 such organizations on CompuServe has a great deal to offer. For many computer owners, the SIGs alone more than justify the costs of a CIS subscription and connect time. (See Figure 8.2.)

FreeTip: Figure 8.2 provides the names of most of the SIGs, but as new computers are produced, that list is certain to grow. To get the most up-to-date list of SIGs, do the following.

Type *GO IND* at the exclamation prompt. This will generate the following menu:

```
INDEX
1 Search for Topics of Interest
2 List ALL Indexed Topics
3 Quick Index List
4 Explanation of Index
Last Menu page. Key digit
or M for previous menu!
```

Key in *1* to search the index and generate the next menu:

```
INDEX
1 Search for Topics of Interest
2 List ALL Indexed Topics
3 Quick Index List
4 Explanation of Index
Last Menu page. Key digit
or M for previous menu! 1
Enter topic (ie. stocks)
: SIG
```

Set your software to capture incoming information and type in the word *SIG* as shown above. This will generate a complete list of all the SIGs currently on the system.

Figure 8.2. The CompuServe Special Interst Groups (SIGs)

The following list includes most of the SIGs on the CompuServe system at the time of this writing. In addition to other standard SIG features, each maintains its own databases. These databases, accessed with the *X* and *XA* commands, always contain information relevant to the SIG's main topic. But even in the non-computer SIGs, they often contain free software as well.

Special Interest Group	*CIS Page Number*
AAMSI (SIG) (Am. Assoc. of Medical Systems and Informatics)	SFP-5
ASCMD (SIG) (Am. Society of Computers in Medicine and Dentistry)	SFP-7
Apple User Group (SIG)	PCS-51
Arcade (SIG)	HOM-138
Ask Mr. Fed (SIG)	MMS-20
Atari (SIG)	PCS-132
Aviation Sig (AVSIG)	SFP-6
CB Interest Group (SIG)	HOM-9
CEMSIG (SIG) (*Computers and Electronics* magazine)	CEM-450
CP/M Users Group (SIG)	PCS-47
Color Computer (SIG)	PCS-126
Commodore 64 (SIG)	PCS-156
Commodore Pet (SIG)	PCS-116
Commodore VIC20 (SIG)	PCS-155
Communication Industry	SFP-35
Computer Art (SIG)	PCS-157
Cook's Underground	HOM-109
Educational Research	HOM-28
Educators' (SIG)	HOM-137
Entertainment (SIG)	HOM-29
Environmental (SIG)	SFP-38
Epson (SIG)	PCS-1
Family Matters (SIG)	HOM-144
Fire Fighters' (SIG)	SFP-36
Food Buyline (SIG)	HOM-151
Golf (SIG)	HOM-129
Good Earth (SIG)	HOM-145

HamNet (SIG)	HOM-11
Heath User Group (SIG)	PCS-48
Hi-Tech Forum (SIG)	CCC-150
IBM-PC (SIG)	PCS-131
ICCA Forum (Independent Computer Consultants Association)	PCS-17
LSI (SIG) (Logical Systems, Inc.)	PCS-49
Legal (SIG)	SFP-40
Literary (SIG)	HOM-136
MNET-11 (SIG) (DEC PDP-11)	PCS-53
MNET80 (SIG) (TRS-80)	PCS-54
MUSUS (SIG) (UCSD p-System)	PCS-55
MicroPro (SIG)	PCS-12
Microsoft (SIG)	PCS-145
Miner's Underground	SFP-44
Multi-Player Game (SIG)	GAM-300
Music (SIG)	HOM-150
National Issues (SIG)	HOM-132
Netwits (SIG)	WIT-100
OS9 (SIG)	PCS-18
Ohio Scientific (SIG)	PCS-125
Orch-90 (SIG)	HOM-13
Outdoor (SIG)	HOM-38
Panasonic (SIG)	PCS-114
Pascal (SIG)	PCS-55
PowerSoft's XTRA-80	PCS-56
Programmer's (SIG)	PCS-158
RCA (SIG)	PCS-57
Religion (SIG)	HOM-33
Ski (SIG)	HOM-36
Space (SIG)	HOM-127
Sports (SIG)	HOM-110
TRS-80 Professional Forum	PCS-21
TRS-80 Model 100 (SIG)	PCS-154
TeleComm (SIG)	PCS-52
Travel (SIG)	HOM-157
VAX (SIG)	PCS-16
Veterinarians Forum	SFP-37

The CompuServe Special Interst Groups (continued)

Whole Earth Software (SIG)	PCS-24
Work-at-home (SIG)	HOM-146
Writers and Editors Forum	PCS-117

Each SIG is managed by one or more SysOps (system operators). Sometimes, as is the case with the Commodore SIGs, the group may be sponsored by a corporation. But usually SIGs are operated by private individuals, much as local users groups are. Running a SIG is a very time-consuming job, and as with local groups, it is often more a labor of love than anything else. Fortunately, CompuServe pays SysOps a small royalty based on the amount of time subscribers spend in their organizations. This has no effect on you as a subscriber since there is no extra connect time charge for using a SIG.

FreeTip: All SIGs can be reached by following the CompuServe menus until you find a menu item for "Groups and Clubs." But with SIGs scattered throughout the system, the most efficient way to get to the one you want is to type *GO* followed by the page number. When you enter a SIG for the first time, you will be asked to enter the name you would like to be known by. Then you will be asked if you want to be added to the membership list. Since you can join as many SIGs as you like, it is usually a good idea to say yes. There will be a pause while your account number is inserted into the SIG's files and then you will be free to roam around at will. The next time you enter a SIG you have joined, the system will automatically greet you by name and deliver any messages addressed to you by other SIG members. (Select the "SIG Options" item from the main SIG menu for more information on customizing these and other SIG features.)

The majority of SIGs are free. However, while you will always be able to use a SIG's messaging function, one or two require a membership fee of about $20 before you will be permitted to access their databases. Before sending in your check, you might consider using the messaging function or CompuServe's E-Mail to ask the SysOp for more information about what the databases contain. As a suggestion, ask the SysOp to provide you with the names of the various XA databases and a CATalogue (a special command) of at least one of them. That way you'll know more about what you're getting for your money. (See *The Complete Handbook of Personal Computer Communications* for tips on using E-mail.)

The Four Areas in Every SIG

Since all SIGs are made possible by the same CompuServe mainframe software, all operate essentially the same way. Each SIG is divided into four general areas. The first area is the messaging function. SIG members can use this facility to discuss a particular topic. Discussions take place over time, usually on an "open letter" basis. All members are free to read each other's comments and to add thoughts of their own. The messaging area is the ideal place to get help when you're having problems with your hardware or when you want to know more about a particular software package you are considering. Any number of people will see your request, and many of them will be able to give you the information you need.

The second SIG function also deals with member-to-member communication. This is the "Conferencing" area, a special section of CompuServe's larger "CB" facility. As its name implies, using CB is very similar to using a citizen's band radio. The main difference is that instead of speaking, you type your comments at your computer. Whatever you type will immediately appear on the screens of every other subscriber currently "tuned" to one of the 40 CB channels. This facility opens a lot of possibilities. Members of MAUG, the Apple SIG, for example, were recently treated to a real-time conference with Steve Wozniak, the man who designed many of their machines.

The third and fourth areas are the "sections" and the "databases." These are the special "side doors" to ACCESS that most new CompuServe subscribers never see. The reason is that the main menu that greets you when you enter a SIG contains only selections related to the messaging function. It says nothing about sections or databases. Although this may change, unless you have the SIG Manual, available through CompuServe's FEEDBACK online ordering facility for about $4, you might not know that these areas exist. (See the FreeTip about a file called EZSIG1.RWJ later in this chapter for what may be a better alternative to the CIS manual.) As it happens, all you need to do is enter *X* for the sections and *XA* for the databases *instead* of a selection from the main SIG menu.

The sections generally contain single long articles or other types of continuous text. A SIG may have as many as eleven of them, and they are referred to as X0, X7, X9, etc. If the SIG maintains a list of BBS phone numbers, the SysOp will typically put it in one of the X sections. The same would be true with lists of local and national users groups. You may also find articles on software, hardware, and book reviews written by various SIG members.

FreeTip: Most SysOps will also make sure that at least one of the SIG's X sections contains instructions for using the SIG. Although

FreeTip continued

the fundamental SIG structure is the same system-wide, there is considerable room for customization within each group. It isn't always the case, but the instruction file is usually placed in the 0 section. To access it, type *X0* from the main SIG menu's *Function:* prompt. Other sections can be accessed the same way.

The Databases are quite different. Often referred to as SIG/ACCESS, each consists of any number of discrete files. These files can be anything. But in SIGs with free software to offer, most of them contain either computer programs or documentation (instructions) for programs. *This*, in other words, is where the free software is stored. There can be as many as ten databases in a SIG, though some may be empty. They are referred to as XA (the *A* is for ACCESS) sections and numbered XA0 through XA9.

The 10 XA databases make the software offerings of the SIG more manageable. SysOps are free to assign any name to an XA database and use it as a way to classify various types of programs. The XA2 database may contain nothing but game programs, while XA3 is devoted to communications software. Because different SIGs have different needs, there is no uniformity among them. The only way to find out what's where is to enter the SIG and take a look. Type *XA0* at the main SIG *Function:* prompt to enter the XA0 database. Then type *XA* at the next prompt you see. This will produce a labeled list of the various XA databases.

FreeTip: Going into ACCESS through a SIG is often the best way to approach things. ACCESS is an essential feature of the CIS system, but it is something of a potpourri. This means that it may take you longer—and cost you more in connect time—to locate a program. By entering through a SIG, you not only gain access to files that are not available through the "main entrance," you also immediately narrow the field to programs pertaining to your machine or interest. There is the added benefit that the SIG programs have usually been tested by another SIG member and possibly even improved or specially modified by still other SIG members. You can use the same commands in ACCESS that you do in SIG/ACCESS, and you should definitely give the "main entrance" a try. But if you are looking for free software, you will almost always be much better off going in through the appropriate SIG.

How to Find the Programs You Want

Don't Ask for Help—Yet

CompuServe's commands are designed to let you locate and retrieve virtually any piece of information stored in its computers. The system also provides extensive "help" files that list and explain each command. But you don't want to see them. Not yet. There are so many commands, command combinations, and permutations that you will be overwhelmed if you try to take them all in.

You can locate and download the software you want with only three commands. These are KEY, S/DES/KEY:, and R. Purists might argue that there are more efficient ways to do things, and there are. But what little this combination loses in efficiency, it more than makes up for in simplicity and ease of use.

FreeTip: You should probably use FEEDBACK (Go-FEE) to order a copy of the "Special Interest Groups and Clubs" manual from CompuServe ($4). But since this manual may be out of date, you might consider creating your own manual by downloading and printing out the online "help" files. Typing <H> and almost any prompt will cause the "help" file pertaining to the feature you are using to scroll up your screen.

However, there may be an even better alternative. In November of 1983, Ronald W. Johnson [70116,1416] prepared and uploaded a complete summary of the commands you need to use a SIG as easily and efficiently (and cheaply) as possible. The date is important because by then CompuServe had begun to implement a number of new commands. The summary exists as two files and is available both in CompuServe's main ACCESS section or in the XA0 (General Interest) database of the Music Forum SIG (HOM-150). To download these files, go to either section and enter *R* (or *TYP) EZSIG1.RWJ*. The second file is EZSIG2.RWJ, and it can be read after the first one is finished.

Searching for free software online can be an enjoyable experience all by itself. It isn't difficult, but it can call for some genuine detective work, a little skill, and some imagination. In other words, to get the best results, your mind, as well as your fingers and keyboard, must be engaged. If you are successful, you will be rewarded with the program you seek. If you fail or if the program you want is not on the database, you will inevitably learn something that you can use the next time. In either case, it will be enormously helpful to be familiar with the general outline of the target before you go in.

All files in SIG/ACCESS have two parts. There is a short section called the "description," and there is the file itself. The description is composed and generated when the file is uploaded by its author. Here, for example, are two descriptions from programs in the XA0 database of the Educators' SIG (HOM-137):

```
[71775,46]
AVERAG.ATR                    21-May-83 2250                 Accesses: 9
  Keywords: AVERAGES GRADES ATARI UTILITY BASIC

   A BASIC-LANGUAGE TEACHER UTILITY THAT PROVIDES AVERAGES
   AFTER USER ENTERS NAMES AND RAW LETTER GRADES. THIS PROGRAM
   SHOULD BE RELATIVELY EASY FOR THE USER TO MODIFY.

[75265,716]
VOICE.DOC                     22-Oct-83 11235                Accesses: 1
  Keywords: VOICEPRINT DEAF SPEECH APPLEPROGRAM DOCUMENTATION

   This documentation supports the VOICE.XEC file in this
   database which contains the VOICEPRINT software. VOICEPRINT
   is an Apple program that lets a speech teacher show voice on
   the screen. It is a useful tool for holding student
   attention and illustrating speech parameters, particularly
   with deaf kids.
```

Much of this is self-explanatory, but the thing to keep in mind is that a description consists of various *individual* components. There is the CompuServe account number of the uploader, the filename and extension, the date the file was uploaded, its size in kilobytes, the number of times the file has been downloaded ("Accesses:"), a list of keywords, and a short description.

The files associated with these descriptions can be located using many of these components. You might, for example, search for all files with .BAS as an extension, or all files contributed under the account number 71775,46. For our purposes, however, the most important components are the keywords.

The keywords are specified by the uploader, and the SIG database maintains a list of them and keeps track of how many times each has been used in a given XA section. You can search one of these databases on the basis of one or more keywords. But that's rather like playing the card game Go Fish: "Let's see, Database . . . Do you have any Ataris?" When you enter the commands to ask this question, the CompuServe computer will go away and check. If it has any "Ataris" it will give the files to you. Otherwise, it will say the computer equivalent of "Go fish!"

For this reason, it is much more efficient to find out what cards the computer is holding before you ask. You can do this with the KEY command. When you enter KEY at the XA database prompt, the computer will yield up its list of keywords. For example, here is a greatly abbreviated version of the KEY file generated by entering that command in the XA4-Programming database of the Apple SIG (PCS-51):

ASSEMBLY	1
BBS	1
C	1
CPM	1
GRAPHICS	2
SSC	1
UTILITY	1
VISICALC	2

The numbers indicate the number of times the keyword appears in descriptions for program files in this database. New Apple users might not know that *C* refers to the C programming language, but most could guess that *SSC* stands for Apple's Super Serial Card, an add-on used to connect a modem, printer, or other serial device. The only caveat here is that since all of the keywords in a description are included, some of the ones you see will refer to the same program.

There are only two other basic commands you need. One will cause CompuServe's computer to display the description, and the other will cause it to transmit the program file itself. When you have picked a keyword from the list, type in *S/DES/KEY:* [keyword] at the database prompt. This will cause the system to *S*can its files for "DES"criptions containing the keyword and then present you with the descriptions.

FreeTip: The descriptions will always tell you something about the file. But since they are composed, often in haste, by many individuals, they tend to vary widely in detail. Ideally a description will tell you whether there is an associated documentation file you should download, any special equipment or software you may need to use the program, and possibly where the program came from (original, from another SIG, from a computer magazine, etc.).

If the description does not give you enough information to make up your mind whether you want the program or not, check the date and the number of accesses. If the file has been downloaded a large number of times, it's a pretty good indication that other SIG members have found it to be useful. Temper your judgment based on how long the program has been on the system. Also, since some

FreeTip continued

SIGs have significantly more members than others, a "typical" large number of accesses in one SIG might be considered small in another.

The descriptions will scroll up your screen without pausing between items, so it is a good idea to have your printer on or to be in "capture" mode or both. When the descriptions are finished, you will be returned to the database prompt. If none of the descriptions tickled your fancy, you may want to enter *S/DES/KEY:* [different keyword] to look for something else.

How to Figure Out a Filename

Every free program in a SIG database is assigned a filename. The first part of the filename will consist of up to six characters, and it will be followed by a period, or a "dot," and a three-character "file extension." As with your own computer, the filename that is assigned to a program is supposed to give you some idea of what the program is all about.

Naturally, some filenames are more descriptive and easier to understand than others. It isn't too difficult to figure out that files with the extensions .BAS, .PAS, or .ASM contain programs written in BASIC, Pascal, or assembly language. But other filenames are less obvious. Generally, there are three main types of filenames you must be concerned with. The first are those that assume some specific knowledge about your particular brand of computer and the free or commercial software available for it. The second are those that end with .HEX or .BIN. And the third are those with the extension .IMG.

Here's a good example of the machine-specific type taken from the XA0 Database in the CP/M SIG (GO PCS-47):

MDM714.INF
MDM714.ASM
MDM714.DOC

You could probably guess that .INF means "information"; that .ASM means "written in assembly language"; and that .DOC signifies a "documentation file." But unless you are part of the CP/M world, you might not know that MDM714 means "MODEM, version 7.14." This is a version of what is undoubtedly the best-known public domain CP/M program, the communications program MODEM7. Since every community of computer owners has its own language and special terms, the only way to familiarize yourself with the meanings of various filenames is to plunge right in and download the descriptions using the commands described earlier. Before long you'll find that you can sling the filename lingo with the best of them.

The second category of filenames are those ending in .HEX (hexadecimal) or .BIN (binary). Though it is not really accurate to do so, SIG contributors tend to use these terms interchangeably. Both refer to a file that consists of nothing but hexadecimal numbers, like this:

```
:20000000C305011E2831C80BAF322D0B215C0011570BCD4A01AF32770B216C00
:200020004A01AF329B0B114A05CD0803215D007EFE20C23B0111E105C3350521
:2000400020C2550111E105C335050E107E1213230DC24C01C911A906CD080321
```

These are hexadecimal numbers arranged in what is known as the Intel format. Other files may use different formats, but they will all consist of the numbers from *0* through *9* and the letters *A* through *F*. These are the 16 characters used to represent any number in the hexadecimal (base 16) numbering system, and that's really about all you need to know about "hex."

However, before you can run any of these programs, you must first convert them into an executable form, and to do that you will need—what else?—a "hexadecimal conversion program" or a "hex converter." Such programs are usually written in BASIC, and virtually every SIG that has hex files in its free software collection will also have the conversion program that is right for your machine. Sometimes there may even be several conversion programs to choose from.

Here are the steps to follow to locate the hex converter programs that are available in any SIG. First, go into the appropriate XA database. A database labeled "Programming" is a better candidate than one labeled "Games," but you may have to look in several databases to find what you want. Second, type in *S/DES/KEY: *CONV** to tell the system that you want it to find key words like "hexconverter," "conversion," "converter," "hex-converter," and any other permutation of "conv" in the database. Third, toggle your printer on or set your system to download the program descriptions that will soon appear. Finally, choose a program and download it with the *R* command as described in the next section.

FreeTip: Hex converters can be among the most valuable programs in your free software collection since they can be used not only with CompuServe hex files but also with hex files found on computer bulletin boards and other systems.

Space does not permit a complete explanation, but in essence hexadecimal files are part of a technique for transmitting machine language programs to and from computers that are not equipped

FreeTip continued

for binary transfers. (See Chapter 7.) The author of the program creates a machine language program with an assembler or compiler and then uses a hex converter to translate it into the hexadecimal format. Because it is simple ASCII text, the resulting file can easily be uploaded to any communications system.

As long as you have a hex converter program, you can just as easily download the file and transform it back into its original machine language form. Note that many hex files conclude with "Checksum=" followed by some number. In most cases you will want to leave that phrase and number in the file when you turn it over to the hex converter since the hex converter uses that information to verify that no errors occurred when you downloaded the file. (The last hexadecimal numbers in each row of the file are usually the sum of the other numbers in the row. The converter program adds these numbers up and compares the total with the checksum.)

FreeTip: Since most hex converters are available in BASIC, you probably will not need any additional software to run them. But BASIC can be very slow. Consequently, in some SIGs you may find that the same conversion program is available in both BASIC and in hex versions.

If you download both files and use the BASIC program to convert the hex file, the result will be a hex converter program that runs at machine language (or compiled BASIC) speeds. You can then put the BASIC version away and use the machine language version from then on.

The third category of files you may encounter are .IMG or "image" files. The term is short for "memory image," and it refers to a file that is an exact copy of a program as it existed in the memory of its author's computer. Although you may be able to download some of them as you would a .HEX file, these are designed to be used with CompuServe's Vidtex™ personal computer communications software. Vidtex is explained in a special section near the end of this chapter, and it is certainly a program you should look into. For now, we can simply say that Vidtex and .IMG files are CompuServe's answer to the binary transfer, error-checking capabilities of the XMODEM protocol described in Chapter 7 and Appendix A.

How to Download a Program

When you see the description of a program you want, you have only to enter: *R* [Filename.Extension] at the next prompt. The *R* stands for "Read." For example, here is the result of an R command entered in PowerSoft's XTRA-80 SIG, a group specializing in Radio Shack computers (PCS-56). The *Key digit:* prompt is the last line of the database's menu. The file we were after is called RECV.100. Notice that file transmission began immediately.

```
Key digit: R RECV.100

100 'RECV reads a file from the Mod
105 '100 RS-232 port and writes the
110 'data to a file. F$ is the Mod
115 '100 End-of-File character.
120 '        -bob b. [70030,137]
125 '
130 DEFINT A-C,I-L:C$="":CLS
135 F$=CHR$(26)
140 MAXFILES=2:INPUT"FILENAME:";N$
```

(etc.)

FreeTip: Older documentation and some online help files may mention the CATalog and TYPe commands. Although these will probably be supported for some time to come, they have been replaced by *S* ("Scan") and *R* ("Read"). This is part of an ongoing upgrading of CompuServe's software that will eventually be implemented system-wide. If you find that *S* and *R* do not work in a SIG, use *CAT* and *TYP* instead.

Vidtex users, please note that when using ACCESS or SIG/ACCESS, the command to enter is *DOW*. You can use *R* to read a file as well, but only *DOW* will activate the B Protocol and other Vidtex features.

Putting It All Together

Here are the steps to follow when you want to locate and download programs from a SIG. These will work for any SIG, but we're going to use the Commodore-64 SIG as an example. The Commodore SIG can be entered directly by keying in *GO PCS-156* at any CompuServe exclamation prompt. However, because Commodore Business Machines sponsors an "information network" on CompuServe, we'll go in that way instead. The commands you should enter are in italics and indicated by the arrows.

(Main CIS exclamation prompt)
...or M for previous menu!: *GO CBM-1* ←———— The target page.

Commodore Page CBM-1
COMMODORE INFORMATION NETWORK'S
MAIN MENU
1 Intro/Survival Kit Menu
2 New Updates To CIN
3 HOTLINE (Ask Questions) Menu
4 Product Announcements
5 Bulletin Boards (SIGs)
6 Commodore Magazine Articles
7 Directory (Dealer & User)
8 Commodore Tips
9 Commodore Product Line
10 User Questionnaire
. Last menu page. Key digit
or M for previous menu.. =!*5* ← Select the SIGs.

Commodore Page CBM-6
Bulletin Boards Menu
1) VIC-20 Bulletin Board
2) Commodore 64 Bulletin Board
3) CBM Bus Machines BBS
. Last menu page. Key digit
or M for previous menu.. =!*2* ← Select the C-64 board.

Thank You for Waiting
Your name: *Puddin'tain* ← Your Name Goes Here.

Do you wish to be added to the
member list at this time? *Yes* ← By all means, sign up. It costs nothing.

Inserting name and ID...
Welcome to Commodore 64 SIG, V. 2C(7)

Name: Puddin'tain 70000,000
Last on: DD-MMM-YY 18:33:44
High msg#: 0
You are user number 159569
System contains messages
39189 to 39666
Brief bulletin:
Enter blank line for menu:

Function menu:
1 (L) Leave a message
2 (R) Read messages
3 (RN) Read new messages
5 (B) Read bulletins
6 (CO) Online conference

```
9 (OP) Change your SIG options
0 (E) Exit from this SIG
Enter selection or H for help: XA
```

Note that XA is not on the menu.

```
Database for which Section:
0 1 2 3 4 5 6 7 8 9 0
```

Enter *0*, even though you don't know what it contains.

(Ah it's the HOTLINE.)

```
XA 0 - HOTLINE (General) :
1 BRO Browse thru files
2 UPL Upload a new file
3 EXI Exit to Commodore 64 SIG
4 HEL Help
5 XA Change database
Key digit: XA
```

The goal here is to produce the list of XA database sections that will follow.

```
Which Section:

  0 - HOTLINE (General)
  1 - Vendor Section
  2 - Software
  3 - User Group
  4 - Languages/FORTH
  5 - Manual Updates
  6 - CP/M Section
  7 - Games (Software)
  8 - Vidtex only PubDom.
  9 - Pseudo .IMG Files
? 8
```

(Now we know what there is to choose from.)

All the programs on the SIG are public domain. But from reading messages and bulletins on the SIG, we have learned that this XA database has over 500 programs, including the entire collection that Commodore Business Machines donated to the public domain.

```
Using Section 8 database.
XA 8 - Vidtex only PubDom. :
1 BRO Browse thru files
2 UPL Upload a new file
3 EXI Exit to Commodore 64 SIG
4 HEL Help
5 XA Change database
Key digit: KEY <----
```

Note that KEY is not on the menu. This generates a list of keywords (not shown), one of which is GAME. Then the same menu, with the *Key digit:* prompt, appears again. (Menu not shown)

```
Key digit: s/des/key: game <----
```

The crucial "scan descriptions for key word" command.

```
[70436,1050]
DAMBUS.IMG     10-Dec-83 33455(13176) Accesses: 437
  Keywords: WAR GAME BOMBING
  This is Commodores Dam Busters.C2 game from there public
  domain series. It has been upgraded to run on all 64s and
  has had the bugs removed. Uploaded with Vidtex by Rick R.
```

(Menu not shown)

```
Key digit: DOW DAMBUS.IMG <----
```

More descriptions will follow, but when they are finished, the same menu and prompt will appear. If you are running Vidtex, enter *DOW* and follow the prompts this generates to download the file.

Helpful Hints

The same procedure can be used to locate and download programs from any SIG on CompuServe. As you become more experienced, you will be able to use a broader range of commands to find the things you want. Here are some points to keep in mind and a few additional commands you might try.

- Don't forget that you can get help at almost any prompt by typing *HEL*. The fact is that only a small fraction of the choices available to you are on the menus, and the ubiquitous *Key digit:* prompt can be very misleading.

- Consider using both your printer and your capture buffer while you are online. Toggle your printer on when you are about to receive information, like keywords, that you will need in your next command. But toggle it off after that. Printers can be very slow. Some communications software is designed to send X-OFF and X-ON signals to a remote database to enable it to match the screen display to the rate of printout. Consequently leaving your printer on for an entire session can increase the time you spend online and raise your total bill. It is better to use a buffer to capture material you want to save, write the buffer to disk, and print out the resulting file *after* you have signed off.

- When you enter a SIG for the first time, try typing *MI* at the main menu prompt. If the SIG maintains a file of *M*embership *I*nformation, this command should cause the system to provide it. You might also try *V* at the same prompt for a list of SIG members and their expressed interests.

- In the above example we used a rather roundabout way to find out how the SIG labeled its XA databases because this technique will always work. In some SIGs you can enter *SN* for "Section Numbers" at the main menu to generate a list of labeled databases. Eventually this command will be available system-wide. You can go to any Database section by entering *XA* followed by the number you want at the *Key digit:* or at the SIG main menu prompt.

- Theoretically the X sections and the XA databases are supposed to correspond. Thus if there were a Software X Section and a Software XA Database, the section would contain only messages from SIG members pertaining to software, while the Database would hold the actual programs. (The messaging function requires that a message be put into a particular section.) In practice, few SIGs follow this procedure. Consequently, if you want to get to know a SIG, be sure to look at the X sections as well as the databases since they often contain nondatabase related information. (Enter *X* at the SIG main menu prompt. Then "pick a number.")

- If you decide to select BROwse from the XA menu, the system will first prompt you for the /AGE: of the file. You may hit <ENTER> or type in the age in number of days. Then it will prompt you for keywords (/KEY:). Again, hit <ENTER> or type in a keyword.

  Starting with the most recent submissions, the system will present the description of a file and a menu to let you you read or download it or move on to the next description. Note that if you elect to read a file, the system will ask you if you want to read it again when you are finished.

- Don't forget to use your imagination. If you want a CP/M program, the CP/M SIG (PCS-47) is the obvious place to go. But remember that many machines can run CP/M, even if it is not their native operating system. Consequently, you will find CP/M software in *many* SIGs. If you need to convert a program from your machine to another, be sure to look in the SIGs for *both* machines.

  Finally, if you use VisiCalc, Lotus, dBASE, SuperCalc, or some other program utilizing templates, worksheets, or command files, be sure to look in the SIGs for all the machines capable of running those programs. An IBM user might not normally consider the Apple SIG as a source of software. But the same VisiCalc templates can be used with both machines.

FreeTip: We have said next to nothing about CompuServe's online software shopping service, but it is something you might want to look into. Called Softex™ and accessible by typing *GO PCS-45*, the system is capable of directly downloading programs into your Vidtex-equipped machine. (Vidtex is a necessity here.) You may or may not be interested in any of the CompuServe products, but if you own a TRS-80 Model I or Model III and are tired of typing in programs from *80-MICRO* magazine, then you should know that many of them are available here. Since you will have read about the program in the magazine, you will know exactly what you are getting.

A SIG Software Sampler

To give you a better idea of the wide range of free software that is available on CompuServe, we have selected programs from eight SIGs. The descriptions following each program are based on those prepared by the submitter, slightly edited for reasons of space. Unlike the free software available on computer bulletin board systems, which may or may not be there the next time you call, the programs submitted to CompuServe SIGs tend to remain on the system. Thus there's a good chance that the programs cited here will be in their respective SIGs whenever you sign on. Please keep in mind that this is only the tiniest fraction of the literally thousands of free programs available on the system.

AAMSI (MED-SIG) *SFP-5*

DIFF.BAS
Keywords: VIC-20 WHITECELLS DIFFERENTIAL

Program for the Commodore VIC-20. Redefines certain keys, enabling you to use the VIC as a white cell differential counter.

DOSAGE.BAS
Keywords: DOSAGE AMINOGLY BASIC

Written in Microsoft Basic—so it can be run on many machines—by Richard B. Asher MD, [70110,523], this program calculates aminoglycoside dosage from pharmacokinetic equations that consider patient characteristics and aminoglycosideserium levels.

FIND.BAS
Keywords: BBS BULLETIN SEARCH TRS

A program for the TRS-80 that will search the full BBS.TXT for the numbers of medical bulletin board systems around the country. You must download BBS.TXT to use this program.

Apple User Group (SIG) *PCS-51*

DB5.FP
Keywords: DATABASE5 DATABASE

This is Database+5, a powerful, public-domain database management system (DBMS). Requires four files. Download DB5.FP and save to disk as Database+5; DB5SRC.FP as Datasearch+5; DB5STR.BIN as Datastrings; DB5GAR.BIN as Datagarbage. The names on disk are important. DB5DOC.TXT gives complete documentation.

ALDCAP.FP
Keywords: DATA CAPTURE AUTO LOG ON MICROMODEM

Program to modify DATA CAPTURE 4.0 to auto log on to CompuServe. A variation of The Source log-on routine modified with CIS's auto log-on program.

FINONE.VC
Keywords: APPLEWARE VISICALC FINANCE

Visicalc financial functions, part one. Includes compounding and discounting of sums and annuities, amortization functions, and a demonstration model. Download to your system and load into VisiCalc using '/SL'. See also FINTWO.VC.

Atari (SIG) *PCS-132*

LOGO.ATR
Keywords: ATARI LOGO DEMO PROGRAM 128 COLORS

A present from TAPS, the Toronto Atari Programmers Club to SIG Atari. A VERY impressive graphics demo. Try it, you'll like it.

TIME.CRE
Keywords: ATARI CLOCK DISPLAY

This program will display a clock face on your screen, with moving hands, including a second hand. For a special treat, LIST the program then let me know how you think I did THAT.

SQ.DOC
Keywords: ATARI SQ USQ DOC

Documentation for file squeezing programs SQ and USQ (unsqueezer). SQ squeezes any file to a smaller size using Huffman algorithm.

Color Computer (TRS-80 CoCo SIG) *PCS-126*

GARFLD.CC
Keywords: GARFIELD COMIC GRAPHIC DRAW PICTURE CAT

Digitized picture of Garfield.

R2D2.CC
Keywords: R2D2 ARTOODETOO STAR WARS HIGH RESOLUTION GRAPHICS

Picture of R2D2.

ENTAIN.MUS
Keywords: MUSIC COLOR CC COCO COMPOSER KOMPOSER COMPILER

This is my song that I typed in using the COMPOSER PROGRAM. It is: "The Entertainer" (theme from "The Sting") by Scott Joplin! It requires the COMPOSER PROGRAM to use. Enjoy!!!

Commodore 64 (SIG) *PCS-156*

DISKCK.IMG
Keywords: DISK UTILITY GENERAL

This program will:
1. Give you a BAM of your disk.
2. Check all files for errors.
3. Check for bad track and sectors
4. Recover scratched files.

Written by Jim Butterfield.

DISKWO.IMG
Keywords: 1541 UTILITY DOS DISK

This is a menu driven program that does the same as the DOS wedge. Its advantages over the wedge are:
1. It allows characters the wedge won't take, like a comma.
2. It is in BASIC, so it won't muck up any other programs. (Good for using C-64 Aid.)

Written, uploaded, and submitted into the public domain by Jeff Leyser

UNLOAD.HEX
Keywords: CPM CPM COM TO HEX

This is UNLOAD from the CP/M SIG. It converts .COM back to .HEX files. Uploaded using VIDTEX 4.0A.

Computer Art (SIG) *PCS-157*

INDEM.IMG
Keywords: C64 DEMO RASTER INTERRUPT

Use this interrupt demo program to explore the fun, but little known world of Display List Interrupt Requests!!! The program displays a multitude of Star Ship Enterprises, using only a few Sprites!

LACE.ATR
Keywords: ATARI GEOMETRIC GRAPHICS8

A short (30 second) geometrical demo illustrating the artifacting capabilities of the ATARI and (possibly) the artifacting capabilities of the human mind.

KYBJOY.FP
Keywords: APPLE KEYBOARD JOYSTICK MUSIC BINARY

Turns APPLE into music KEYBOARD, also JOYSTICK input for special effects. Machine language/binary code. Just "EXEC" this file once you have it stored to your disk.

CP/M Users Group (SIG) *PCS-47*

ACTREC.DOC

Keywords: AR Accounts Legal Super-Calc

This is a neat accounts receivable template for a small law firm, accounting firm, or any other organization that has only a few hundred invoices out at a time. Requires Super-Calc-2.

PIPXFR.ASM

Keywords: CPM PIP INP OUT RDR PUN MODEM HANDSHAKE TRANSFER

This overlay to PIP adds RDR:/PUN: transfer via the INP: and OUT: special device names. The protocol operates successfully with 2MHz 8080's connected via 9600 baud serial ports, with the OUT: from one machine correctly transferred into the INP: and thence to a file of another. Operation of the technique and its use of echo as a way to match speed between sender and receiver is described by Steven Fisher in the July 1983 MICROSYSTEMS.

ACATMS.BIN

Keywords: APPLE MICROSOFT SOFTCARD MODEM NOVATION APPLE CAT

COMPLETE terminal program for the Novation Apple Cat II running under Microsoft Softcard CPM (see ACATPC.BIN for the AppliCard version). Includes auto dial, tone or pulse, Christensen XMODEM protocol and bulk ASCII file transfer. Based on MODEM 903 and 7xx.

IBM-PC (SIG) *PCS-131*

MISTOX.HEX

Keywords: STOCKS LOTUS 1-2-3 123

MISTOX is a LOTUS 1-2-3 worksheet that is completely menu driven and allows one to "What If?" their stock portfolio. Written by Steve Maller. MISTOX.HEX should be converted to MISTOX.WKS using either HC.COM or CVTHEX.

DOWDIF.HEX

Keywords: VISICALC STOCK MARKET DOW JONES DIF LOTUS 123

DOWDIF is a program that converts files retrieved from the Dow Jones News/Retrieval Service to DIF specifications. The resulting DIF file can be read by VisiCalc, LOTUS 1-2-3, and other programs. It allows investment analysis, and with

1-2-3 it allows charting. Requires 64K, comm software, a wordprocessor, and a DIF compatible spreadsheet. DOWDIF is a User Supported (contribution requested) program.

123KEY.DOC
Keywords: LOTUS 123 KEYPAD PROKEY NUMERIC 123KEY

Explanation of 123KEY.PRO, a file of key definitions to be used with Lotus 1-2-3 and PROKEY. This keydefs file will allow you to use the numeric keypad.

FPLOT.BAS
Keywords: GRAPHICS MATHEMATICAL FUNCTION PLOTTING

This BASIC program will plot mathematical functions in polar, Cartesian, and rotated Cartesian (3D) coordinate systems.

Why You Should Consider CompuServe's Vidtex™ Program

Two considerations are paramount to anyone who wants to obtain free software over the telephone. Since even a fraction of a second of static on the phone line can cause communications errors that will render a received program useless, the first consideration is accuracy of transmission. The second is the ability to receive binary files, since many of the best programs exist in fast-executing machine language form.

As discussed elsewhere, the XMODEM binary file transfer protocol answers both of these needs for users of computer bulletin boards. On the CompuServe system, the Vidtex protocol and Vidtex personal computer communications software plays a similar role. The program costs about $40 and is available for virtually every brand of computer. (See Appendix A for a description of features not described here.)

Error-checking is handled by the proprietary CompuServe "B Protocol" that both the firm's mainframes and Vidtex-running personal computers support. The firm also has has an "A Protocol" designed for use with simple ASCII files. This may be supported by some earlier versions of Vidtex on some computers, and you may find public domain programs that will give you access to it.

However, most CIS subscribers will use a package that supports the B Protocol. This protocol can be used with *any* kind of file. Since accuracy is just as important in a stock quote as it is in a program, CompuServe's MicroQuote™ also supports B Protocol transfers, as does Softex™, the firm's direct-delivery online software shopping service.

Machine language binary transfers are handled in one of two ways. The first method is to use the hexadecimal/machine language conversion technique described earlier. Vidtex has a built-in hex converter program that is activated when you specify a filename with the .BIN filename extension. This converts machine language programs into hex when uploaded from a personal computer and reconverts them into machine language when they are downloaded. (If you do not have the Vidtex program, you can download .BIN files and convert them yourself with a hex converter, but no error-checking will be performed during the transmission.)

The second binary file transfer option is especially intriguing. This method uses machine-specific "image" files that enable you to transfer free programs just as if your computer were one disk drive and the CompuServe mainframes were another in the same computer. Both .BIN and .IMG files consist of hexadecimal representations of machine language. Where image files differ is in the extra, machine-specific information they contain.

For example, before an image file transfer takes place, CompuServe's software asks your Vidtex package for the brand and model of your computer. When the transfer begins, your software sends not only the file itself, but also information from the disk directory regarding the file's type and size. All of this is stored in the CompuServe .IMG file.

When you download an image file with Vidtex, the process works in reverse. The CompuServe mainframe will ask your software for the computer's make and model. If the information tallies with what's in the file, the transfer will proceed automatically. (The CompuServe DOW, for "download," is intended exclusively for use with the Vidtex program.)

Depending on your version of the program, a series of numbers or numbers and plus signs will appear on your screen as the transfer takes place. (Each number represents the transfer of a 32-byte block, and the numbers cycle from 0 through 9 and back.) The program will be converted to machine language and written directly to disk as it is received. When the process is over, "*** File Transfer Completed! ***" will appear and you will have an exact copy of the program as it originally existed on its author's disk. If the information does not match, the CompuServe computer will either issue a warning that the program may not run on your machine and give you the option of aborting the transfer, or it will refuse to transmit and abort on its own.

Vidtex Limitations

Forty dollars is not a lot of money to pay for a program with the capabilities of Vidtex. Indeed a number of Commodore SIG members maintain that it is the best communications program for their machines and consider it a steal at the price. The more expensive, more feature-filled IBM/PC version wasn't issued until December of 1983, but shortly thereafter .IMG files began to appear in the IBM SIG's databases. Whether Vidtex will become a "standard" remains to be seen, but clearly it will make your life easier if you plan to tap CompuServe's free software resources frequently.

At the same time, it is important to be aware of the program's limitations. Because it does not support the XMODEM protocol, you will not be able to use it to obtain machine language programs from BBSs and RCPMs. Nor can it be used for transferring programs and files directly from one computer's disk to another's by cabling the two machines together. You can load a file into a buffer and transmit it from there, but the file can be no larger than the buffer itself.

If at all possible, spend some time poking around in the SIGs before deciding whether to buy Vidtex or not. Any simple terminal program can be used for this purpose. If such a program did not come with your computer, you can probably obtain one for your machine from one of the national or local users groups mentioned elsewhere in this book. In the course of your explorations you may find that the software you are most interested in doesn't require Vidtex at all. Or you may find that everything you want is a stored as a Vidtex image file. If that's the case, you'll find Vidtex a major convenience. You might also use a SIG's messaging function to ask members for their advice and opinions. If you are primarily interested in free software, this is an excellent way to spend the hours of free connect time that come with your CompuServe subscription.

Finally, whether you are a Vidtex user or not, you should be aware that the program files in the various SIGs are not always precisely named. For example, in some SIGs the extension .BIN and .HEX are used interchangeably. In others it is possible to find files labeled .IMG that have not been uploaded with Vidtex. Part of this is due to the fact that a term like *image* has different meanings. Technically it has nothing to do with the CompuServe Vidtex format at all. It is simply the memory image of a machine language program expressed in hexadecimal form. But to Vidtex users it means both this and a "machine-specific" Vidtex file. In addition, earlier versions of Vidtex did not offer the same sophisticated file transfer described earlier. The only way to sort this out is to explore a SIG's databases to get a feel for the conventions its members use.

Counting the Cost

The software on CompuServe isn't completely free, of course. Any more than the programs you obtain from a local users group or other organization are free. When using CompuServe or any other online service, you are charged for every minute you spend on the system. And whether you obtain your programs from CompuServe or a users group, there is a media (floppy disk or cassette tape) cost.

The least expensive way to get free software is through a users group. A users group will charge an average of $6 for a diskful of programs, including the disk they supply and a copying charge. Let's assume that the disks for your computer are formatted to hold 160K. To download 160K of programming from a SIG on CompuServe would cost from $4.80 (1200 baud, standard rate) to $8 (300 baud, standard rate). To this one must add the minimum cost per sign-on (10¢ to 21¢ at standard 300/1200-baud rates) and the hidden cost of "post-production processing" on your part. Most users group programs come to you ready to run. Downloaded files may have to be "word processed" to clean them up, and programs may have to be converted from hex to machine language.

It is important to keep the cost in mind. On the other hand, nothing can beat the "instant delivery" (and instant gratification) of downloading from the system. Obtaining a disk by mail from a users group could take two or three weeks. Nor should one overlook the immeasurable benefits of being able to confer with other individuals who own the same computer, regardless of their geographical location. One word of sound advice from a fellow SIG member about what hardware or software to buy or avoid can save you enough time and money to pay for your subscription many times over.

The tips and techniques presented in this chapter and in *The Complete Handbook of Personal Computer Communications* can help you keep your connect time charges at a minimum. You may find the following tables useful as a quick reference when deciding whether to download a program or not. To see how many kilobytes a program occupies, look at the program's description. The number between the date and "Accesses:" is the file's size in bytes. Some .IMG and .BIN files will have a number followed by a second number in parentheses. The first number is the file's size in hexadecimal format and the one to use when estimating the download cost. The second number is the number of bytes the file will contain once it has been downloaded, converted, and stored on disk.

CompuServe Connect Time Charges

	Prime Rate (8 AM – 6 PM)	*Standard Rate* (6 PM – 5 AM)
300 Baud	$12.50/hr = 21¢/min	$6.00/hr = 10¢/min
1200 Baud	$15.00/hr = 25¢/min	$12.50/hr = 21¢/min

No charge for connection via CompuServe's ComLink network. A $2 per hour surcharge is added for Telenet, Tymnet (DataPac), or Uninet access. Above rates apply to contiguous states and Canada. Rates for Alaska and Hawaii are higher. There is a minimum charge of one minute's worth of connect time (10¢ to 25¢) each time you sign on.

What Will It Cost at 300 Baud?

Program Size (in Kilobytes)	*Time Required*	*Prime Rate*	*Standard Rate*
1K	0.5 min.	$0.10	$0.5
16K	8 min.	$1.60	$0.80
32K	16 min.	$3.20	$1.60
64K	32 min.	$6.40	$3.20

What Will It Cost at 1200 Baud?

Program Size (in Kilobytes)	*Time Required*	*Prime Rate*	*Standard Rate*
1K	0.13 min.	$0.04	$0.03
16K	2 min.	$0.64	$0.48
32K	4 min.	$1.28	$0.96
64K	8 min.	$2.56	$1.92

...9...

The Source: *The Magic of User Publishing*

The Source is a full-featured database owned and operated by the Reader's Digest Association. The Source and the CompuServe Information Service (CIS) both came to life in 1979, but they were founded for very different reasons. This more than anything else is responsible for their distinctly different personalities, and for the differences in the free software you will find on each system. CIS was begun as an adjunct to CompuServe's primary remote data processing business. During the evening hours, after the banks and other financial institutions who used this service had closed up shop for the day, a significant percentage of CompuServe's computing capacity lay idle. Today's CompuServe Information Service developed out of a desire to make that power available to personal computer enthusiasts at very low rates. The Source, on the other hand, was from the very beginning intended to be a round-the-clock "information utility."

Consequently, although this is changing, CompuServe has always had more of a computer hobbyist orientation, while The Source has tended to attract businesspeople and non-programmers. The Source, for example, makes it possible for subscribers to exchange programs and other information through "SHAREFILES," but this facility lacks the sophistication of CompuServe's ACCESS. Special Interest Groups (SIGs) are well-developed and extensive on CompuServe but have only recently been added to The Source. Source SIGs have all the message exchange and database features of those on CompuServe, and many people may find them somewhat easier to use. But things are just getting started and, as of this writing, there are only three such organizations.

As a result, while many public domain programs are available in various nooks and crannies of The Source, you will not find the same depth of free software there that you will on CompuServe. Yet what The Source may lack in quantity, it makes up for in quality. Many of the programs here are quite good, and some of them will fill your ears with music, and your eyes with dazzling color graphics. In addition, you may find that it is somewhat easier to download software from The Source, since the sections with programs to offer tend to be menu-driven. Instead of entering a series of commands as you must in a CompuServe SIG, you are usually presented with a list of available programs and asked to enter the menu item for the ones you want.

Finally, while there are programs here for anyone who can run BASIC, CP/M, Forth, VisiCalc, or Pascal, the support for some brands of equipment is especially strong. There is an Epson Graftrax printer SIG, for instance, with a library of graphics software. And the support for Apple computers is so good that, if you own one, it might be reason enough to take out a Source subscription. (There's even a Source "private sector" database open to members of the Washington state–based super group, CALL-A.P.P.L.E. See Chapter 5.)

If you're one of the 2.4 million people who own a Texas Instruments computer, you will be happy to know about the support and more than 2,200 free programs available to you through The Source's TEXNET database. (The sponsors of this database confirm that TEXNET will continue, stronger and better than ever, even though the manufacture of TI computers will not.) And computer owners of every persuasion will find that the main system bulletin board (POST) offers a quick and easy way to learn about free software available for everything from a DEC Rainbow to an Osborne Executive.

A Quick Overview for New Users

The Source calls itself "America's Information Utility," and as you might guess, there's much more to the system than the free software collections we are about to discuss. Among other things, The Source offers what is probably one of the most powerful and convenient electronic mail systems in the industry. "SourceMail" or "SMAIL" is much more flexible and easier to use than the CompuServe system. Consequently, Source subscribers tend to use the phrase "Contact me via SMAIL" more freely than their CIS counterparts. It's either that or the fact that a Source "TCA123"-like account number is easier to remember and type than a "71234,567"-type CompuServe number. One way or another, this is something you will encounter frequently as you use the system, and it would be well worth your time to learn how to take advantage of the mail facility.

FreeTip: Here's a quick tutorial in SourceMail basics. You can reach the mail feature by following the menus. But to send a letter to someone any time the spirit moves you, you need to know the individual's account number, and you need to be at the Source Command Level. Do the following:

FreeTip continued

1. Type *QUIT* (or *STOP*) at the next available prompt, and continue to respond that way until you see this on your screen: ->.
2. Type *MAIL SEND TCA123*, where *TCA123* is the recipient's account number.
3. Respond to the resulting *Subject:* prompt with a clever, precious, or merely descriptive phrase.
4. When you see *Enter text:* begin typing your message.
5. When you have finished, generate a fresh line by hitting <ENTER>. Then type: *.S* (for "send") and hit <ENTER> again.

To return to what you were doing, type *QUIT* at the mail prompt, then type *MENU* at the resulting arrow prompt. This will return you to the Source Main Menu, allowing you to select the items that will take you back from whence you came.

The Source offers many other communications options as well. You can key in and send a Western Union MailGram™, dictate a phone message and have it transcribed and delivered via SourceMail, or send a single "hard copy" letter through the U.S. Postal Service's E-COM facility. (The cost is $1.35 for the first 41 lines, including postage. There is no required minimum number of letters.)

There is also a sophisticated computerized conferencing facility ("PARTICIPATE"), up-to-the-minute news from United Press International, stock quotes and financial information services, the Management Contents business publications database, a wide selection of online games, and more. The Source is described in much greater detail in *The Complete Handbook of Personal Computer Communications*. In this chapter we are going to be looking primarily at a single aspect of the system (User Publishing), but here are the main things you need to know:

- The Source, like CompuServe, is a time-sharing system consisting of many large computers. The Source uses Prime computers and a customized version of the PRIMOS operating system, while CompuServe runs on mainframes from Digital Equipment Corporation.

- The Source is based in the Washington, D.C., suburb of McLean, Virginia, where all the women are strong, all the men good-looking, and all the children above average. But anyone with a communicating computer and a modem can contact the system, regardless of the individual's physical location. (The author has received SourceMail letters from such far-flung locations as Melbourne, Australia; Haifa, Israel; and Paris, France.)

- Source subscriptions are available through most major computer stores. All subscribers receive 4K of storage on the system (equivalent to about two double-spaced typewritten pages; additional storage space is extra) and the monthly newsletter "SourceWorld." There is a monthly minimum charge of $10, $9 of which is credited against usage while $1 goes for account maintenance. All costs, including the initial $100 subscription fee, may be charged on a major credit card. The Source confirms that the 30-day, money-back guarantee it has long offered is still in effect. (See Figure 9.1 for more information.)

New User's Survival Kit

There are at least five ways to get where you want to go on the system, and all of them are explained in *The Complete Handbook of Personal Computer Communications.* However, most subscribers use one of two main techniques. The easiest is the "menu approach." When you sign on to The Source, you will be greeted by the Main Menu. By choosing selections from this menu and entering other selections from the subsequent menus that will appear, you can move to virtually any part of the system. The second technique, the "command approach," is faster and therefore less expensive. This is the method we will use in this chapter.

> **FreeTip:** If you are a brand new user, you will be better off staying with the menus for the time being. The Source, like any other database, takes a little getting used to. Although there are times when you will have to dip into the command mode, wait until you are comfortable with the menus and know your way around a bit better before switching to that technique exclusively. Remember, you can always go to the Command Level (->) by typing *QUIT* at a menu prompt, and you can always return to the Main Menu by typing *MENU* at the Command Level.

The Source supports many commands designed to make it easy for you to control the actions of the host computer. However, here are the ones that you *must* know to use the system effectively:

- <BREAK> This is the key to hit when you find yourself in the midst of something you want to get out of. When it receives this signal, the system will return you to a menu prompt or the Command Level.

- [<CONTROL><P>] Acts like <BREAK> and can be used if your computer does not have a <BREAK> key. Note that CompuServe uses a Control-C, while The Source uses Control-P.

- [<CONTROL><S>] Causes the onscreen scroll to stop temporarily by sending an X-OFF.

- [<CONTROL><Q>] Restarts an onscreen scroll by sending an X-ON.

- HELP When entered at a menu prompt or at a "-MORE-" pause, this will almost always generate a list of the commands available to you at that point. At the Command Level, enter *HELP*, followed by a space, followed by the name of the Source feature you are interested in. (See the FreeTip below.)

- OFF To sign off the system and stop the connect time meter from running, enter *OFF* at the Command Level. If you are using the menus, you must first enter *QUIT* to reach the Command Level (->).

Figure 9.1. Subscription Information for The Source

The Source
1616 Anderson Road
McLean, VA 22102
(800) 336-3330
(703) 734-7540

Initial subscription: $100; 30-day money-back guarantee.

Availability: Computer stores or from The Source.

Hours of operation: 24 hours.

Costs: Daytime (7 AM – 6 PM)
$20.75/hour for 300-baud service.
$25.75 per hour for 1200-baud service.

Evenings and Weekends (6 PM – 7 AM)
$7.75/hour for 300-baud service.
$10.75/hour for 1200-baud service.

These rates apply to the continental United States and Canada. Rates from Alaska and Hawaii are slightly higher. Telecommunications network charges are included in the above rates. The Source is accessible via Telenet, Uninet, or the firm's own Sourcelink network. Tymnet access was discontinued in April of 1984.

There is a minimum charge of 25¢ each time you sign on.

Monthly minimum fee: $10 ($1 for account maintenance; $9 credited against usage).

Comments: All charges are billed to your major credit card. Each subscriber receives a monthly statement detailing connect time used. If you have not bought your modem and communications software yet, be sure to watch for special promotional offers for these products in the computer magazines. A major modem manufacturer recently offered a free Source subscription (as well as a certain communications handbook) with the purchase of one of its units. If you own a Texas Instruments computer, be certain to tell your dealer that you want a "TI" Source account number. You will need this if you want to access the special TEXNET free software database. Although you can always switch later, it will be more convenient for you if you start out with a number like this. Call The Source at (800) 336-3366 (or at one of the numbers above) for more information. Also, see the TEXNET section later in this chapter.

FreeTip: Over 250 "help" files are available to you on The Source. Many are displayed in response to a request for help when you are using the menus. But some are accessible only from the Command Level. If you are a new user, it would be an excellent idea to print out the names of all such files. This will keep you from wasting time and money trying to guess whether the system has a particular help file. Do this:

1. Get to the Command Level.
2. Set your computer to download information.
3. Type: *HELP LIST*.

This will produce an alphabetized list of all the help files available on the system. Write your file to disk, and print it out after you sign off. If you store the printout with your Source manual, it will always be available for quick reference.

How to Find the Programs You Want

The free software on The Source is stored in three major areas: User Publishing, SHAREFILES, and the special TEXNET database for TI users. User Publishing is as characteristic of The Source as the SIGs are of CompuServe. As its name implies, it offers individuals an opportunity to publish articles, poems, commentary, and other pieces they have written. Unfortunately, the term "User Publishing" is rather misleading, for this area also serves as an umbrella for many features that are not quite what one would expect to find under this label. A more accurate definition of User Publishing, or "PUBLIC" as it is known on the system, is necessary.

User Publishing

In essence, PUBLIC provides an opportunity for any individual or group to offer its services through The Source. Thus, in addition to the subscriber-supplied poetry and at least one electronic novel, you will also find companies with software and computer equipment to sell. There are also at least two online magazines featuring information of interest to IBM/PC and PC/jr owners (*Real Times*) and Apple users (*S.A.U.G. Magazine*), an online computer matching service (Dial-a-Date), J. Baxter Newgate's weekly crossword puzzles, and much more. Altogether, there are are over 30 major User Publishing categories, and more are being added all the time.

In this chapter we will look at those User Publishing features known to have free software for you to download. However, there are a number of points to be aware of when using any PUBLIC feature. Each is operated and maintained by an individual or organization who has signed a contract with The Source agreeing to be responsible for all computer storage costs and other charges associated with the feature. In return, The Source pays the sponsor a royalty of 10 percent or more of the billable connect time subscribers spend using the feature.

This fact has a number of implications. First, it means that it is in the best interests of the sponsor to offer information, services, and free software that will attract a large number of users and encourage them to return frequently. Second, it means that although most PUBLIC features can be used at no additional cost, some sponsors may charge a membership fee to help defray their expenses. Finally, while The Source reserves the right to approve the contents of PUBLIC features, operators are free to implement customized control software. Consequently, the format and available options in some PUBLIC features may differ slightly.

SHAREFILES and POST

The SHAREFILES feature on The Source provides subscribers with a means of transferring programs and other information stored in their "personal filing cabinets" (computer storage space) to other users. For the creator of the file this is a two-step process. First the file must be uploaded into the filing cabinet, then the individual must enter the necessary commands to make it accessible to other users. Downloaders have the option of viewing the file on their screens or transferring it to their own filing cabinets to be read later. (For more information on how to use SHAREFILES, enter *HELP* at the Command Level, followed by *SHAREFILES*. Then enter *HELP GETSHR*. And later, *HELP PUTSHR*.)

Unfortunately, while the transfer system works quite well, there is no easy way to know what sharefiles are available. There is no SHARE-FILES database to search on the basis of keywords, filenames, or dates, as is the case with CompuServe's ACCESS program. The only way to learn of a free software program stored as a sharefile is for the uploader to tell you that it exists. Thus, most uploaders announce their sharefiles on the main Source bulletin board, POST. Since POST notices *can* be searched on the basis of keywords, that is what you must do to learn of the existence of any sharefiles of interest. (We'll show you a quick way to do it later in this chapter.)

TEXNET

As mentioned, the special TEXNET database is accessible only to those with Texas Instruments computers. To enter this section, your Source account number must begin with "TI." (If you already have a different account number, you may switch at no charge.) In addition to making available more than 2200 public domain TI programs, each of which can be downloaded to your computer whenever you like, TEX-NET offers a number of features designed to take advantage of the unique capabilities of TI equipment. For example, TEXNET supports the use of the TI Solid-State Speech synthesizer for those who want to *hear* as well as read the information coming into their computers. In addition, you will find many programs in the database to help you write customized software for that device yourself. The database also offers special color graphics functions that can produce onscreen pictures, diagrams, and charts. These features are not available in any other part of The Source.

Perhaps most important of all in light of the withdrawal of Texas Instruments, Inc., from the home computer market, TEXNET is not only alive and well, it is thriving. TEXNET is now operated by SOFT-MAIL, Inc., in partnership with the International 99/4A Users Group, the organization that started the service several years ago. Conversations with Don Bynum of SOFTMAIL and Charlie LaFara of the TI users group confirm that exciting things are afoot for TEXNET and TI users. We'll look at them in more detail later in this chapter.

Figure 9.2. The Menu Approach

If you choose to use the menu approach when moving around on The Source, here are the paths to follow to reach the software libraries in User Publishing and the bulletin board in POST. The items on various menus are subject to change, of course, so it is best to think of these as examples. More than likely, however, the titles of the menus themselves ("Creating and Computing," etc.) will remain the same. These are the names we will use when referring to specific menus in the text.

THE SOURCE MAIN MENU

1 NEWS AND REFERENCE RESOURCES
2 BUSINESS/FINANCIAL MARKETS
3 CATALOGUE SHOPPING
4 HOME AND LEISURE
5 EDUCATION AND CAREER
6 MAIL AND COMMUNICATIONS
7 CREATING AND COMPUTING
8 SOURCE*PLUS

Enter item number or HELP

CREATING AND COMPUTING

1 MICROLINE
2 USER PUBLISHING
3 SOURCE MANUALS
4 TEXT EDITOR
5 FILE TRANSFER TO THE SOURCE
6 PROGRAMMING
Enter item number or HELP *2*

MAIL AND COMMUNICATIONS

1 MAIL
2 CHAT
3 POST ←——— **Search for SHAREFILES.**
4 PARTICIPATE
5 MAILGRAM MESSAGES
6 ECOM MESSAGES
Enter item number or HELP *3* (***Results not shown.***)

WELCOME TO USER PUBLISHING

1 PUBLICATION CATEGORIES ←——— **See next menu.**

2 MEMBERS-ONLY PUBLICATIONS ——— **S.A.U.G. Program Libraries/SIGs.**
3 ALL ABOUT USER PUBLISHING
4 COMMENTS BY READERS/WRITERS

```
5 BEST-SELLERS
6 NEW PUBLICATIONS
7 PUBLICATION INDEX          <——— See Figure 9.3
Enter item number or HELP 1

USER PUBLISHING CATEGORIES

1 THE WORLD OF COMPUTING     <——— See next menu.
2 SERVICES
3 USING THE SOURCE
4 GAMES AND CREATIONS
5 MAGAZINES AND JOURNALS
6 NOVELS
7 THINGS FOR SALE

Enter item number or HELP 1

THE WORLD OF COMPUTING

1 TRADEWINDS              CL3035
2 PUBLIC ACCESS SYSTEMS   TCU583  <——— Large searchable BBS phone list.
3 APPLE CITY              TCD912  <——— Apple magazine and software.
4 THE MUSES               TCP831
5 S.A.U.G. MAGAZINE       TCA265  <——— Apple magazine.
6 PRODUCT REVIEWS         TCY617  <——— VisiCalc templates.
7 REAL TIMES MAGAZINE     TCS091  <——— IBM/PC and PC/jr magazine.
Enter item number or HELP
```

Note: You can always return to the *previous* menu by entering *P* at a menu prompt instead of making a selection. Depending on where you are at the time, entering *QUIT* or *STOP* will either take you back to the first menu of a feature, or it will take you to the Command Level.

Entering *MENU* at any prompt will usually take you back to The Source Main Menu.

FreeTip: There is one command you absolutely must enter before you begin to download software on The Source. Unless you specify otherwise, Source users who are online at the same time can interrupt you to ask if you would like to engage in a real-time CHAT. This is a friendly gesture and something you should try yourself. But you do not want to see: *** CHAT FROM TCA123 *** appear on your screen in the midst of a download. If this happens, you will have to start all over again. To prevent it, do the following:

1. Get to the Command Level
2. Enter: *CHAT-OFF* (Note the space before the hyphen.)
3. Enter *MENU* or some other command to be on your way.

Be sure to do this as soon as you sign on for a software-hunting session. If you don't, you will have to leave the User Publishing area, execute the above commands, and return to User Publishing to download your program. (For information on how to make the system automatically turn CHAT off when you sign on, see the explanation of C__ID files in *The Complete Handbook.*) To enable CHAT again, type *CHAT-ON* at the Command Level.

FreeTip: There is one other feature you should know about. Though less of a problem than a CHAT interruption, turning off the *-MORE-* prompts before you begin a download can eliminate the need to remove them later. Most areas of The Source are set up to present a *-MORE-* prompt after displaying 24 lines. Hitting <ENTER> will cause the next 24 lines to scroll up. The prompt can be supressed, however, if instead of hitting <ENTER>, you type in *NOCRT* and then hit <ENTER>. The system will come back with a final *-MORE-*. Respond by hitting <ENTER> again, and the scroll will continue uninterrupted.

The *-MORE-* supression only lasts as long as you are using a particular feature. If you are in APPLE CITY and then go to TELERESOURCES, you will have to remember to enter *NOCRT* again. (If *NOCRT* does not work, try *NOMORE* or *HARDCOPY*.) Be sure to take this step at your first opportunity—before you get to the point where you are ready to download a program.

How to Download Software from User Publishing

You can reach all User Publishing features by following the menus shown in Figure 9.2. And if you are more comfortable with the menus, by all means take that approach. Since each User Publishing area offers its own internal menus, however, you can combine the best of both worlds (and save connect time charges in the process) if you use this procedure:

1. At The Source Main Menu prompt, type *QUIT* to get to the Command Level.

2. When the arrow prompt (->) appears, type *PUBLIC* [Location Number]. See Figure 9.3 for location numbers. With some User Publishing programs, you can add the word DIRECT to the above string. This will let you bypass the two-paragraph Source disclaimer

that normally appears when you enter User Publishing. This will take you directly to the target area, where you will be able to use the feature's internal menus.

The First Step: Download the Index

Before you begin your software quest, take a moment to download the index of User Publishing categories. Follow the menus until you reach "Welcome to User Publishing" or type *PUBLIC* at the Command Level. Then enter the selection for the publications index. Capture the results and store the file to disk. Then print it out after you are offline. If you keep the printout with your Source manual, you will always know the location numbers of the features you want to use.

User Publishing is a growing category, however. So to stay on top of things you might want to repeat the above procedure every few months or so. You might also want to search the POST User Publishing category for announcements of new additions of possible interest. To help you get started downloading free software immediately, and to give you a glimpse of the non-software features available, we have printed a recent User Publishing index in Figure 9.3. You might want to use this as a guide in the beginning, and download your own copy later.

Figure 9.3. User Publishing Categories and Location Numbers

The following index of The Source's User Publishing area includes the title of the feature, the location number you should enter after typing *PUBLIC* at the Command Level, and the SourceMail address (account number) of the person responsible for each feature.

TITLE	LOCATION NUMBER	PUBLISHER
APPLE CITY	113	(TCD912)
CHRISTOLOGY COURSE	124	(STI016)
CLASSIC & EXOTIC CARS	173	(CL3309)
CLEARPOINT INT'L. NEWS	158	(TI2560)
CROSSWORD PUZZLES	142	(ST9912)
DIAL-A-DATE	122	(TCA550)
DICHECK	132	(TCC744)
EATER'S DIGEST	156	(STY542)
ELEPHANT WALK ENTERPRISES	172	(TCT170)
IMAGE MICRO CATALOG	171	(ST7367)
INDEPENDENT RECORD RELEASES	175	(STX453)
JOBHUNTER'S HANDBOOK	126	(STV709)
THE MUSES	151, 114	(TCP831)
MYLAR'S WARP	161	(MDR002)
NEWSBYTES	155	(STH256)
NEW TECH TIMES	125	(BBI599)
ONLINE EDUCATOR	157	(ST6588)
OXBRIDGE LEGAL FORMS	123	(STN250)

User Publishing Categories and Location Numbers (continued)

PAR MT. TELEGRAPH	153	(TCS780)
PRODUCT REVIEWS	116	(TCY617)
PUBLIC ACCESS SYSTEMS	112	(TCU583)
REAL TIMES MAGAZINE	117	(TCS091)
RIDEXCHANGE	121	(ST0926)
S.A.U.G. MAGAZINE	115, 133	(TCA265)
S.A.U.G. LIBRARIES	22	(TCA265)
S.I.G.O.P. LIBRARY	21	(TCV176)
SOURCETREK	152	(TCE054)
TELERESOURCE	174	(ST3899)
TRADEWINDS	111	(CL3035)
VAULT OF AGES	141	(TCY971)
W_I_N_K MAGAZINE	154, 131	(TCV176)

"DELETE Filename"—The Most Crucial Money-Saving Command

No one knows how many Source subscribers are unintentionally paying storage costs for material that they never wanted to save because they are not aware that it has been placed in their personal filing cabinet. But one can guess that the number is large. This is not a nefarious plot on the part of The Source to secretly squeeze additional revenue out of subscribers. It is more on the order of a thoughtful feature that can go wrong if subscribers don't understand how it works.

Here's the problem. When you are in User Publishing or sending SourceMail or using many other Source services and there is a problem on the communications line, the system tries to recover as much of what you were doing as possible. The same thing can happen if you issue a BREAK signal at an inopportune time.

In both cases, the system will store as much of the text or program as possible in a "temporary" file within your personal filing cabinet. These files are given names that begin with *T$* ("tee-dollar") and end with some four-digit number. But they aren't really "temporary" since they will stay right where the system put them—at a cost of 50¢ per 2K per month—until you delete them.

This "safety feature" works quite well, as long as you are aware that the system takes this action and as long as you remember to regularly check your filing cabinet for T$ files. However, the file manipulation commands used by The Source are among its most complex features. They are definitely not for the squeamish or tender-hearted. Consequently, many subscribers *never* check their files. And the charges mount up month after month.

Ideally, "temporary" files should really *be* temporary. But until The Source implements a procedure that will automatically delete them after a certain number of days, you will have to take the responsiblity yourself. This is not difficult. The hardest part is remembering to do it. Here are the steps to follow:

1. Get to the Command Level.

2. Enter <F> for a complete description or <L> for a quick list of filenames. In both cases the filename will be the last item to appear.

3. Note the complete names of any T$ files.

4. Type *DELETE T$*nnnn, where the *n*s represent a four-digit number.

You do not necessarily have to do this every week or every month. The key thing to remember is whether or not the system behaved in a strange manner, whether you had difficulty signing off, and whether there were any communications line problems or "network errors" during your online session. If any of these things happens, be sure to check your filespace for any T$ files at the next opportunity.

Transferring Control to User Publishing . . . Please stand by . . .

Apple City

Focus: All models of Apple computers.

Coordinator: Walt Marcinko, TCD912.

How to Get There: PUBLIC 113 DIRECT.

Cost of Membership: None.

What you will find:

```
                * ==========*
                  APPLE CITY
                * ==========*
       (C) 1984 BY WALT MARCINKO (TCD912)
                 MAIN STREET
                 -----------
         1 . . .  What's New DD/MM/YY
         2 . . .  Welcome To Apple City
         AS . . . APPLE SQUARE
         PL . . . PROGRAM LIBRARY
         AG . . . ART GALLERY
         GS . . . GENERAL STORE
```

Command:

PROGRAM LIBRARY
1 . . . How to Use Library
2 . . . Sounds of Apple
3 . . . Kinetica #4
4 . . . Disk Map / Clean
5 . . . Music - Bach Preludio
6 . . . Music - Bach Gavotte
7 . . . Music - 'Sylvia'
8 . . . Music - Beethoven
9 . . . Music - Schubert Moment
10 . . . Music - Schubert Scherzo
11 . . . RAMdisk //e
12 . . . Catalog Sorter
13 . . . Super Menu
14 . . . Invaders Game
15 . . . Fast Copy

ART GALLERY
1 . . . Visitor's Guide
2 . . . Beethoven (TCY761)
3 . . . J. S. Bach (TCY761)
4 . . . Space Shuttle Launch (TCD912)
5 . . . Satellite (CL0774)
6 . . . Shuttle Landing (CL1312)
7 . . . King Tut (TCD912)
8 . . . Receiver
9 . . . Shipper
10 . . . Display
11 . . . Documentation

Comments and Considerations: Apple City is without a doubt one of the outstanding features in User Publishing. Walt Marcinko and his assistants, Hyman Himem, Loni Lomem, and Victor Vector, Director (all of 6502 Main Street, Apple City, U.S.A.) have done a superb job of organizing, formatting, and maintaining a database and program library that is both interesting and easy to use. The free software collection is changed and updated regularly, and all the software is tested both before and after it is uploaded. Mr. Marcinko personally downloads every program to make certain that it works as it should before transferring the file to the Apple City library.

The very first time you enter Apple City, be sure to download the "Welcome to Apple City" file, since this will give you an overview and command summary. From then on, be certain to download the "What's New" file for a summary of the new programs and files that have been added to various locations. It's always fun to explore, but this will give you a map.

You should also pick up the file explaining how to use the Program Library, and you'll need both the "Receiver" file and the "Documentation" file from the Art Gallery. The high resolution graphics files are stored in a compressed format to save storage space and download time. By running the "Receiver" program on your machine, you can expand each file to its original form.

The download procedure is straightforward and the step-by-step instructions supplied at the beginning of each file make it easy. Unlike many online sources of free software, Mr. Maricinko places a description of the program you are about to receive and any additional points you should be aware of at the beginning of the file. You are then given the option of downloading the program or returning to the menu.

There is only one serious omission, and that is a lack of an explanation of the Apple EXEC command required to process each program after you have captured it. The documentation at the beginning of each program does tell you to save the download in the form FILENAME.TXT and they type *EXEC FILENAME.TXT* from Applesoft BASIC. But the standard documentation that comes with each Apple computer spends very little time on this command, and new owners may have difficulty puzzling it out.

How to "EXEC" a File

Since you will encounter the term "EXEC" both here and in the other Apple-based features in User Publishing, it may be worth taking a moment to explain how it works. There are only a few things you need to know. First, EXEC tells your Apple to take its instructions from a textfile and enter them into memory just as if you were typing them yourself at the keyboard. This is rather like a player piano responding to a punched paper piano roll. If the file contains the lines of a BASIC program, EXEC-ing it produces the same results as if you had sat there typing every line.

Better yet, if the BASIC program is so designed, it can be used to *build a machine language program file*. This is yet another solution to the problem of communicating binary files discussed in Chapter 7, and most of the programs in Apple City use this technique. When you EXEC them, they poke bytes into memory. When you RUN them the first time, they automatically record the memory image they have created as a binary file on disk. From then on, you have only to type *BRUN FILENAME* to load and execute the program at machine language speed.

The FP you will see at the beginning of these files makes certain that your computer is in Applesoft ("floating point") BASIC and that its memory is clear. The MON command tells the computer's internal MONITOR program to listen up and take notes. The NOMON command at the end of most programs turns the monitor program off. For more information, see the *Apple DOS Programmer's Manual*.

"The Sounds of Apple"

If you want to see how much fun online free software can be, download one of the music programs from the Apple City Program Library. They will knock your ears off. The Bach Preludio, for example, reproduces one the selections from *Switched On Bach*, the album that introduced the Moog synthesizer to the public more than a decade ago. The sound is so good that if you didn't know better, you would think you were listening to the album and not the Apple.

The program called "Sounds of Apple" is a special "front end" program created by Mr. Marcinko. It will present a menu to allow you to select each of the other songs in the library by pressing a single key. You can use "Sounds of Apple" with a single music program, but obviously you must first download and EXEC any selection that you want to be able to select from its menu.

A word of caution is in order, however. Mr. Marcinko makes a point of keeping Apple City fresh and up-to-date, so you may not find these specific programs when you pay your first visit. There will almost certainly be other music programs, however. And if the past is any guide, they will be of the same high quality. [Be sure to check the General Store for information on ordering the "Best of P/D" (public domain)disks prepared for Apple City users.]

The Independent Record Release Index

Focus: Information resource and contact point for musicians, agents, and others in "the biz."

Coordinator: PAN (The Performing Artists Network of North America), STX453.

How to Get There: PUBLIC 175.

Cost of Membership: None.

Comments: This is not a place one would normally look for free software. Indeed the database has only one program, but it's quite interesting and well worth considering. Look for "FREE-SOFTWARE" on the PAN menu that greets you when you enter. The program is called "BACH to BASIC," by Perry Leopold, and it is designed to let you compose music from your computer keyboard. Notes are represented by their respective letter keys. There are options for selecting tempo and octave, and once a song has been composed, it can be saved to disk and played or altered at any time. We ran it on an IBM/PC with an Amdek Color II monitor and found the color graphics to be better than many commercially available programs. Impressive.

The program is written in a "generic" dialect of Advanced BASIC and intended to be run on many different computers. There are a few minor problems, however, that illustrate the kinds of things you can expect to encounter when downloading any kind of generic free software. One problem was caused by a communications error. Somewhere along the way "PRINT" became "RINT" in line 1030, and the computer did not like that when it began to run the routine that starts there.

Typos can be fixed with a BASIC editor or word processing program. But other problems can be more serious. When the program began executing another routine, for example, the computer returned an error message indicating that there was a RETURN without a GOSUB in line 1430. If you are fluent in your computer's BASIC, this is not too difficult to fix. But adapting the program for your machine could be a problem if you are a new owner. Consequently, before paying to download this program (about five minutes at 300 baud), make sure you have a users group or friend to turn to for help.

S.A.U.G. Magazine

(Source Apple Users Group)

Focus: Apple computers.

Coordinator: Craig Vaughan, Software Sorcery, TCA265.

How to Get There: PUBLIC 115 DIRECT.

Cost of Membership: None.

What You Will Find:

Source Apple Users Group
File Directory

Article #	Name	Reading Time
1	WHAT.IS.SAUG	0:40
2	FILE-CATALOG	2:08
3	APPLESOFT-TUTORIAL	0:09
4	ACCOUNT-LIST	1:25
5	COMMANDS	0:05
6	ABBREV.COMMAND	1:37
7	LONG-LINES	0:52
8	PRINTING.ONLINE	1:00
9	INSURANCE	1:41
10	APPLE.//E	7:24
11	GENERAL.MGR.PATCH	0:57
12	WORDSTAR.APPLE///	1:18
13	RS232.INFORMATION	3:23
14	E-COM	0:42
15	DAJAX	0:42
16	ERROR.TRAPPING	2:22
17	USER.KEYS	2:08
18	APPLE.SERVICE	5:00
19	REGIONAL.CENTERS	0:37
20	DISK.COMMANDS	1:52
21	MACH.LANGUAGE	7:00

```
22  BLOWN.PASCAL.DISKS          3:57
23  ONERR.GOTO                  3:08
24  APPLESOFT.BUGS              3:02
25  VIDEO.GLOSSARY              3:06
26  APPLE.PIE                   0:45
27  OKIDATA/APPLEWRITER         0:37
28  JOEL.COMDEX                 1:48

You may enter a list of Article
numbers separated by spaces.
```

Comments and Considerations: This feature is most likely to appeal to Apple owners with a strong interest in programming and the technical aspects of their machines. Most of the filenames in the directory are descriptive enough to be meaningful to Apple owners, and we will not go into them here. S.A.U.G. is a member of the International Apple Core (see Chapter 5). It is operated under the supervision of Craig Vaughan of Software Sorcery, Inc. Mr. Vaughan and his firm are responsible for the ABBS Apple bulletin board software discussed in Chapter 10. In addition, as the former technical director of The Source, he is quite familiar with the system's ins and outs and unpublished commands.

All Source subscribers are free to use *S.A.U.G. Magazine,* and we can recommend the "ACCOUNT-LIST" file on the menu to everyone. It contains an extensive list of the SourceMail addresses for people employed by and otherwise involved with the utility. Most of the available free S.A.U.G. software will not be found here. It is located in the S.A.U.G. Library, a feature requiring a $10 membership fee. You'll find more details in the "WHAT.IS.SAUG" file.

S.A.U.G. Library

Focus: Apple DOS, BASIC, Forth, Pascal, CP/M.

Coordinator: Craig Vaughan, Software Sorcery, TCA265.

How to Get There: PUBLIC 22 DIRECT.

Cost of Membership: $10 a year.

What You Will Find:

```
Please select a function
1) PASCAL and CP/M Library
2) DOS, BASIC, AND FORTH Library
3) SAUG 'Disearch' Program
4) Quit
```

DOS, BASIC, AND FORTH Library		
Program #	Name	Listing Time
1	CATALOG	0:45
2	A.EDITOR	5:59
3	A.COMPACTOR	2:46
4	A.REGATTA	3:18
5	A.POINT&FIGURE	2:09
6	FORTH.SCREEN	2:09
7	FORTH.LIFE	1:49
8	VISI-PRINT	0:50
9	BLOAD.UTIL	0:29
10	A.M/L	1:49
11	A.BILL-CHECKER	2:22
12	A.CALENDAR	3:50
13	A.STOCK-TRADER	4:36
14	A.HIRES.DEMO	0:13
15	A.MENU.PRGM	0:44
16	A.FILEREADER	0:15
17	A.VERT.ANT	3:31
18	A.HIRES.ERSE	0:06
19	B.SILNT.BOLD	0:16
20	A.CHEKBKBAL	1:13
21	A.POLAR	0:50
22	A.ERR.HANDLR	1:59
23	A.STRINGIO	1:16
24	A.BARGRAPH	3:07

PASCAL and CP/M Library		
Program #	Name	Listing Time
1	CPM.INDEX.ASM	33:05
2	CPM.INDEX.DOC	6:13
3	EPSON.TEXT	5:56
4	COMPARE.TEXT	7:58
5	CLOCKDOC	3:15
6	CLOCKSTUFF	1:44
7	CLOCK	4:35
8	ACLOCK4	5:04
9	QUICKSORT	0:29
10	SCREENCNTL	0:34
11	PICO-ADVENTURE	4;35
12	DVGREETING.TEXT	0:23
13	SPEC.CHAR.TEXT	0:52
14	DVGREETING.DOC	0:43
15	CATALOG	0:36
16	FASTIO.TEXT	4:55

Comments and Considerations: As the onscreen prompts will advise you, the first thing to do when entering this feature is to download the catalogue files that appear on both menus. Here is a short sample of what they contain:

CHEKBKBAL - Checkbook balancer.
STOCK-TRADER - A good stock market simulation.
HIRES.DEMO - Hi-res graphics demo.
POINT&FIGURE - Hi-res point & figure stock charting.
EDITOR - A program to edit diskettes at the BYTE level.

Generally speaking, none of the programs on either menu are anything to get excited about. But there's a reason why the collection appears pretty lackluster. And things are about to change. At this writing, the S.A.U.G. Library has only recently come under its present management, and changes have yet to be implemented. As Mr. Vaughan writes in a letter to all S.A.U.G. members: "We plan to add a regular monthly newsletter for members only and to increase the software library. To do this we need your help and support. If you are interested in providing material for either the library or the newsletter, please contact us via SourceMail." Mr. Vaughan can be reached at TCA265 or care of Software Sorcery, 7927 Jones Branch Drive, Suite 400, McLean, VA 22102.

S.I.G.O.P. Library

Focus: Special Interest Group bulletin boards.

Coordinator: Licensed SysOps.

How to Get There: PUBLIC 21.

Cost of Membership: Determined by SysOp, average of $20.

What You Will Find:

Contents of the S.I.G.O.P Library

ITEM #	NAME	
1	SIGBOARD.TXT	Explains SIGBOARD concept
2	APPLE-III.SIG	SIG for Apple III users
3	CP/M.SIG	SIG for CP/M (tm) users
4	GRAFTRAX.SIG	SIG for Epson/Graftrax Users

Comments and Considerations: A company called SigNet Services, Ltd., has developed a Source-based software package that makes it possible for individuals or organizations to create their own online special interest groups. The SysOps (system operators) license the software from SigNet, and SigNet manages the technical aspects. However, because of the financial details of the license agreement, most SysOps must charge an annual membership fee to recover their expenses. The SigNet software provides both a sophisticated message exchange system and a database for the storage of free programs and files. But while anyone can scan the messages in the CP/M SIG or GrafTrax SIG, only members may use the databases. The Apple /// SIG is completely closed to nonmembers.

For more information on the other two SIGs, type *M* (for "membership") at one of the internal prompts. Or contact:

CP/M SIG
ARM Associates
P.O. Box 652
Fairport, NY 14450
SourceMail: TCD877

GrafTrax SIG
C. Edward Chapman
P.O. Box 3386
Alexandria, VA 22302
SourceMail: TCV176

Other User Publishing Features to Consider...

- Product Reviews (PUBLIC 116).
  As its name implies, this is a database containing published reviews of

various computer hardware and software products. It also contains a number of VisiCalc templates. We found the database difficult to use and notably lacking in explanations and instructions. Perhaps things will improve in the future.

- Public Access Systems (PUBLIC 112).
This is an extensive keyword searchable database of BBS and RCPM telephone numbers. Definitely worth a look if you are interested in finding a bulletin board system near you or a system specializing in a particular subject or computer.

- *Real Times* magazine (PUBLIC 117).
This is an excellent feature and an ideal source of information for IBM/PC and PCjr owners. Editor and creator Tom Kashuba (TCS091) is a computer professional with both extensive technical knowledge and impressive writing skills. Mr. Kashuba also takes great pains to keep his publication current. (*Real Times* carries an average of seven columns a month and is updated on a weekly basis.)

  Within hours of the announcement of the IBM XT, for example, *Real Times* had a complete description and analysis online and ready for its readers, making it the first publication in North America to carry news of that computer. *Real Times* responded with equal rapidity when the PCjr was announced in November of 1983. (Look for *Real Times* to become a major source of PCjr support and information as that computer comes on stream.)

  In addition, every experienced subscriber will be interested in Mr. Kashuba's SourceAid articles explaining some of the system's little-known commands and features. You may occasionally find short routines and helpful bits of code in the various articles, but since *Real Times* is not a major source of free software, we have not featured it here. (Be sure to download the main "help" file for information on the customized commands and features Mr. Kashuba has added to this User Publishing area.)

- Teleresource (PUBLIC 174).
This is an online shopping service offering namebrand floppy disks and software at discounted prices. Inexpensive ($10) game and other programs are available for direct download into your machine. There are also a number of free programs (BIORHYTHMS, BANNER, GUNNER, etc.) provided as a promotional offer. Unless otherwise specified, all programs are written in generic BASIC. The menus and instructions are easy to understand and follow. Just remember that you must "mark" the software you want as you review the descriptions, then return to the menu and select the "download" option. The programs you have selected will be transmitted in succession.

The POST/SHAREFILES One-Two Punch

As we have said, the only practical way to learn of the existence of free software stored in an individual's SHAREFILES area is to scan the POST bulletin board for announcements. POST is also an excellent way to discover other sources of free software, for there are many people with libraries or programs to swap or trade.

POST has a number of advanced features, but for our purposes you need only remember one command: *POST S K SOFTWARE*. If you type this at the Command Level, the resulting list should contain every relevant notice on the POST bulletin board. Alternatively, you could follow the menus to POST, enter *S* for "scan" when prompted for your pleasure, enter *K* for "keyword" at the next prompt, and finish up by entering *SOFTWARE* as your keyword.

Either approach will generate a listing similar to that shown below. There are only two other things to remember. The most efficient technique for using POST is to first scan the notices, select those you wish to read, and then read each one in succession. Since the first 22 lines will begin to scroll off your screen as soon as you hit <ENTER> at the *-MORE-* prompt, it is important to write down the item numbers of the notices you want to read before continuing. When all the items have been listed, you may type in all of the item numbers you have selected. Separate them with commas or spaces.

The second thing to be aware of is that The Source automatically purges all notices that are more than two weeks old. So it can be worthwhile to check POST regularly for new announcements. Alternatively, you might limit your search to just those notices POSTed after the date of your last search. See your Source manual for instructions.

One of the advantages of scanning for SOFTWARE is that you are virtually certain to hit every free software notice, regardless of its location on the board. The disadvantage is that you will also locate many notices that are not relevant to your quest. So read carefully.

Here is a greatly abbreviated version of what you can expect to see:

```
* 1   TCA157 FREE OSBORNE 1 SOFTWARE!(OSBORNE)
  2   ST3030 EDUC.SOFTWARE (AD)(APPLE)
  3   STR087 HELP WITH MODEM SOFTWARE(IBM)
* 4   BKP129 DEC LA50 PRINTER SOFTWARE-FREE(DEC)
  5   STU938 WANTED USED SOFTWARE FOR IBM-PC(IBM)
  6   BBG328 COMMUNICATION FOR COMMODORE 64(SOFTWARE-WANTED)
  7   BBL950 HAM RADIO CW AND DXCC SOFTWARE(HAM-RADIO)
  8   BBL568 APPLE SOFTWARE FOR TRADE OR SALE(APPLE)
  9   STP429 INFOCOM TRADE TI-PC(SOFTWARE-SALE)
  10  BBK363 INFOCOM GAME EXCHANGE DESIRED(SOFTWARE-WANTED)
  11  BBB214 PEACHTREE TO LOTUS CONVERSION(SOFTWARE-WANTED)
  12  BBB214 KERMIT WANTED(SOFTWARE-WANTED)
```

```
13  BBL845 DEC RAINBOW SOFTWARE(DEC)
14  STX453 FREE SOFTWARE!!!(SOFTWARE-SALE)
15  BBL092 MODEL IV SOFTWARE TO EMULATE DEC(TRS-80)
16  STG833 VIC20 & COM. 64(SOFTWARE-SALE)
17  STX453 FREE MUSIC PROGRAM AVAILABLE(SOFTWARE-WANTED)
18  TCD912 "BEST OF P.D." (APPLE)(SOFTWARE-SALE)
19  ST2256 MEDICAL MANAGEMENT DRG/CAP(SOFTWARE-SALE)
```

We've marked the two notices we'll look at with an asterisk. At the appropriate prompt, you would merely type *4,1* and hit <ENTER> to read the notices in that order. In each case the bulletin's header will appear and you will be given the opportunity to either read the complete text or move on to the next notice on your list. Here are the two examples we've chosen:

```
Category:DEC
Subject:DEC LA50 PRINTER SOFTWARE-FREE
From:BKP129
Posted:DD MMM 9:57 pm

<N>ext,<PO>st, or Return for text-

MENU DRIVEN IN MBASIC 86.
GENERATES THE ESCAPE SEQUENCES NECESSARY TO GIVE YOU THESE EXTRA
FEATURES:
6 HORIZONTAL PITCHES
6 VERTICAL PITCHES
STANDARD, BOLD, & ENHANCED TEXT
UNDERLINE OPTION
ALSO SUPPORTS FORM LENGTH,TOF & NON-TRUNCATED TEXT.

SEND BLANK DISKETTE & RETURN POSTAGE TO:
RICK NOVACKY
14569 AVERY CIRCLE
E. LIVERPOOL, OHIO 43920

AND WHY NOT INCLUDE ONE OF YOUR FAVORITES?
-More-

Category:OSBORNE
Subject:FREE OSBORNE 1 SOFTWARE!
From:TCA157
Posted:DD MMM 7:45 pm

<N>ext,<PO>st, or Return for text-
```

```
*****************************************************************
*                FREE PROGRAMS FOR THE OSBORNE 1!               *
*                          by Greg Dahl                         *
*                               —                               *
*                   "User supported software"                   *
*              try any program with no obligation               *
*                               —                               *
*                GL—a General Ledger System                     *
*                   written in dBASE II                         *
*          WSPATCH3— updates to Wordstar ver. 2.26              *
*                               —                               *
*             VMAP2—gives variable map and cross                *
*                   references for BASIC programs               *
*          BCSQUASH—reduces size of BASIC programs              *
*                   by removing blanks, comments                *
*          DBSQUASH—reduces size of dBASE II programs           *
*          MULTREG— performs multiple regression                *
*                               —                               *
*     Type CRTLST SFILES>TCA157>FREEPROGS at command            *
*                level for more information                     *
*****************************************************************
```

Notice the phrase beginning "CRTLST SFILES..." in the above box. This is your key to obtaining more information about the user supported software Mr. Dahl has to offer. Get to the Command Level and enter the specified string. Mr. Dahl's "FREEPROGS" file will begin to scroll onto your screen.

TEXNET for TI Users

TEXNET was started by Mr. Charles LaFara, the founder and president of the International 99/4A Users Group profiled in Chapter 5, and much of the free software available from that group can be downloaded from TEXNET. The service is now operated by SOFTMAIL, Inc., a joint venture of Mr. LaFara's group and several other individuals. We spoke to both Mr. LaFara and Mr. Don Bynum, the head of SOFTMAIL, and learned that great things are planned to support TI owners and make TEXNET better than ever. However, at this writing the details are in the process of being finalized, and neither gentleman was free to discuss them.

The following information is taken directly from the online description of the TEXNET service (pre-SOFTMAIL). If you are a TI owner, you're sure to find it interesting. Be sure to request a "TI" Source account number should you decide to buy a subscription, since this is your key to getting into TEXNET. There is no additional charge for using this service. For the latest information type *HELP TEXNET* at The Source Command Level.

SPECIAL FEATURES OF THE TEXNET SERVICE INCLUDE:

TI SOFTWARE EXCHANGE

- A VAST SOFTWARE LIBRARY WHICH CAN BE "DOWNLOADED" TO THE DISK MEMORY SYSTEM OF THE TI HOME COMPUTER FOR LATER USE...FREE OF CHARGE!

TI-CHAT

-AN ENHANCEMENT TO THE SOURCE CHAT CAPABILITY, TI-CHAT ALLOWS TEXNET SUBSCRIBERS TO HAVE THEIR CHAT MESSAGES SPOKEN WITH THE TI SOLIDSTATE SPEECH(TM) SYNTHESIZER.

COLOR, SOUND, AND GRAPHICS

-ON THE TEXNET INFORMATION SERVICE, TI HOME COMPUTER OWNERS CAN ALSO VIEW GRAPHIC FEATURES, SUCH AS PICTURES AND DIAGRAMS. USE OF THE SOLID STATE SPEECH(TM) SYNTHESIZER ALLOWS TEXNET SUBSCRIBERS TO HEAR TEXT SPOKEN ON EITHER THE SOURCE OR THE TEXNET SERVICE.

OTHER FEATURES OF THE TEXNET SERVICE INCLUDE:

TI-NEWS -- AN "ELECTRONIC NEWSLETTER" FOR ALL TI HOME COMPUTER USERS' GROUPS;

TI-SERVICE -- A KEY-WORD-ACCESSED LISTING OF TEXAS INSTRUMENTS EXCHANGE SERVICE CENTERS;

TI-USERS -- A WORLDWIDE DIRECTORY OF TI HOME COMPUTER USERS' GROUPS.

IN ADDITION, TEXNET SUBSCRIBERS GAIN ACCESS TO ALL THE PROGRAMS, SERVICES, AND FEATURES OF THE SOURCE.

FreeTip: If you would like more information on TEXNET, you will be best off contacting Mr. Bynum directly, instead of calling The Source. Write to:

Mr.Don Bynum
SOFTMAIL, Inc.
P.O. Box 745
Rockwall, TX 75087
SourceMail: TI0004

...10...

Going By the Boards: *BBS and RCPM Free Software Delivery Systems*

There is probably no better example of microcomputer technology in the service of people than the network of personal computer bulletin board systems that is rapidly spreading across the North American continent and around the world. These systems, each of them a mini-database and message exchange, have the potential to add a new and exciting dimension to human communication. But they also hold enormous quantities of free, public domain software.

The concept behind a bulletin board system (BBS) is not difficult to understand. It is based on the ability of a computer to accept commands and input from any "port" its owner selects. With the right software, you can run a computer with a light pen, a bar code reader, a joystick, or a "mouse." All of these devices usually communicate with the machine through an RS-232 serial port, but they are relatively recent developments in the microworld. One of the first techniques for running a microcomputer from something other than the "console" (keyboard) also used an RS-232 port. And that, of course, was to use a different computer's keyboard connected to the system via modem and telephone.

In computerist terms, it is a rather simple matter of running a short program that "initializes" the RS-232 port (tells the UART what baud rate and other parameters to use) and reassigns the machine's "I/O" (pronounced "eye-oh"; input/output). Add an auto-answer modem, and you're in business. Some commercial communications packages offer this option as a standard feature, primarily for executives who want to access their desktop machines from home.

This is exactly what Chicagoans Ward Christensen and Randy Suess did with a NorthStar computer in February of 1978 when they created the first computer bulletin board system, CBBS #1. Since that time nearly 1,000 other computer owners have "brought up" boards of their own. Virtually any kind of computer can be used as a "host" system.

But while all are based on the same fundamental concept, the software that drives them can be quite different.

Historical Highlight: How the First Board Came to Be

In human terms, 1978 is not that long ago. But in the personal computer industry it is ancient history. The first personal computer, the MITS Altair, was introduced—in solder-it-yourself kit form—in 1975. Floppy disk drives were virtually unheard of, and if you did hear of one—and its price—you wished you hadn't. Yet by 1976 Christensen had successfully coupled his Altair to a set of drives and was busily writing programs in 8080 assembly language. As assistant software librarian for CACHE (Chicago Area Computer Hobbyist Exchange), an early users group, Christensen was naturally interested in promoting both group communications and the distribution of public domain software.

By 1977 Christensen and Suess were sending messages and programs between their two computers. And at some point the idea for a bulletin board system developed. The original idea was to use a computer as the electronic equivalent of a cork and thumbtack bulletin board to allow CACHE members to exchange messages. And that was the system that went on the air on February 16, 1978.

The system was based on a NorthStar computer and was ostensibly designed exclusively for messaging. (The basic NorthStar system in 1978 included a Z80A, 32K RAM, single 70K floppy disk drive, and a 12-slot S-100 motherboard. It sold for $2,315, and you had to add your own monitor and keyboard.) There was a secret feature, however, that only a few people knew about at first. Christensen included a module designed to work with his MODEM program to allow callers to download public domain software.

CBBS #1 is still up and running today, and recent reports indicate that the system has logged over 100,000 callers. Ironically, considering Ward Christensen's crucial role in developing the XMODEM protocol, the file transfer feature was removed from the board early in its history due in part to limited disk space. Thus when you see a system designated "CBBS," you can assume that it is a wonderful place to meet and greet online friends, but it is probably not the best place to look for public domain software.

FreeTip: The term CBBS™ has been trademarked and officially refers to the bulletin board messaging software now available for most CP/M systems. The cost is $50. For more information, contact:

FreeTip continued

Mr. Randy Suess
CBBS 5219 West Warwick
Chicago, IL 60641

The Major Dividing Line

Bulletin board host software can range from a bare-bones package that merely connects the computer to the phone line when its modem answers a call to advanced $300 packages that endow the host with attributes as sophisticated as those of The Source, CompuServe, or some other commercial database. As a free software hunter who is likely to be accessing a wide range of systems, it's important to know the difference. In this growing "network nation" the main dividing line falls between RCPM ("Remote CP/M") systems and BBSs.

Whenever you see a board designated as an RCPM, you can assume that the host computer is running the CP/M operating system and that the machine has been programmed to allow you to enter DOS commands as if you were typing on its keyboard. That means you can change logged disk drives or USER areas on the same drive. You may be able to PIP a file, call for a STATus report, or type MBASIC at the DOS prompt to run MBASIC.COM and do a little programming.

If all of this sounds like gobbledy-gook to you, then you should not use an RCPM system. And that's the point. Although other boards may allow you to do the same things, all boards designated "RCPM" use this approach, and many of them *require* it. Few things are more frustrating than to connect with a board, read the greeting message welcoming you to the system, and then be presented with the naked CP/M prompt: A0>. If you type "Help," and the system responds with "HELP?" it is your signal to sign off and stop the long distance meter from running, for you will never find your way around the board.

FreeTip: Many RCPMs include help files and may well respond with a list of commands when you type that word. But most SysOps—the "system operators" who own the host computers—are less than thrilled about having a non-CP/M user tying up their boards. Some have even instituted a little test to quiz callers on the name of a certain dynamic debugging tool or other standard CP/M utility before allowing them to proceed.

The RCPM approach is a very efficient way to run a system. The remote access software requires very little storage space on the SysOp's disk, and as long as the caller knows what to do, it is an easy way to transfer public domain software. This, in fact, was one of the main reasons Christensen and Suess set up CBBS #1 in the first place. For less computer-wise individuals, however, the bare-bones approach clearly presented a problem. Consequently it wasn't long before some SysOps began writing "user friendly front ends" for their boards. The "front end" software provided menus, help files, and other features to make the board easier to use. Sophisticated messaging functions were also added, making it possible for one caller to leave a note on the system for another caller (or everyone) to read at the next sign-on.

SysOps also began to make articles, tips, essays, and other textfiles available. And some of them began to sell the software they had written to other users interested in bringing up a board on the same brand of computer. Over time a new category of remote access system began to evolve, a category we will refer to as BBSs. It is always difficult to generalize when dealing with personal computers, but "generally" a BBS will be a non-RCPM system that offers menus, help functions, and other features similar to those found on a commercial database. BBSs will have software collections for you to download, but many tend to emphasize the messaging function.

FreeTip: We have chosen BBS to refer to a generic, non-RCPM system. However, other terms *are* used. The two you will encounter most frequently are PAMS for "Public Access Message System," and RBBS for "Remote Bulletin Board System." Occasionally you will even see the term "RCPM-RBBS" attached to a phone number. This usually signifies an RCPM system with a messaging function front end.

An RCPM, on the other hand, may offer a messaging function, but it may also have a significant portion of the SIG/M and CPMUG public domain library online at any time. (See Chapter 2.) If the public domain program you want isn't available when you sign on, ask them. Many RCPM SysOps will make sure that it's there for you the next time you call.

Bulletin Board "Families"

The BBS category is quite large, but it can be subdivided on the basis of the particular bulletin board program a given system uses. The ABBS (Apple Bulletin Board System) program from Craig Vaughan's

Software Sorcery is designed for the Apple II, as is Bill Blue's PMS (People's Message System) package. Forum-80 is Bill Abney's program for the TRS-80 Models I and III, and ST80-X10 is a host program for the same machines written by Lance Micklus. AMIS is a public domain program for the Atari 800. RBBS-PC is a free program for the IBM/PC, and HOSTCOMM is a commercial package for the same computer. The list goes on.

The important thing to remember is that just as no two word processing programs use the same commands to accomplish the same thing, no two BBS host programs share the same set of commands. Each type of host program, and all the systems that use it, can be thought of as a separate bulletin board "family." If you know how to use one ABBS, you know how to use all such boards, regardless of their locations. For someone who wants to access many different families of boards, though, keeping straight all the commands each requires can be a problem. We'll tell you what kinds of commands to look for when you sign on to a BBS, and we'll show you how to use an RCPM. But first let's take a look at the kind of software you can expect to find.

The Truth About Downloading Bulletin Board Software

You are likely to find virtually all of the most popular public domain programs that are available for your machine on a BBS or RCPM. There are scores, and perhaps hundreds, of programs to give you some form of directory of your disk. There are print spoolers, mailing label producers, games, graphics generators, amateur radio-related programs, and complete computer languages. There are also VisiCalc and SuperCalc models, dBASE II command files, and Lotus 1-2-3 worksheets, and much more. But in most cases *it does not make sense to obtain these programs from a bulletin board.*

Bulletin board systems are well worth getting excited about. But in their enthusiasm for the hundreds of megabytes of free software now available on the boards, many proponents overlook simple matters of practicality and economics. At a communications speed of 300 baud, a 16K program will require eight minutes to download (two minutes at 1200 baud). If you assume that an out-of-state call costs you an average of 25¢ for the first minute, and 18¢ for every minute thereafter, that 16K program will cost you about $1.50 in long distance charges at 300 baud.

This is only a rough approximation, of course. And it does not include the time you spend signing onto the system, reading bulletins from the SysOp, and reviewing the selection of available software. Admittedly, $1.50 is not a great deal to pay for a program that you want—until you realize that you could obtain six to ten programs of a similar size from one of the local users groups or national organizations cited in previous chapters for about $6. If your disks are double-sided, you could obtain *20* programs for the same $6. (Again, these figures are approximations and will vary depending on your system's disk format.)

Alternatively, you could sign on to CompuServe, locate the identical public domain program in the appropriate special interest group (SIG), and download it at 300 baud for 80¢. (See Chapter 8.)

Clearly, downloading public domain software from a bulletin board can be one of the most expensive ways to obtain it. If there happens to be a board you like within your local calling area, the cost will be less. But the days when one could remain online with a nearby bulletin board for an hour at a cost of three to five cents are rapidly drawing to a close. All phone companies are scheduled to institute "measured service" for local calls in the future. Everyone will be charged on the basis of total connect time, regardless of where you call.

FreeTip: Many bulletin boards and RCPM systems will tell you the estimated transmission time for whichever program you select and then ask you whether you want to continue with the download. Unless otherwise stated, you can assume these speeds refer to a rate of 300 baud, the speed most bulletin boards use. Others will display the size (in bytes) of a program as part of its description. Translating "byte size" into transmission time and multiplying it by the applicable long distance charge can help you decide whether to download the program or not. (Or whether you have time to go fix yourself a sandwich while the download is in progress.)

Here's how to perform the translation:

300 baud = 30 characters/second = 30 bytes/second
= half a minute per 1,000 bytes (K)
= 1 minute for every 2K

1200 baud = 120 characters/second = 120 bytes/second
= about 8 seconds per 1,000 bytes (K)
= about a quarter of a minute (15 seconds) for every 2K

When Does It Pay to Use a Bulletin Board?

This hard-nosed, dollars-and-cents approach is not meant to discourage you from going online with a variety of BBS and RCPM systems. If there is no users group near your home, and you are not willing to wait for a national organization to send you a disk, then you may have no alternative. It is simply important to be aware that there *are* less expensive ways to obtain the same major public domain programs.

Small programs, unique little utilities, and patches are another matter. In many cases a bulletin board will be the only practical way to obtain this kind of software. For example, the first versions of PC-TALK, Andrew Fluegelman's Freeware™ communications program for the IBM/PC, did not support the XMODEM protocol. Since Mr. Fluegelman makes this BASIC program available in both interpretive and compiled form, it did not take long for XMODEM-supporting BASIC patches to appear on the IBM/PC bulletin boards. (PC-TALK III now supports XMODEM. See Chapter 11.) For many people, downloading the patch and merging it with their copy of PC-TALK was the quickest and easiest way to upgrade the program.

Public domain authors have created all manner of utility programs to perform highly specialized tasks. Many of these are designed for various forms of file manipulation or to provide detailed information about a disk. Most were written because their authors needed to solve a particular problem—and should you ever face the same problem, they can be invaluable. Although most programs of this type eventually make their way into users group software libraries, a bulletin board can be a convenient way to obtain them when you are in a hurry.

Finally, you may discover programs that are unique because of their local flavor or subject matter. You are not likely to find RED.BAS, a program that plays the fight song of the Washington Redskins football team while putting on a nifty color display, anywhere else but on Washington, D.C., IBM/PC boards and in the local users group library. Similarly, a bulletin board specializing in coin or stamp collecting, alternate energy sources, or medical topics is likely to be the best place to find software dealing with these interests.

FreeTip: How can you discover the kind of software you're likely to find on a given board? Users group members and club newsletters are good sources, as are the various computer magazines. (*PC World*, a magazine for IBM owners, carries a regular column devoted to IBM boards, including a "Bulletin Board of the Month" section that usually presents a directory of the board's programs.)

There is one book, however, that no one who wants to work the boards should be without. *The Computer Phone Book*™ by Mike Cane (NAL/Plume, $9.95) provides essential information and short descriptions of several hundred BBS and RCPM systems across the continent. The book is unique in that Mr. Cane has paid an electronic visit to each system and recorded the kinds of things he found on each. The book includes multiple indices to let you locate a board by location, by special interest, and by whether or not it is known to offer downloadable software. This last index is especially valuable because it can save you from spending time and money on boards that are primarily messaging systems.

A monthly update is available ($20 a year in the U.S. and Canada) from the author. Contact:

Mr. Mike Cane
The Computer Phone Book
175 Fifth Avenue, Suite 3371
New York, NY 10010

Cracking the Computer Culture Code

If you look at most lists of bulletin board phone numbers, you will notice that they are classified by the type of computer that serves as the host system. This is important for two reasons. First, it alerts you to the family of BBS software the board is running (where that fact is known) and thus enables you to bring yourself up to speed on the sets of commands you will need before you call. Second, it makes it easy to locate boards that are likely to specialize in software for your brand of computer. Some boards carry programs for many different computers, regardless of the type of host system. But if you are a new user, your online efforts are likely to be more fruitful if you concentrate on hosts of the same brand.

You may not be aware of it, but if you have just bought a computer, you have also just enrolled in a specialized foreign language class. Every brand of computer is surrounded by its own culture. And while some are stronger than others, each has its own language. You may know the meaning of *bytes, RAM*, *disk sectors*, and many other general computer terms. But do *Num-Lock*, *SSC*, *PMMI*, *LDOS*,and *1541* have a familiar ring? If you recognize one of these terms, the chances are that you will not recognize the others because each is from the argot of a particular computer brand culture.

FreeTip: In the interests of cross-cultural pollination: *Num-Lock* is a key on the IBM/PC keyboard; *SSC* stands for an Apple Super Serial Card; *PMMI* is a Potomac Micro Magic Incorporated modem popular among CP/M users; *LDOS* is an alternative TRS-80 operating system from Logical Systems, Inc.; and *1541* is the name of a popular disk drive for the Commodore 64.

This is more than a computer version of Trivial Pursuit®. The filenames and program descriptions you will encounter on bulletin boards will incorporate these terms, and you will be expected to know what they mean. The best way to crack the code of your own computer's culture is to jump in and nose around a bit. If you're not a member of a users group and do not yet subscribe to any computer magazines, downloading articles and tip sheets (as well as programs) from BBSs is an excellent way to get your feet wet. Total immersion may not be necessary, but until you become familiar with the terms, you will neglect to download important programs or mistakenly download others that you cannot use.

The Two Crucial Programs to Download First

The bulletin board world uses three important and interrelated techniques to distribute software. But unless you are a card-carrying member of the cognoscenti, it will take you a while to discover them on your own. Here they are.

The first technique is the XMODEM binary file transfer protocol. Every RCPM system expects your communications software to support this protocol, and many other boards require it as well. For more information, see Chapter 7 and Appendix A.

The second is hexadecimal conversion. If your communications software does not offer a binary transfer mode to let you download machine language programs directly, you may be able to download the same program as an ASCII hexadecimal file. A hexadecimal file uses the digits from *0* through *9* and the letters *A* through *F* to represent the binary numbers of a machine language program. But it can not be run directly. You must download it and then use a hexadecimal converter program to turn it back into its original machine language form.

"Hex converters" are usually written in BASIC, so they can easily be run by almost anybody. You can recognize them by their filenames, many of which include *hex*, *convt*, *hc*, or some related term. The converter programs will usually have a file extension of .BAS, while the hex file programs will usually end with .HEX. See Chapter 8 for more details regarding hex converters in general.

FreeTip: A hex converter written in BASIC will work quite well, but it may operate more slowly than you would like. Often the solution is to first obtain a BASIC hex converter and then obtain the hexadecimal version of that same program. This will enable you to create a fast-running machine language version of the hex converter. Alternatively, you could obtain a machine language version from a users group. If you are a CP/M user, for example, you might look for a program called UNLOAD.COM. This program will convert a .COM file assembled from hex from machine language back into the Intel hex format.

The third technique revolves around the "squeeze" and "unsqueeze" twins. To be a SysOp is to be perpetually concerned about storage space. The articles, programs, and features on a system can take up a lot of room, and on an active board there is a constant stream of new messages to store. As one SysOp says, "If you aren't careful, you can fill up a 20-meg hard disk in no time at all." (A 20 megabyte hard disk can store the equivalent of 125 single-sided floppy disks formated at 160K each.)

To help conserve storage space, many SysOps use a program incorporating data compression techniques to reduce the space required to store a textfile or program by as much as 75%. You can usually tell if the program you are interested in has been "squeezed" by checking the filename extension for a *Q*. Thus, MODEM7.ASM (a full-sized assembly language version of MODEM7) would become MODEM7.AQM after being passed through the squeezer. PROG.DOC (a textfile documenting PROG) would become PROG.DQC. And so on.

Squeezing a program is good for the SysOp's disk space and good for you, since it will take less time to transmit in its compressed form. But as with .HEX files, a squeezed program will do you no good if you do not have a program to unsqueeze it. Consequently, you should make a point of downloading an "unsqueeze" program as soon as possible, perhaps even during the same session used to obtain your hex converter. Look for files with names like UNSQUEEZE or USQ-19. (Note that the "squish" programs found on some boards are not the same as the "squeeze" programs. SQUISH.BAS, for example, is an IBM/PC program that will remove REMarks from a BASIC program so that it takes up less space on disk. But it does not compress the data that remains.)

FreeTip: To keep callers from running a machine language program on their systems, RCPM SysOps usually rename .COM files as .OBJ files. They will also remove the standard CP/M operating system module REN.COM to prevent pranksters from renaming files. (Remember, with an RCPM system, the caller is the console as far as the computer is concerned.) Consequently, if you find a file with a name like USQ.OBJ, download it using your comm program's binary transfer mode and the XMODEM protocol. Then

FreeTip continued

rename it to USQ.COM with your own REN.COM on your own system.

FreeTip: How can a program or textfile be squeezed? The technique requires two basic components: a set of special codes and a table that can be used to translate those codes into the original characters they symbolize. In the ASCII code set even a blank space is represented by a character (ASCII decimal 32). That means it takes up just as much room as a letter or any other character. Suppose every paragraph in a long article stored on disk was indented five spaces. If you could replace those five spaces with say, an ampersand (&) and a number (5) to indicate the number of spaces symbolized, you could reduce the number of characters per paragraph from five to two. What required five characters of disk space before could now be represented by: &5.

A data compression program will automatically perform this kind of substitution on the file you hand it. But before it is finished, it will build a conversion table and record it with the file. The "unsqueeze" program simply looks at that table and goes through the file making the necessary conversions, expanding &5 to five space characters, and so on.

Perhaps the best known series of rules for compressing data is the "Huffman algorithm." Based on an article published by D. A. Huffman in 1952, this algorithm uses a related, but different technique to compress data by factors of 75% to 40%, depending on the type of file.

The Top Ten Sources of BBS Phone Numbers

The top ten of anything is always debatable. But listed below you will find ten excellent sources of BBS and RCPM telephone numbers. If you discover other sources, please feel free to contact the author at the electronic or U.S. mail addresses at the back of this book.

- "The Online Computer Telephone Directory" (OLCTD). Compiled by James A. Cambron and issued quarterly, OLCTD contains one of the most accurate lists of BBS and RCPM phone numbers available, thanks to proprietary software developed by Mr. Cambron. Before each issue goes to press, Mr. Cambron's computer automatically dials each of the 500 or more numbers in its file. BBS systems that are still up and running are "saved"; numbers that have been disconnected are flagged for editing. For more information, contact:

OLCTD
P.O. Box 10005
Kansas City, MO 64111-9990
CompuServe ID: 70040,414

One year (4 issues): $9.95.
Two years (8 issues): $15.95.
Overseas (U.S. funds only): Add $6.00 to the above rates.

- NewsNet. The OLCTD is also available on the NewsNet database. This means that you can scan articles for keywords on the latest BBS developments and instantly generate a list of numbers for the area code you are most interested in. See *The Complete Handbook of Personal Computer Communications* for more details or contact:

NewsNet
945 Haverford Road
Bryn Mawr, PA 19010
(800) 527-8030
(215) 345-1301, in Pennsylvania

- "Plumb." Edited and published by Ric Manning, this monthly newsletter features the "Hot 100," a list of boards that in the estimation of Mr. Manning are especially interesting. There are notes on the subjects the various boards specialize in, and commentary as well. Contact:

Ric Manning
"Plumb"
P.O. Box 300
Harrods Creek, KY 40027

One year (12 issues): $20.00

- Magazines. As mentioned previously, *PC World* magazine carries a monthly column devoted to IBM/PC BBSs. Magazines that do not have regular columns often carry articles with sidebars containing BBS numbers. One good source is *The Computer Shopper*. This publication carries a list of numbers in every issue. It is available in your local bookstore magazine rack or on the newsstand. Call: (305) 269-3211 for subscription information.

- Books. A growing number of books are being published on the BBS phenomenon. Here are three of them you might consider.

Hooking In: The Underground Computer Bulletin Board Workbook and Guide
by Tom Beeston & Tom Tucker
175 pages; $12.95 at your local bookstore, or
$14.95 postpaid (check, Visa/MC) from
Computerfood Press
31754 Foxfield Drive
Westlake Village, CA 91361

This book contains hundreds of bulletin board numbers as well as reproductions of the Main Menus and complete command explanations for many major BBS families. We learned from Tom Beeston that of the nearly 1,000 BBS phone numbers the authors collected and called, more than half had been disconnected. The 400-plus numbers included in the book were verified as operational systems at the time of publication. A caller's log section is also provided for noting what you find on various systems. The book is especially strong in tips and advice for using RCPM systems. An annual edition is planned.

The Small Computer Connection
by Neil L. Shapiro
Micro Text Publications, Inc.
McGraw-Hill Book Company
1221 Sixth Avenue
New York, NY 10020
190 pages; $15.95

Includes much of the online documentation and command summaries provided by major bulletin board families as well as an extensive list of BBS phone numbers. As with *Hooking In*, this book can save you the time and expense of downloading those command summaries yourself.

The Computer Phone Book™
by Mike Cane
New American Library
1633 Broadway
New York, NY 10019
450 pages; $9.95

An excellent directory of what to expect to find on hundreds of BBS and RCPM systems. See FreeTip earlier in this chapter for more information.

You may also find books designed to offer a directory of *specific* pub-

domain programs available on various boards. This is a laudable goal, but it may be impossible to achieve. Many SysOps will maintain a central core of popular programs, and these will be available at all times. But part of the vitality of the public domain is that new software is constantly being introduced. Only a very few SysOps own the storage capacity to make significant portions of public domain collections available at all times, and they may charge an annual membership fee for access privileges.

- Local and national users groups. The newsletters published by such organizations can be wonderful sources of BBS numbers. See Chapters 3 and 5 of this book for more information.

- CompuServe special interest groups (SIGs). There are over 60 SIGs on the CompuServe system covering an exceptionally wide range of interests and computer equipment. Many of these "electronic clubhouses" maintain files of relevant magazines and BBS numbers. (See Chapter 8.)

- The PAMs List on The Source. Bill Blue, creator of the People's Message System bulletin boards, maintains a list of hundreds of BBSs on The Source. One can search the list on the basis of area code or system type. Follow the menus to User Publishing or type *PUBLIC* at the Source Command Level. (See Chapter 9.) This list is also available in the ACCESS section of CompuServe. (See Chapter 8.)

- POST on The Source and BULLET on CompuServe. Both The Source and the CompuServe Information Service have system bulletin boards that can be scanned for keyword references. ("BBS" is always a good choice.) New SysOps are interested in spreading the word about their systems, and many of them place announcements and descriptions on these two boards.

- Finally, bulletin boards themselves are one of the best sources of additional BBS numbers. Almost every BBS or RCPM system maintains a file containing such numbers, and some even have free search programs for you to download with the list and use to locate boards of your choice when you are offline.

Bulletin Board System Basics

Although each bulletin board family handles things a bit differently, they have a number of things in common. Indeed, if you are interested only in obtaining software, a typical BBS session can be broken down into about six steps. The steps for using an RCPM system are similar, as we'll see in the next section.

Before You Dial the Phone . . .

This may seem elementary, but before you go online, take a moment to prepare:

- Make sure your printer has plenty of paper. A printer that runs out of paper in the midst of an online session can cause problems for your communications software.

- Check the available space on the floppy disk you plan to use for recording. Better yet, always start with a properly formatted blank disk. There is no way you can know beforehand how much material you will want to download from a given board. It is not a bad idea to have *several* formatted disks close at hand.

- Start by choosing boards within your own area code. And if you are new to the game, pick ones that use your brand of computer as a host. If you are not able to get on any of these boards, branch out to other nearby area codes.

- If you have not used your communications software recently, you might want to review its major commands. If you have a list of the commands required by the BBS family you will be calling, review that as well.

- Set your communications parameters to:

300 or 1200 baud		300 or 1200 baud
Full duplex		Full duplex
8 Data bits	*or*	7 Data bits
No parity		Even parity
1 Stop bit		1 Stop bit
(8/N/1)		(7/E/1)

Although some boards operate at 7/E/1, the trend is toward 8/N/1. Use the eight-bit setting first and if you find that you are getting strange characters on your screen, switch to 7/E/1.

Initialization and Sign-on

When you dial the phone, the BBS modem will answer and begin issuing a high-pitched tone (if you are running at 300 baud). Your modem will respond with a tone of its own and you will be connected. More than likely, you will immediately see a question appear on your screen. But if the modem connection has been made and nothing appears, try hitting <ENTER> once or twice to tell the other system that you are there. That will normally cause the text to appear.

Next, you will be asked a number of questions to enable the remote system to match your computer's requirements. You may be asked whether your computer can handle upper and lower case and whether or not you need "line feeds," for example. Whenever two machines are communicating, one of them must be set to add a line feed character to each carriage return to prevent succeeding lines of text from over-writing each other. Normally you should set your communications software to add the line feed, but if you can't do this, any remote system that asks this question can do it for you.

You may also be asked how many "nulls" you need. A null is a time-wasting signal intended primarily for callers using a teletype-like machine as a terminal. These machines have no display screen, and their printing elements tend to be rather slow. By adding one or more null codes to each line of text, the remote system can give the printing element time to return to the left margin before it must deal with the next line. A single null is 30 milliseconds, but if you are using a computer it is doubtful that you will need any, even if you have your printer toggled on. If you find that your printer fails to print the first few letters of a line ("drops characters"), however, you will have to experiment to determine the number of nulls needed to correct the problem.

Next you will be asked to enter your name and the city and state you are calling from. (Be sure to use your state's official two-letter designation as many systems will not recognize the complete state name.) You may be asked for your phone number as well. SysOps request this in case the the system goes down while you are online and they need to contact you about what happened so the problem can be corrected. On systems requiring passwords for "privileged user status," the SysOp will usually phone you to make sure you are who who you say you are before giving you a password. With the preliminaries out of the way, a greeting message similar to the following will appear:

```
*****************************************************
....................WELCOME ....................
        TO THE APPLE BULLETIN BOARD
                    AND
       INFORMATION EXCHANGE SYSTEM
=================================
               ABBIES V. 4.2

               HIGHSEAS, OK
```

```
YOUR INSTANT SOURCE OF ALL APPLE
RELATED INFORMATION...

APPLE HARDWARE AND SOFTWARE REVIEWS

PROGRAMMING TIPS

SOFTWARE BUGS, REMEDIES AND RELEASES

NEW PRODUCTS AND APPLICATIONS

PERSONAL MESSAGES AND GENERAL BULLETINS

FEATURE ARTICLES AND SOFTWARE
::::::::::::::::::::::::::::::::::::::::::::::::::::::::::::::
RICHARD BOLITHO, H.M.R.N. (ret.)

ADVENTURER-AT-LARGE

DARING DEEDS IN THE FACE OF IMPOSSIBLE

ODDS; DEFEATING FRENCH EMPERORS, OUR

SPECIALITY. CALL FOR AN APPOINTMENT.
```

System Bulletins and Main Menu

You may then see a series of annoucements and bulletins covering the hours the BBS is available, special commands to use, the date and time of the next local users group meeting, etc. This material may also direct your attention to recently added or updated files. And, because many SysOps are justifiably proud of their equipment, there may be a description of the system's configuration. If this information is provided, pay particular attention to the number of disk drives or other measures of storage capacity. A single or double drive system is not likely to contain many programs, particularly if the board has an extensive messaging facility. You may not want to spend a great deal of long distance connect time searching for software on such a system. Do not simply hang up the phone, however. Wait until you get to a menu or prompt that will let you exit in an orderly manner.

Many systems will automatically check to see if someone has left a message addressed to you. Then the board's main menu will appear:

```
IF CONFUSED--TYPE --> ?
FOR COMMAND SUMMARY

OR TYPE '?ALL' FOR FULL DESCRIPTIONS
OF SYSTEM FUNCTIONS
```

```
  *** ABBIES FUNCTION PROMPT CODES ***
> DENOTES COMMONLY USED FUNCTION

  A=APPLE 40 COLUMN
  B=LIST SYSTEM BULLETINS AGAIN
>C=CHAT WITH SYSOP
  D=DUPLEX SWITCH (ECHO/NO ECHO)
>E=ENTER MSG
>F=FEATURE ARTICLE DIRECTORY
>G=GOODBYE(LEAVE SYSTEM)
  K=KILL(ERASE) MSG
  L=LINE FEED (ON/OFF)
  N=NULLS (SET AS REQ'D)
  P=LIST CURRENT PRIVILEGED USERS
>Q=QUICK SUMMARY OF MESSAGE HEADERS
>R=READ ENTIRE MESSAGE OF CHOICE
>S=SEARCH MESSAGES (SUBJECT)
>T=TIME, DAY, AND DATE
  X=EXPERT USER
>?=PRINTS THIS AGAIN!
  DOWNLOAD=DOWNLOAD SOFTWARE TO YOUR SYSTEM
  UPLOAD=UPLOAD FILES/SOFTWARE TO THIS SYSTEM

  FUNCTION:

  (A,B,C,D,E,F,G,L,K,L,N,P,Q,R,S,T,X,
  DOWNLOAD, UPLOAD,?)?
  CHOOSE A FUNCTION BY LETTER ==>
```

We have used an ABBS system as an example because it is generally acknowledged to be one of the most "friendly" and easy-to-use bulletin board packages. It also offers a good way to show how boards within the same family can differ. As with all good commercial software, the ABBS program is constantly being updated and improved with new capabilities and additional features. In addition, many SysOps have purchased the basic ABBS program but may or may not have incorporated the optional NEWS (displays a list of files available for reading), CONF (lets users switch between sets of messages), and UPLOAD and DOWNLOAD modules. Finally, a SysOp can usually customize a BBS package, and most of them do in some way. You may thus encounter ABBS systems that ask you to enter *?ALL* for a complete command summary, while others ask you to enter *HELP*. You will find similar variations within other families.

The only way to become comfortable with a given BBS family is to sign on to many systems and pay attention to what you see. Fortunately, the majority of the commands a given BBS package requires will be the same on every system. The command to activate an optional feature will not conflict with one of the standard commands, so in many cases you can simply ignore them.

FreeTip: The first time you sign on to a board in a particular family, it can make good sense to make downloading the complete help file and command summary your first goal. Ideally your communications software should be able to capture information in a buffer and print it out at the same time. If you do not already have a list of commands, you will want to refer to the printout in the course of the same session. But if you take the extra step of saving the summary in a capture buffer and recording it to disk after the summary has stopped, you will later be able to use your word processing program on the file. You might want to move certain key commands to the top of the page where they will be easy to find the next time you are online with the same type of board, for example.

You may even want to create your own BBS documentation and log book by collecting BBS command summaries and notes in a three-ring binder. This can save you the time and expense of repeatedly downloading the same command summary every time you sign on.

Getting a Directory and Downloading a File

Up to this point, you haven't had to do much work since the board has carried you along automatically. When you see a prompt asking for a command, however, it's time to get busy. The first thing to do is to check the main menu for anything that looks like it might give you an overview of what is available on the system. Since many of the menu items will probably be concerned with the messaging function, locating the directory command may not be easy. Do not be misled by "quick summary" or "scan" commands as these are intended to help callers locate particular messages.

Some systems offer menu selections like ".DIR" (directory), but often the download and directory functions will be combined. For example, a board might include "Download Menu Selections" as one of its main menu options. If you select this option, the system will probably produce a subsidiary menu listing all of its available programs. The menu may end with a prompt requesting you to enter the item number of the program you want. Other prompts may then appear to guide you through the downloading process. On a BBS it is *usually* safe to simply enter the download command and follow the resulting menus. But on an

RCPM system, in contrast, a similar command may produce a simple prompt instead of a menu. You will be expected to know the name of the file you want the system to send you and enter it at that time. Regardless of the system you use, *do not forget to download the documentation files associated with the program.*

FreeTip: As mentioned earlier, the software available on BBSs is often identical to that available through users groups and other sources. Public domain software flows in both directions, however, and if you are interested in publishing a program you have written, uploading it to a BBS is one of the best ways to ensure the widest distribution.

Many users groups across the continent regularly check relevant boards for new contributions. And new programs circulate on disk within the SysOp community. At most major computer trade shows, for example, the system operators will get together for a private meeting to exchange information and programs uploaded to their boards.

Exiting Properly

When you have finished downloading the software you want, *do not simply hang up the phone.* Instead, enter the proper command—often *G* for "good-bye"—to officially sign off. (If you merely hang up when you have taken what you want, you may prevent the host computer from resetting and preparing for the next caller.)

At that point you may be asked if you would like to leave a private message for the SysOp. This would be the courteous thing to do, particularly if you have downloaded a lot of material from the individual's system. The message does not have to be very long. Even a simple "Thank you" will be appreciated.

How to Use an RCPM System

There are three tricks to using an RCPM system. The first is an adjustment in mental attitude. You should always be aware that, while there may be a few menus, an RCPM is *not* a menu-driven system like CompuServe, The Source, or most BBSs. The only way to obtain public domain software from most RCPM systems is to run the remote computer as if you were sitting in front of it instead of using your own machine.

The second requirement is a familiarity with the standard commands required by the CP/M operating system. You do not have to know all the permutations of PIP (the file copying module) or DDT (the debugging module). But you must know how to move from one drive and user area to another, how to get a directory, and how to view or download a file. These are not difficult commands to master and, since most callers will be CP/M users, they should not pose a problem. (There is little reason for a non-CP/M user to call an RCPM since none of the software will be usable.)

The third trick is to be aware of certain conventions, procedures, and files most RCPM systems have in common. A knowledge of these common programs and files and what they are designed to do can make your session much more rewarding.

Signing On and "Entering CP/M . . ."

The RCPM sign-on procedure is similar to that found with most BBSs, and we will not repeat it here. RCPM systems are intended primarily for the distribution of public domain software, but some have incorporated a messaging function. These are usually called RBBS/RCPM or MINI-RBBS/RCPM systems. Other variations on RBBS may also be used. If there is a messaging function, the first thing you see will probably be a menu. One of the items on the menu will usually read: "C= Exit to CP/M." If there is no menu, you will probably find yourself in the "CP/M environment" as soon as you sign on.

One way or another, this is where you have got to go to gain access to the board's software collection. Most boards will notify you by printing "Entering CP/M . . ." as they make the transition. At that point, you will receive some variation of the standard CP/M DOS prompt: *A0>* or *A>*. The system will then wait for you to enter a CP/M command. The *A0>* prompt signifies that you are logged onto drive A, user area 0.

Changing Logged Drives and User Areas

Under CP/M a "user area" is equivalent to a "directory" level in MS-DOS 2.0 or IBM/PC DOS 2.0. (Your computer's operating system may not have an equivalent.) The easiest way to think of user areas is as partitioned sections of a single floppy disk. CP/M supports up to 16 different user areas (0–15) on a disk, and each has its own directory. Thus if you are logged onto A0> and you type *DIR*, you will get one list of files. But if you are logged onto A7> and you enter the same command, the list will be entirely different. In order to access a file or run a program, you must be logged into the user area where it is stored.

To move from user area 0 to user area 7, type *USER 7* at the *A0>* prompt. This prompt will then be replaced with: *A7>*. Use the same technique to move to any user area on the same drive. To change your logged disk drive from A to B, type *B:* at the *A>* prompt. The prompt will then be replaced with *B0>*.

With a little practice, you'll find that you can easily move from one drive to another or from one user area to another as you roam around the system. Although you will inevitably have to change your logged drive during an online session, with some systems you may not have to worry about user areas. CP/M permits user areas on any type of disk drive, but the technique is most often used with a hard disk. If the system has a hard disk drive, it may *appear* to have four or more floppy drives in addition to drives A and B. You do not have to understand this to use the system. Simply treat drives C, D, E, F, etc., like standard floppy drives.

TYPE-ing and Finding Out What's Where

As mentioned, you can call for a directory of any drive and user area by entering *DIR*. But on a large system, doing this for each possible storage area would be an major chore. Fortunately, most RCPM systems will have a file called DISKMENU.DOC that presents the contents of all the drives and user areas in the system. Normally this file will be stored on drive A, user area 0, the location most boards start you at when you enter CP/M. To obtain a copy of this file, open your own computer's capture buffer and enter: *TYPE DISKMENU.DOC* at the *A0>* prompt. (If you do not have a capture buffer you will have no choice but to toggle your printer on, though this will slow things down considerably.)

Once the complete file has been displayed and the *A0>* prompt has appeared again, enter *BYE* to sign off the system. Review the DISKMENU.DOC file at your leisure, circling the files you want and their disk and user area locations. This will enable you to efficiently download everything you want the next time you call the system.

Before signing off, you might also consider another utility commonly found on RCPM systems. This is WHATSNEW.COM. This program will give you a list of all the files that have been added or deleted from the A0 section, starting with a date you specify. If a copy of the program exists on other disks and areas, you can use it in those locations as well. Remember, this is a program, not a TYPE-able file. Therefore you have only to enter *WHATSNEW* at the prompt.

If you are just getting started in public domain software, you might use WHATSNEW to see if there is a new version of MODEM7 or some other popular CP/M program on the system. But many of the newest programs are highly specialized. You will be much better off if you concentrate on starting your library with the standard programs cited on the CP/M Gems List in Chapter 2.

The most efficient way to do this is to use another utility program commonly found on RCPM systems. This is FILEFIND.COM. Again, note that this is a program, not a file to be displayed. FILEFIND is very simple to use, and it can save you enormous amounts of time. If you know the exact name of the file you are looking for, at the *A0*> prompt you can type: *FILEFIND FILENAME.EXT* (where FILENAME.EXT is your target file). The program will then search through all user areas and disk drives for a file that matches your specifications.

Entering an exact filename, however, may not be the best approach. Since different versions of the same CP/M program have similar but different names, if you search for MODEM7.DOC and the file exists on the system as MODEM714.DOC, the program will not locate it. Nor would it find MODEM7.DQC, the "squeezed" version of that file. Consequently, to increase the chances of locating the file you want, you should use the FILEFIND program's "wildcard" feature. This allows you to enter an asterisk to represent any number of characters or a question mark to represent any single character. See Figure 10.1 for the results of using FILEFIND to locate all the documentation files on an RCPM system.

> **FreeTip:** The disk directory produced by entering the *FILEFIND *.DOC* command in Figure 10.1 will be familiar to most CP/M users. Others may find the "user area" numbers that follow the drive designations slightly confusing. If you are familiar with MS-DOS 2.x (or IBM/PC DOS 2.x), you can simply think of *A6:* as drive A, directory 6, since a CP/M user area is roughly similar to an MS-DOS directory. If you are familiar with neither of these operating systems, just think of *A6* as one drive designation, *A4* as another drive designation, and so on. An RCPM system will usually start you out on drive A0. To change your logged drive and user area, simply type the proper designation at the prompt and hit <ENTER>.

Figure 10.1. Using FILEFIND on an RCPM

Here's an example of how the CP/M utility FILEFIND can help you locate files, regardless of where they are on an RCPM system. With the exception of the first FILEFIND and FILEFIND *.DOC, all of the text below was generated by the RCPM system.

```
A0>FILEFIND

FILEFIND ver 11.1
Type CTRL-C to abort

Usage: FILEFIND <filename.type>

      You must specify the file(s) you
      want to find. Ambiguous file names
      may be used.

      Examples: FILEFIND MOD*.D?C
                FILEFIND *.A?M

A0>FILEFIND *.DOC

FILEFIND ver 11.1
Type CTRL-C to abort

A0:CHANGES  .DOC A0:INDEX    .DOC A0:SQ/USQ   .DOC A0:LBR      .DOC
A0:SYSUSE   .DOC A0:THIS-SYS .DOC A0:CAT      .DOC A0:XMODEM   .DOC
A0:TYPE     .DOC A0:XFER     .DOC A5:LITL-ADA .DOC A6:MBOOTA86 .DOC
A6:XDIR-A86 .DOC A7:FTHCPM   .DOC B0:DASM     .DOC B0:PURETEXT .DOC
B5:FRND1X   .DOC B5:XC       .DOC B8:COMMSN   .DOC B8:BIBLIO   .DOC
C0:APHALT13 .DOC C0:SPELL-11 .DOC C0:UMPIRE   .DOC C0:SCRAMBLE .DOC
C0:SUB-FIX  .DOC C0:DD       .DOC C0:DUTIL    .DOC C1:CHEAT    .DOC
C1:EL-E     .DOC C1:MYDDBIOS .DOC C1:SCRAMBLE .DOC C1:SYSMON   .DOC
C3:NZRASFIX .DOC C4:REFORM   .DOC C4:XLATE2   .DOC C6:DATABASE .DOC
C6:MAILLIST .DOC D0:CALLWAIT .DOC D4:DIAL     .DOC D7:TVKILL   .DOC
D8:PACMAN   .DOC D8:ALIENS   .DOC D9:ATYPE    .DOC D9:AUTOLOAD .DOC

A0>
```

FreeTip: Use FILEFIND to locate the essential "unsqueeze" program mentioned earlier. You probably will not need a hexconverter since CP/M's LOAD.COM module converts files from .HEX to .COM files. However when you begin uploading programs of your own, you may need the public domain program UNLOAD.COM that converts .COM files to hex. Try *FILEFIND USQ*.** or *FILEFIND US*.** first. If these do not work try FILEFIND U*.*. Almost all filenames for this program begin with U, but the more ambiguous the specification, the more files the program is likely to find, and the longer the process will take.

TYPESQ, the Temporary Unsqueezer

TYPESQ.COM is another time- and money-saving RCPM utility. Unlike USQ.COM, this program does not create an unsqueezed disk file.

Instead it sends its unsqueezed output to the display screen. If you are ever in doubt about whether you want to download a squeezed file, you can use TYPESQ to take a quick look at it before ordering the system to send it to you. Programmers typically place a description of their programs in REMark or similar statements at the beginning of their work. Thus by watching the first few lines of output, you may be able to get a better idea of what the program is designed to do and whether you want it.

For example, suppose you saw a file called DATABASE.DQC, a squeezed version of a .DOC file. And suppose that the TYPESQ program is located on drive C, user area 6. To run that program and look at DATABASE.DQC, you would first move to C6 and then enter: *TYPESQ DATABASE.DQC* at the DOS prompt. Here is what you might then see:

```
A0>C6
C6>TYPESQ DATABASE.DQC

Ctrl-S pauses, Ctrl-C Aborts.

TYPEing file DATABASE.DOC (200 lines MAX)

TARBELL DATABASE MANAGEMENT SYSTEM March 23, 1978

The main theme of this system is to provide a common set
of programs that help the user create, modify, and
access data files for a variety of needs. In this way,
the system can be better tailored for a particular
situation, and ...(etc.)
```

Note that you may enter a <Control>-<C> to abort the transmission and return to the DOS prompt at any time. This might be a good idea even if you want to download the file. Since a squeezed file can be considerably smaller than an unsqueezed one, it will take less time to download. Just be certain that you have the unsqueezer program to translate it.

How to Use XMODEM

Finally, there is the matter of XMODEM.COM. You will find more details on this nearly legendary program and protocol in Appendix A. Here, however, are the nuts and bolts of actually using it:

- Your communications software must include XMODEM support. A simple binary transfer or some other protocol will not work. And you must be communicating at 8/N/1.

- You must know the exact name of the file you wish to download, in most cases. There are versions that support additional features, but in the beginning things will be simpler if you specify the exact name. Use your DISKMENU.DOC printout as a reference.

- You must know which disk drive and user area holds the XMODEM.COM program. Remember, when you are on an RCPM system you are using the remote computer to run programs, and you cannot run a program if you are not logged onto the location that contains it. Again, DISKMENU.DOC should be your guide.

- Remember that "XMODEM isn't just for programs anymore." Indeed it never was. Any kind of file, text, or program, squeezed or unsqueezed, can be downloaded error-free with XMODEM.

Here's what to do:

1. Sign on to the system and go to the disk and user area containing XMODEM.COM.

2. At the DOS prompt type in: *XMODEM S A7:FILENAME.EXT* Note that A7 is the location of the program. Substitute the appropriate drive letter and user area for the file you want. *S* means "send."

3. The system will come back with something like this:

```
FILE OPEN - SIZE nn (nnnnn) sectors
SEND TIME: nn minutes, nn seconds at 300 baud
TO CANCEL: Use Control-X
```

4. At that point the remote system is ready and waiting for your machine to issue the proper signal. Enter the commands required by your own comm package to begin an XMODEM transfer. This may be something like: *R B:FILENAME.EXT*. The *R* stands for "receive" and *B:* is the disk drive you want the file to be recorded on.

5. The transfer will now begin, and your software will keep you informed of the progress by displaying the number of blocks of data received on your screen.

6. When the transfer has been completed, you will be returned to the RCPM's DOS prompt. At that point you may enter *BYE* to log off and reset the system for the next user. Or you may use XMODEM to transfer another file.

Conclusion: Don't Be a "Taker"

Unbelievable as it may sound, there are actually computer-owning creatures who call up bulletin boards for the sole purpose of trying to wreck the system. This is not funny. It is not cute. It is in no way excusable, regardless of the age of the individual. It is pure malevolence.

Most SysOps are able to take countermeasures. Some BBSs have the kind of built-in protection you would expect to find in a Pentagon computer. Indeed, in light of recent security breaches, the "boys in the brass hats" could undoubtedly profit from a SysOp-sponsored tutorial.

Many of the protective measures involve incorporating additional code in the BBS software. But there is a growing trend toward more overt methods of limiting access. More and more bulletin boards require passwords, for example, and some require the payment of a membership fee. There is also a trend toward imposing a time limit on each caller. (When your time is up, the board will automatically disconnect you.)

Not all of these steps are in response to the system wreckers. Many of them are the result of a breach of another sort, a breach in the unwritten contract between SysOp and caller. It is not at all unusual for a SysOp to have invested six to twelve *thousand* dollars in the equipment necessary to operate a top-flight board. And while no individual would remain a SysOp if he or she did not enjoy it, few callers are aware of the endless labor that is involved.

Even fewer would be willing to tie up their own computers as host systems for however many hours a board is on the air. But that is exactly what a SysOp does. In the absence of expensive multi-tasking software, a computer that is hosting a bulletin board cannot be used for any other purpose.

The SysOps invest their money and give their time and effort voluntarily. They *want* you to call their systems. Many are more than willing to help you with your computer-related problems, whatever they may be. Even if it means answering the same questions over and over again. But they hope callers will contribute something of their own that will in some way strengthen the board and enrich the bulletin board community.

And it *is* a community. A bulletin board represents a cooperative effort among people all over the continent. As such it is perhaps the first truly people-oriented application of personal computers. The potential benefits for everyone are enormous, but they can only be fulfilled if communication works in both directions.

When you're new to the BBS/RCPM community, no one expects you to do anything but download programs and other material. But as you gain more experience and become comfortable working the boards, any contribution you can make would be appreciated by everyone. As one SysOp puts it, "You don't have to be a programmer. But if you see a program on another board that you feel is of value, download it from there and upload it to another board. Help spread it around."

Because it is beyond the scope of this book, we have not discussed the messaging functions offered by virtually all BBSs and many RCPM systems. But you should definitely take the time to learn how to scan, read, and post messages. (Download the "Help" file most systems provide.) A bulletin board's message collection can be a rich source of tips, ideas, and imaginative solutions. The manuals that come with your computer and software do not always mention all of the available features. (There are undocumented commands in IBM/PC BASIC and many other packages, and every computer has its little quirks.) If you discover something about your computer or your software, don't keep it to yourself. Post an account of what you have found on a board and share your knowledge.

By being a "giver" as well as a "taker," you and everyone else who is online will benefit. In this chapter we have given you the keys to the bulletin board kingdom. Please don't abuse them.

...11...

IBM/PC, PCjr, and Compatibles: *The Freeware™/Shareware Phenomenon*

How would you like an IBM PCjr Entry Model computer (list price $669) for free? That's not really possible, of course, but thanks to the Freeware™/Shareware phenomenon, you can get the next best thing. For a total of $155 you can obtain a communications, a database management, and a word processing program for your PCjr, or other IBM computer. Even at a mail order discount, you would have to pay approximately $800 for three commercial programs of similar power, and in many cases you would not receive the same quality of user support. Your net savings: $645. Almost enough to pay for a PCjr, or to pay for a PCjr Diskette Drive ($480) and an IBM PC Compact Printer ($175).

If you already own programs in those three categories, perhaps you'd like an implementation of Logo patterned on the one developed by Terrapin, Inc., for the Apple II for $35? Or a statistical package for $25? An "Extended Batch Language" that incorporates many of the features found in VisiOn, DesQ, StarBurst, and ProKey for $30? An extensive "desktop manager" for users of Lotus 1-2-3 for $25? And if you are interested in both learning more about assembly language and in obtaining a powerful assembler, you might want to look into CHASM (CHeap ASseMbler) for $30 before you plunk down $100 for the IBM Macro Assembler.

Perhaps best of all, each of the programs we've mentioned comes with something better than a money-back guarantee: You do not have to pay a dime for the software if you find that you don't like it and decide not to use it. Your total initial cost is five to ten dollars per program for the disk, disk mailer, and postage—or less, if you copy the program from a friend. After that, it's up to you whether you want to pay for the software or not. If you think you've died and gone to PC heaven, rest assured. Your disk drives are still spinning. You have merely entered the world of Freeware, Shareware, and "user supported" software for the IBM/PC.

But wait a minute. Over $600 worth of professional quality programs for free? Can they *really* be that good? Where's the catch?

There is no catch. The "contributions" to pay for the software are purely voluntary. And yes, PC-TALK III (communications), PC- FILE III™ (database management), and PC-WRITE (word processing) really are that good—as articles and reviews in *PC World*, *PC* magazine, and other publications have frequently pointed out. We've called these programs "The PC Big Three" since the functions they perform are among the four essentials needed for any well-rounded personal software library. [The fourth, an electronic spreadsheet (PC-CALC), has recently been issued but was not available for review at this writing.] They are also the best known of all the programs offered in this way. In this chapter we'll show you how to obtain the Big Three, as well as many other high-quality, low-cost programs for your IBM/PC, XT, PCjr, transportable, or IBM-compatible computer.

Definition of Terms

"Freeware™" is a term coined and later trademarked by Andrew Fluegelman, author of the communications program PC-TALK III and the originator of the concept. The idea is simplicity itself: the software is made available in unprotected (copyable) form, and everyone who finds the program useful is asked to send its author a contribution. In the case of PC-TALK III, the suggested contribution is $35. Those who send in the money receive update information and have the opportunity to obtain the latest versions of the program as new features are added by the author.

This has proved to be a remarkably successful way of putting needed software into the hands of computer owners, and other program authors have adopted the method as well. However, since no one else can legally use the trademark "Freeware," a new term had to be created. A growing number of authors appear to have settled upon "user supported," often abbreviated "U/S." The size of the requested donation varies with the program, but U/S software is essentially the same as Freeware™.

The term "Shareware" was coined by Bob Wallace, author of the word processing program PC-WRITE, to describe the technique he invented for distributing this software. As with Freeware or U/S software, the program is made available through users groups, bulletin boards, and by the author himself. But instead of a donation, you are asked to send a registration fee to Quicksoft, Mr. Wallace's firm. The registration fee for PC-WRITE is $75, but you get a lot for your money.

The uniqueness of Shareware centers around what happens next. You are encouraged to make copies of your PC-WRITE disk and share them with friends or anyone who needs a good word processor. If any of these individuals decides to register the program, Quicksoft will pay you a sales commission of $25. According to Mr. Wallace, one SysOp who offers the program on his bulletin board system has already made several hundred dollars this way. The feature that makes it all work is the serial number associated with each copy of the PC-WRITE program. More than likely, you will have obtained your copy from some other user and it will bear that individual's serial number. When you register the program with Quicksoft, you will be asked for that number so that the individual may receive a commission. You will then be given a number of your own, and a disk containing that number will be mailed to you. Following Quicksoft's instructions, you can even insert the number into your copy of the program immediately, though a disk will be mailed to you in any case. Your name and number are put into a computer. (Bob Wallace uses PC-FILE to keep track of these things.) From then on, all of the copies you make will bear *your* number, and you will be paid a $25 commission every time anyone registers one of those copies.

Although the Shareware approach makes it possible for the number of copies of PC-WRITE to expand geometrically, it is not a pyramid scheme as some have alleged. The $25 is a sales commission paid on each copy of the program that you "sell." Since each registered user receives a unique serial number, no one receives a percentage of the sales of subsequent generations of copies.

Freeware, Shareware, and U/S Fundamentals

There is some background information that can be important to anyone interested in obtaining and using Freeware-type programs. That's what we'll present in the following section. However, we suggest that you jump ahead to the sections labeled "The PC Big Three" and "Other User Supported Programs" before reading the following material. If the software is of interest to you, come back here for nuts-and-bolts information that applies to all such programs.

On-Disk Documentation

A natural concern of anyone considering any powerful program is the quality and quantity of the documentation (instruction manuals) provided. Unlike some of the public domain programs we have discussed elsewhere, all of the programs discussed in this chapter come with documentation. In many cases, and especially with the Big Three, the quality is excellent. One can always quibble, but to anyone who has struggled through the abstruse tomes provided by many commercial software houses, these manuals will come as a breath of fresh air. Generally they are conversational in tone and quite complete. Their authors, though programmers themselves, are aware that they are speaking to average computer owners, not to other programmers.

All documentation exists as text files on the same disk that holds the program. You will need a printer to generate hard copy, of course, but there is no need for a word processing program or any additional software. Each of the Big Three authors provides instructions for printing the program's manual, usually in a file with a name like README.TXT that you can list on the screen. Andrew Fluegelman provides a batch file that guides you in listing the documentation to the screen and using the [<CONTROL><PRINT SCREEN>] function to generate a hard copy. Bob Wallace provides his 100-page manual on disk in a file that has been squeezed using data compression techniques. He includes a utility program to expand the file to its regular size and provides instructions for printing it out.

Of the Big Three, Jim Button's approach with PC-FILE is the easiest to use. The PC-FILE manual is about 32 pages long, and it too is stored in compressed form. But Mr. Button includes a program called DOC.EXE to list the "unsqueezed" version to the printer. What's more, the instructions are right on the label of the disks he makes available, so it's easy to print the manual before doing anything else.

"User Support"

The expression "user supported" software arose as a substitute for "Freeware" because that term is legally off limits to all but the holder of its trademark. It is a vague and confusing term that ranks as one of the greater sins computerists are in the process of committing against the English language.

"Vendor support" or "dealer support" in the microworld refer to the information, software and manual updates, and help provided by the software house that created a program, or by the retailer who sold it. At this writing, "user support" has come to mean at least two things. First, it refers to the financial support of the program's author by users who have made a voluntary contribution. And second, it refers to the activities of the community of computer owners who actively use the program. As we saw in Chapter 4, dBASE II, VisiCalc, and other commercial programs have attracted people who are interested in exploring the possibilities of this software by creating command files and spreadsheet templates and by exchanging information with other users. The same thing has happened with a number of Freeware-type programs, only here the involvement can be even greater since in some cases the authors make the source code available.

> **FreeTip:** If you're new to computing you may not completely understand why this is so significant, or what the difference is between "source code" and "object code." Here's the short answer.
>
> A computer can only act upon or run object code. For all intents and purposes, object code is "machine language" consisting of nothing but thousands of 1s and 0s. Source code can be thought of as the English-language equivalent. It consists of the words of the program you write in BASIC, Pascal, or some other computer language. Object code can be produced in at least two ways. It can be created "on the spot" as the source code program is run. (This is what happens when you run most BASIC programs.) Or it can be created once and stored in a file. This is what happens when you use a compiler to translate BASIC source code program into object code.
>
> For our purposes here, the crucial difference is this: If the author makes the source code available, you or anyone else with a knowledge of BASIC (or whatever language the author used) can change it, add features, and generally customize it to your own needs. It is readable text, after all. If the author supplies only the object code—the output of a BASIC compiler, for example—the program cannot be changed or altered.
>
> It is important to point out, however, that user supported programs are not in the public domain. The authors hold the copyrights. You can modify the software, pass the programs around, or do almost anything else you like except offer them as Freeware or Shareware yourself.

In some cases, this has stimulated the growth of an almost clublike community of users focusing on a particular program. Membership is open to everyone. You have only to obtain a copy of the software, and usually one of the "club members" will be happy to give you one. "Club members" share a common dialect—they are thoroughly familiar with the program and its features and with the commands used to activate them. They thus tend to communicate in a shorthand that is all but unintelligible to the uninitiated. They also exchange information and ideas on how to use the program more effectively.

As mentioned, these activities parallel those of dBASE II and VisiCalc users, or, in the public domain, those of the community that has grown up around MODEM7, the CP/M communications program. But this is something special, and if you are considering a Freeware-type program, it is important for you to be aware of it.

Two examples will suffice. Andrew Fluegelman makes available both the source code and the object code for PC-TALK III. The program is written in BASIC. The object code is the product of a BASIC compiler and thus runs much faster, an important factor when you are communicating at 1200 baud. This is a particularly considerate "user-oriented" step since the compiler software necessary to produce your own object code can cost as much as $300.

But the availability of the source code is just as important. For one thing, it provides an excellent tutorial in how to write a good communications program. We know of one bulletin board SysOp, for example, who was involved in creating a public domain BBS program. The SysOp freely credits Mr. Fluegelman's code for suggesting some of the ideas and techniques that were eventually incorporated in that public domain program.

Similarly, when it became known that the Hayes Smartmodem 300 could be "pushed" beyond its 300 baud rating and made to communicate at 450 baud, "club members" quickly created and distributed the necessary patches to the BASIC PC-TALK program to enable this feature. Other individuals have altered or added other features to customize PC-TALK to their special needs. Can you imagine doing the same thing to dBASE II, VisiCalc, or any commercial communications program?

The second example concerns PC-FILE, the database management program. On Disk 89 ("Tools") of the PC/SIG public domain collection discussed in Chapter 6, there is a program called PC-LIB.BAS. (The program is undoubtedly available from other sources as well.) This software is designed to help you keep track of the programs in your "library." It asks you to insert one disk after another, and in each case it reads the directory of files on the disk and places the resulting text in a single master file. As the documentation points out, the resulting file is structured to be compatible with the PC-FILE program. When you have finished inserting disks, you can thus use PC-FILE to alphabetize every filename in your library, or use the program's search feature to locate particular files. Since PC-LIB attaches the disk number or title to each filename when it creates the main file, it is easy to locate the correct disk. "User support" of this type can thus make your copy of PC-FILE even more useful.

The Most Important Feature of "User Support"

The biggest advantage of the U/S distribution technique may be the opportunity it provides for direct contact between the end user and the program author. When you as a registered user phone Quicksoft for help with PC-WRITE, there's a very good chance that Bob Wallace himself will answer the phone.

Similarly, Jim Button reports that "Someone sent me a letter on The Source the other night and said 'I just found an obscure bug in PC-FILE. When I try to do this with it, it does that.'

"I wrote him a quick note that said, 'Fine, I'll check into it.' I signed off The Source and brought up PC-FILE and sure enough, the guy was correct. There was a bug. Next I pulled out the source code and made a simple patch. Then I sent him a corrected disk.

"But not only that, I changed the distribution file so that everyone from then on would receive the updated, fixed version. There have been times when I've thought the bug was important enough that I've gone back and notified all my registered users and said 'There's a bug there, and here's how to avoid it or here's how to get an update.'

"Using the standard approach, if I were distributing PC-FILE through a publishing company, you'd only see one update a year. So I think the user community benefits from the author being able to go in and make those fixes and get out another update right away."

The unique benefits of user-to-author-to-user communications flow in both directions. Mr. Button says that in many cases the direct feedback he gets from users has helped him design a better program and make important improvements.

"So many people are using PC-FILE," he says, "and they all follow my instructions. At the beginning of the program I have a screen that says 'I'd really love to hear your ideas and needs. Let me hear from you.'

"I get wonderful letters. Tons of them. And many of them say, 'Gee, I wish PC-FILE would do this or I wish it would do that.' I can't ignore those letters. I keep reading them, and if I hear a suggestion two or three times, I think, 'Hmm. I wonder if I could get that feature into the code.'

"The old brain starts churning and pretty soon I've got the source code back out again and I'm working out a way to add some new feature."

Many large software companies listen to the users of their products, but the nature of a large organization insulates the creator of a program from the people who are using it. Clearly, user supported software is different.

A Special Note to Owners of IBM Compatibles

If you own an IBM compatible like the Compaq, Corona, Hyperion, Eagle, Radio Shack 2000, or an Apple computer equipped to emulate an IBM (See Appendix B), or some other machine, there is good reason to believe that you will be able to use most of the software described in this chapter. The only way to be absolutely certain is to test the program. Since the programs are available for free or for the cost of a disk, this should not pose a major problem.

If you are a programmer, and if the source code is available, you may be able to make any necessary modifications yourself. The BASIC source code for PC-TALK III is available to everyone. The Pascal source code for PC-WRITE is available to registered users. PC-FILE is available in its compiled form only. Since many other U/S programs are written in Microsoft BASIC, a language that is probably available on your machine, the alterations needed to make them run may be very minor. It all depends on whether the program uses BASIC functions that are unique to the IBM and whether they can be duplicated with your version of Microsoft BASIC.

If you are not a programmer, the best approach is to obtain your copy through a users group, preferably one with a SIG specializing in IBM-compatible computers. Once such organization is the Capital PC group profiled in Chapter 5. You will undoubtedly find others with similar SIGs. Check in your local area first.

Please do not contact the program's author. Most of them have their hands full simply supporting equipment made by IBM. There are at least three other steps you might take. You could place a notice requesting information on the IBM/PC section of the main Source bulletin board. (See Chapter 9.) You could place a similar information request in the IBM/PC SIG on CompuServe. (See Chapter 8.) Or you could contact IPCO via CompuServe or regular mail and ask that your information request be run in "IPCO Info." (See Chapter 6.) You may be able to take advantage of other points of access discussed in this book as well. One way or another, if a version of a Freeware-type program exists for your IBM compatible, you'll find it.

The PC Big Three

Since the IBM Big Three are likely to be of the greatest interest to the greatest number of people, we'll look at these programs in more detail. Then we'll provide contact information and descriptions of the growing array of other programs available to you via the U/S approach. Before we begin, however, there are three things to be said concerning

PCjr compatibility, the availability of the software, and the variations in the support provided by the authors.

PCjr Compatibility

We have spoken to the authors of each of the Big Three programs and learned that PC-TALK III, PC-FILE III, and PC-WRITE will run perfectly on the PCjr with a single disk drive and 128K of internal memory. Here is a quick rundown:

- PC-TALK III requires 64K of RAM to run the interpreted BASIC version; 128K is required for the faster compiled version. Both require a communications card and modem, of course. The files on the distribution disk occupy 280K.

- PC-FILE III is available only in its compiled version and requires 96K of RAM; 128K or more memory is recommended since the program grabs and uses all the memory it can get its hands on and runs faster and better as a result. The files on the distribution disk occupy 190K.

- PC-WRITE is available in its compiled version (though registered users receive the Pascal source code as well) and is so tightly coded that it requires only 64K of RAM. The files on the distribution disk occupy 150K.

Earlier versions of TALK and FILE can also be run with 64K. However, although these versions are still widely available, they do not include the latest features. PC-TALK II, for example, does not support XMODEM protocol file transfers (see Appendix A). PC-FILE Version 9.1 permitted a maximum of 4,000 records per database, but PC-FILE III (Version 1.0) permits 9,999 and has many other enhancements as well.

Thus, if you are interested in the PCjr, you will really need the Expanded Model (128K, one disk drive; $1,269). If you have an Entry Model (64K, no disk drive; $669), you can add the standard double-sided disk drive (360K) for $480. That will give you what you need to run PC-WRITE and the earlier versions of the other Big Three programs. However, since the 64K RAM and Display Expansion (80 columns) card that completes the upgrade costs only $140, many users will want to add that as well. All of these programs will run better with more available memory.

These figures are the IBM list prices current at this writing. To save you doing the addition, the cost difference between upgrading an Entry Model or purchasing the Expanded Model is only $20. IBM did not become what it is today without knowing how to price its products.

FreeTip: Regardless of the model you have purchased or are thinking about buying, you may want to wait as long as possible before adding a disk drive, extra memory, a printer adaptor, a communications card, or any other peripheral. If the precedent set by the IBM/PC and other models is any guide, there will soon be many "third party" (non-IBM) suppliers, whose products may be better suited to your needs than those available from "Big Blue."

One excellent way to stay on top of what's available for the PCjr is to consult the latest copy of *PCjr Magazine* or *PCjr World*. You can find these on your local newsstand, or contact the addresses below for information on the latest subscription rates:

PCjr Magazine
Ziff Davis Publishing Co.
One Park Avenue
New York, NY 10016

PCjr World
555 De Haro Street
San Francisco, CA 94107

Program Availablity

Of the Big Three programs, the easiest to obtain is PC-WRITE, since you can either send a check for $10 or phone Quicksoft and charge the cost to your major credit card. If you want a free copy of Mr. Fluegelman's and Mr. Button's programs, you'll have to get it from a users group or one of the other sources cited elsewhere in this book. Alternatively, you can save yourself some time and immediately gain the benefits of becoming a registered user if you simply send a check for the requested contribution. Mr. Fluegelman and Mr. Button will then send you the latest version of their programs. This is what we would advise, though it is our suggestion and not that of the program authors.

Both gentlemen have asked us to emphasize that they can no longer place their software on disks you supply as they have done in the past. Their programs have become so popular that they no longer have time to fill such requests, and if you send them a disk, it will be returned to you unopened.

Other Sources

You can obtain the Big Three and many other U/S programs from a variety of other sources. The most convenient single source we have found is Richard Petersen's PC/SIG described in Chapter 6. The cost is $6 per disk, plus $4 per order for shipping and handling. Mr. Petersen has assembled a large portion of the U/S software available. Indeed, he reports that many U/S authors send him their programs because PC/SIG makes it easier for them to get the software distributed.

Other sources include IPCO and the Capital PC Users Group. Both organizations require you to be a member and charge $6 to $8 per U/S disk, postage and handling included. (See Chapters 6 and 5, respectively.) At this writing neither organization offers as comprehensive a selection as PC/SIG, though that will undoubtedly change. Other IBM users groups and super group SIGs cited elsewhere will also have the programs, as will your local group.

FreeTip: Users groups and other organizations offer a convenient way to obtain several U/S programs by placing a single order. If you like the software, you can then send the requested donation to the author.

This approach makes a lot of sense for most of the non–Big Three programs for which updates and improvements are usually not made as frequently, if at all. However, if you are interested in one of the Big Three, you will probably be best off if you contact the author directly and order your disk from him.

This may be less convenient than placing an order with a users group, but it is the only way to be assured of receiving the most up-to-date version. And since all three authors have some kind of "staff" to help them, there is a good chance that you will receive your program sooner.

FreeTip: Very important. Do not—repeat—do not try to order the Big Three programs by contacting a single author. Each is independent of the other and each has his own operation. At one time both TALK and FILE were offered under the Freeware banner. But this is no longer true. Messrs. Fluegelman and Button are still good friends, but both report that things simply became too complicated. Consequently, both have asked us to emphasize that Mr. Button is the man to contact for PC-FILE and Mr. Fluegelman is the man to contact for PC-TALK.

Support

When you pay $150, $500, or $700 for a commercial communications, word processing, or database management program, part of what you are buying is "support" from the software house, the retailer, or both. (You may not always receive all the support you pay for, but that's another story.) When you obtain public domain software, on the other hand, support is one of the things you must do without.

Freeware, Shareware, and U/S programs fall somewhere in between. In the first place, it is unreasonable to expect any of these authors to answer your questions if you have not sent in your contribution and become a registered user. Although they may answer you in any case, common courtesy demands that you fulfill their modest requests and send them a check. All three of these programs are a steal at triple their price.

As a registered user of PC-WRITE, you are entitled to telephone support, and the people at Quicksoft will happily answer your questions. You can reach Mr. Fluegelman and Mr. Button by mail. (Please do not send inquiries to *PC World* or *MAC World*, the magazines Mr. Fluegelman edits.) Be sure to print out and read their instruction manuals first. If you still have a serious problem, by all means send them an electronic or paper letter.

> **FreeTip:** If you have never considered a communications, database, or word processing program before, you may not be familiar with the features described in the following profiles of PC-TALK, PC-FILE, and PC-WRITE. You will find the information you need, however, in the Toolchest section of *How to Buy Software.*

PC-TALK III — Communications

The Headlands Press, Inc.
P.O. Box 862
Tiburon, CA 94920

Author: Andrew Fluegelman.

Requires: 64K for interpreted BASIC version and 128K for compiled version. Both are supplied on the distribution disk. Program can be run with a single-sided disk drive. DOS 1.0, 1.1, and 2.x are supported.

Length of Manual: 70 pages.

Requested Contribution: $35

How to Obtain: Distribution files total 280K. Contact a users group or other source cited elsewhere in this book for a free copy. Or send the requested donation to the address given above. Do not send the author a blank disk as it will be returned unopened.

Comments and Features: How good is PC-TALK III? According to a recent survey conducted by McGraw-Hill's Datapro Research, Inc., business users ranked PC-TALK among their favorite and most frequently used programs. At least three presidents of commercial software firms across the country have told us that they feel the pressure from PC-TALK and consequently cannot charge what they had planned for their commercial communications programs. Other individuals in the commercial software industry are less than enthusiastic Fluegelman supporters for similar reasons.

There is an important—even revolutionary—dimension to the appearance of products like PC-TALK. It represents a unique combination of the tenets of both Karl Marx and Adam Smith. Affordable microcomputers have put "the means of production" in the hands of "the workers," at least those "workers" with more than a thousand dollars to spend. At the same time, in the best traditions of competition and the free market, the products they have created and offered have driven down the prices of competing products.

There are arguments on both sides of this issue. Certainly one can be sympathetic with the commercial firm that invests money and pays wages and taxes to create its products in the expectation of making a profit, but who can deny the "better mousetrap" philosophy that has been responsible for the success of so many entrepreneurs?

FreeTip: As it happens, influenced by PC-TALK, in February of 1984 a commercial firm introduced a "better mousetrap." It's called SYSCOMM/ABSCOMM and it is produced by Microlife. According to Jerry Shipman, the firm's president, the package will do everything PC-TALK will do. But it also includes features like these:

- A batch transfer option to allow you to send a range of files using the XMODEM protocol. You can use *.* or wildcards, for example. The person on the receiving end does not even have to be there since the sender can handle everything automatically.

- A feature called POLITE that produces two windows on your screen and allows both computer operators to talk back and forth while file transfers are taking place.

- Complete auto-log on for any database. You tell the program when you want it to place the call and give it the file containing your account number, password, and other information. You can then leave and go about your business. This one's really impressive since the program will send its response only after it receives the database sign-on prompt you have specified.

You can even select your own colors. There is an excellent 70-page illustrated manual designed to fit into a three-ring IBM documentation binder. Users receive telephone support and free updates. The cost of the package: $40.

The program runs under any version of DOS and requires an 80-column display and 128K of memory. It also runs on the Columbia, the Eagle, and other IBM compatibles. For information contact:

Microlife, Inc.
P.O. Box 340
Jessup, MD 20794
(301) 799-5509

PC-TALK III is a full-featured smart terminal program capable of communicating with remote databases, corporate mainframes, and nearby computers connected with a null modem cable. It can run as slowly as 75 baud and as fast as 9600 baud with anywhere from four to eight data bits at even, odd, space, mark, or no parity. It can both send and receive files directly from disk, without the need to first load them into a buffer. It supports the XMODEM binary file transfer protocol. There is also a straight binary file transfer mode for use when you want to transfer machine language files to a directly cabled machine that does not support XMODEM.

At any one time, you may also specify up to three ASCII characters to be either stripped (thrown away) or converted to some other character as they are received. This is useful if the remote database or mainframe is programmed to send an end-of-file character (ASCII 26) or some other troublemaker at the end of each paragraph or block of text. Unfortunately, this "translation table" feature represents "half a loaf." Though it is not necessary for most applications, one would hope that PC-TALK would eventually be able to convert characters on output as well as on input since this can make it easier to "talk" to computers running a less flexible program.

> **FreeTip:** Here's an excellent example of the support for PC-TALK provided by the "user community." The following notice from one TALK user to another appeared as a message on one of the bulletin board systems operated by the Capital PC Users Group in Washington, D.C.:
>
> > The Dow Jones News/Retrieval Service sends ASCII characters 30 and 31 with the prompts resulting in some wild cursor ups and downs. To avoid the problem, I set up the PC-TALK Dialing Directory to include character stripping. When asked if you want stripping, respond *Y*, specify the following: 030/013/031/010/127/000, and press <ENTER> . . . Hope this helps.

The printer can be toggled on and off to generate a hard copy printout of text as it comes in over the communications line. And a "snapshot" of the screen can be dumped to the printer at any time, or if you like, you can dump the screen to a disk file. There is an upload pacing option that allows you to order the system to pause a specified amount of time after sending each line. This can be important when you are uploading a file to The Source, CompuServe, or some other remote computer. When these systems are heavily loaded (lots of users checking their mailboxes and chatting via CB), their mainframes can miss some of the characters you send them because their processors are off handling someone else as the characters come in.

You can take time out to look at the contents of a disk file before sending it without leaving the communications mode. You can even erase files without ever going out to DOS.

There are other features, of course, but two deserve special mention. On is the Dialing Directory. This is a list with room for up to 60 names and phone numbers, as well as the communications parameters, character stripping/converting, and other options you have specified for each entry. Designed to be used with an auto-dial modem, this makes it possible for you to record your favorite bulletin board, database, and other phone number once and "dial" them at the touch of a button from then on. You have only to type in the desired item number from the Dialing Directory menu.

PC-TALK III defaults to Hayes Smartmodem support, but you can easily make it issue the auto dial and other commands that non-Hayes modems need to see. There is even an automatic redial feature that will cause the system to dial the specified number once every minute (or at any interval you specify) until a connection is made. When the target phone picks up, the system will sound an alarm to notify you to return to the console.

> **FreeTip:** Note that there is no reason why you must limit your use of the auto dial feature to phoning other computers. You can easily use your system to keep dialing the chronically busy phone number of your broker, a theater box office, the customer "hotline" provided by the vendor of a commercial software package, your editor, or a real human being.

The second feature worthy of special note is the "string loadable keys" option. PC-TALK III lets you assign "strings"—like your CompuServe account number, your CompuServe password, or some other frequently used sequence of characters—to up to 40 different keys. The program uses the function keys <F1> through <F10> as one set of 10 and combinations of those keys and the <ALT>, <SHIFT>, and <CONTROL> keys for three additional sets of ten. Key assignments can be made on the spot, or they can be stored in a file and loaded in each time you boot the program.

Additional features include display of elapsed time for any call, an instantly available "help screen" command summary, the ability to send a true BREAK signal ("regular" or "sustained"), X-ON/X-OFF support, and error messages. The only important thing this package appears to lack is a "character prompted uploading" feature that would cause it to send a line of text only after it received a specified "prompt" character from the remote database or mainframe. When the other system cooperates, this is a more accurate way of uploading files than pausing at the end of every line since the remote system won't issue the prompt until it is ready to receive a line of text.

Future Enhancements?

One of the most fascinating things about PC-TALK is the wonderful sense of community that Mr. Fluegelman and his program have created. As he points out in his documentation, "This version of PC-TALK has incorporated the suggestions of many users who made modifications to earlier versions. Some of these earlier modifications were posted on bulletin boards and became, in effect, 'standard' modifications to the earlier program. There are still many more useful modifications which could be made, and we would like to encourage this grassroots improvement process. . . . Program lines form 10000 have specifically been reserved for this purpose."

You will want to read the rest of this section of the documentation yourself for advice on how to go about submitting "mods" (modifications) to the program. But we thought we'd ask Andrew Fluegelman himself what he had in mind in the way of future enhancements. Here's what he said:

"There are a few minor things that I might stick in mainly to support weird modems. I hear about people who have modems that are just nowhere near being Hayes-compatible as far as the auto-dial feature goes. So I might generalize that a little bit. If I were to come out with a major new version, the last obvious thing to stick in there would be a 'scripted operation' feature.

"With this feature you could say 'At midnight, log onto The Source and download these files. Then check PARTI for any messages. Then get me the day's closing price of April wheat futures. Then log off.' It really wouldn't be that hard to program, and I think I'll probably do it some day when I have time."

PC-FILE III™ Database File Management

Mr. Jim Button
P.O. Box 5786
Bellevue, WA 98006
Source: CL2925
CompuServe: 71435,2012

Author: Jim Button.

Requires: 96K, minimum, but 128K is recommended. "You'll see a sizeable speed improvement. The sort will also run faster. Your maximum record length will increase. Beyond 160K of memory, no improvement will be noticed." Can be run on a single-sided 160K drive. Operates under DOS 1.1 and and 2.x.

Length of Manual: 32 pages

Requested Contribution: $45.

How to Obtain: Distribution files total 190K. Contact a users group or other source cited elsewhere in this book for a free copy. Or send the requested donation to the address given above. Do not send the author a blank disk as it will be returned unopened.

Comments and Features: PC-FILE III is *not* a relational database management system (DBMS) like dBASE II. Technically, it is a "file management" program that can more properly be compared to VisiCorp's VisiFile, IUS's EasyFiler, and similar commercial programs. (You'll find an explanation of the difference in Chapter 16 of *How to Buy Software.*) Like its commercial counterparts, PC-FILE does an excellent job of keeping track of and manipulating information. For people who do not need the power (and complexity) of a program like dBASE, PC-FILE can be an excellent choice.

Information Management/PC-FILE Basics

All information management systems can be divided into several main functions. "Data entry" is the process of typing in the information you want to keep track of. It could be employees, names and addresses, telephone number, recipes, customers, or any other collection of individual but related pieces of information. Each "big" piece of information is called a record, but it is often divided into smaller pieces called fields. Your first name, last name, middle initial, house or apartment number, street name, city, state, ZIP code, and telephone number might constitute a single record, while each of the information components we've just listed would be a field.

PC-FILE III lets you create up to 9,999 records per database file. That's a lot of products, part numbers, employees, or coins in your coin collection. Each record may have up to 41 fields (first name, last name, ZIP code, etc.). And each field may have a maximum of 65 characters. A single record may contain a maximum of 1,440 characters.

These figures assume an 80-column display. If you have a 40 column display, then the maximum field length will be 25 instead of 65 characters and the maximum number of fields per record will be 21 instead of 41.

"Data retrieval" is the process of finding the records you have typed into your "database" file and either displaying them on the screen again or sending them to the printer or both. This is usually done on the basis of what's in a particular field. You can say, "Find me every record with 'John' in the field called 'FIRSTNAME' . . . Find me everyone who lives on 'Elmwood Glen Drive' . . ." and so on.

PC-FILE lets you get at your information based on the contents of any field. You can specify the entire string as your search criteria ("Elmwood Glen Drive") or just a part of it ("wood"). Retrieval specifications can also be much more sophisticated. For example, you can say

"Give me the records of all employees who have worked for the firm for more than five years but less than ten years OR have had five years work experience elsewhere AND have had advanced training in biomechanics." In all, you may specify a total of ten "and/or" comparisons.

"Sorting" a database means just what you think it means. Individual records are rearranged (or appear to be rearranged) on the basis of the information stored in one or more of their fields. PC-FILE lets you sort your records on the basis of the contents of up to ten fields. You can thus tell the program to sort first on the basis of a person's LASTNAME and, within that list, on the basis of ZIP code, and within that list, on the basis of digits five through seven of the PHONE field, and so on. The program can sort approximately 400 records a minute.

"Printing reports" refers to the process of generating some kind of hard copy containing some or all of the information found in the records of your database. You might want to print out address labels, for example, containing just the name and address of each person in your database, but not their telephone numbers. At another time, you might want just a list of people and phone numbers, but no address information. When you print reports with PC-FILE, you can specify both the specific fields each report will contain and where the information will appear in the page or label.

FreeTip: One of the crucial questions to ask about any information management system is "What happens if I want to add more fields to my records or make longer fields after I've entered my data?" The random access files used by PC-FILE and similar programs make it easy to quickly locate individual records, but the technique requires you to specify the number of fields and the character length of each before you begin entering data. This causes the program to allocate a certain amount of space for each record and in effect locks you into that format.

With some programs, if you later decide that you want to add new or longer fields to each record, you could be out of luck. You will either have to live with what you've got or design a new database format and re-enter all of your data.

PC-FILE solves this problem with its CLONING feature. In effect, you can design a new database format with additional and longer fields and tell the program "Take all the information from my old database and insert it in the proper locations in the new format."

"Goodies" and Other Features

The manual does a good job of explaining the program, though if you're a brand new computer user you will probably have some initial difficulty understanding what's going on. Chapter 16 of *How to Buy Software* will help, as will rereading the manual and playing with the program. If you are a new user, be sure to follow Mr. Button's instructions and print the manual before doing anything else, since you are likely to be lost without it.

If you have had more experience, however, you will find that the program is so easy to use that you can plunge right in and begin defining your database immediately. When you're finished naming your fields and specifying their lengths, simply hit <ENTER> at the next "Field Name" prompt, and you're ready to begin typing in data. When you've finished hit <ENTER> again when the next blank record appears, and you'll be presented with an easy-to-follow menu of options.

Mr. Button is constantly adding features and otherwise improving his program. And since contributing users are notified of major enhancements and given the opportunity to obtain copies of the new program for $10, this represents a major incentive to send in the requested contribution. (As *InfoWorld* columnist Doug Clapp once wrote: "If you use PC-FILE and don't send Jim Button a check, the guilt will kill you. And it should.") The last version of the original PC-FILE program was Version 9.1. In January of 1984, Mr. Button issued PC-FILE III, Version 1.0, a major enhancement. Here are just a few of the "goodies" Mr. Button added to an already outstanding program:

- Optional "data encryption" with a security code.

- "Calculated" report fields. Up to 20 fields can now be added, subtracted, multiplied, or divided by other fields or constants.

- PC-IMPOR implemented to bring DIF files such as the data files created by VisiCalc™, "mail merge" files such as those used by WordStar™, or files created with a word processing program *into* your PC-FILE database.

- Enhanced PC-EXPOR to "export" PC-FILE records not only to VisiCalc, DIF, and mail merge formats, but also to a word processing format. Among other things, this feature lets you use PC-FILE data with Lotus 1-2-3™, Multiplan™, and other commercial programs.

- Automatic entry of data into date, time, and "empty" fields.

- Floating point (scientific-notation) numbers can now be used in numeric fields and will be sorted and totaled correctly.

- And more, of course.

FreeTip: One of the changes made with PC-FILE Version 9.1 was a switch to the Microsoft BASIC compiler. According to Mr. Button, this "yields smaller size programs, and programs which should be more compatible with other MS-DOS computers." When we spoke with Mr. Button, we also learned that a version of PC-FILE is available for Osborne owners. "I've made it available . . . but the Osborne has pretty well died," Mr. Button said. "This is PC-FILE Version 8.6 which is quite an old version. I converted to the Osborne because Osborne BASIC and IBM/PC BASIC are almost identical. It's still available. And I'm still receiving checks from the Osborne community, but it has never been anything like the number of IBM users." If you own an Osborne or know someone who does, "Tell a friend."

The Genesis of PC-FILE

Jim Button is a professional computer consultant and systems analyst with over 17 years' experience in the field. His speciality is mainframe and minicomputer operating systems. He wrote PC-FILE because he needed it himself. "I had an Apple at the time," he said when we spoke to him recently. "I needed to print some mailing labels and to keep track of some names and addresses for a church membership file. So I sat down and said, 'How am I going to do what I need to do here?' I roughed out a crude little program that would do all of the things I wanted, but while I was at it I said 'Well I might as well make it a database type of approach so that if I have to use it for anything else, I can use the same program. That would have been in about 1979 or 1980.

"Then I kept enhancing that program for my own needs. And when the IBM came out I said 'Well, I'm going to sell the Apple and get the IBM and I've got to have that program on it. In the conversion process I added some more things. And as I gave it to friends and associates here in the Seattle area, they'd say 'Gee, we wish you would do this or wish you would do that.'

"By the time I started distributing it with the user supported approach, the program had been on the IBM for quite a while, and all of the updates that I had added had used commands and language types of statements that are available only on the IBM. To convert it back to the Apple, although I considered it many times, would have been a very large project. Even though it came from there originally, only about a third of the progam as it now stands was original Apple code. I'm not even sure that the Apple could handle it."

FreeTip: We asked whether the fact that PC-FILE is written in Microsoft BASIC wouldn't make it possible to bring it over to a wide number of machines. "Absolutely," he said. "The problem's not the code, it's lack of time. My consulting work keeps me busy eight hours a day, and when I get home at night I have to answer all my phone calls, read all my mail, answer all the letters, and make sure everything got distributed as it was supposed to. By then it's bedtime.

"The idea of putting PC-FILE on the TI, the Wang, and all those other computers is tempting, since it would be so easy to do. But I just have not had the time."

FreeTip: If you're technically inclined, you'll be interested to know that Mr. Button uses Microsoft BASIC and the Microsoft BASIC compiler to produce his programs. "Since the Microsoft compiler doesn't support all of the features of IBM BASIC, I had to code some screen handling routines in assembler to get it converted to the Microsoft compiler. But the advantage was that since it doesn't support all those game type things, the object code produced by this compiler is many K smaller. That makes PC-FILE III run faster, and the more compact code lets people with only 64K work with bigger databases.

"The compiler works fine with DOS 1.1 and 2.0, but it does not support things like tree structures and 'change directory' commands. But that's okay as long as you run the program out of the same directory that holds your data."

At this writing, there is no BASIC compiler to support all of the features added by DOS 2.0. However, the day after such a product becomes available, it's a good bet that Mr. Button will have his source code out and be adding code to take advantage of those enhancements.

Mr. Button said that he originally bought his Source and CompuServe subscriptions so that he could advertise the program on the main bulletin boards of those two systems. "That's the only form of advertising I have ever used. I don't run the announcement anymore. But back in the early history that's the way I got the distribution started."

We asked about the logistics of filling orders for PC-FILE and supporting the program and learned that it amounts to nearly a full-time job for several members of the Button household. "My son fills the orders," Mr. Button says. "That gives him a job to help him earn money for college. John is seventeen, so he'll be leaving soon. I'm going to turn it over to his brother, Steven, who is fourteen."

Mrs. Button is also on the case, working almost full time screening incoming mail and handling many of the replies. The Buttons have turned one bedroom into a combination office/computer room. "We had to expand and buy another PC," Mr. Button explains. "I found that there was so much time spent using our original machine for copying that I wasn't able to get on and do any more program development."

Asked if he purchased a stripped-down model to do the copying, Mr. Button laughs and says, "Well we intended to, but we ended up upgrading it to almost the capacity of the original PC so we could have flexibility. Either one can be used for copying and both have the power I need for program development."

Finally, we asked about the continuing stream of PC-FILE improvements, extra features, and enhancements that flows from Mr. Button's computers. "I don't do the updates with the idea of somehow keeping PC-FILE 'competitive.' While it wouldn't be impossible for someone to create an equivalent program, it would be difficult to do, and it isn't likely that someone else would try this approach.

"What motivates me is just pride in what I've created and that large body of users out there that I would like to keep happy. I think the sense of community and author-user communication that develops is one of the big benefits of the User Supported or Freeware approach." Thousands of people approve of Mr. Button's work. And evidently his local church does too, since they've still got him doing the address labels that got him started on the program years ago.

PC-WRITE — Word Processing

Quicksoft
219 First N. #224
Seattle, WA 98109
(206) 282-0452
Visa and MasterCard accepted.

Author: Bob Wallace

Requires: 64K, minimum. Allows editing of about six pages at a time. With 128K or more, you can edit about 31 pages at a time. Requires a minimum of one single-sided (160K) disk drive. Will run under DOS 1.0, 1.1, and 2.x. At this writing the program does not support a 40-column display and thus cannot be conveniently used with a color television. Bob Wallace says that this feature is not that difficult to add and he will do so if there is sufficient demand.

Length of Manual: 100 pages; includes an index.

Requested Contribution: $75.

How to Obtain: Quicksoft will send you a copy of the latest version for $10. You may phone the above number and charge this to your credit card or write and send the firm a check. You may also register at the same time, charging $75 to your credit card, but you do not have to do this to obtain a copy.

Comments and Features: Any IBM owner who doubts that it is possible to obtain commercial quality programs for as little as $10 has only to order and run a copy of PC-WRITE to be convinced. It is difficult to decide which is more dazzling—the program's speed, Mr. Wallace's lavish and effective use of color, or the bushel basket of "goodies" and extra features he has tucked into the extraordinarily compact code.

Perhaps one should expect no less from someone of Mr. Wallace's gifts and experience, but still, it dazzles. Bob Wallace began designing text processors in 1969 while a student at Brown University. He holds a master's degree in computer science, and, in 1978, he was one of the first dozen people to join a little Bellevue, Washington, firm called Microsoft. While at Microsoft he designed the language and architecture, wrote the compiler front end, and wrote much of the runtime for Microsoft's MS-Pascal. Since this is one of the fastest and most powerful languages for the IBM/PC, and since no one knows its ins and outs better than Mr. Wallace, it was the natural choice when it came time to create PC-WRITE.

FreeTip: As explained earlier, when you become a registered user you are entitled to a $25 sales commission any time someone registers a copy of your program. That means your total cost could be $50 or lower, depending on how many copies you "sell." Whether

FreeTip continued

or not you ever "sell" a program, you will receive a printed, spiral bound copy of the manual, the latest update of the program, telephone support, and a copy of the Pascal and assembler source code. According to Mr. Wallace, "There are enough people interested in 'source.' For some, it adds an extra value to registration, even if they don't know how to write programs themselves."

The source code supplied is complete and well commented, though much of it is in assembly language. If you know what you're doing and have the necessary compiler and assembler software, you can modify the program to suit your needs.

FreeTip: The $10 distribution disk comes with a file called MANUAL.CRN (for "crunched"). This is identical to the printed manual you will receive when you register the program, except that, being disk-based, it may be slightly more up-to-date. To "uncrunch" this file, you must use the supplied EXPAND.COM utility.

There is an instruction file on the disk to tell you what to do, but it assumes a double-drive system. These instructions may be updated to accommodate PCjr users, but in case they aren't on your copy, here is what you need to know. The two files mentioned above, plus the expanded translation of the manual, occupy slightly more than 250K. This means you will have enough room on a single 360K disk. Copy EXPAND.COM and MANUAL.CRN onto a formatted blank disk. Then at the DOS prompt type *EXPAND MANUAL.CRN MANUAL.DOC* and hit <ENTER>.

If you have a PC, XT, or another computer equipped with enough memory for an electronic disk drive, copy the above two files into "drive C," put a blank disk in drive B, and at the DOS prompt for drive C type *EXPAND MANUAL.CRN B:MANUAL.DOC* and hit <ENTER>. This will greatly speed up the "uncrunching" process and save you from giving drive A a workout.

The Question of Quickness

PC-WRITE is a full-screen editor like WordStar™ or MultiMate™, of course. As you create your text, you can move quickly and easily from any spot to any other spot and back again, whether the "spots" are separated by a single line, a paragraph, or all of the pages in the document. You will be most aware of PC-WRITE's blinding speed whenever you want to go from the first line to the last line of a multi-page document. When editing a 60K file in memory (about 31 double-spaced pages), you go top-to-bottom in a single second. The screen simply flashes, and there you are. Some leading commercial programs can take anywhere from 3 to 10 seconds to accomplish the same thing.

The program's "search and replace" feature is equally quick. We tested it using a 55K file consisting of 30 pages of text. The time required to replace every occurrence of the word *the* with the word *banana* was under two minutes. The program reported that it performed 728 replacements. As an experiment, we conducted the indentical test using a major commercial program. And to give the commercial contender every benefit, we ran it from a hard disk drive and copied the textfile into an electronic disk. The time required to do what PC-WRITE accomplished in two minutes was nine minutes and 20 seconds.

Independently Scrolling Windows

PC-WRITE offers many convenient "whistles and bells," far too many even to list here. However, there is one feature you absolutely must know about. At any time, you can split your screen into two windows. You simply move the cursor to the place where you wish the dividing line to occur and hit <F2>. A "margin" or "ruler line" will then appear at that spot. To scroll through your text, you move the cursor into the desired window and hit the appropriate keys. While you're doing this, the second window will remain "frozen." You can easily switch from one window to another. Any editing changes you make in either window will be saved just as they would be if the text filled the entire screen.

You might use this feature to keep reference material on the screen in one window while you worked in another, but that is one of its lesser applications. Far more important is the fact that you can use PC-WRITE's windows to combine one file with another, or to pull blocks of text out of one file and insert them into the one you are currently creating. In other words, you can tell the program that you want to edit two different files at the same time. Thus if you have gotten to page 4 of a report and decide to insert a table of figures or several paragraphs from page 15 of a file that you created last month, you can easily perform the "cut and paste" operation with PC-WRITE windows.

Color, Color, Color

In some computer industry circles, the mania for color displays is so pervasive that one can have the best program in the world and "It don't mean a thing if it ain't got red, blue, and green." Consequently, the use of color, while it may help move computers and sell software, is often gratuitous. Although one could alter PC-TALK III to display text in color, the program does not suffer from displaying text in black and white. The same might be said of PC-FILE.

But a word processing program is different. Because you spend a great deal of time concentrating on the text that is displayed on the screen, the imaginative use of color can be a real asset.

Although PC-WRITE can be used with a monochrome display, it really shines if your system is equipped with a color monitor. (On a monochrome display, special text that would otherwise be in color is shown with reverse highlighting.) You can select any combination of colors you like, including colors for: the border, the background, normal text, the text you mark as a block to be moved or deleted (conditional), the same text after you have decided to confirm the marking, the keys on the "Help" screens, the text on the "Help" screens, and three other possibilities. Needless to say, this can make text creation (writing) both fun and easy.

Upgrades and Enhancements

The copy of PC-WRITE we tested is Version 1.4, but as you read this, Version 2.2, a major upgrade according to Bob Wallace, should be available. According to Mr. Wallace, Version 2.2 "has horizontal scrolling and printer support for special fonts. For example, when you hit [<ALT-B><B> at the beginning or end of a word, that inserts what's called a 'font character.' The text between the font characters is actually brighter, so you can see it. (You can elect to have the font characters displayed on the screen, or not.) When the text goes to your printer, the font characters tell the printer to use bold or compressed print, to add an underline or to use a strike-out (this draws a line through a word and is especially important for lawyers), or to use double underline or super- and subscripts, and so on. The program will support just about any special printing feature.

"I am also including more 'Help' screens. In Version 1.4 there is only one 'Help' screen, but Version 2.2 has nine. This means you can really get started right away and do quite a bit without even looking at the manual." A spelling checker and a mail merge feature are planned for the near future.

FreeTip: If you are technically inclined, you may be interested in knowing how Bob Wallace modified his program to make it completely compatible with the PCjr.

"I didn't have to do anything to make it run on the PCjr. I undid something. I was playing a trick with the keyboard. Basically I pretended NUM-LOCK was on all the time. And I would go and turn it on again if someone tried to turn it off. Then I would interpret the keys coming out the reverse of the way they would normally be interpreted. I was going to all that trouble for two reasons. One, I wanted to get the center *5* key on the numeric keypad to do something. And second, I wanted the <INSERT> key to repeat.

"But I finally decided it wasn't worth all the extra trouble, so I just took all that stuff out. When I was doing that it meant I couldn't work well with ProKey and it wouldn't work on the Junior. Now it runs perfectly—though the PCjr is inherently slower than the PC 'Senior.'

"That was all I had to do to get it to run on the Junior. But I did do a couple other things. To use the Function keys on the Junior, you have to hit the <FN> key and one of the digits. But on the regular PC I also use the <SHIFT> and a function key for various things. That meant that to do the same thing on the Junior, someone would have to enter three key strokes: <FN>, <SHIFT>, and a digit. That seemed like a lot of keys. In Version 2.2 I modified things so that instead I use <ALT> with a digit."

As an additional note, there are two versions of 1.4. One of them supports the Junior and the other does not, though Mr. Wallace sent out a patch to all 1.4 users and clubs that had the program. To make certain that you obtain the latest version, order your copy directly from Quicksoft.

Like the other two IBM Big Three programs, PC-WRITE is clearly worth your consideration. The only major flaw we can find is the fact that, at this writing, the program does not make it easy for you to generate form letters. But then, neither do many commercial word processors.

FreeTip: If you are interested in obtaining PC-WRITE for your company or your school system, you should know that Mr. Wallace has an especially enlightened attitude about making multiple copies of the program. "I will be selling the printed manuals sepa-

FreeTip continued

rately," he said. "They will cost $25 apiece, or $15 in quantity. These will be useful in a corporation or a larger company. Or in a school. The organization would have to register at least one copy of PC-WRITE, though there is probably not much incentive for them to register the additional copies they will make. But they would probably like to have a manual at each work station that uses the program."

PC-CALC—The Fourth Shoe

With the release of Jim Button's PC-CALC electronic spreadsheet program in May of 1984, the final component of a complete Freeware/User Supported library of productivity software for the PC fell into place. Mr. Button is making this program available through users groups and the other channels used for Freeware-type programs. As with PC-FILE III and PC-DIAL (see below), you can also order a copy from the author by sending the requested $45 contribution.

Though not available for review at press time, here is a quick rundown of PC-CALC's major features. (If your spreadsheets are unfamiliar to you, see Chapter 15 of *How to Buy Software* for an explanation of the following terms and suggestions on how you might tap a spreadsheet's power.)

- 36 columns
- 255 rows
- Variable column widths
- User-selectable colors
- Ability to move and insert rows and columns
- Complete online "Help" facility accessible with the F-keys
- Largely patterned after SuperCalc™ in format and prompts

Mr. Button says that PC-CALC does not support the DIF file storage format that is designed to let DIF-supporting programs share data. However, PC-CALC does include an interface that will let you import and export data to PC-FILE. This means you can develop information with PC-CALC and transfer it to PC-FILE for sorting and other manipulations. You can also transfer information prepared with PC-FILE into PC-CALC.

One of the most interesting features of the PC-CALC package supplied by Mr. Button is a 30-item questionnaire designed to elicit comments from users regarding the features they would most like to see incorporated in future releases. Mr. Button indicated that the ability to sort data within the PC-CALC program itself may be one such future enhancement.

Other User Supported Programs

As one might expect, the success enjoyed by the IBM Big Three has encouraged other programmers to try the Freeware/User Supported distribution technique. Listed below are ten user supported programs that are likely to be of value to many IBM owners. These are not the only U/S programs available, but they are some of the best we know of. In most cases, you can obtain a copy by sending a blank, formatted disk, disk mailer, address label, and return postage to the program's author. However, many may be available from users group libraries, computer bulletin board systems, and other sources as well.

Because Richard Petersen's PC/SIG, profiled in Chapter 6, is perhaps the closest thing to a "library of record" in the IBM/PC free software world, you might want to check there first. Since you may want to obtain a program immediately, we have provided the PC/SIG disk number to use when placing your order. At this writing, PC/SIG does not offer all of the programs cited below, but that will undoubtedly change. Send for the catalogue for the most up-to-date list. Here is the necessary address and ordering information:

PC Software Interest Group (PC/SIG)
1556 Halford Avenue Suite #130
Santa Clara, CA 95051
(408) 730-9291
Visa and MasterCard accepted.
California residents, add 6.5% sales tax

Catalogue: $5.95, including postage

Disks: $6 each, plus $4 per order for shipping and handling.

CHASM (CHeap ASseMbler) 8086 Assembler

Mr. David Whitman
136 Wellington Terrace
Landsdale, PA 19446

Order: PC/SIG Disk 10; or from author (recommended).

Comments: The above address for Mr. Whitman is current as of February 1984. (Older copies of the program give his former address at Dartmouth.) The copy we looked at was Version 1.9, but we have learned from talking to Mr. Whitman that Version 3.14 has recently been released. The requested donation is $30. Though not a macro assembler, this program will do many of the things that the IBM Macro Assembler program ($100) will do and some things that it will *not* do. Because Mr. Whitman is a skilled writer as well as a programmer, his documentation is outstanding. CHASM thus offers an excellent way to learn more about assembly language at a very reasonable price. If you find that you like it, you will undoubtedly want to purchase the IBM product, but you may find yourself using both programs. Here is what Mr. Whitman had to say about his creation:

"Because CHASM produces code that can be immediately run on your machine, as opposed to an intermediate module that must be linked, it is well suited for self-contained pure assembly language programs. Also, the IBM assembler makes it nearly impossible to write subroutines for BASIC. CHASM now supports two independent ways of easily getting subroutines into BASIC programs.

"This is not a fault of the IBM product. It's just that the tool is not the right tool since it produces the wrong output to be appropriate for BASIC. For its part, CHASM produces the wrong output to be appropriate for Pascal.

"I've written an implementation of the UNIX WC filter in CHASM. I've also written a utility which senses the size of a formatted disk and then passes that information back to DOS to set the error level. I use this every time I make a copy of CHASM for someone since it automatically senses the size of their disk. It automatically determines what files I give them. If the disk is formatted for DOS 2.0, it gives them some extra files since there is more room on the disk. You cannot do that through BASIC.

"I'm pleased to say that many people have told me the CHASM documentation is easier to understand than IBM's. On the first page of the IBM manual, there is a phrase like 'Welcome, experienced programmers . . .' My first page says, 'If you're a beginner, print this other file to help you along.'"

In the best do-it-yourself tradition, Mr. Whitman reports that he began writing CHASM while in the midst of his Cornell Ph.D. thesis. "I was going crazy and I wanted something else to do. I had always wanted to get into assembly language, but I couldn't afford the $100 dollars for the IBM product. Since I had a BASIC interpreter, I wrote an assembler in that. It was a lot of fun.

"I read about Andrew Fluegelman's program and the Freeware concept. Here I was with 1,000 lines of code that I had done for my own purposes, and it occurred to me that many others might not be able to afford the IBM Macro Assembler either."

Just as Bob Wallace uses PC-FILE to keep track of registered PC-WRITE users, Dave Whitman uses PC-FILE to generate mailing labels when he announces a major upgrade to his program. "And when I post an advertisement on CompuServe, it's PC-TALK that is doing the 'talking.'"

FreeTip: Dave Whitman also offers a small utility called NUMZAP that may be of interest to users of the IBM BASIC Compiler. This program will strip all unused line numbers in a BASIC program, that is, line numbers that the program does not GOTO. Without NUMZAP, you would probably have to go through your BASIC program to figure this out yourself. Mr. Whitman indicates that removing unused line numbers can result in a 20 to 30 percent reduction in the size of the compiled code. The program is available under the U/S approach. Suggested contribution: $15.

CHASM was originally available only in its interpreted BASIC form. But in the fall of 1983 Dave Whitman introduced the compiled version. The compiled version is copyrighted and is available only to registered CHASM users. Mr. Whitman has asked us to emphasize that he will accept formatted disks only.

COMM PLUS Patch for IBM Asynchronous Communications

MicroCorp
913 Walnut Street
Philadelphia, PA 19107

Send formatted disk or $6.

Comments: This program adds uploading and downloading capabilities to the IBM Asynchronous Communications program. It also provides full printer support, expanded and improved error checking, optional support for the Hayes Smartmodem, and allows you to load strings of characters into your function keys. Originally sold as a commercial product, it is now available as a U/S program.

THE DESIGNER Graphics/Animation Creator

Jan B. Young
767 N. Holden St.
Port Washington, NY 53074

PC/SIG Disk 69

Comments: The PUT and BLOAD commands in IBM BASIC can be used to display and animate pictures and designs on your screen. Although crucial for games and other forms of animation, they can be used to add some pizzaz to any BASIC program. You might create a signature image showing your name or a picture and include it at the beginning of all the programs you write, for example. Both PUT and BLOAD, however, require images that have already been created and exist either in memory or in a disk file.

THE DESIGNER makes it easy for you to create and record those images without doing any programming. It generates files for backgrounds ("screens") and movable characters ("sprites") in a form that can be used by those BASIC commands. This frees you to concentrate on the artistic aspects of what you are creating instead of worrying about writing code.

You can select high or medium resolution and choose from one of two palettes. You are then presented with a blank screen with a tiny dot at its center. Using the cursor control keys, you can then draw lines and shapes, lifting and moving the "pen" much as you would with a Logo turtle.

There are commands to automate the creation of straight lines, diagonals, arcs, circles, and grids. The ten function keys are used to scale (enlarge or reduce) the figure, store and retrieve sprites and backgrounds, and include text in your screens. There are extensive online help files, and a BASIC demonstration program is provided to aid you in learning how to incorporate sprites and backgrounds in your own program.

First issued in April of 1983, this is a very impressive piece of software. The version we tested suffered from inadequate error trapping and recovery, but once you learn the ropes this should be less of a problem. Since it is written in interpreted BASIC it is also a mite slow. (The program uses dynamic array dimensioning and thus cannot be compiled.)

The documentation is copious and well written. This program will clearly be a boon to anyone interested in exploring the color graphics and animation possibilities of an IBM computer. You will need color graphics support and a color display. The requested contribution is $25.

DESKTOP LOTUS 1-2-3 Worksheet

Microcomputer Management
45 Drum Hill Road
Concord, MA 01742

Order: PC/SIG Disks 64 and 65 (double-sided); or send two formatted double-sided disks to the above address. If you send the requested $25 contribution, the author will supply the disks and postage.

Requires: Lotus 1-2-3 Version 1A and 192K.

Comments: This is a desktop aid for executives who use Lotus. According to the author, "Amongst other things, it contains macro and menu-writing for 1-2-3. All choices are user-modifiable." We have not used this program, but the word from the free software grapevine is that it is quite good.

EPISTAT Statistical Analysis

Tracy L. Gustafson, M.D.
1705 Gattis School Road
Round Rock, TX 78664

PC/SIG Disk 88

Requires: Color graphics and 64K; 96K is even better.

Comments: This is actually a collection of programs written in BASICA for statistical analysis of "small to medium-sized data samples" (less than 1,000 observations per sample and less than 28 data samples). Included are programs to enter, append, and edit data, as well as programs to perform several transformations. The disk contains 23 files, including HISTOGRM.BAS to create graphs of data samples on a high resolution screen. "Some of the programs emphasize epidemiologic and medical applications (but) these tests also apply to many other types of data." The requested contribution is $25.

Extended Batch Language (EBL) High-level DOS enhancement

Frank Canova
Seaware Corp.
P.O. Box 1656
Delray Beach, FL 33444
(305) 276-5072

Order: Send $5 to the above address.

Comments: According to Ken Goosens, writing in the January 1984 issue of "Capital PC Monitor," Extended Batch Language (EBL) is "an incredibly powerful product . . . that allows you to write 'drivers' for your machine so that you can configure how your software is going to interact with you. Putting up menus and prompts is a snap. From it, you can run nearly all applications, so that you can integrate all those programs you have that were never designed to work together into one environment. You can pass data from one program to another. You can make programs that run automatically without any input from you, by passing stored keystrokes to it. When programs give you messages on the screen . . . the extended batch facility can read these messages and be programmed to react accordingly . . . the only single product I know that gives you more total control over your machine is assembly language."

At a later point in his review, Mr. Goosens says, "The commercial products which are comparable to EBL are VisiON, DesQ, and StarBurst . . ." As Mr. Goosens points out, the program combines "elements of ProKey, menu generators, the batch facility built into DOS, and numerous utilities."

We called Frank Canova for more information, and he explained, among other things, that you might use EBL to create menus that would appear when you booted up the system. For example, if you had WordStar stored in one hard disk directory, dBASE II in another, and VisiCalc in a third, you could prepare a menu that offered these three choices. EBL would accept whichever choice you entered and would issue the proper DOS commands to take you to the appropriate directory. It would then issue the command needed to start the desired applications program.

This only scratches the surface, however. As Mr. Canova points out, EBL is very similar to BASIC in its programming approach, and anyone who is familiar with that conventions of the language should have little trouble using it. Among other things, EBL can:

- Control the display attributes of the screen (blink, intensity, reverse video, color).
- Exit to DOS at any time.
- Read commands and responses from the keyboard.
- GOTO a labeled command.
- Call DOS subroutines.
- Locate target files using either a unique filename or wildcards, regardless of the drive that holds them.
- Assign values to DOS variables.
- Execute integer arithmetic operations.
- Handle strings and substrings.

Mr. Canova is an IBM employee, and he has that firm's permission to offer this program, which he created in his spare time. The program came about because of Mr. Canova's familiarity with the VM 370 operating system. VM (virtual machine) includes a well-known facility called EXEC, which is so powerful that many VM users end up writing almost everything within its confines. "I really liked those VM features," Mr. Canova says, "and I felt a need for them on my PC. I wasn't sure at first that the PC would support them.

"The necessary programming 'hooks' into the operating system were never listed as being available, and for a long time it looked as though VM-like features would not be possible. But I decided to disassemble DOS and take a look for myself. I discovered that it wasn't too difficult to do." Although originally designed for use with DOS 1.1, EBL also works with 2.x and all versions of PC-DOS or MS-DOS.

FreeTip: The program Mr. Canova used to disassemble DOS was not some "special" IBM tool. It was ASMGEN.COM, a public domain disassembler that generates IBM Macro Assembler source code from an executable file. The program and accompanying documentation are available on PC/SIG Disk 93.

Mr. Canova said that one of the most popular applications for EBL is the creation of menus such as the one described earlier. "DOS 2.x will accept 'return' codes from an applications program to pass control back to DOS. The problem is that very few applications programs use them. I would guess that only about one percent of all programs actually generate a return code that DOS 2.x can use.

"EBL makes your batch language 'smart.' It is capable of actually looking at the text and error messages an applications program generates and responding accordingly."

Mr. Canova will send you a disk containing EBL as well as several demonstration files and samples for $5. The requested contribution to become a registered user is $30 and it provides a 70-page hard copy manual with examples, tips, and descriptions, plus a password that will admit you to Mr. Canova's BAT BBS bulletin board. This board operates at both 300 and 1200 baud and serves as a clearinghouse for information concerning Extended Batch Language and as a source of many user-contributed tips, tricks, and applications. Though formerly available for a limited number of hours, it is now online round the clock.

Free Software Synergy

One of the EBL features many people will find most useful is the program's ability to read the screen and respond accordingly. Here's a good example of that feature in particular and of what might be called "free software synergy" in general.

We wanted to find a way to make an IBM/PC and intelligent modem dial the phone and sign on to The Source or CompuServe at a preset time—automatically, with no human intervention. A commercial communications program offering this capability might cost hundreds of dollars and might require the purchase of an add-on "clock/calendar" board. But with free software you can do it for a fraction of that price, with or without a special board.

First we downloaded a free hexadecimal conversion program from the IBM/PC SIG on CompuServe. (See Chapter 8.) Then we downloaded one of the free clock programs available on that SIG and converted it to an .EXE file with the hex converter. Clock programs of this sort typically display a small digital clock in the upper right corner of the screen. They set themselves to match the computer's internal clock, the same clock you set when you first turn on the system.

The next step was to create a batch file for EBL to use. The batch file told EBL to prompt the user for the desired sign-on time and then to "watch" the clock display on the screen. When the digital display matched the specified time, EBL issued the command needed to activate PC-TALK III. EBL then issued the commands PC-TALK requires to dial the phone and work through the sign-on process.

Since EBL commands are accepted by a program just as if they were entered from the keyboard, you can include the keystrokes you would normally use to check your Source or CompuServe mailbox, obtain the latest price quote on a range of stocks, or do any of the other things you might want to accomplish with an online database. As long as you know what commands must be issued to a given database, EBL can handle it for you. It can also save incoming material to disk, toggle the printer on and off, or use any feature offered by your communications software.

Signing off the database can be handled in a number of ways. As explained in *The Complete Handbook of Personal Computer Communications*, your CI_D file on The Source can be used for this purpose. For CompuServe and other databases not offering this capablity, you can tell EBL to issue sign-off commands and terminate communications after a specified amount of time.

Since EBL can also issue one or more beeps, it can be used in conjunction with the same free clock program to turn your IBM computer into an alarm clock. (You need only tell EBL to beep repeatedly instead of activating a communications program at a specified time.) Even more impressive results can be achieved by using a widely available free program called TUNE.EXE. This program by Jeff Garbers can play a funeral dirge, the theme from *Close Encounters of the Third Kind*, and several other songs. It makes a nice substitute for a "beep" in an EBL-based alarm clock.

GINACO Utilities 56 Utilities and Subroutines

GINACO
10708 Santa Fe Drive
Sun City, AZ 85351

Order: PC/SIG Disk 66 (double-sided)

Comments: This is a real "goodies" package containing something for nearly every PC user. Among the highlights are a mailing label creator, a utility to disable all input keys except those needed by your program, a check-ledger reconciliation form sheet, a disk drive head cleaning program, a hex-to-decimal converter, a random number generator for use with game and other programs, a yes/no subroutine, and a program to clear a designated area of the screen.

There is even a program called BLUEMENU.BAS to let you easily select and run all of the programs on the disk. The requested contribution is $15.

LADYBUG LOGO Language Implementation

David N. Smith
44 Ole Musket Lane
Danbury, CT 06810

CompuServe: 73145,153

Order: PC/SIG Disk 94, or from author.

Requires: 128K, color graphics, and one single-sided drive (two are preferred, however).

Comments: According to Mr. Smith, LADYBUG is a graphics language based on LOGO Turtle Graphics. It offers most of the graphics, procedure-making, and control commands found in the Apple II implementation done by Terrapin, Inc., and is similar to other Apple versions as well as those for the Texas Instruments and TRS-80 computers. The version is described in the book *Logo for the Apple II* by Harold Abelson (McGraw-Hill, 1982).

The disk comes with the main program and a 60-page manual (on disk), as well as 20 different "procedures." These include: CIRCLES, MATH, POLLY, PROFILE, RAIL, RAYS SOUNDS, SPIN, SPIRAL, SNOWFLAKE, and DRAGON. The requested contribution is $35.

PC-DIAL™ Communications
(Also known as "1-RingyDingy™" or "1RD.")

Jim Button
P.O. Box 5786
Bellevue, WA 98006
SourceMail: CL2925
CompuServe: 71435,2012

Order: PC/SIG Disk 77 or from author.

Requires: 64K (with DOS 1.0 or 1.1); 96K with DOS 2.x. One disk drive; RS-232 port; 80-column display

Comments: You just know what the first question has got to be: "What's the difference between PC-DIAL and PC-TALK III?" Here is what Jim Button said when we asked:

"PC-TALK III is strongest in having the dialing directory. The program supports that much more completely than does my program. My program's strong points are, first, its simpler dialing directory, and second, the fact that it can easily handle the Hayes and any other type of modem.

"I think the strongest feature of all, however, is its ability to call up a wide variety of databases and to log on to each one almost automatically. With PC-DIAL you set up a kind of script of how you get into any online service that you use. Each script is a complete file, so you can make it as long as you want. The first line sets the communications parameters. The next line might be a command to your auto dial modem. The next might be your Telenet terminal type, followed by the address of The Source, followed by your Source log-on ID and password.

"You can send each string of characters—each 'record' in the file—by hitting the same key in succession. You can also skip over records and respond from the keyboard if need be.

"After you get logged in, there are other pre-recorded strings you can send. You can either bring in a different script file to handle this, or you can press a key that tells the system to 'go down and search for MAILCK in my log-in script file.'"

PC-DIAL is available only in its compiled form, and in addition to supporting the standard X-ON/X-OFF protocol, it also supports XMODEM. You can open and close a capture buffer that automatically dumps to disk or appends incoming information to a pre-existing file. You can set up a file that will filter or convert incoming characters, communicate at as fast as 9600 baud, change the colors on your display, and move back and forth among different DOS 2.x "directories."

The on-disk manual is 16 pages long. The suggested contribution is $25. Mr. Button indicates in his documentation that he does not foresee a large number of updates to the program. PC-DIAL "was designed with the 'KISS' ('Keep It Simple, Stupid') principle in mind. Although it employs a simple and straightforward approach to communications, its capabilities surpass those of some of the more expensive communications programs on the market today."

ULTRA-ZAP Disk Utilities
ULTRA-FORMAT
ULTRA-FILE

FreeSoft Ultra-Utilities
P.O. Box 27608
St. Louis, MO 63146

Requires: 64K; one single or double-sided disk drive; an 80-column display

Order: Send one blank, formatted, double-sided disk, or two single-sided disks, to the above address.

Comments: We have not used this package and do not know what the suggested contribution is. However, the programs sound interesting. Here is what FreeSoft has to say about the ULTRA utilities.

There is now available a three-volume set of IBM-PC utilities that do everything the NORTON UTILITIES do and much, much more.

The package includes:

- Ultra-Zap: Program for displaying/modifying disk sectors and file sectors, copying disk sectors, searching for byte or character sequences in disk or file sectors, filling or zeroing disk sectors, and interrogating diskettes to display their protection techniques. This program can work on any disk sector, regardless of protection, etc.

- Ultra-Format: Can format standard or copy-protected disk tracks, also can repair files containing "flaky" sectors by placing a fresh format on a track without erasing prior data.

- Ultra-File: Program for displaying all directory information about a disk file, assigning or removing SYSTEM or HIDDEN status to a file, building files from scratch, resurrecting accidentally erased files, and selectively killing files from a menu (FAST!).

Freeware™, Shareware, U/S, and the Future

The increase in individuals adopting the user supported approach has had at least two effects. On the one hand it has stimulated an outpouring of more good software. Since these programs are generally more sophisticated and powerful than those found in the public domain, and are often comparable to commercial software, they are almost always worth many times their authors' requested contributions.

On the other hand, the very fact that this distribution technique exists has led other individuals to tack a "User Supported" notice and contribution request onto an otherwise ordinary public domain program. Unfortunately, these programs may or may not offer the extra quality that one normally expects when an author requests a contribution. What's more, similar programs of comparable or better quality may be available as "plain vanilla" public domain software.

You may also find U/S software that has become somewhat outdated or at least less useful than it once was. For example, IBM PC DOS 1.0 and 1.1 do not support a graphics screen dump to your printer. When those were the only versions of DOS available, a U/S screen dump program filled a critical need for many users. If you own DOS 2.x, however, such a program is no longer necessary since this version of the operating system includes a file called GRAPHICS.COM that does the same thing.

Since all U/S programs are available for the cost of a floppy disk, postage, and a disk mailer, you have little to lose if the software does not live up to your expectations. At the same time, however, the growing number of user supported programs and the variability in quality raises a difficult question. Some computer owners will take everything they can get. The thought of supporting a program's author by sending a contribution never even crosses their minds. Others are more than willing to show their appreciation for a useful program.

We have tried to present some of the best programs offered under the Freeware approach. But you will undoubtedly encounter others that are what might be called "substandard." The danger is that if the number of these U/S programs becomes too great, the entire idea of user supported software may lose its luster. If every author requests a donation, regardless of the quality of the program, even the most honest user may feel disinclined to contribute to anybody.

Without user support, however, there would be little incentive for any programmer to exert the extra effort needed to produce a superior Freeware-type product. This has not happened yet. But in the future it seems likely that the Freeware equivalent of "caveat emptor" will become increasingly heard.

...12...

The Treasure Trove: *Unusual and Little-Known Sources of Free Software*

There are many sources of free software that are more or less off the beaten path. They are not users groups, though they may have libraries of users group–supplied software. Some are individuals, some are organizations. Their programs, while not expensive, may not always be free. Each of them offers unique variations on the user-written, free software theme. The one thing they have in common is that most people haven't heard of them.

In this chapter we'll look at a number of interesting sources for Apple software; at APX, a division of Atari that markets user-written software (and awards a $25,000 cash prize for the best submission each year); at a firm that adds color and sound and otherwise improves public domain programs for the Commodore 64; at a commercial communications program and a database management program for TRS-80 Model III and Model 4 owners that is now available for free; and at the CoCo Freeware Clearinghouse for owners of Tandy's Color Computer.

We'll introduce you to SOFTSWAP, a prime source of free educational software for most major brands of computers. You may also be interested in what two pioneering public libraries are doing in the field, possibly with an eye to establishing similar projects in your locality.

If you are a serious investor, you will be interested in the investment-related software available free to members of the Microcomputer Investors Association. Finally, we'll show you how SofTraders™ can put you in touch with other individuals who have software they would like to exchange for programs you may have.

Apple

ADVENTURE Game

Jeff Jacobsen
Frontier Computing, Inc.
P.O. Box 402
Logan, UT 84321
CompuServe: 72446,2557
SourceMail: STT637

Requires: 48K and one disk drive; DOS 3.3. Runs on Apple II, II Plus, and //e and most Apple look-alikes.

Cost: Send $10 to the above address; disk will be sent to you via First Class Mail.

Comments: This is the classic Colossal Cave *Adventure*, a public domain game developed by Willie Crowther and Don Woods at MIT. The original game was written in FORTRAN and brought up on a DEC PDP-10 (minicomputer). Intended to serve as a demonstration of artificial intelligence, the program acts as your "guide" through the cave. You can ask questions regarding your surroundings and issue instructions to tell the guide where you want to go and what you want to do.

The program made such a hit that, as Tracy Kidder points out in *The Soul of a New Machine* (Atlantic, Little-Brown, 1981), it "traveled widely, like a chain letter, from coast to coast among computer engineers and buffs." When microcomputers came along, bringing it over into the microworld was a natural step.

Jeff Jacobsen's version is a complete implementation. There are over 130 rooms, 15 treasures, 40 useful objects, and 12 obstacles or opponents. A perfect score is 350. What makes Mr. Jacobsen's game unusual is that he has written exceptionally tight code enabling him to pack the entire game into 48K of RAM. This means that when you play, the entire game loads into your Apple memory, and it makes for faster play. In contrast to other versions, there is no need in this one for the computer to periodically go out to disk to bring in some portion of the game required to respond to your commands.

Mr. Jacobsen says, "I wrote it more or less on a bet to prove that I could do it and make it fit into 48K. I didn't know what to do with it once I got it finished, but hated not to share it." You can sample more of his work in the *Eamon Adventure* series offered by the Apple Avocation Alliance described elsewhere in this book.

Diversi-DOS DOS 3.3 Enhancement

DSR, Inc.
5848 Crampton Ct.
Rockford, IL 61111
(408) 877-1343

Distribution fee: $5.

Registration fee: $25.

Comments: Diversi-DOS reads, saves, loads, and writes faster than Apple DOS 3.3. It also includes a "type-ahead" keyboard buffer. This sets aside a certain portion of your machine's memory to store keystrokes so that they will not be missed by the computer when the machine is busy doing something else, like reading a disk. There is also a printer buffer or "print spooler" that lets you load text into memory and tell the machine to send it to the printer at whatever speed the printer will accept. This frees both you and the machine to move onto another task while the printout is taking place.

According to the documentation, Diversi-DOS modifies the standard version of Apple DOS 3.3 that resides on the first three tracks of a formatted disk. You place Diversi-DOS on the target disk once, by selecting the appropriate item from the main Diversi-DOS menu, and from then on it loads in whenever you boot the disk. DSR indicates that it has a license from Apple to distribute the portions of the DOS 3.3 code present on the Diversi-DOS master disk.

The firm's distribution approach is somewhat unique. This is a copyrighted program. It is not public domain software. But it may be distributed by any club, company, or individual for a charge of up to $5, provided that it is made clear that an additional $25 fee must be sent directly to DSR. (This program is available from the Apple Avocation Alliance.) The registration fee is to be paid within two weeks of receiving the program.

According to the supplied documentation: "This method of distribution offers tremendous advantages. The cost of Diversi-DOS is less than one half of what it would be if distributed conventionally. Also, you can test the program before you pay."

Telephone Software Connection, Inc. Free Software Online
P.O. Box 6548
Torrance, CA 90504
(213) 516-9430
TELEX: 469635

24-Hour Modem Lines: (213) 516-9432 (300 baud; 8 data bits; no parity.)

To Obtain Software: Connect with modem line or send $5 for disk.

Comments: This firm, headed by Edward Magnin, is one of the leaders among companies that deliver commercial software to home computers over the telephone. As Mr. Magnin points out, this technique not only keeps costs down—a typical program costs about $25—it also makes it easy for registered users to receive online updates to the software they have purchased. The system can accommodate many users at one time, so there's a good chance that you'll get through the first time you call. When you sign on you will see that in addition to the commercial software, there are a number of free programs.

Some of the free programs are demos and tutorials intended to highlight the firm's commmercial products. But others are completely workable free programs. The software is made available in two ways. If your computer is equipped for communications, you can phone the firm's modem number and download the programs directly into your Apple. (To purchase a program at the same time, you merely enter your major credit card number.) Alternatively, you can send $5 to the above address and request the free software and demos that are available on the system. Note that if you purchase a program on disk, you pay the $5 in addition to the price of the software itself—and you receive all the free software and demos as well. As Mr. Magnin says, this barely covers the cost of the disk, disk mailer, postage, and handling.

What free programs are available? Here are several of the online descriptions that you will see on your screen when you sign on:

```
ANALOG CLOCK ....................$ FREE
A TIMELY GIFT FOR THOSE WHO HAVE EITHER
THE APPLE CLOCK OR THE SUPERCLOCK II.

MICROMODEM FLAGS ..............$ FREE
EXPLAINS THE USE OF THE MICROMODEM
FLAGS. INCLUDES SAMPLE CALCULATIONS.

SHAPE TABLE DEMO ...............$ FREE
SEE WHAT CAN BE DONE WITH THE SHAPES
YOU CREATE USING OUR 'SHAPE BUILDER' &
'SHAPE EDITOR' PROGRAMS. REQUIRES ROM
APPLESOFT (OR LANG. CARD).

CALL TSC ..........................$ FREE
USE THIS PROGRAM NEXT TIME YOU CALL US.
WILL AUTOMATICALLY DIAL OUR NUMBER AND
LOG YOU ON. (REQUIRES MICROMODEM OR
APPLECAT WITH ROM)

DESK CALCULATOR II TUTORIAL ....$ FREE
A NO-RISK WAY TO SEE WHY YOU NEED OUR
DESK CALCULATOR II.
```

If you plan to order these or other free programs on disk, it is a good idea to request the first two programs by name since they are not normally placed on disks that are mailed out by the firm. (See the table at the end of this section.) "These two programs are available free over the phone," Mr. Magnin said, "but if someone asks for them on disk, we'd be glad to send them along with the other free programs and demos.

"Micromodem Flags, incidently, is a program that documents the binary flag locations of the Micromodem board. You can do an awful lot by poking numbers into those locations, but nobody knows what number to poke in there. If you want to turn on the keyboard, the terminal mode, or transparency, for example, you poke a certain value. But this program asks the user, 'Do you want the keyboard on or off?' and says, 'Okay, poke this number into that location.' It can help people write their own programs.

"The Shape Table demo program shows you what you can do with shape tables. It doesn't necessarily sell our programs, but if you know you can do something with shape tables, then you might want to buy our Shape Builder program." Shape tables allow you to draw images on your screen and save them to disk. The shapes can then be reloaded and moved around under program control. There are many helpful REMARK statements in the demo program that can provide an excellent tutorial in using shape tables. The cost of the commercial Shape Builder program is $25. It requires ROM Applesoft or the language card.

Mr. Magnin suggests that everyone download CALL TSC first. "This gives people a way of calling us automatically. But a lot of people have taken that program and modified it to be a sign-on program for other services. The code that makes the program look for our prompt 'What is your first name' can be modified to whatever The Source or CompuServe requires." The program is written in Applesoft and is easily listable. In effect, it can be turned into a free general purpose communications program.

There is also a commercial communications program called TELEPHONE TRANSFER II ($75) that supports a cyclic redundancy-checking binary file transfer protocol. We mention this because one of the free programs is TELEPHONE LINKER, a communications program that enables a second Apple to *receive* programs transmitted by an Apple running Telephone Transfer II.

There is also a free program called DOS UPDATE that was featured in *CALL-A.P.P.L.E.* magazine. "That was an experiment we tried where one of our programmers wrote an article for the magazine and included a listing. It was available for free in the magazine, then we made it available for free over the system so people wouldn't have to type it in themselves."

DOS UPDATE allows you to permanently modify DOS and save the results to disk. You have to do your own peeking and poking to the image of DOS loaded into memory—say, to make it accept CAT for CATALOG as the command to generate a disk directory—but when you are finished you can write the results back to disk. This way the modifications to DOS on that disk become permanent.

We found the Telephone Software Connection online service well-prompted and easy to use. The only drawback is that it runs at 300 baud, though 1200-baud capabilities will be added in the near future. Mr. Magnin had a vast knowledge of the inner workings of an Apple computer and a genuine concern with the problems faced by the new user. As a sidenote, if you have written a program and are considering marketing it, you might want to explore the possiblities of selling it through this firm. Mr. Magnin said that free-lance programmers have written about half of the software the company sells.

Here is the complete list of free programs and demos available on disk or over the phone. The list is current as of this writing, but it will undoubtedly expand in the future. Don't forget, a disk costs $5.

These programs are placed on every disk:

#1 CALL SC
#12 DESK CALCULATOR II TUTORIAL
#22 DESK CALENDAR II TUTORIAL
#26 PROGRAMMERS LIBRARY TUTORIAL
#44 VIDEO LIBRARIAN TUTORIAL
#49 TELEPHONE LINKER
#65 CHECKWRITER TUTORIAL
#65 PRIORITIZER.DOC

You must request these programs by name:

#2 TEST
#6 ANALOG CLOCK
#7 MICROMODEM FLAGS
#14 UPDATE DESK CALENDAR II
#17 SHAPE TABLE DEMO
#34 VANDAL FOILER
#42 DOS UPDATE
#51 TELE-FRIEND
#57 MANY MINIFLOPPY FILE FINDER

Atari

APX — User-written software

ATARI Program Exchange
P.O. Box 3705
Santa Clara, CA 95055
(800) 538-1862

In California: (800) 672-1850
(408) 727-5603

Visa and MasterCard accepted.

Catalogue: $2.

Comments: APX programs are inexpensive, averaging about $25 each, but none of them is free. However, nearly all of them are written by individual Atari users and submitted to APX for review and distribution. Programs that are accepted earn their authors a royalty based on mail-order sales. But the real incentives are the prizes that APX awards for outstanding programs each quarter.

At this writing, there are four prize categories: Consumer (entertainment and personal development), Home Management, Learning, and Systems/Telecommunications. There are first, second, and third prizes in each category, consisting of Atari hardware, software, and other equipment valued at $750 to $3,000. APX also awards a cash prize of $25,000 to the author of the best program of the year. In the spring of 1984, APX introduced an additional contest focusing on programs written to use Atari peripherals such as the Trak-Ball, the 1200 Color Printer, the speech synthesizer, or any Atari modem. Prizes are from $1,000 to $3,000 worth of equipment, and the grand prize is $5,000 in cash.

This is a very impressive operation, both in concept and in execution. The four-color catalogue is over 70 pages long and contains nearly 200 programs. Given at the beginning of each item in the catalogue are the name of the program, the author, the recommended audience or age group, and the language the software was written in. In many cases there will also be a four-color reproduction of a sample display generated by the program. Short "Review Comments," a list of hardware requirements, and ordering information are also provided. Best of all, the catalogue doesn't stint on program descriptions. The average length ranges from 250 to 500 words, enough to give you a good idea of what the program will or will not do for you, and whether or not you should order it.

Although most programs are written by one individual, quite a few have joint authors. There is also at least one husband-and-wife team. Here is a sampling of titles and prices.

Title	*Medium*	*Price*
Home Inventory (Keep track of your valuables.)	Disk	$24.95
Bowler's Database (Detailed records of each bowler's performance.)	Disk and Tape	$17.95
Piano Tuner (Learn piano tuning, tone generation, and ear training.)	Disk and Tape	$29.95
Mapware (Create and store high-resolution world maps.)	Disk	$24.95
Microsailing (Sail through four courses that teach tacking and jibing.)	Disk	$17.95
Atlas of Canada (Quizzes you on Canadian provinces, capitals, and landmarks.)	Disk and Tape	$24.95

Of special note are the programs supplied by the Minnesota Educational Computing Consortium (MECC). This is an organization formed to assist users and educators throughout the Minnesota school system (elementary through college) in using and coordinating computer resources. MECC has developed a wide range of classroom-tested educational software that is available for free to Minnesota residents and at very low prices to residents of other states.

All MECC programs come with documentation prepared by MECC members and include materials for background and suggested follow-up activities. Here are some highlights, with recommended grade levels:

Metric and Problem Solving (2-6) Learn the metric system through computer games.

The Market Place (3-8) Four simulation games for teaching economic concepts.

Geography (4-10) Four programs quiz you on names and locations of cities, states, countries, and continents.

Earth Science (5-12) Earthquake epicenters, mineral identification, solar distance, and star patterns.

Music Series (Terms and Notations; Rhythm & Pitch; Scales &

Chords) Theory, drill, and practice. Student selects difficulty level desired.

These and other MECC programs available from APX all require 16K and the ATARI BASIC Language Card. Each program sells for $29.95, and they are available only on disk.

FreeTip: MECC has similar programs for other computers as well, and you can contact them directly for ordering information and to receive a copy of their catalogue. Write to:

MECC Distribution Center
2520 Broadway Drive
St. Paul, MN 55113

(If you live in Minnesota, be sure to request the catalogue for Minnesota residents.)

Commodore 64

Almost-Free-Software — Enhanced Public Domain Software

The Friendly Computer Shop
78 Main Street
Littleton, NH 03561
(603) 444-2668

Catalogue: Free.

Comments: The Friendly Computer Shop carries an extensive line of commercial software for the Commodore 64 (130 to 140 programs at any given time), but it also offers Almost-Free-Software PAKs. These are individual disks containing 10 to 12 programs each. There are at least six PAKs, containing a total of nearly 60 C-64 programs, and as many as 200 to 300 more are planned for the future. The cost is $25 per PAK, postage included.

The programs themselves are in the public domain. What makes them unusual is that David Wheeler, one of the store's managers, has taken the time to debug them and, when appropriate, to write additional code that adds sound and color. Here is a list of the six PAKs in the collection at this writing:

PAK I
Backgammon
Monopoly
Hangman
U-Boat
Murder Mansion
Yahtzee
Master Mind
Draw Poker
Skeet
Limerock

PAK II
AFO
Blackjack
Concentration
Quick Reaction
Lem
Labyrinth
Frog
Word Guess
Checkers
Artillery

PAK III
Monopoly
Magic Piano
Biorhythm
Time Card
Titrate
Murder Mansion
Hawaii
Ferry
Date Book

PAK IV
Decimals
Percent
Division
Arithmetic
Dart
Fractions
Powers
Integers
Hex Demo
Small Math

PAK V
Vectors
Planes
Lines
Conics
Linear Systems
Matrix Solution
Triangle Solving
General Anova
Heat Solver
Root Finder

PAK VI
Grammar
Antonyms
Definitions
Speed Read
Q's & Z's
Spelling
Mad Lib
Microtyping
Word Ladder
Computer Poetry

We tested PAK I and would recommend it to anybody with a Commodore 64. The *Hangman* game is challenging and has good graphics, but the real star is *Monopoly*. This is a very complete implementation of the classic board game, complete with color, sound, and surprises. There is no argument over who will be the banker—the computer handles and keeps track of all transactions. This makes it possible to complete a game in perhaps seven hours, instead of seven days when playing the board version. The only limitation is that the game can handle only two players.

TRS-80 Models III and 4

MicroCorp
913 Walnut Street
Philadelphia, PA 19107
(215) 627-7997
Visa and Mastercard accepted

Programs: For DataMaster (a complete database management system) Model 4 owners send $15 for three disks. Model III owners send $15 plus proof of purchase of LDOS. (LDOS, LDOS manual, and the three DataMaster disks are available for a total of $59.)

For Intelliterm (a communications program) send $6 to cover disk, disk mailer, and postage.

Comments: These programs represent a truly impressive value. DataMaster was advertised in *80 Micro* magazine and sold for $300. Intelliterm originally sold for $150. The programs are not public domain software but are being made available because MicroCorp has changed its focus from Radio Shack computers to those made by IBM. They are available "as is," and no support will be provided.

DataMaster is a powerful menu-driven database management system that is quite capable of serving the needs of many small- to medium-sized businesses, to say nothing of the home user. It contains far too many features to detail here. However, highlights include an exceptionally fast sort of database records and easy access to LDOS commands without the need to leave the program.

Perhaps most impressive of all, however, is the module that allows you to design your data entry form right on the screen. There is no need to specify the number of characters you want to allot for each field. You merely move the cursor and the program takes care of the rest. DataMaster makes it easy to create an onscreen duplicate of whatever printed form you may now be using. In addition, it places the full power of the BASIC language at your disposal when you specify search criteria or otherwise manipulate records.

Intelliterm is also a powerful program. It does not support XMODEM, but it has many desirable features. One of these is a "split screen" mode that segregates the text you type at your keyboard from the text coming into the communications port. You can adjust the split screen bar to any position within two lines of the top or bottom of the screen. Translation tables or filters, both incoming and outgoing, are also supported. There is also a direct disk-to-disk transfer mode for use when communicating with a second computer that is also running Intelliterm.

The author wrote the original documentation for both programs but is not connected with the software or with MicroCorp in any way. Nor are we responsible for whatever form the documentation may now take. At the same time, however, we have no qualms about recommending both programs to Model III and Model 4 owners, particularly at prices as low as these.

TRS-80 Color Computer and Compatibles

The CoCo Freeware Clearinghouse — Assorted Programs
P.O. Box 1084
Morgantown, West Virginia 26507
(304) 599-4493

CompuServe: 70305,723

MCI Mail: FREEWARE

Catalogue: Send self-addressed, stamped envelope for "INFO-PAK." (Two INFO-PAKS are available, one for users and one for program authors interested in offering their software.)

Comments: Donald Barber has a very interesting idea. He has established The CoCo Freeware Clearinghouse to serve as a central meeting point for authors of CoCo software wishing to distribute their programs on a voluntary contribution basis and users wishing to obtain same. Mr. Barber told us that the Clearinghouse began operations in December 1983 with the release of its first program, *Flight from Grimdar* by Steven D. Richards. This was followed shortly thereafter by the ALP Toolkit (Program number 301) package that consists of a two-pass assembler, documentation, and related files. Here's what Mr. Barber told us about his operation:

"The CoCo Freeware Clearinghouse is designed to handle software for the TRS-80 and TDP System-100 Color Computers produced by Tandy, and the Dragon 32/64 (a work-alike from Great Britain, soon to be produced here in the U.S. by Tano). I hope to include programs for all different levels and types (4K, 16K, 64K, Color BASIC, Extended BASIC, and Disc Extended BASIC) and of every nature (games, utilities, telecommunications, etc.). Considering the programs that are now undergoing review, it looks like we will have something for everyone."

Programs may be obtained by sending a blank cassette tape or formatted disk and a postage-paid return mailer along with your request for a specific program. "Please mention the program number. Send no money now. However, after you have received the CoCo Freeware Program and you use or otherwise enjoy the program, please make a contribution in the amount of your choice. Your contribution will be forwarded to the author. Please don't feel that your contribution would be too small. Sometimes the fact that someone cared enough to send a little something matters more to the author than the amount received. When making a contribution, please mention the program number."

Here is the INFO-PAK description of Program #101:

FLIGHT FROM GRIMDAR. *NEW* *RAINBOW CERTIFIED* You are the only survivor of a vast human task force. Your only goal: SURVIVE! Your only means: Pilot a Grimdarian starship back to Earth! Requires 16K Extended BASIC. Disk Compatible.

Unique Sources and Contact Points

SOFTSWAP
San Mateo County Office of Education (SMERC)
Library and Computer Center
333 Main Street
Redwood City, CA 94063
(415) 363-5470

Catalogue: Send $1 to the above address.

Cost: $10 per disk.

Computer Using Educators (CUE)
CUE MEMBERSHIP
P.O. Box 18547
San Jose, CA 95158

Cost: $8 per year; includes CUE Newsletter containing announcements of all new SOFTSWAP programs.

Computers Supported: Apple, Atari, CompuColor, IBM, PET, TI 99/4A, and TRS-80. (Others may be added.)

Comments: SOFTSWAP is the brainchild of Ann Lathrop, Library Coordinator for SMERC. It began as an exchange of instructional software at the Asilomar Math Conference in 1979. Programs were contributed by individuals participating in the conference and placed in the SMERC library in the spring of 1980. Many of the computer manufacturers who were contacted agreed to loan the library complete systems. And before long The Microcomputer Center began to take shape.

Today The Microcomputer Center at the San Mateo Library serves as a central meeting place for residents interested in personal computers. But visitors come from all over the state and from many other states, Canadian provinces, and foreign countries as well. Any visitor is free to copy any of the programs in the SOFTSWAP library.

That's more or less Part I of the program. Part II concerns how the free software library has been built over the years and how it continues to expand. Originally, the idea was to create a clearinghouse for educational software written by educators throughout the state and throughout the country, and the association of Computer Using Educators (CUE) was closely involved in this from the start. One educator would send in an original program and receive a free disk of other programs in exchange. This arrangement still exists.

SOFTWSAP proved so popular, however, that the policy was soon broadened. Today anyone may submit a program and swap it for a disk of other free software. In addition, the large number of requests for programs from people outside the San Mateo area led to the establishment of a mail order procedure in the spring of 1981. Now it is possible for anyone to order a disk for $10, though of course you'll want to have the catalogue first. Ms. Lathrop estimates that by April 1983, SOFTSWAP had mailed out over 8,000 disks as exchanges or sales.

Although it receives no outside funding and is operated by CUE volunteers, SOFTSWAP is different from most computer users groups in that it supports a wide variety of computers, and places a strong emphasis on educational software. Most programs in the library are short, stand-alone instructional units. Many are drill-and-practice oriented. You will find few purely recreational games or computer utilities. Every program is evaluated by at least two professional educators before being added to the collection. Corrections are made, where necessary. The documentation may be expanded. And other steps are taken to make sure that each program meets the CUE/SOFTSWAP standard. Only then is a program made available on disk.

There are programs dealing with science, math, social studies, foreign languages, language arts, music, educational games and logic, driver education, and utilities of interest to teachers. A list supplied by SMERC indicated that as of April 1983 there were nearly 45 Apple disks, 7 for the PET, 5 for TRS-80 computers, 70 for Compucolor machines, and 4 for the Atari. Those totals have certainly grown since then.

Your first step in plugging into SOFTSWAP should be to send for the catalogue ($1). But you should also consider becoming a member of CUE. Not only does the CUE newsletter periodically publish summaries of new programs in the SMERC library, it also contains many educational programs, tips, access points, and other information important to anyone interested in educational software and in the role of microcomputers in the classroom.

How to Help Your Own Local Library

On anyone's list of institutions essential to civilization, libraries have to rank right up there with an assured food supply and a workable justice system. Unfortunately, they are chronically underfunded. Many would like to establish software collections, but they lack the money, personnel, and experience to do so.

You can help. It may not be necessary to establish a fully equipped resource center like the one in San Mateo. A simple donation of disks you have assembled from the various sources cited in this book may be more than enough to get things started. Since disks can be loaned by the library just as if they were books, there is no need for the library to have computer equipment or someone with computer expertise.

You might consider placing each disk in a clear plastic notebook insert of the sort designed to accommodate an 8½-by-11-inch piece of paper. You could print out a directory of the programs on the disk on a single page and insert that as well. There would also be room for the library's circulation and "Due Date" forms, either inside the package or taped to the outside. Finally, since these sheet protectors are designed to fit in a three-ring notebook, they would be easy to store on a shelf. With properly marked tabbed notebook dividers, each disk would also be easy to locate anytime someone wanted to borrow it.

Naturally it is vital to discuss the plan with your local librarian first. But with this as a beginning, there is virtually no limit to what can be done. For example, if you have a dual disk drive system, you might consider preparing classified free software collections (games, utilities, education, etc.) from the miscellaneous disks you receive from users groups and other sources. You could use the techniques described elsewhere in this book to locate nearby computer users groups for each major brand of machine and enlist their aid. (The person who serves as a group's software librarian will be an especially valuable contact, able to provide pointers on organizing the library's collection.)

If there are no groups nearby, you might consider forming a committee of computer owners and making each responsible for obtaining software for a given type of machine. If the response is good, you might also see about working with the library to obtain machines from computer manufacturers. Note that this requires a much greater commitment on the part of the library since space must be allocated for the machines, policies will have to be established, and someone will have to be put in charge of the computer area.

> **FreeTip:** The Apple Computer Company has long been the leader in making its equipment available at reduced prices to schools and educational institutions. IBM has recently begun to follow suit. Most other major computer manufacturers are interested. This is not pure altruism, of course. It makes sound business sense, for the computer a student becomes accustomed to using in school is the one he is more likely to purchase when the time comes.
>
> Policies and contact points differ with each company. If you have difficulty locating the correct person to contact, write to the president. (Use the library's resources to locate the individual's name.) If the library has its own stationery, you might want to consider using that (or having someone at the library send the letter).
>
> You may also find that local computer stores will respond favorably to your request for a loan of equipment. And, although many will not be able to afford to donate a machine, they may be willing to make a machine available at cost.

Though it isn't likely that you will be able to take a tax deduction for your time, in many cases you will be able to deduct the cost of the media you donate to a library. So save your receipts, and in all cases, check with your accountant.

If you would like to see what some local libraries have been able to accomplish, perhaps to obtain ideas for your own program, there are at least two places to contact, one in Chicago and the other in Wenatchee, Washington. Both have information packets they can send. Since their time is limited too, you should request these instead of asking for replies to specific questions.

The Chicago Public Library—North Pulaski Branch

Although other branches in the Chicago library system also have computers, the most elaborate program may be the one created by Patrick Dewey at the North Pulaski Branch. With funds supplied by the Friends of the Chicago Public Library, Mr. Dewey purchased a complete Apple system. He assembled his software from users groups, SOFTSWAP, and MECC (see the FreeTip under the Atari section above).

The system is kept in a separate room, and an appointment is required for each one-hour session. The software does not circulate, but patrons are free to bring their own disks and copy any programs of interest. To prevent the system from being monopolized by children playing games, use of arcade-style software is restricted to two hours a week on Wednesday afternoons. Brand new users are given a brief orientation and printed instructions.

Mr. Dewey has also set up a computer bulletin board system using People's Message System (PMS) software. This runs on the same computer during the hours that the library is closed. Book and software reviews and announcements concerning the computer center are available on the system.

For more information, contact:

Mr. Patrick Dewey
North-Pulaski Branch Library
4041 West North Avenue
Chicago, IL 60639

North Central Regional Library

The North Central Regional Library in Wenatchee, Washington, has a different approach. It has incorporated disks of public domain software in its Mail Order Library operation. According to the literature we received, this "experimental program was started the first week in January 1983 [as] an innovative approach to rural library service. . . . Users choose software from a catalogue, place their orders on prepaid postcards, and then receive diskettes in a cardboard mailer with return postage and label inside."

According to one official, "When we started we did a week of testing and then took the jump and presented the service at a local computer fair. The response we got was staggering." The program assigns an accession number to the software and the programs are assigned to a general category for the catalogue. The circulating period is about three weeks.

There are over 190 disks, representing a large chunk of the available public domain software for Apple, Commodore, and Timex/Sinclair computers. Since many of the disks are "flippies" with a full complement of programs on both sides, the actual number of volumes is probably close to 400.

It is important to emphasize here that the library serves only its surrounding area. Depending on where you live, you might be able to take advantage of this program by requesting the software through your local library's interlibrary loan program. However, for most readers it will not make sense to do so. You will be better off getting the software from the sources described in this book.

Anyone interested in setting up a similar program at a local library, however, would do well to contact Dean Marney, the software library program coordinator. This is an impressive program and there is much to be learned from this library's experience. Contact:

Mr. Dean Marney
Software Library Coordinator
North Central Regional Library
238 Olds Station Road
Wenatchee, WA 98801
(509) 663-1117

Investment Software

The Microcomputer Investor
Dr. Jack M. Williams
The Microcomputer Investors Association
902 Anderson Drive
Fredericksburg, VA 22405

Send $5 for Information Packet.

Participating Membership: $50 plus one publishable article per year.

Library Membership: $50/year. Contact on library stationery and be sure to include library phone number.

Comments: The Microcomputer Investors Association is a nonprofit, professional association of men and women who use personal computers to manage their investments. *The Microcomputer Investor* (*MCI*) is the organization's journal. At this writing, it is published twice a year, though quarterly publication is a possibility for the future.

Founded by Jack Williams in 1976, this association has a unique membership requirement. In addition to the $50 annual dues, each member must commit to preparing one publishable article during the year. This is done to encourage genuine participation and to promote the dissemination of the special knowledge and experience each member has to share. At first blush, this seems like a rather stiff requirement, but Jack Williams assured us that it is not difficult to fulfill.

"There is absolutely no minimum or maximum. I've received articles that were near 100 pages and, although it is very unusual, I've received—and printed—articles that were only one page long. Needless to say, they were very good articles. What we prefer is something around 10 pages. And as long as the topic is something likely to be of interest to your fellow professional investors, almost any topic will be fine." Book reviews, investment-related hardware and software reviews, reports on an interesting investment-related application you have developed or are familiar with, and similar topics are all acceptable.

Perhaps most important of all for our purposes here, over 50% of the articles appearing in *MCI* contain complete investment-related programs. Here are some sample titles taken from recent issues:

The Option Writer's Evaluator
Geometric Projections of Trends
Advances, Declines, and the Composite
Using VisiCalc with Call Options
Buy and Sell Timing for Commodities
Testing Price Movement Strategies
Call Option Deltas
DPV & ROR
The Fourier Transform
A Commodity Graphics Program for the Apple II
A Conversion Program for CompuTrac Data

Jack Williams says that each program-containing article has an introduction citing the language and the required computer and/or peripherals, as well as a description of the technique that the program implements. "Virtually all of these programs are available to association members on diskette for the cost of the media and postage alone. The association requires that everyone who submits a program also submit a diskette to our software librarian. The last time I checked, I believe the number was over 100 diskettes, and since our librarian has a modem, some members arrange to contact him and download the software they want over the phone.

"Many of the program listings are between two and three pages long, but others run 12, 15, or even 20 pages. If you want a program and for some reason the librarian does not have it on file, members can always write the the author of the article to get a copy."

If you are serious about both investing and personal computing, it would be well worth your while to invest $5 in the Information Packet the association makes available. This includes a complete description of the group, a membership application form, and photocopies of the tables of contents of all previous *MCI* issues. Back issues are available to members at a cost of $25 each. The topics are intriguing and the free programs are plentiful.

Swapping Commercial Software

SofTraders™ International
1610 Shomaker Drive
Murphysboro, IL 62966
(618) 687-4799
Visa and MasterCard accepted (add 5% to prices below)

Monthly Catalogue: $2 in the U.S.; $5 non–U.S. air mail delivery. (Catalogue cost may be deducted from first order.)

Catalogue and Access to One Trader: $5; $8, non–U.S.

Catalogue and Listing: $5 Standard Listing; includes five program titles. Five additional program titles may be listed for $1. Non–U.S. residents, add $3 per order for air mail. (Volume discounts are also available.)

Comments: SofTraders is not a source of free software, but it can save you money. According to George Wayne, Executive Director of SofTraders:

"When you consider the cost of just a few games or educational programs, not to mention the more expensive business applications, it is clear that few users can afford to tie up their money in software that no longer suits their purpose.

"Exchanging software is the most cost-effective approach. Unlike reselling used software, which rarely brings more than 50% of the original investment, software exchanges enable traders to replace their progams with others of equal cost. Coupled with the fact that traders are easier to find than buyers, trading is a practical and economical approach.

"SofTraders offers all computer owners the opportunity to exchange progams directly with other users. SofTraders expands the personal trading network of its clients by providing them with the names, addresses, phone numbers and other access information for the traders they select.

"SofTraders requires no annual dues . . . no extra fees . . . no membership requirements. Costs are not based on the number of programs traded or their value. SofTraders allows users to make their own trading arrangements. Once in touch with each other, users freely trade as many programs as they can . . . as often as they want. Invaluable advice, information, ideas and solutions are also exchanged."

As you can gather, SofTraders serves as a central clearinghouse to bring together individuals with programs to trade for others they want. Here are two sample listings:

TRADER: 138A LOCATION: New York
SYSTEM: VIC-20 Tape
HAVE: Cartridge: Adventureland, Voodoo Castle
Tape: Draw, Fire, Krazy Kong
WANT: Skramble, Grave Robbers, River Rescue, Key Quest, Paratrooper

TRADER: 123A LOCATION: Michigan
SYSTEM: Atari 400 16K Tape
HAVE: Cartridge: Space Invaders, Star Raiders
Tape: Apple Panic 16K, Crossfire 16K, Shamus 16K, Preppie 16K, Milliped 16K (old DOS)
WANT: Games. Anything different.

To get in touch with these individuals, you send SofTraders $5 per trader. You receive access information, and then it is up to you to contact the individual and work out the trade. The cost to list your own "haves" and "wants" in the catalogue is $5. This includes the listing of five program titles. You may list five additional titles for a dollar. The catalogue we looked at included listings for the following machines: Apple II Plus, Apple //e, Apple ///, Apple compatibles, Atari 1200, 800, and 400, Commodore 64, Commodore VIC-20, IMS, Osborne, IBM/PC, and TRS-80 Models I and III.

Finally, SofTraders guarantees that "you will be able to arrange at least one trade with each person you select (within three months) or you may select another trader at no cost."

Appendix A
The XMODEM File

MODEM7, the popular communications program discussed in Chapter 2, is the paradigm of public domain software. Thousands of hours have been spent on its development. Scores of skilled programmers have generously donated their time and creativity to adding features and improvements, fixing bugs, and producing versions compatible with nearly every brand of computer. As it exists today, MODEM7 is on a par with many commercially available communications programs. But in the best public domain tradition, it's yours free for the asking. There is no finer example of "computer power to the people" than MODEM7.

As you know from Chapter 7, the XMODEM protocol supported by MODEM7 and other programs is crucial to anyone who wants to send binary program files from one computer to another. In this appendix we'll present an overview of how the protocol works. We'll also show you how to get a copy of MODEM7 that has been configured for your CP/M-running machine and point you in the direction of some non-CP/M programs that support the XMODEM protocol. Finally, we'll look briefly at VIDTEX™, a powerful communications program available for Commodore, Apple, IBM, and other computers.

How Does XMODEM Really Work?

Accuracy of information transmission and reception is a problem all communications systems must deal with. How often, for example, have you been taking down an address over the phone and said, "Is that *B* as in *boy* or *P* as in *Papa*?" and had the other party "retransmit" the ambiguous character? In the future, the accuracy of communications will be even more critical. The time is rapidly approaching when you and your personal computer will point a little 18-inch dish receiver at the sky and download information and software from a satellite in geosynchronous orbit above your home. When that day arrives, some type of error-checking protocol will be essential. In all likelihood the protocol chosen will be conceptually similar to XMODEM, just as XMODEM is based on concepts developed in the past.

The XMODEM protocol supported by MODEM7, by PC-TALK III, and by similar programs, uses a technique called "cyclic redundancy checking" or "CRC." If you look this term up in a computer dictionary, you will probably be confused by the definition. The following explanation should be easier to understand. Please keep in mind that XMODEM is both the name of a public domain CP/M program (described later) and the file transfer protocol it uses. In the following discussion, "XMODEM" means the protocol, not the specific program.

As you know, a file transfer protocol is designed to make sure that every binary digit in a machine language or other file is accurately received by your system or by the remote computer. To do this, XMODEM chops a file up into 128-byte units called "blocks." The transmitting computer assigns a number to each block and adds up the ASCII values of each byte as it is sent. When the last byte in the block has been sent, the computer divides the total of the ASCII values by 255. This division yields a quotient and a remainder. The transmitting computer throws away the quotient and sends the remainder down the line to the remote computer. The number that is sent is called a "checksum."

For its part, the remote computer adds up the ASCII values of each byte as it is received and performs the same division after the 128th byte in the block. If the remainder matches the checksum, it knows that the block has been received accurately. So it stores the information away and says, "Okay, send me the next block."

If the two checksums do not match, the receiving computer says, "We've got a problem here, boss. Better send that last block again." If the block is still faulty, the process will be repeated until a total of ten attempts have been made. Should the last attempt fail, the program will abort the transfer.

If everything goes well, the transmitting computer will finish up by sending a special signal indicating the end of the transmission. When it receives that signal, the other computer will close the file and finish storing it on disk.

Control Codes Make It Possible

There are other CRC protocols, of course, just as there are other non-CRC error-checking techniques. But all CRC protocols use the same general approach. Where they differ is in the details. These include the size of the blocks, the divisor or constant they use to generate the checksum, the number of times they will retry a transmission, and the control characters the two computers use to talk to each other.

A complete discussion of control characters or "codes" is beyond the scope of this book. Unless you're a programmer, all you really need to know is that control codes are part of the standard ASCII code set and that each has a special meaning in the field of data communications. For example, under XMODEM the sending computer needs to see a NAK (Negative Acknowledge; Control-U) from the receiving computer before it will start the transfer. The receiving computer, for its part, won't send this code until it is ready to receive the file. Each 128-byte block begins with an SOH (Start Of Header; Control-A) to signal the beginning of a block. An ACK (Acknowledge; Control-F) is used to indicate that a block was received correctly. An EOT (End Of Transmisson; Control-D) is sent to say, "That's all folks. Close the file." Fortunately, your computer handles all of these codes automatically.

Block Numbers

For the sake of simplicity we have left one other detail until now. This is the matter of block numbers. Obviously it is crucial for both computers to be synchronized so that each is dealing with the same block of data at the same time. Consequently, immediately after sending SOH, the transmitting computer will send the number of the block it is about to transmit. This tells the other computer to get ready to receive block 1 or block 3, or whatever. To make sure that the block numbers are transmitted correctly, each is followed by its "ones complement." This is a term from binary arithmetic, and it need not concern us here. In XMODEM, the ones complement is derived by subtracting the block number from 255. The receiving computer checks to make sure that the two numbers add up to 255. If they don't, it knows that something—noise or other electrical "hits" on the phone line—has affected its synchronization with the remote system. This prevents the receiving computer from inadvertently recording the same block of data under two different block numbers. In a text file that mistake would be minor, but in a program it would be disastrous.

Since it can sometimes help to see things graphically, you might want to look at the following diagram based on one supplied by Ward Christensen. You can think of a "timeout" as pause and reset. Under XMODEM the receiving computer spends ten seconds watching for information on the data line and then "times out." It stops looking, sends a NAK to tell the other computer that it hasn't received anything yet, and then starts watching again. The block numbers following <SOH> are in hexadecimal notation.

XMODEM: How the Data Flows

The following diagram shows the sequence of events that take place during an XMODEM transfer. Three blocks are shown. We've used HEX1, HEX2, and HEX3 instead of the actual hexadecimal numbers to make the blocks easier to identify. Notice that HEX1 is transmitted flawlessly, but that a "line hit" garbles the first transmission of HEX2, causing the Sender to retransmit. The checksum, sent with each block, is symbolized by <nn>.

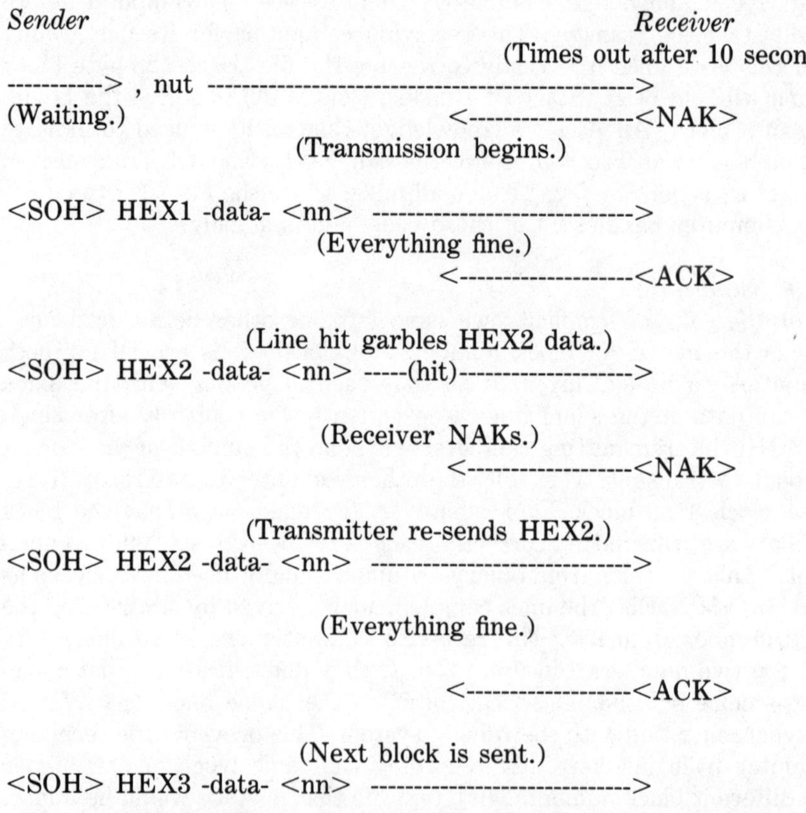

FreeTip: The original versions of MODEM-related programs used a simple checksum instead of the CRC bytes described above. The checksum was calculated by simply adding up all the bytes in a block and sending that number to the remote computer. The CRC technique is much more accurate and can be found in versions 4.3 and beyond. Most RCPM systems now support CRC, but you probably won't have to worry about those that do not. The most recent versions of the MODEM terminal program will attempt

CRC with the remote system, but if the RCPM fails to acknowledge, your program will automatically switch to the older method in most cases. If it doesn't, there will be a command you can enter manually to cause it to do so.

MODEM7xx, XMODEM, BYExx, and Other Programs

As you review catalogues of public domain CP/M software, it isn't lways easy to tell what each program is designed to do. This is espeially true when you are looking for a communications program because here are so many of them. Generally speaking, however, here are the uidelines to follow.

Any time you see a filename containing MODEM, MODM, MD, or ome other variation that does not include an X, you can assume that it s a smart-terminal communications program. The first program of this ype was called MODEM. It was quickly followed by updated versions s programmers added features, fixes, and improvements. The seventh ersion, MODEM7, represented a major overhaul of the Ward Chrisensen original by Mark Zeiger and Jim Mills. It is significant because eiger and Mills added user friendly menus, an auto-dial telephone diectory, a batch file transmission option, and many other features. Alnost all of the modem programs in the various libraries are based on his version.

The numbers following the alphabetic characters signify the version umber. Thus MODEM714 means "MODEM, version 7.14." Prefixes re often used to indicate versions that have been customized for paricular modems or computers. SMODEM37 and SM-MODEM7 are for se with the Hayes Smartmodem. APMODEM22 is for a CP/M-running pple computer.

All versions of MODEM7 support the XMODEM protocol. But when MODEM or some variation is used in a filename, the program is probbly the file transfer module designed to be used by a bulletin board rogram. For example, there are a number of programs that incorpoate some variation of the word BYE in their filenames. These are buletin board programs designed to turn a computer into an RCPM ystem. BYE67 is intended for use with the Potomac Micro Magic Inorporated (PMMI) modem, a popular board-mounted modem used with -100 systems. DCHBYE57 will do the same thing for users of a D. C. Iayes modem. But in both cases, the RCPM systems must also have he appropriate version of an XMODEM program if their SysOps want o permit downloading of machine language files.

How to Get MODEM7 and XMODEM Protocol Support

MODEM7 can be run on literally hundreds of makes and models of personal computers, and if your machine can run CP/M, there's an excellent chance that you'll find a version for your equipment already in the public domain. For those with IBM/PCs or MS-DOS–running machines, there are public domain translations of MODEM7. Other non-MODEM7 public domain programs also offer the XMODEM protocol and there are several excellent commercial packages that incorporate it as well. Finally, while XMODEM has yet to become available on some computers, there is an outstanding package from CompuServe called Vidtex™ that enables machine language transfers via the "B protocol" of the CompuServe system. In the following section we'll give you the information you need to pursue each of these avenues.

Start with Your Local Users Group

Although the code used in the basic MODEM7 program will work on almost any CP/M-running machine, as with most commercial software, minor modifications may have to be made to "install" the program for each brand of computer. The hexadecimal addresses of various ports may have to be changed, for example, and the key assignments may have to be customized. It may also be desirable to incorporate additional code designed to take advantage of the special capabilities of your equipment.

If you can handle 8080 assembly language, you can install the program yourself. But you should be aware that the source code for MODEM7 can only be assembled by MAC™, the macroassembler from Digital Research (about $100). The assembler that came with your CP/M package cannot do the job.

The do-it-yourself approach may be good exercise. But most CP/M users will probably be better off obtaining a version of MODEM7xx.COM for their machines from a local users group. To run this, you need only type in the word MODEM7 (or some other filename) at your DOS prompt. If there is no group in your area, contact one of the super groups cited in Chapter 3.

The group approach is the easiest and cheapest way to obtain the program. Computer and modem configurations can differ so widely that it is hard to make generalizatons. However, while a "standard" version of MODEM7 may work on your machine, you will probably not be able to take advantage of features like auto-dial if the software hasn't been customized. For this reason, try to obtain your copy from a group or SIG specializing in your brand of computer. The chances are excellent that their version will fully support your machine.

The quickest way to obtain a copy of the latest version of MODEM7 is to sign on to CompuServe and go into the CP/M SIG. This procedure has many advantages, the most important of which is Irvin Hoff. Mr. Hoff (CompuServe ID: 72365,70) has done an incredible job by creating what is in effect a national one-man support service for MODEM7. He has prepared a documentation file that is must reading for every current or prospective MODEM7 user. The file may be called MDM714.DOC. To be certain of finding the most up-to-date version, however, use the BROwse command described in Chapter 8. Key in *BRO MDM7??.DOC* at the *Function:* prompt. The transmission time is about 27 minutes at 300 baud, 7 minutes at 1200 baud.

Equally important, Mr. Hoff has prepared a master version of MODEM7 and over 40 machine-specific overlays you can use to install the master program for use with your equipment. There are overlays for most major native CP/M machines, of course. But Apple owners who are equipped for CP/M and Baby Blue–equipped IBM/PC owners will find that Mr. Hoff has not left them out in the cold. Mr. Hoff also provides an instruction file to show a novice user how to merge the overlay with the master.

FreeTip: The master file was created by running the assembly language source code of MODEM7xx through Digital Research's MAC assembler, so there is no need for you to own that program. As Mr. Hoff points out, most users will not need the MODEM7 source code at all. The preassembled master program exists as a text file in hexadecimal form. The filename will be in the form MDM7xx.BIN, where the *x*s signify the latest version. The overlays are written in assembly language and ample comments are included to guide you in entering the correct information. DDT, SID or some other debugger can be used to create an executable .COM program from the hex file. The overlay assembly language file can be processed into a hex file by the standard assembler (ASM.COM) that comes with most CP/M packages. The two programs can be merged using DDT or another debugger.

All of the modem-related files are in the Communications section of the CP/M SIG on CompuServe. Follow the instructions given in Chapter 8 to go into the SIG. Type *XA* at the *Function:* prompt, then key in *0* (the number of "Communicatons"). Next, key in *BRO MDM7??.???* to obtain a list and short description of the relevant files. The information in these files will get you plugged in and guide you to the other files you need.

Other Public Domain Sources of CP/M MODEM7

If you have difficulty obtaining the program from a local or super group, and if you do not yet have a subscription to CompuServe, you might want to contact one or more of the sources listed below. The following list is largely based on personal research, but it is by no means intended to be comprehensive. If you learn of additional verified sources, please write to the author care of St. Martin's Press.

Apple CP/M

Apple Avocation Alliance, Inc.
2111 Central Avenue
Cheyenne, WY 82001
(307) 632-8561

Send $2 for their catalogue ($3 for overseas shipment). The disks you want are numbers CP/M 04 and CP/M 05. Disks are $3 each and contain approximately 12 other programs. Add $2 for shipping and handling per order.

DEC Rainbow 100 and 100+

MDG and Associates
4573 Heatherglen Court
Moorpark, CA 93021
(805) 529-5073

Send $5 for a Rainbow disk containing MODEM7, as well as approximately 40 popular CP/M utilities. A game called DECMAN and a 22K file of RCPM systems is also included.

DEC VT-180 Computers

Mr. Larry Cole
10228 Parkwood Drive
Kensington, MD 20895

Send $5 for disk, copying, and postage. Mr. Cole soon plans to market programs to read, write, and format IBM/PC floppy disks on the DEC VT-180.

Heath/Zenith/"Baby Blue"
Mr. Robert Todd
1121 Briarwood
Bensalem, PA 19020

Complete CPMUG, SIG/M, and CP/M for IBM/PC owners with “Baby Blue” Z-80 boards in virtually all Heath/Zenith formats. Write for details.

Kaypro/Xerox 820

Sheepshead Software
P.O. Box 486
Boonville, CA 95415
(707) 463-1833

MODEM7 from CPMUG volumes 79 and 84, patched for Kaypro users. Cost is $16 per volume for SSSD and $12 for SSDD. Volumes include many other CP/M programs. Visa and MasterCard phone orders accepted.

NEC PC8000, Eagle I–III, and Zorba Portable

Mr. James Love
AWM American Micros
3493 North Main Street
College Park, GA 30337

SMODEM37-MODEM7 and several public domain programs. Contact by mail only. Send a formatted disk and $10.

Osborne

FOGHORN
Box 3474
Daly City, CA 94015-0474
Voice: (415) 755-4140
Modem: (415) 755-2030

With nearly 6,000 members worldwide,this is truly a Super Osborne Group. Yearly membership is $24, including monthly newsletter. Contact for name of group nearest you. Or join and purchase MODEM7 disk, $5 for members.

Superbrain and Compustar

Mr. David Steidley, President
Omnitech
50 Baltusrol Way
Short Hills, NJ 07078
(201) 376-6406

MODEM7 operates on all models of Intertec Data Systems's Superbrain and Compustar computers, with the exception of the new Superdensity. Cost is $8 (includes shipping). Disk comes with file of several hundred BBS phone numbers.

TRS-80

Mr. J. Cramer
Box 28606
Columbus, OH 43228-0606

Catalogue of free CP/M and free non-CP/M programs to run on Radio Shack computers. Your computer must be equipped for CP/M to run MODEM7.

Vector Graphic

L. M. Hammer
San Mateo Camera and Photo Supply
1933 South El Camino Real
San Mateo, CA 94402

MODEM7 for Vector Graphic computers.

Public Domain XMODEM Support for Non-CP/M Machines

Apple, Franklin, and Compatibles

See Term-Exec in the commercial products section below.

Atari

Michigan ATARI Computer Enthusiasts
(M.A.C.E.)
P.O. Box 2785
Southfield, MI 48037
(313) 338-6837

With over 1200 members worldwide, this is one of the largest Atari groups. It is homebase for Jim Steinbrecher, author of AMODEM, the XMODEM-supporting program you need. M.A.C.E. will thus undoubtedly have the latest version, though your local group may have it as well.

Membership is $20 per year and includes a subscription to the monthly *M.A.C.E. Journal* and access to the public domain software library. Catalogue available to members for $1. First disk or cassette is $6, subsequent ones are $5 each.

Commodore

See Bufterm and Vidtex™ in the commercial product section below.

MS-DOS Machines

Joseph Boykin, President
SIG/86
International MS-DOS Users Group
47-4 Sheridan Drive
Shrewsbury, MA 01545
Home: (617) 845-1074
Office: (617) 366-8911 Ext. 3216

300 baud modem: (617) 842-1435
1200 baud modem: (617) 842-1712
Hours: 11PM to 6PM (Eastern time)

Mr. Boykin reports that the group is hard at work converting MODEM7 to 8086 assembly language. When finished, the program will be available in the SIG/86 library.

You must be a member to access the library. Individual: $18 per year. Users groups: $15. Software: $10 for 8-inch SS/SD or 5-inch DS/DD members. Be sure to specify disk size.

IBM/PC and PCjr

PC-TALK III or PC-DIAL
(See Chapter 11.)

Both programs support the XMODEM protocol and will run without modification on an IBM/PC or XT. Andrew Fluegelman's PC-TALK III requires a 128K machine to run in its fastest, compiled version but only 64K to run the interpretive BASIC version. Suggested contribution: $35.

Jim Button's PC-DIAL™ (or "One-Ringy-Dingy"), available only in a compiled version, requires a minimum of 64K under DOS 1.0 and 1.1 and a minimum of 96K for use with 2.0, 2.1, and higher versions. Suggested contribution: $25.

The Long Island Computer Association
P.O. Box 71
Hicksville, NY 11802

Annual membership is $12. Includes subscription to "The Stack" monthly newsletter. This group has the complete PC/BLUE collection put together by the New York Amateur Computing Club. MODEM7, adapted from CP/M, is on PC/BLUE volume 37. Cost is $3 for members.

PC Software Interest Group (PC/SIG)
1556 Halford Avenue, Suite 130
Santa Clara, CA 95051
(408) 730-9291

The PC/BLUE MODEM7 program mentioned above is on Disk 4. A newer version (MODEM.COM) is on Disk 81, and One-Ringy-Dingy (1RD.COM) or PC-DIAL is on Disk 77. Cost is $6 per disk, plus $4 per order for shipping and handling.

Overseas orders, add 10% or $10 (whichever is greater) to the above total. California residents, add 6.5% sales tax.

Complete catalogue: $5.95, postage included.

Texas Instruments

Mr. Ralph Fowler
P.O. Box 383
Kennesaw, GA 30144
Modem: (404) 425-5254

Mr. Fowler brought up the first TI-99/4A BBS (T.I.B.B.S.) in the fall of 1983. The system does not support XMODEM, but should that protocol enter the world of the 99er, Mr. Fowler is certain to be one of the first to know. If you're interested in establishing a T.I.B.B.S. of your own, Mr. Fowler is also the person to contact as he is the author of the code.

XMODEM Support in Commercial Software Packages

Many versions of MODEM7 and similar public domain programs are accompanied by excellent DOC (documentation) files. But this is not something you can count on. The program has been worked on by many different people, and some programmers are more conscientious than others about documenting what they have done. Consequently, you may find the instructions less than complete. If you are a member of a local users group, this should not pose much of a problem since your fellow computer users will be able to help you. But this may not be as convenient as calling your retailer or even the software house responsible for a commercial program. And if you don't belong to a users group, you may have no readily available source of support. This can be particularly vexing if you are a new computer owner and you run into one of your first bugs.

For example, here is a message from Mark Graybill of MDG and Associates commenting on the version of MODEM7 for the DEC Rainbow 100. The comment appears at the beginning of the documentation file:

> I have used this version for about 6 months and have found some bugs. One is that you must type the commands in upper case letters for them to be recognized...Also, don't believe the onscreen prompts that say "Carriage Return" for "no change." You still have to enter one of the values displayed.

To someone with a little computer experience these bugs are simply one more set of details and exceptions to remember. But to a new computer owner who has just finished struggling through the CP/M manual, they can be quite discouraging. Unfortunately, the worst is yet to come.

As it happens, there is an undocumented bug in this version of the program that makes it necessary to *space once before entering your choice of baud rate and other communications settings*. (If you type in your choice where the onscreen prompt tells you to, you will get an error message. Repeat the process, and you will get the same message. There is no apparent way to get out of this loop.) As a new computer owner, and with no vendor to call, you might assume that you were at fault and give up on the program completely.

Once you get this software going, however, it is powerful. In addition to offering speeds of up to 9600 baud and supporting the XMODEM protocol, it will give you a disk directory, let you erase files, and provide access to other DOS functions. These are convenient features that many commercial programs do not include.

Pros and Cons of Commercial Comm Programs

There can be no question that purchasing a good commercial communications program is the best alternative for many people. The average price for a full-featured comm program has dropped in recent years to between $100 and $150, and in the future such programs may be even less expensive. This is a reasonable level, particularly in light of the excessive prices being charged for other applications software. However, compared to a copy of MODEM7 for as little as $5, any commercial program is going to seem expensive.

It's important to consider, however, what your time is worth, as well as the various kinds of communicating you will be doing. Public domain programs may not include the features essential to communicating with a mainframe, for example. Or they may not be as easy to use when sending TWX and telex messages. In addition, a growing number of software houses are integrating word processing, remote access (BBS), and modules that permit automatic, unattended operation with their products. Similar modules may be available in the public domain, but by the time you obtain the necessary disks you may find that you have more time and money invested than you anticipated.

Commercial programs will contain fewer bugs, offer more extensive documentation, and provide the additional features you may need for your other online activities. Most important of all, reputable vendors will be there to answer your questions and to help you get out of trouble should you have problems with the program. They will also make sure that the software is properly customized for your equipment (computer, modem, and disk format) and provide you with reasonably priced updates should new features be added.

As long as you are aware of the pluses and minuses, there is no reason why you can't start off with a public domain communications program and see how you like it. Ideally it should be one that is recommended and supplied by your local users group. If you have trouble using it or if you find that it doesn't offer all the features you need, you can always consider a commercial program. The worst that can happen is that you'll have invested several hours and spent about $5 on a floppy disk. The hours will not be recoverable, but you can always erase the disk and use it for something else.

Seven XMODEM-Supporting Commercial Programs

If you decide to purchase a commercial program, you may find that one of those listed below will provide all the features you need. With the exeception of Crosstalk™, none is heavily advertised. But all are offered by reputable vendors with long experience in the communications field and a thorough knowledge of their product. The features offered by these programs are too numerous to summarize here, but all seven support the XMODEM protocol. There are undoubtedly other equally fine commercial programs available for your computer. As a smart consumer you should investigate all of them. The comments below present only a few highlights designed to help you decide whether to send for more information. In every case, be sure to contact the vendor for more details before sending any money. For more help in choosing a commercial communications program, see *How to Buy Software* by Alfred Glossbrenner (St. Martin's Press, NY).

Bufterm
Quantum Software
Suite 31-B
5252 NE 6th Avenue
Ft. Lauderdale, FL 33334
(305) 776-7421
6 PM–10 PM (EST)
CompuServe: 74275,1154
Visa and MasterCard accepted.

Systems supported: CP/M-equipped Commodore 64.

Cost: Release 2, the version with XMODEM support, is $45, plus $2 shipping and handling.

Comments: This is a menu-driven program written entirely in Z80 and 6510 assembly language for fast execution. You can open and close the capture buffer at will and write its contents to a CP/M file at any time. Files may also be uploaded from the buffer. The program gives you full control over the colors on your screen and permits you to call for a disk directory or erase files without returning to DOS. Release 1 sells for $30 and does not include XMODEM support. Release 2 offers all of the above features, plus XMODEM.

COPYLINK™
U.S. Digital Corporation
5699-D SE International Way
Milwaukie, OR 97222
(503) 654-0668

Systems supported: IBM/PC and compatibles; any CP/M machine.

Cost: $100 for complete package with one format; $130 for complete package with any two formats. Discount of 40% given on quantities of five or more.

Comments: XMODEM support; top speed of 19,200 baud; batch send and receive; answerback; remote access (RCPM-like) function; control character filters; online help files; access to DOS commands; string-loadable keys; dialing directory; sophisticated automatic log-on and information retrieval capability; many customizable features.

CROSSTALK™
Microstuf, Inc.
1845 The Exchange, Suite 140
Atlanta, GA 30339
(404) 952-0267

Systems supported: IBM/PC and compatibles; any CP/M machine.

Cost: $100 (at a discount).

Comments: Long a popular program in the eight-bit CP/M world, the more powerful 16-bit version may be the best-selling comm program for the IBM/PC. Top speed: 9600 baud; very readable manual; can preview file before sending; batch send and receive; string-loadable function keys; control character filters; user-selectable line turnaround character; answerback; auto-redial; auto-dial, log-on, and information retrieval capability; IBM 3101 and DEC VT-100 emulation; sophisticated remote access feature with password protection; and more. XMODEM support began with Version 3.4, issued in January 1984.

Intelliterm™
MicroCorp
913 Walnut Street
Philadelphia, PA 19107
(215) 627-7997

Systems supported: IBM/PC.

Cost: $150 for standard package; $325 with MultiLink™ multi-tasking.

Comments: Particularly well-suited for use with IBM/XT or other hard disk-equipped PC. XMODEM support; top speed: 9600 baud; user adjustable split-screen separates incoming and outgoing characters; auto dial and dialing directory; unique simultaneous bidirectional file transfer capability; echo-paced transmission option; user-selectable capture buffer size and buffer auto dump; automatic printer initialization strings; label source of data on printer feature; includes complete word processing program and complete BBS program; extra cost MultiLink option permits running BBS module or other programs as background task, freeing foreground for other applicatons.

The author wrote the original documentation for this program but has no connection with the program or with MicroCorp. Nor are we responsible for whatever form the documentation may now take. At the same time, we have no hesitation about recommending that you consider Intelliterm. It is a powerful, imaginatively conceived program at a very reasonable price.

MITE, MITE/86, and MITE/MS
Mycroft Labs, Inc.
P. O. Box 6045
Tallahassee, FL 32314
(904) 385-1141

Systems supported: Any CP/M computer; any IBM/PC or MS-DOS computer.

Cost: $150 for MITE (CP/M); $195 for MITE/86 (CP/M-86) and MITE/MS.

Comments: Preinstalled versions available for over 100 computers. Top speed: 9600 baud; supports CLINK/CROSSTALK and Hayes protocols as well as XMODEM; remote access feature; special Western Union TWX mode lets computer replace TWX terminal; easily readable manual; completely menu-driven; string-loadable keys; auto-redial; line turnaround character; echo-paced transmission; control code character filters; access to DOS commands.

SYSCOMM/ABSCOMM
Microlife, Inc.
P.O. Box 340
Jessup, MD 20794
(301) 799-5509

Systems supported: IBM/PC, PCjr (128K), Columbia, Eagle, and other MS-DOS machines.

Cost: $40.

Comments: At this writing, SYSCOMM/ABSCOMM has barely been advertised at all, making it one of the great but little-known values in the IBM/PC world. SYSCOMM is the main terminal module. ABSCOMM is a module that permits unattended file transfers. At your direction, ABSCOMM will either answer the phone and permit a caller to log onto your system or it will dial a number at a preset date and time. Once a connection with another ABSCOMM-running system has been made, your system will download whatever files you have specified and sign off.

The package also includes EDCOMM, a menu-driven module that makes it exceptionally easy to configure SYSCOMM and ABSCOMM control files. See Chapter 11 for more information on this program.

TermExec™
Exec Software, Inc.
201 Waltham Street
Lexington, MA 02173
Voice: (617) 862-3170
Modem: (617) 863-0282 (a Net-Works™ board)

Systems supported: Apple II+, Apple //e, Franklin, and other Apple "clones"; DOS 3.3 and PRODOS.

Cost: $80.

Comments: XMODEM support; top speed: 1200–2400 baud; online HELP feature; send and receive files as large as disk capacity; unique "backscrolling" lets you review text that has already scrolled off screen; 80-column emulation on Apple IIe; batch command files; completely automated log-in and data capture at user selected time of day, with no need for a clock; macro commands files; full-screen editor with search capability for word processing mode; remote access (BBS) feature; full ASCII code for Apple IIe; licensed Diversi-DOS, access files up to nine times faster than with 3.3; automatic upgrade support available through Exec BBS; discount on BRS After Dark subscripton; Echo II/Text Talker support.

All of the above vendors care about their customers, but Drs. Elizabeth and Patrick O'Neil, president and chairman of Exec Software, communicate a particularly strong sense of mission. They appear to be dedicated to making it as easy as possible for Apple users, Franklin users, and users of compatible computers to access the power of the electronic universe. The software and the support their firm provides clearly bear this out.

FreeTip: For reasons of space, we have not considered the following four packages. But you should, since you may find they offer just the combination of features you need. As CP/M-based packages, each will run on literally hundreds of computers. All support XMODEM.

AMCALL ($150) and MCALL-II ($125) from:

MicroCALL Services
P.O. Box 650
Laurel, MD 20707
(301) 776-5253

ASCOM ($176) from:

Dynamic Microprocessor Associates
545 Fifth Avenue
New York, NY 10017
(212) 687-7115

COMMX ($100) from:

HAWKEYE GRAFIX
23914 Mobile
Canoga Park, CA 91307
(213) 634-0733

RCPMLINK ($50) from

Wizard of OsZ
P. O. Box 964
Chatsworth, CA 91311
(213) 709-6969

Vidtex™—Protocol Transfers and an Industry Standard?

Apple	IBM/PC and compatibles
Atari	Kaypro
Coleco Adam	Osborne
Commodore PET	TI 99/4-A
Commodore 64	TRS-80—all models
CP/M generic	. . . and most other machines
Franklin	

Vidtex™ is both a program and a set of conventions, standards, and protocols, created by CompuServe Information Service and either marketed by them or licensed to computer manufacturers. Versions are available for virtually every brand of computer, and with one exception, all are priced at $40. The exception is the IBM version. Also known as The Professional Connection™, this program uses Vidtex as the "kernel" for a more powerful program. Its list price is $90.

Vidtex does *not* support XMODEM file transfers. Instead it offers CompuServe's "B Protocol," a set of procedures designed for the error-free transmission and reception of binary files via the CompuServe system. The package can thus not be used to download most BBS and RCPM machine language files, though of course ASCII BBS files pose no problem. Vidtex is designed to let computer owners use CompuServe as a common meeting ground for the exchange of programs.

As a CompuServe spokesman points out, "Bulletin boards are wonderful, but once you dial out of your local calling area, it becomes cheaper to use a database such as ours. That's a major thrust of our business. We absorb the 'LD'—the long distance charges—making it cheaper to use CompuServe at ten cents a minute than to pay for a toll call." The rate referred to is CompuServe's cheapest 300-baud rate ($6 per hour) at this writing. The comparable 1200-baud rate (currently $12.50 per hour) is about 21 cents per minute.

The Vidtex Standard

Vidtex has been consciously designed with the goal of establishing a de facto industry standard for communications between personal computers and commercial databases. Every version thus supports the same set of features and responds in the same way to commands issued by the remote computer. Here are some of the more important features it offers:

- Automatic log-in and information retrieval via recorded command files or "scripts."

- Internal menus and HELP pages.

- Up to ten string-loadable function keys.

- Complete ASCII code set (eight-bit) capabilities.

- Page "send-ahead" stores eight or more screens of information the first time they are transmitted in a RAM buffer; any screen can be viewed instantly without waiting for retransmission from the remote system. Particularly well-suited for maps, grids, and multiscreen online games like Command Decision.

- Will respond to cursor positioning and color graphics commands from host computer to create special video effects.

The CompuServe "B Protocol" is part of the Vidtex standard. This protocol allows the error-free communication of three types of files, each of which has a special filename extension on the CompuServe system. Text files (.TXT) are simple ASCII. Binary (.BIN) files can be used to transfer tokenized (compressed) BASIC programs and data files, as well as machine language programs written for a particular microprocessor (as distinct from a particular brand of computer using that microprocessor). Machine language programs of this sort must have been customized for use on specific machines.

Perhaps most interesting and useful of all are the image files (.IMG). These are machine-specific binary files that require no customization to run on your computer. During an image file transfer, the Vidtex package automatically inserts all of the information needed to create the memory image of the file as it is intended to exist on your machine. This image is identical to the one that would be created were you to load the same program from a floppy disk.

Before initiating a transfer, the CompuServe mainframe will interrogate your little micro to make sure it knows that the machine is not an enemy spy. It won't ask for Babe Ruth's batting average or who's buried in Grant's Tomb, but it will find out what kind of computer you are using. If the .IMG file is not designed for your machine, it will not be transmitted.

Special Note for Commodore 64 and Coleco Adam Owners

Commodore Business Machines, Inc., found Vidtex so impressive that it has concluded a licensing agreement with CompuServe permitting it to offer it as a ROM-based, plug-in cartridge. If this is not on your dealer's shelves, it should become available shortly. In the meantime, the disk version is available directly from CompuServe. (You can use a bare-bones terminal program to access the system and place your order through FEEdback.) The disk version might be your best alternative in any case, since C- 64 ROM cartridges are limited to 16K. This is enough to support all current Vidtex features, but 16K may not offer enough room should there be future enhancements.

CompuServe has confirmed plans to offer Vidtex on the Coleco Adam home computer. There are no other details as of this writing, but one might guess that it will first become available for use with the high-speed tape system or the new Coleco disk drives, with a ROM-based version to follow. Watch the computer magazines and check with your dealer for further information.

Appendix B
How to Quadruple Your Free Software Library

Quadruple? Maybe not quadruple. Maybe you can *quintuple* your free software. Then again, maybe you will only be able to double the number of free programs available to you from, say, 3,000 to 6,000. One way or another, though, there is little question that you can greatly increase the amount of free software available to you, regardless of the machine you own. Maybe you own an Apple, an Atari, or a Kaypro, and would love to be able to run the free IBM software described in Chapter 11. If you're an IBM owner, there may be Apple programs you'd like to use. And what about running those same Apple programs on your Commodore 64? Wouldn't it be great if everyone could use the programs on the CP/M Gems List in Chapter 2, as well as the thousands of other free CP/M programs in the SIG/M library? In this appendix we'll show you how to do it. And, for those computer owners who are considering equipping their machines for CP/M, we'll present a quick guide to that operating system that will help you appreciate the free programs cited in Chapter 2.

We are happy to report that all of the above "switcheroos" can be effected today. And they won't necessarily cost you a month's rent, either. A Commodore 64 can be equipped to run the free programs in the CP/M libraries for about $50. If you have an Apple, you can gain access to the same libraries for about $95 ($60 if you're handy with a soldering iron). Other switcheroos are more expensive. If you own an IBM/PC, Compaq, or Columbia and are interested in running either CP/M-80 or Apple programs, you can buy what is in effect a 64K Apple or CP/M computer on a single board for about $475 at a mail order discount. The point here is this: *Today any brand of computer can run software written for any other brand of computer.*

Only a short time ago a statement like that would have been branded as rank heresy in the microworld. If you were to utter it in public, your disk drives would be seized immediately, your computer power supply would be permanently disconnected, and you would be sentenced to a life of playing *PacMan*. Today the statement is only a slight exaggeration because of the universality implied by the word *any*. Nothing in personal computing is ever universal. But then, nothing is impossible either. If the computer you own cannot at this point be equipped to run another machine's software, wait. The necessary circuits have probably already been designed, and as is the case with all new computer equipment, the product is undoubtedly "scheduled to ship next quarter."

Switcheroos!

How is It Possible?

If you're an experienced computerist, you probably have more than an inkling of how the above bits of magic are done. If you've just bought your computer, you may be subject to a brief mental *crise* since one of the first things all new computer owners learn is that "nothing is compatible."

It is true that personal computers (and the people who bought them) have been plagued with incompatibility. One machine couldn't use another's software, or if it had that capability, there was no simple way to get the programs into the target computer since it couldn't read the other machine's floppy disks. Now at long last, things are changing. Incompatibilities still abound, but more and more products are being created to overcome them.

One such product is the Uniform program described in Chapter 5. This software allows a given computer to read the floppy disk formats used by dozens of different computers. The switcheroos we'll focus on here represent hardware or hardware/software solutions to even more serious incompatibility problems.

To understand how an IBM/PC can be made to run Apple software, or vice versa, there are several general computer-related facts you must be aware of. The first is that the computer sitting on your desktop or in your den is not a monolithic appliance. All of the pieces may be in the same "ergonomically designed" box (easy to work with and at least moderately pleasing to look at), but in reality your machine has more in common with a component stereo system than with refrigerator. It would be difficult to rip the compressor out of your refrigerator and install it in someone else's icebox, but you can easily plug your speakers into someone else's stereo.

Similarly, a computer consists of many discrete components. These include the keyboard assembly, the CRT or television display, rows and rows of memory chips, the floppy disk drives, and so on. Like the pieces of your sound system, these components can often be mixed and matched. Are you fed up with how slowly your Commodore 1541 disk drive loads a program? No problem. Any number of firms can sell you a different drive that will operate at more than double the speed. Need more memory for your Apple? Fine. I'll just give you some of the RAM chips in my IBM. Not everything is interchangeable, of course. But you might be surprised at how many functionally different computers contain identical components from the same suppliers.

FreeTip: If you own a Commodore 64 and are thinking of adding a floppy disk drive, you would do well to consider non-Commodore suppliers before automatically buying a 1541 or similar C-64 compatible drive. Because they tramsmit information in serial fashion (one bit at at time), Commodore drives are notoriously slow. For approximately $250, or just a bit more than you would pay for a 1541, you can get a parallel (eight bits all at once) drive that operates at least twice as fast. Many companies sell this equipment, but here is at least one place you can contact for more information:

Concorde Peripheral Systems, Inc.
23152 Verdugo Drive
Laguna Hills, CA 92653
(714) 859-2850

If all of these pieces are generally interchangeable, what is it that makes an IBM/PC an IBM/PC, or an Atari 800 an Atari 800? The answer lies in the most important component of all, the microprocessor that is the "brain" of every computer. You may hear this referred to as the computer's CPU (central processing unit) or as "the chip." Other more specific terms may also be used. But as with the brain and the human body, all of the other components in the system exist to support this tiny piece of etched silicon.

The microprocessor is the only component in a computer that does any real work. The disk drives bring information in for the microprocessor to work on and record the results once it has finished. The memory chips serve as large temporary storage areas for information that the microprocessor needs. And the CRT and printer serve to display what it accomplishes.

If you're new to computing, the key thing to remember is that there are many *types* of microprocessors. An Apple //e uses a MOS 6502A, IBM/PCs and compatibles use an Intel 8088, and many CP/M based machines use a Zilog Z80. For our purposes here, we can think of each microprocessor as a craftsman from a different country. Each can use the same tools—the disk drives, memory chips, and CRT display— but each understands only his native language. If you want to ask an Italian craftsman to do something, you've got to speak Italian. To get a French craftsman to do the same thing, you must speak French. If you and your program do not use terms the computer's microprocessor can understand, the chip will not respond.

The only way to run a program written for the IBM/PC is to use the IBM's chip. The only way to run an Apple program is to use the Apple's chip. And that is exactly what a switcheroo makes possible. A switcheroo is simply a way of installing another computer's CPU in your machine. You might think of it as a brain transplant. The beauty is that both the chip your computer came with and the new chip can usually use the same disk drives, keyboard, CRT, and other support components. When used in this way, the second microchip is called a "co-processor."

Variety of Products

The devices we've called "switcheroos" typically consist of a circuit board that is designed to plug into your machine at some point. If your computer has internal expansion slots like the Apple or the IBM, the board may plug in there. If you have a Commodore 64, one of the external ports will be used. If you have an Atari, you will need an add-on interface box with expansion slots designed to accept such cards.

The switcheroo board may contain just the desired microprocessor CPU and some support circuitry. Or it may include an additional 64K or more of RAM. In some cases you may be able to use this extra memory when operating your computer in its native mode. In other cases the extra RAM will be reserved for the co-processor's exclusive use.

Some switcheroos include a brace of floppy disk drives and a different disk controller circuit board. A special disk containing software to activate the foreign processor may be needed. In other instances, the co-processor board remains dormant until it senses one of its disks in the drives. When it comes to life, it may assign your machine's native processor the task of watching the keyboard or handling other input/output functions. Or it may cut the main processor out of the circuit completely. Other techniques may be used as well.

Finally, some computers come from the factory with two microprocessors. The DEC Rainbow 100 has both an Intel 8088 (IBM) and a Z80 (CP/M), for example. But the all-time champ to date is the Dimension 68000 (Micro Craft Corp., Suite 241, 4747 Irving Boulevard, Dallas,

TX 75247). The basic machine is built around a Motorola 68000 microprocessor and sells for about $4,000. For an additional $400 each, the firm will supply co-processor boards that allow the Dimension to run Apple, TRS-80, CP/M-80, IBM/PC, or CP/M-86 programs. If each co-processor is a foreign craftsman, this machine is a regular United Nations.

Does it Make Economic Sense?

Does it make sense to buy a co-processor board just to be able to run free software? It depends on the cost of the boards or conversion packages, the quality of the free programs you want to run, and the specific commercial programs you want to use. The Commodore 64 is a good example. Commodore owners can pay $50 (at a discount) for a Commodore-supplied CP/M cartridge. Or they can buy the Convert 80 package from Estes Engineering for $600. (See listing below for contact information.)

Convert 80 includes a Z80B microprocessor, a disk controller card, 64K of RAM, two RS-232 serial ports, two parallel ports (one of which is Centronics-compatible for use with many major brands of printers), the CP/M operating system (Version 2.2), and a 5¼-inch Shugart floppy disk drive. (A package with an 8-inch drive costs $150 more.)

When you consider that the Commodore 64 itself sells for only $200, that seems rather like buying a very inexpensive car and then spending all the money you saved loading it up with options. Wouldn't one be better off buying a more expensive computer in the first place, one that included such features as standard equipment? "It depends," said Rick Estes, president of Estes Engineering. "Convert 80 uses the C-64 as a terminal to get information in and out of the computer we supply. And our add-on board really is a self-contained computer. Two hundred dollars is a very low price to pay for a computer terminal."

When you compare the $450 that you might pay for a C-64 ($200) and Commodore disk drive ($250), to the $800 ($200 for the C-64 and $600 for Convert 80), and factor in all of the extra ports and features, Convert 80 begins to look like a very good deal—if your goal is to obtain an inexpensive CP/M computer.

Untold numbers of Apple owners have paid from $200 to $400 for the Z80-based Microsoft Softcard that gives their machines the power to run WordStar and other popular CP/M programs. Indeed, at least one authority maintains that there are more CP/M-running Apple computers than any other single brand. The fact that the Softcard or a similar Z80 card also gives them access to the large public domain CP/M libraries is an added bonus. When the IBM/PC was introduced and software was relatively scarce, many people paid $600 for the Baby Blue card that let them run CP/M software. An enhanced Baby Blue, as well as a card called Big Blue (discounted price: $480) from another company, is still available today.

If you decide to go shopping for a switcheroo, just bear in mind that a number of different packages (and prices) may be available for your machine. Read the magazines that are published for your brand of computer. Look for ads and product reviews. Contact the manufacturer for brochures and information. And if there is a computer users group in your area, by all means ask its members for their suggestions.

A complete catalogue of available switcheroos is beyond the scope of this book, so the following list represents a sampling of some of the products offered by some manufacturers. It is intended to show you some of the different approaches that are used, and to serve as a source of contact points to get you started. At this writing, the trend is just beginning. So keep your eyes peeled for the new products that are sure to be offered in the future. All prices are subject to change, of course. And discounts may be available.

Some Important Switcheroo Points

Here is some information that will help you understand the features offered by some of the products listed below. All of these points are explained in greater detail in *How to Buy Software.*

- There are at least two reasons why many switcheroo boards include 64K or more of RAM. Sometimes the architecture (internal design) of the target computer makes it difficult for a co-processor to use the memory you already have. And sometimes that memory can be used, but doing so markedly slows down the operation of the co-processor. It can thus be more efficient for the co-processor to have its own on-board memory.

- An electronic disk or RAM drive is a portion of a computer's memory that is set aside to imitate a floppy disk. This greatly increases the speed with which you can use your computer, and often a switcheroo package will include the special software that makes it possible.

- MS-DOS (Microsoft DOS) is for all practical purposes the same as PC-DOS (IBM/PC). A large percentage of the free and commercial programs written for one of these operating systems will run on the other.

- CP/M 3.0 is the newest version of the operating system created by Digital Research. CP/M 2.2 is the most widely used version. Version

3.0 includes many additional features, but the company confirms that any program written for 2.2 will run under 3.0. The reverse is not necessarily true, however. (See the Quick Guide to CP/M later in this appendix.)

FreeTip: A word needs to be said about the various versions of the Zilog Z80 microprocessor that are offered by many switcheroo suppliers. The main difference among them is one of processing speed (also called "clock speed"). A chip's speed is measured in megahertz (MHz) or millions of cycles per second. Here is how the various versions stack up:

Z80	2.5 MHz
Z80A	4.0 MHz
Z80B	6.0 MHz
Z80H	8.0 Mhz

You will not notice the difference in all programs, but in some, the faster the chip, the faster your computer will respond. It is important to remember, however, that the memory chips and peripheral devices in a computer must be matched to the CPU's clock speed. Consequently, a switcheroo package may include additional circuitry to slow down its microprocessor when necessary to match the speed of the computer's other components.

FreeTip: Another way to expand the free software available to you is to translate programs from one version of a computer language into the version that is acceptable to your machine. This is most frequently done with programs written in BASIC.

The BASIC supplied by Microsoft Corporation is so widely used that it has become the de facto standard BASIC. And just as Latin served as the basis for French, Italian, and Spanish, MS-BASIC is the foundation for countless machine-specific versions of the language. Thus, you usually have a lot to work with right from the start.

The amount of effort involved in translating a BASIC program will vary. In some cases the program can be run "as is," and you have only to download it into your machine via the phone line or a direct computer-to-computer connection. At other times you'll have to write short subroutines in your computer's BASIC to accomplish what the program accomplishes with some machine-specific statement. Other programs are so dependent on their native computer that you will not be able to translate them.

The various steps can be quite involved, but without question everybody's first step should be to buy *The BASIC Handbook* by David A. Lien. This is the bible of the BASIC language. It contains capsule explanations of nearly every important word in over 250 versions of BASIC. And Mr. Lien is such a good writer that it is a pleasure to read. The book is available at most major bookstores, but you can also order directly by sending $19.95 plus $1.65 for shipping and handling to the address below. (For foreign air mail shipment, send $10 instead of $1.65; U.S. funds on a U.S. bank, only.)

COMPUSOFT Publishing
1050-E Pioneer Way
El Cajon, CA 92020

FreeTip: For more information on performing BASIC translations, be sure to check your computer's BASIC manual. The IBM BASIC manual, for instance, addresses the subject in its Appendix D. You might also consider the computer magazines. George Stewart, the technical editor of *Popular Computing*, has an excellent article called "Translating BASIC Programs" in the September 1983 issue of that magazine. If you do not have a copy, ask someone in your local users group. Users group newsletters are another good source of translation tips. When you join a group, whether as a local or remote member, you might ask if the subject has been covered and if back issues are available.

We can recommend at least one other book as well. Written by Larry Noonan, the *Basic BASIC-English Dictionary* ($10.95) provides complete cross-referencing information and tips for translating the BASICs used by the Apple, the Commodore PET, and TRS-80 computers. Look for it in your bookstore or contact:

dilithium Press
P.O. Box E
Beverton, OR 97075
800-547-1842
Visa and MasterCard accepted

Atari, Big Board, Kaypro, Osborne, Xerox 820, Zorba

SWP, Inc.
2500 East Randol Mill Road
Arlington, TX 76011
(817) 469-1181
Visa and MasterCard accepted

CP/M Conversion
IBM/PC Conversion

Comments: If you own one of the above listed computers, this company (formerly known as Software Publishers, Inc.) can sell you what you need to run CP/M-80, CP/M-86, or MS-DOS (IBM/PC DOS) software. Atari is a special case, so we'll look at that system first. If you own an Atari 400 or Atari 800, you can buy SWP's expansion box interface, the ATR8000, for about $350. This includes both a serial port and a parallel port for use with a modem and/or printer, as well as interfaces for up to four floppy disk drives (any type or size) and a special interface for the Atari 810 drive. Also included is 16K of RAM for use as a printer buffer.

If you want to run CP/M-80 2.2 on your Atari, you can then add a Z80 card containing 64K of memory and the operating system software. If CP/M is your primary interest, though, you will be better off purchasing the ATR8000 and this option as a package. The cost is about $500, complete.

The other computers listed above all support CP/M-80 as their native (supplied by the manufacturer) operating system and can thus run most public domain CP/M software. Owners of these machines who want to be able to use software written for the IBM/PC, for machines running MS-DOS, or for machines running CP/M-86, have two options. You can either buy SWP's expansion box and install the firm's Co-Power-88™ co-processor board, or buy the board alone and install it in your own system.

Co-Power-88 comes with an Intel 8088 microprocessor, 256K of RAM, electronic disk software, MS-DOS Version 1.25, and CP/M-86. The cost is about $500. (The version of MS-DOS for the Kaypro 10 is Version 2.11 and the total cost is about $600.) If you buy the expansion box as well as this package, the cost is about $1,000.

As an interesting side note, SWP has licensed the manufacturing rights to its Co-Power-86 board to Kaypro, though the product is available from both firms. The co-processor boards that enable the Morrow and the Access Matrix to run MS-DOS and CP/M-86 are also SWP products, though they are available only from those computer manufacturers.

Orbital Systems CP/M Conversion
5225 East Heran Road
Scottsdale, AZ 85254
(602) 996-5064

Product: E-Z CARD.

Price: $90, assembled; $60, do-it-yourself.

Key Points: Contains no additional memory chips; makes use of Apple's internal memory. Runs at about 3.58 MHz. No software is supplied.

Microsoft Corporation CP/M Conversion
10700 Northup Way
Bellevue, WA 98004
(800) 426-9400

Products: Softcard ($345) and Premium Softcard IIe ($395).

Key Points: Regular Softcard is for non-//e Apples; includes Z80, CP/M-80 Version 2.23 software, Microsoft BASIC Interpreter, utility program package for using CP/M on the Apple, and complete instructions and documentation.

Premium Softcard IIe is for Apple //e only; includes CP/M software, 64K of RAM, and an 80-column card capability.

Digital Research, Inc. CP/M Conversion
160 Central Avenue
Pacific Grove, CA 93950
(408) 649-3896

Product: The CP/M Gold Card (64K RAM) and Disk Cache (additional 128K RAM and supporting software).

Price: $775, complete; $495, without Disk Cache.

Key Points: DRI's first hardware product. Runs on all Apple models and can be placed in any slot. Includes Z80B offering three times the speed of Z80-based boards, CP/M Version 3.0 (CP/M Plus), 80-column display capability when running CP/M, and 64K of memory.

Disk Cache option includes additional 128K of memory (for total of 192K) and special software for completely user-transparent (you won't be aware of it) disk emulation. More sophisticated than plain RAM or "electronic" disk. Reads and writes to floppies automatically.

Personal Computer Products, Inc. CP/M Conversion
16776 Bernardo Center Drive
San Diego, CA 92128
(714) 485-8411

Product: Appli-Card.

Prices: Z80A (4 MHz), $295; Z80B (6 MHz), $375; Z80B with 128K RAM extender, $395.

Key Points: Choice of Z80 processors; Can be used on all Apple models, any slot; includes CP/M 2.2, 64K RAM, 70-column upper- and lowercase capabilites, on-board expansion port for more memory or other interfaces; 2K PROM (programmable read only memory) expandable to 8K; special utility program package, including ADOSXFER to transfer files between Apple and CP/M format. Additional 128K RAM extender can be used as an electronic disk.

Rana Systems IBM/PC Conversion
21300 Superior Street
Chatsworth, CA 91311
(800) 421-2207
In California: (800) 262-1221
SourceMail: TCT654

Product: Rana 8086-II.

Price: $1,795.

Key Points: Includes two 360K disk drives, disk-controller board, and co-processor board. Co-processor board contains Intel 8086 chip (compatible with IBM's 8088, but a "true" 16-bit processor; clock speed is 5.0 MHz). Also included are 256K of RAM, expandable to 512K.

System automatically detects difference between Apple disks and IBM disks when supplied Rana drives are used. Standard Apple drives cannot read IBM formatted disks.

Commodore 64

Pioneer Software, Inc. Apple Conversion
#217-620 View Street
Victoria, BC
Canada V8W 1J6

Product: AP Modular Pak.

Price: "Under $500."

Key Points: AP Bus contains eight standard Apple II peripheral slots plus four C-64 expansion slots; AP "CPU" Card plugs into its own slot on the AP Bus and handles all Apple II to C-64 conversions; AP DOS Card converts a Commodore 1541 disk drive into an Apple II compatible drive.

According to *RUN* magazine, "any program designed for the Apple II will now run on the C-64. All Apple II peripherals function the same as they would connected to an Apple II."

Special Note on Commodore 64 CP/M Conversions

As mentioned earlier, Commodore 64 owners wishing to run CP/M software have at least two routes open to them. As you might expect, however, there is a trade-off between price and convenience. The least expensive alternative is to purchase the Commodore CP/M cartridge and CP/M disk. The list price is $70, but we've included contact information for a firm that will sell it to you for about $50. The more expensive, more convenient alternative is to purchase a co-processor/disk drive combination like Convert 80 from Estes Engineering ($600), also listed below. Here is what you need to know when making up your mind.

The problem centers around the Commodore 1541 disk drive and its relatives. Because the drive uses an unusual format, it can be difficult to obtain free CP/M software on a disk that the 1541 can read. Limited quantities of this software may be available on Commodore disks from computer users groups. But at this writing few of the firms that specialize in providing free CP/M software for many different computers offer a Commodore drive–compatible format.

The two alternatives cited above represent the two major solutions to this problem. If you were to buy the Commodore CP/M cartridge and equip your machine for communications, you could download a large percentage of the available free CP/M programs by calling an RCPM bulletin board or by accessing the CP/M SIG on the CompuServe system (see Chapters 10 and 8, respectively). Or you could connect your C-64 to a CP/M-running computer with a null modem cable and pump the software directly into your machine. Either way, the programs can be captured and recorded on your Commodore disk for use any time thereafter.

Your cost, then, would be $50 for the CP/M cartridge, $100 for an RS-232 cartridge interface and a 300-baud modem, and about $45 for an XMODEM supporting CP/M communications program like Bufterm (see Appendix A), for a total of $195. That may sound like a lot, but don't forget that it includes a communications capablity. With a different communications program, you can use the same equipment to download free Commodore-specific software.

The more convenient alternative is to add a CP/M co-processor board and use a standard disk drive in place of the 1541. This will allow you to obtain and use free CP/M software on disks that have been formatted for a Xerox 820, a Kaypro II, or some other machine. The Convert 80 package is even available with a standard 8-inch drive that will let you use the CP/M disks supplied by SIG/M and other sources offering free software in the standard IBM 3740 8-inch format. (See Chapter 2.) Other CP/M conversion packages that also use a non-Commodore disk drive may be available, but all of them will cost considerably more than the less expensive alternative.

FreeTip: Here's an idea that may be of interest to any enterprising C-64 owner interested in starting a small business. If you wanted to, you could use your C-64 and equipment supplied by Estes Engineering to start your own CP/M downloading service. The Convert 80 package we have been discussing can be equipped with *both* a standard 8-inch drive and a 5¼-inch drive.

Rick Estes, president of the firm, says, "We supply a software package with Convert 80 called 'ES Install.' This lets you specify the disk parameters such as the number of tracks and the number of bytes per sector needed to create virtually any format. We do this all the time, since we frequently have to transfer a customer's program from say the Kaypro format to an 8-inch system, or vice versa."

The manual includes the format specifications for the Kaypro II, Xerox 820, TRS-80 Model II, Televideo 920, and several other machines. But according to Mr. Estes, "You can do any format. You just have to know what formats you are trying to transfer the software to and from. This is not the same approach used by the Uniform program, although that program runs quite well on our equipment. We provide a menu that lets you actually change the operating system routine so that it can run the specified drive."

The cost for the Convert 80 package with both an 8-inch and a

5¼-inch drive is about $1,000. To this you must add the $200 that you probably paid for your C-64 and the cost of the SIG/M CP/M library on 8-inch disks. Assuming you decide to obtain 100 SIG/M volumes at $6 apiece, your cost will be $600. Throw in another $200 for advertising, blank disks, disk mailers, and miscellaneous supplies, and the total comes to $2,000. That covers just about everything you need to start your own downloading service. When you consider that the specialized computers used by large commercial firms to accomplish the same thing can cost several thousand dollars, this would seem to be one of the least expensive ways to get started.

AB Computers — CP/M conversion
252 Bethlehem Pike
Colmar, PA 18915
(215) 822-7727
Visa and MasterCard accepted

Product: Commodore CP/M package

Price: $50

Key Points: Commodore-manufactured CP/M cartridge and 1541 compatible disk containing the CP/M operating system.

One of many firms selling Commodore equipment through the mail, this company has an extensive inventory of C-64 hardware and software and is staffed by very knowledgeable people.

Estes Engineering — CP/M conversion
P.O. Box 753
Salina, KS 67402
(913) 827-0629

Product: Convert 80.

Price: $350 for basic board; from $600 to $750 or more for the board and a disk drive.

Key Points: Convert 80 board contains Z80B able to run at 4 or 6 MHz; 64K RAM; two RS-232 serial ports; two parallel ports, one of them Centronics compatible; disk controller card; CP/M 2.2 operating system.

A variety of disk drives are also available, including 5¼-inch single-

and double-sided and a standard eight-inch drive. For maximum convenience, Estes recommends the eight-inch drive since all commercial and public domain CP/M programs are available in that format.

At this writing, the product is available only directly from Estes.

IBM and Compatibles

Special Note on IBM CP/M Emulation

Both IBM and Digital Research sell a CP/M-86 operating system software package for IBM Personal Computers. However, you should be aware that while it has a similar structure and similar commands, CP/M-86 is written for the Intel 8088 microprocessor. It is not the same as CP/M-80, the Z80 (or Intel 8085)–based version used for most public domain programs. CP/M-80 data files can be read and used by CP/M-86, but one cannot run CP/M-80 programs under 86 without translation.

When the IBM/PC was first shipped, a number of Z80 boards with the CP/M-80 operating system appeared on the market to give IBM owners access to CP/M software. These may still be available, but we have not been able to find any of them mentioned in ads carried by *PC* magazine or *PC World*. The more typical approach in the IBM world is to supply a Z80 board and software that lets the PC emulate CP/M-80 and run programs written to run under its control.

This emulation software takes the place of (and eliminates the need to pay a licensing fee for) the CP/M operating system. This enables you to run many commercial and public domain CP/M programs. But since CP/M itself is not provided, you will not have the CP/M assembler or other modules to work with.

QuCeS Inc. — CP/M Emulation
3 Quces Drive
Metuchen, NJ 08840
(201) 548-2135

Product: Big Blue.

Price: $595, list; about $480 at a discount.

Key Points: Contains a Z80B and 64K of RAM which can be used by your IBM/PC when operating in normal IBM mode. Also, an RS-232 serial port, a Centronics parallel port, a hard disk interface, and a real-time clock.

According to literature supplied by QuCeS, "Big Blue runs CP/M-80 programs on your PC, Compaq, or Columbia without CP/M. . . . Programs provided for emulation, communication and reading most CP/M formats."

Microlog, Inc. CP/M Emulation
222 Route 59
Suffern, NY 10901
(914) 368-0353

Product: Baby Blue II.

Price: $695, list, with 64K RAM installed.

Key Points: Includes Z80B and 64K RAM, expandable up to 256K; clock calendar; parallel port; two RS-232 serial ports; RAM, ports, and clock can be used by both Z80 and 8088 processors.

Software for electronic disk, print spooling, smart terminal and protocol file transfer, and file conversion is included. Also includes Keyfix, a program that lets you load up to 54 PC keys with strings of characters.

Quadram Corporation Apple Conversion
4355 International Boulevard
Norcross, GA 30093
(404) 923-6666

Product: Quadlink.

Price: $680, list; $485 at a discount. Prices for Compaq or Columbia owners, slightly higher.

Key Points: Plug-in board with 6502 microprocessor, 64K RAM, a disk controller chip, and PAL (programmed array logic) chips that emulate an Apple's ROM when loaded with supplied software. Game port for joysticks.

Compaq and Columbia owners will need special cables, available as part of package. At this writing, Quadlink will not operate the Compaq's internal CRT, but will work with an external monitor on that system. No problems reported driving IBM/PC monitors or internal Columbia unit.

Two floppy disks are supplied. One is a boot disk in IBM/PC format to initialize the Quadlink. Other contains Apple DOS 3.3, Integer and Applesoft BASIC, and a menu-driven collection of utility programs.

TRS-80 Computers

Special Note on Tandy Radio Shack CP/M Conversions

With the exception of the Tandy Model 2000, which is built around an Intel 80186 microprocessor and is able to run a large percentage of IBM/PC software, the Color Computer, and the lap-sized Model 100, most Radio Shack computers are built around a Z80A or similar CP/M chip. Models II, 4, 12, and 16 can be "converted" for CP/M by simply inserting the CP/M operating system on disk.

Models I and III, however, require an add-on board and a little handiwork. The products designed for these machines require you to remove the Z80B processor from its slot on the computer's main circuit board, plug it into the add-on board, and plug the add-on board into the slot formerly occupied by the Z80. These boards work quite well, but installing them is not something to be taken lightly. You will have to remove the computer's plastic case, thus breaking the seals and voiding your warranty. And at the very least you will need an inexpensive chip extracting tool. You must also take great care not to bend any of the prongs on the chip when you are inserting it into its new home.

Since these are not Radio Shack products, you will probably not be able to persuade your store's service person to do the job. Instead, you might offer the individual a free-lance assignment to be completed after business hours. You might also contact your local TRS-80 users group to locate someone who can help.

CP/M Conversion for Models II, 12, and 16

Pickles & Trout
P.O. Box 1206
Goelta, CA 93116
(805) 685-4641

Product: Pickles & Trout CP/M.

Cost: $200.

CP/M Conversion for Model 4

Montezuma Micro
Hanger #18
Redbird Airport
P.O. Box 32027
Dallas, TX 75232
(214) 339-5104

Orders Only: (800) 527-0347; (800) 442-1310. Visa, MasterCard, and American Express accepted.

Product: Montezuma Micro CP/M.

Price: $200.

Key Points: Consists of a single floppy disk containing CP/M 2.2, electronic disk software, and MODEM7. Supports 80-by-24 video, reverse video, and direct cursor addressing. Includes INTERCHANGE™, a utility that allows reading, writing, and copying of 20 different disk formats, including IBM, Kaypro, Osborne, and Xerox. Includes FORMAT, a menu-driven utility permitting up to 52 disk formats to be constructed.

CP/M Conversion for Models I and III

The following manufacturers are some of the major suppliers of CP/M conversion hardware and software in the TRS-80 world. Their basic products differ, and some offer a range of additional options. Consequently, we suggest contacting each one for additional information. You might also check the December 1983 issue of *80 Micro* for Terry Kepner's article "CP/M III Ways," and other publications specializing in TRS-80 computers. If there is a users group in your area, be sure to ask members for their opinions.

Omikron Systems
1127 Hearst Avenue
Berkeley, CA 94702

Product: CP/M Mapper I or III Board.

Price: $140 for Model I; $200 for Model III.

Holmes Engineering, Inc.
5175 Green Pine Drive
Murray, UT 84107

Product: VID-80 Board.

Price: $279.

Memory Merchant
14666 Doolittle Drive
San Leandro, CA 94577

Product: Shuffleboard III.

Price: $300.

Hurricane Laboratories
5149 Moorpark Avenue
San Jose, CA 95129

Product: Compactor I and III.

Price: Not available at this writing.

Microcomputer Technologies
1530 South Sinclair Street
Anaheim, CA 92806

Product: CP/M 64K.

Price: $398; CP/M operating system available separately for $120.

A Quick Guide to CP/M

If you are already conversant with CP/M, you will not need this information. However, if you are an Apple, Commodore, or IBM/PC owner considering CP/M, or if you are thinking of buying a CP/M-based computer, the following will be helpful. Since a complete explanation is beyond the scope of this book, we're going to speak telegraphically, without drawing all the lines in between. The following information should be enough to help you make sense of the CP/M Gems List in Chapter 2:

- As mentioned earlier, the brain of any computer is a microprocessor or "chip." If you change the chip, you change the computer.

- The thing that makes each chip unique is its "instruction set." You can think of this as a limited vocabulary of perhaps 40 to 100 "words" or commands. A chip will only respond to words that are in its vocabulary.

- Chips come in families, and every member of a family shares the same vocabulary. The difference is that newer members understand not only the old words but several additional words as well. The family that CP/M users are most concerned with is the 8080 family, and it includes the Z80 and the 8085. The 8080 and 8085 are made by Intel. The Z80 is made by Zilog.

- The 8080 is the oldest of the three. It was the chip that started the personal computer revolution. The Z80 and 8085 represent improved versions with expanded instruction sets. Thus, while programs written for the 8080 will run on all three chips, the reverse is not necessarily true. It all depends on whether the program uses instructions found only in the Z80 or 8085.

- CP/M-80 is designed to talk to 8080 and Z80 chips in their own language. CP/M-86 is designed to talk to a different family of chips, the 8086 family. (As a confusing side note, the 8086 family includes the 8088 chip at the heart of the IBM/PC and its clones.)

- As you know, a personal computer can consist of a chip, video screen, printer, keyboard, communications port, disk drives, and other equipment. But left to their own devices, computers are little more than a collection of unrelated electronic junk.

  CP/M is a software product that ties all of these unrelated pieces together and makes them operate as a system. When a program needs information stored on disk, it is CP/M (the operating system) that sets the disk drive spinning and locates and retrieves the required data. Similarly, when you hit a key on your keyboard, it is CP/M that is responsible for making sure it is displayed on your screen.

- The important thing to keep in mind about CP/M or any other operating system is that they are *programs*. They are loaded into memory and run by the microprocessor just as any other program is. And like any other program, an operating system can be modified or "enhanced" by adding customized "code" (the computerist's word for computer programming instructions).

- This modification, in fact, is what a large number of public domain programs are designed to do. Such programs are called "utilities" because they are tools you use every day to perform routine chores like getting a directory of a floppy disk. Often public domain utility programs are more powerful and more convenient than their official CP/M counterparts.

- Each brand and model of computer is different. Two different machines may have the same chip and use many of the same hardware components. But there is no "standard" configuration.

- The reason CP/M can be used on so many fundamentally different machines is the fact that it consists of a series of software *modules*, each of which "plugs into" the other the way a three-prong adaptor plugs into a two-hole electrical socket.

- The CP/M module that must be customized for each and every machine is called the "BIOS" or "Basic Input/Output System" (pronounced "buy-o's"). This is almost always done by the company that supplies you with the CP/M operating system. For example, your machine might use 8-inch drives, 5¼-inch drives, or a combination of the two; the BIOS must be modified accordingly. Other CP/M modules "talk" to the BIOS, and the BIOS "talks" to the specific hardware.

- To carry this one step further, the programs (or the computer languages you use) "talk" to CP/M, and CP/M "talks" to its BIOS, and the BIOS "talks" to the computer's hardware.

- The result is that as long as the BIOS has been customized for the hardware, almost any program written to run under CP/M (issue the commands CP/M understands) can be run on almost any computer that is built around or equipped with the necessary microprocessor chip (an Intel 8080 or, these days, a Zilog Z80 or Intel 8085).

- You can run a great deal of public domain CP/M software "as is," without the need for changes. Some programs, however, must be modified or otherwise customized to make them run on your machine. Often several versions of a program will be available, each of them configured (customized) for a particular computer or peripheral (auxilliary equipment). Obviously you must make certain to get the version that is right for your equipment.

- Where completely configured versions are not available, you may be able to obtain "patches" or "overlays." These are short, prewritten modules that will handle the customization for you when they are applied to the main program. In some cases, they will come with cookbook-style instructions to step you through the process. At other times you will be on your own and may need the help of a friend.

- Where neither customized versions nor appropriate patches are available, you will have to do the work yourself. The actual amount of work involved usually will not be great, but you must know what you are doing. Until you get the hang of it, the help of someone with more experience will probably be essential.

Version Numbers and the Standard CP/M Package

Like all software of a certain age, CP/M has been upgraded and improved many times. Each time a new release is issued, it is given a different "version" number. Version numbers are indicated by *V. N.n* where *n* signifies a relatively minor change and *N* signifies a major new edition. The mileposts in the CP/M world are Version 1.4, Version 2.2, and Version 3.0. Obviously, the higher the number, the newer the version. Version 3.0 ("three point oh"), also known as "CP/M Plus," was issued in 1983. It includes many enhancements, including graphics capabilities and the ability to address 128K of RAM instead of the 64K limit found with previous versions. Version 2.2 has probably been the most widely distributed and it is still the one most CP/Mers use.

FreeTip: These are all versions of what is now called CP/M-80 to distinguish it from CP/M-86, a version written for a different family of microprocessor chips. If you have an IBM/PC you can run CP/M-86 without adding an extra board, since the 8088 at the heart of your machine is a member of the 8086 family. But this is *not* the same as the CP/M used for most public domain software. To run these programs you will have to add a Z80, CP/M-80–running board.

Since Version 1.4 is one of the earliest releases, most early public domain programs were written for it. Unfortunately, some of these programs may not be usable with Version 2.2. The description of the program will usually warn you of this fact. As a rule, programs written for an older version of CP/M can be used with a newer version, though the reverse is not the case. Sometimes, however, the addition of new features and additional commands can cause incompatibilities. Much depends upon the specific program and the demands it makes of the operating system. The most serious incompatibilities exist in those few early programs written for Version 1.3. These programs tend to be hardware-sensitive and usually will not work without modification.

The Standard CP/M Modules

The standard CP/M 2.2 package includes 17 separate programs. These exist as discrete files on your disk, all of which end with .COM to signify that they are immediately executable machine language programs. No separate language package, like BASIC, is required to run these programs. ERA erases files. DIR lists the names of the files in a specified directory on a disk. REN renames files. And TYPE will display the contents of a file. These are among the operating system programs that are loaded into the machine whenever you "boot" (start up) CP/M.

Other CP/M "system" programs stay on the disk and are brought in only as needed. ED is a "line editor" that allows you to create and alter text one line at a time. You cannot move the cursor all over the screen with ED, as you can with a word processor. ED is intended to be used to create "assembly language" programs (though this can also be done with a word processor).

ASM takes an assembly language textfile and "assembles" the instructions it contains by converting them into a series of hexadecimal numbers. Since a single programming instruction may be translated into many hexadecimal numbers, the resulting file will take up more space on a disk than the textfile containing the "source code." For this reason, many public domain programs are provided in source code (text) form and must be "ASM'ed" by you.

Once you have assembled a program, you must use LOAD to convert the hexadecimal numbers into machine language numbers. Again, the resulting .COM file will be larger than the "hex" file it was translated from. At this point the program is ready to run. DDT, the Dynamic Debugging Tool, can be used for the same purpose, but it is more sophisticated than LOAD and is meant to be used to correct and alter programs while they are running. Finally, PIP (Peripheral Interchange Program) is CP/M's version of COPY in other operating systems. (For more information on other CP/M commands, see your manual or one of the CP/M guidebooks cited in Chapter 2.)

> **FreeTip:** It is worth pointing out that the operating systems provided for non-CP/M computers rarely include the tools one needs to write assembly language programs. They are usually available, of course, but are almost always sold as an extra-cost option (about $75 to $100). Even Digital Research sells a popular assembler (MAC Assembler™) for programmers who need more power than ASM.COM can provide. And occasionally you will encounter a public domain program that can only be assembled with MAC. The description of the program will usually warn you of this requirement.

A Word about Languages

Like an operating system, a computer language is a special kind of computer program. As such, the language software itself must be written to run on a particular microprocessor *and* under the control of a particular operating system. A language program may be able to execute the same commands as other versions of the same language, but it must meet these two criteria.

Just as many Apple owners use Applesoft BASIC and many IBM owners use IBM/PC BASIC or Advanced BASIC, CP/M owners use

EBASIC, CBASIC2, or MBASIC. EBASIC (or BASIC-E) was written by Gordon Eubanks while he was in the Navy. Because it was developed using government facilities, it was automatically placed in the public domain. It is available through CP/M users groups, and possibly from computer manufacturers and suppliers of CP/M. CBASIC and CBASIC2 were Mr. Eubanks's next efforts. Privately developed, CBASIC2 is available from Digital Research.

MBASIC is Microsoft BASIC. The company has officially changed the product's name to MS-BASIC as part of its campaign to increase Microsoft's corporate visibility. This is the same firm responsible for IBM/PC BASIC, as well as the IBM/PC operating system, PC-DOS, and the generic version, MS-DOS. It is also a leading provider of CP/M and Z80 plug-in cards for Apple computers (the Softcard™).

Almost every other major computer language is available in a CP/M-compatible version, and some of them have spawned dedicated users groups of their own. These groups also have public domain libraries, many of which interlock with the CP/M collections and are available from both places. (The C Users Group, the Pascal-Z group, and the Forth group are especially well represented.) You'll find a number of major language-specific users groups described in Chapter 4, so we won't discuss them here. There is one BASIC point to be made, however, and that concerns the difference between EBASIC and CBASIC2 on the one hand and MBASIC on the other.

MBASIC works the same way most other BASICs do: You load BASIC and write and run programs. EBASIC and CBASIC2, in contrast, create "semi-compiled" programs. The process is as follows: 1. You write a BASIC program with a word processor or line editor. 2. You run EBASIC (BAS.COM) against the program to create a hexadecimal file called PROG.INT. (Though the expression is not strictly accurate, this is sometimes called "compiling" the program.) 3. To execute the program, you must then use RUN.COM (or CRUN.COM for BASICC2) and PROG.INT. The final step must be repeated each time the program is run. You will find public domain CP/M software written in (and requiring) both of these languages.

FreeTip: For more information on CP/M, lists of CP/M users groups, and information and announcements from Digital Research, you may want to look at two new online features available via The Source (see Chapter 9) and CompuServe (see Chapter 8). To access these DRI-sponsored features, type *MICROLINE* at the Source Command Level (or follow the menus to the "Creating and Computing" section), or type *DRI* at any CompuServe exclamation prompt.

Appendix C
Free CP/M Software Distribution Points and Club Contacts

To improve the efficiency of distributing free CP/M software, SIG/M has established a number of regional distribution points. We have edited the list to include at least one contact point per listed state. To obtain the complete list, send $2 for U.S. mailing, or $2.50 for foreign mailing, to SIG/M at the address under New Jersey, below. It may be more convenient for you, however, to contact one of the individuals listed here. If you are not interested in CP/M but merely want to locate a nearby users group, these people may be able to help you.

The official SIG/M Regional Distribution Points are those names marked with three asterisks (***). These individuals will be able to supply you with the same 8-inch disks you can obtain from SIG/M, and most will have the entire SIG/M library in their possession. SIG/M would like to establish more distribution points, so if you're interested in taking on this responsibility, contact Mr. Robert Todd at 1121 Briarwood, Bensalem, PA 19020; (215) 752-4604. SIG/M strongly advises computer owners to use its distribution points whenever possible instead of ordering directly through SIG/M headquarters. (If your state or country is not included here, see the following supplemental list prepared from material in the DRI section of CompuServe.)

Here is the paragraph with which SIG/M begins its list of distribution points:

> The following organizations or individuals can provide copies of SIG/M volumes. Their charges, as far as we know, are the same as SIG/M itself ($1/Vol copying charge or $5/Vol with disk furnished, plus shipping).

SIG/M Distribution Points

California

Kelley Smith
CP/M-Net
3055 Waco Avenue
Simi Valley, CA 93063

8-inch, Osborne, Kaypro

Jim Ayres
Apple CPMUG
Small Computer Users Group—Marin
301 Poplar Street
Mill Valley, CA 94941

8-inch, Apple, Otrona

Charlie Foster***
Pascal/Z Users Group
SIG/M West Coast Coordinator
7962 Center Parkway
Sacramento, CA 95823

Trevor Marshall***
3423 Hill Canyon Avenue
Thousand Oaks, CA 91360

Colorado

A. J. Lundquist***
Denver Amateur Computer Society
Box 633
Broomfield, CO 80020

Connecticut

Henry B. Rothberg
1 Laticrete Park North
Bethany, CT 06525

8-inch, North Star, Vector

Florida

John Irwin
Miami Amateur Computer Group
9159 S.W. 77th Avenue
Miami, FL

Georgia

Charlie Wells***
Atlanta Computer Society
465 Northgate Pass
Atlanta, GA

Hawaii

Jim Yuen
919 Luna Helu Street
Kailua, HI

Illinois

Jim Mills
CACHE/CPMUG
824 Jordan Place
Rockford, IL 61108

Louisiana

Home Branch
Heath UG of New Orleans
703 Valence
New Orleans, LA 70115

Massachusetts

Dave Mitton***
New England Computer Society
13 Swan Street
Arlington, MA 02174

Michigan

Keith Peterson***
Box 309
Clawson, MI 48017

Minnesota

Secor/Thomas
CPMUG of Minnesota
854 120th Lane NW
Coon Rapids, MN 55434

New Hampshire

Steve Peterfreund
Microprocessor Association
Box 3438
Nashua, NH

DEC Rainbow

New Jersey

SIG/M Main Office
Box 97
Iselin, NJ 08830

New York

Henry Kee
SIG/M Editor/Librarian
NYACC
42-24 Colden Street
Flushing, NY 11355

North Carolina

Elliot Wheeler
Box 713
Mt. Holly, NC

Ohio

J.C. Kramer
CP/M-ASCO of Columbus
Box 28355
Columbus, OH 43228

Osborne, Xerox, Omikron

Pennsylvania

Robert Todd***
Zenith/Heath Coordinator
1121 Briarwood
Bensalem, PA 19020

Rhode Island

Dean Kelcher
11-B Sandy Point Road
Portsmouth, RI

South Carolina

Jim Colligan
157 MacGregor Drive
Summerville, SC

Texas

Fred Pfafman***
2320 Heather Hill Lane
Plano, TX 75075

Al Whitney***
SIG/M-South Central Coordinator
2003 Hammerwood
Missouri City, TX 77489

Virginia

Stan Levine
CP/M Users Group of Washington, D.C.
2053 North Abington Street
Arlington, VA 22207

Dave Holmes
Digital Interest Group in Tidewater
Box 1708
Grafton, VA 23692

Washington

George Blat
Northwest Computer Society
8016 188th Street SW
Edmonds, WA 98020

Dave Rabbers-Ballard
CP/M Users Group
6551 16th Avenue NW
Seattle, WA 98117

SIG/M International

Australia

Bill Bolton***
Box 80
Newport Beach, NSW 2106

Canada

Dave Bowerman***
West Coast Computer Society
Box 4031
Vancouver, BC V6B 3Z4

Jud Newell***
4691 Dundas Street West
Islington, Ontario M9A 1A7

Japan

Fukuoka Toshio
Futabacho 1-15-4
Tomakomai, Hokkaido

Netherlands

Hank Berkoudt
CP/M Groep
Hesselskamp 4
Rotterdam 3085 SM

United Kingdom

J.D. Millne
Inpholink Ltd.
Front Street West
Bedlington Northumberland
England NE22 5UB

Derek Fordred
CPMUG of UK
72 Mill Road
Hawley, Dartford
Kent, England DA2 7RZ

Venezuela

Hans Stauffer
Caracas Computer Club
Apartado 66394
Caracas 1061A

or

Hans Stauffer
M-105
Box 520010
Jet International Airport
Miami, FL 33159

Singapore

Alex Chan
745 Mountbatten Road
Singapore 1543

Maresh Kapoor
Patel Computer Systems PTE
27058 OCBC Centre
Chulia Street
Singapore 0104

South Africa

Peter Briggs
Transvaal Amateur Computer Club
Box 2513
Kempton Park 1620

The Digital Research Incorporated Users Group List

The following list of CP/M users groups was developed from information found in the special area which Digital Research, Inc., (DRI) sponsors on the CompuServe system. You can reach this section by typing *GO DRI* at the CompuServe exclamation prompt. If you are a Source subscriber, the equivalent DRI feature is MICRONET. Type *MICRONET* at the Source Command Level. DRI has no official connection with the following groups.

The list has been edited to mesh with the SIG/M list above, with the goal of providing contact points for states and countries not on that list. Please note that the individuals and groups listed below are not official SIG/M distribution points for public domain CP/M software, though many of them will be able to supply it or put you in touch with someone who can.

North America

Alaska

Dennis Harris
Juneau CP/M Users Group
361 Distin #107
Juneau, AK 99801

Oregon

CP/M Users Group Northwest
1346 NE 28th Street
Portland, OR 98323

Wisconsin

Michael von Schneidemesser
CP/M Users
Department of AG Economics
427 Lorch Street—B3
University of Wisconson
Madison, WI 53715

International

England

David Powys-Libbe
CP/M Users Group (U.K.)
11 Sun Street
Finsbury Square
London, England EC2M 2PS

Ireland

CP/M Ireland
Gardner House
Ballsbridge
Dublin 4, Ireland

Germany

Guenter Musstoph
PascaL/MT Users Group
Schiemmelmannstr 37G
D-2070 Ahrensburg
West Germany

Japan

CP/Club
c/o MSA KOBAYASHI or NISHIJIMA
6th AY Building 3-2-2,
Kitaaoyama, Minato Ku
Tokyo 107, Japan

Glossary

Explanations of computer terms are rather like the threads you might pull from an article of clothing. Some are discrete units that can be pulled out cleanly, but others run throughout the entire garment and produce far more cordage in the form of subsidiary explanations before the job is done. You will find a complete unraveling in *How to Buy Software*. Here we will focus on just those terms you are most likely to encounter when reviewing free software catalogues, contacting users groups and other points of access, or otherwise moving about in the free software world. If you don't find the term you're looking for here, check the Index.

acoustic coupler: A type of modem designed to transmit and receive data through a telephone handset. The handset is placed in a cradle consisting of two rubber cups, one for the earpiece and one for the mouthpiece. Sometimes called a "data set." Used mainly in offices, hotel rooms, and other places where a direct modem-phone line connection is not possible.

ANSI: American National Standards Institute, an organization of computer professionals responsible for setting standards for everything from floppy disk quality to computer languages.

ASCII: Acronym for American Standard Code for Information Interchange. Pronounced "as-key." Used in virtually all personal computer data communications, the ASCII code set consists of 128 numbers ranging from *0* to *127*, each of which has been assigned a particular meaning. ASCII is a seven-bit code (seven binary bits are required to represent each number). However, because each character is usually transmitted with a parity bit, it is sometimes referred to as an eight-bit code.

assembler: A program that translates English-like assembly language instructions into the 1s and 0s of machine language. A program written in assembly language must be assembled before it can be run on a computer. "Assembler" is sometimes used in place of "assembly language," as in "That program is written in Z80 assembler."

A single assembly language instruction typically translates into only one or two machine language instructions. A "macro assembler" gives a programmer more bang for the byte since it allows him to write a single "macro instruction" that will be translated into several ordinary assembly language instructions before being converted to machine language. Some free programs require the use of the appropriate macro assembler since they include instructions a standard assembler cannot translate.

auto-dial/auto-answer: A feature offered by more expensive modems. The auto-dial feature allows you to dial your telephone by typing the numbers from the keyboard. This feature also lets you use communications software to record phone numbers on disk and dial each by pressing a single button.

baud: A unit for measuring the speed of data transmission. Technically baud rates refer to the number of times the communications line changes states each second. Strictly speaking, baud and bits per second are not identical measurements, but most nontechnical people use the terms interchangably.

Bell-compatible: A term used to describe modems. The term means that the audio tones issued by the modem meet Bell Telephone standards. Variants of the term include Bell 103–compatible (standard for 300 baud modems) and Bell 212A–compatible (standard for full duplex, 1200 baud modems).

binary file: File containing machine language as opposed to simple text. The file may be a directly executable program such as those created by compilers and assemblers. Or it may be a BASIC or other program that has not been recorded in a simple text format. Word processing programs usually store their text in binary files containing both text and machine language codes. Because a special procedure is needed to transfer binary files over the telephone, it is important to use communications software that offers this capability.

bit: Acronym for "*bi*nary digi*t*." The smallest unit of information in the computer world. Eight bits together are called a "byte," and four bits are called a "nibble."

boot: Short for "bootstrap," a reference to a computer's ability to "pull itself up by its bootstraps" as it automatically loads in the operating system software. In the CP/M world "cold boot" refers to turning the power on and loading the operating system, while "warm boot" refers to reorienting the system by hitting <CONTROL>-<C>.This must be done whenever you change disks. Generally, to "boot a program" means to load it into the computer and begin running it.

buffer: Any portion of your computer's internal memory that is set aside by a program as a temporary "holding tank." In a word processing program, the software may create a "type-ahead" or "keyboard buffer" to allow you to type faster than the computer can display characters on the screen. It may also create a buffer to hold the blocks of text you want to move from one page to another. A communications program may set aside a "capture buffer" into which you can pour incoming data instead of waiting for the printer to print it.

bug: Broadly speaking, any kind of malfunction, whether of hardware or software. One explanation for the origin of this term involves the doorbell-like relay circuits that were used to create the first computers. This type of switch works by causing a bar of metal to physically move toward an electromagnet. It is thought that a moth or some other insect at one time managed to get in the way of the contact and cause the computer to malfunction. Whether true or not, the logbook for one of the early computers built under the aegis of the Department of the Navy has a desiccated moth pasted into it with a notation in the computer operator's handwriting that he had found a bug in the system.

byte: Eight binary digits. Because it takes eight bits to represent a single letter or other character using the ASCII code set, the word *byte* is often used synonymously with *character*.

carriage return: Whatever results when you hit your <ENTER> key.

CBBS: Computer Bulletin Board System. The name of what is generally acknowledged to be the first bulletin board program (written by Ward Christensen and Randy Suess).

Christensen protocol: The XMODEM file transfer protocol explained in Appendix A.

co-processor: A second microprocessor chip or "brain" in a computer. Some co-processors are designed to handle special functions under the control of the main processor. Others are designed to take control of the computer when it is operating in a certain mode. Best example is the Z80 co-processor many computer owners add to their systems in order to run CP/M.

code: Computer programming. Could be BASIC, Pascal, assembly language, or any other type of programming.

compiler: Special software to translate BASIC and other computer programs into machine language. Compiled programs run much faster, but the compiled version cannot be examined or changed.

CPU: Central Processing Unit. The main microchip or "brain" in a computer.

CRC: Cyclic Redundancy Check. Technique for making sure a given block or quantity of information has been accurately read, written, or transmitted. An important component in communications error-checking protocols, but used internally as well when computers read or write to disk.

database: Any collection of related information, like the addresses and phone numbers in your little black book. Also, short for "online database," such as the collections of information maintained by CompuServe and The Source.

DB-25 connector: A 25-pin or 25-socket plug used to connect a computer to a modem or serial printer.

diode: The manner in which most programmers, and everyone else for that matter, would prefer to leave this life.

documentation: The instructions for using a program, computer, or piece of computer equipment.

DOM: Disk of the Month. The International Apple Core and other users groups prepare a disk of free software each month and make it available to their members.

DOS: Disk Operating System. Pronounced "doss." The special software that insulates a program from the demands of your computer's hardware. Thanks to DOS, a program does not have to worry about the kind of disk drives, display, or other equipment your computer uses. A DOS must be written for a particular microprocessor chip. CP/M-80 is a DOS that runs on computers built around a Z80 chip, for example, while MS-DOS (IBM/PC DOS) runs on computers equipped with an 8088 chip.

downloading: Transferring computer programs and other information via a communications link. With a communicating computer you can download programs from CompuServe, for example. The term also refers to transferring programs from one floppy disk format to another. Thus a "downloading service" can transfer free CP/M software from an 8-inch disk to a 5¼-inch disk that you can use in your machine.

DRI: Digital Research, Incorporated. The creators of the CP/M operating system and other commercial software products.

flippy disk: A regular floppy disk that has information recorded in a single-sided format on both sides. Requires the cutting of a second write-protect notch in the cardboard envelope that holds the disk itself. Not available commercially. Strictly do-it-yourself.

hex or hexadecimal: This is the base 16 numbering system. In the decimal system there are ten digits (*0* through *9*) to use in expressing a number. In "hex" there are those ten digits plus six letters (*A*, *B*, *C*, *D*, *E*, *F*). The main advantage of the hexadecimal system is that it is easier to read and deal with than the 1s and 0s of the binary system.

It also lets you express the same number in less space. For example, the decimal number 14 can be expressed in binary as 1110 or in hex as E. Similarly, a number that would require sixteen 1s and 0s to express in binary form can be written in hex as "89AD."

hires or hi-rez: Short for "high resolution."

homebrew: Originally, any computer that was designed and built from scratch using off-the-shelf parts. Later, any computer sold in solder-it-yourself kit form. The term is rapidly receding into the "MITSy" past of personal computer history to take its place beside the legends of young men building best-selling computers in their parents' garage.

keyword and keyword search: A single word you feel is likely to be included in any database file on a particular subject. A keyword is usually a word that comes as close as possible to describing the topic or piece of information you are looking for. In a keyword search, the database computer scans its files looking for a match between the keyword and the words in the file. Matches are often called "hits."

kilobyte: A unit of 1,000 bytes, or more precisely, a unit of 1,024 bytes. But no one ever worries about the 24 bytes. One kilobyte or "K" of memory can hold 1,000 characters or about half a double-spaced, typewritten page.

line feed: A special signal that causes the paper in a printer or text on a screen to advance one line.

listing: A printout of a computer program. To get a listing of a program, you must have its source code. Since most public domain software is supplied in source code form (instead of being compiled or assembled), you can usually change or modify the public domain programs to suit your needs.

machine language: The only language a computer understands. Represented by 1s and 0s, machine language consists of nothing but binary digits (bits). Machine language programs are directly executable, meaning you can simply type the name of the program to make it run.

media: Floppy disks, cassette tapes, or any other material used to store computer programs and information.

megabyte or "meg": A unit of one million bytes (actually, a thousand kilobytes or 1,024,000 bytes). Abbreviated "MB."

megahertz: A measurement of the speed with which a microprocessor acts on each instruction. Equivalent to one clock pulse, cycle, or instruction per millionth of a second. Abbreviated "MHz." The higher the megahertz of the CPU, the faster your programs will run. The only time you need to consider a CPU's megahertz rating is when you are equipping a computer with a co-processor and a choice of speeds is available. This is often the case when adding CP/M capabilities to a machine.

microprocessor: The microchip a computer is built around. The microprocessor or CPU is the computer's brain. It is the only component that does any real computing, and everything else exists to support it. Computer programs must be written for specific microprocessors, which is why you cannot run an Apple program on an IBM unless you equip the IBM with the microprocessor used in Apple computers.

mod: Slang term for "modification." Because most public domain programs can be altered by their users, you will frequently hear of people "adding mods" to a piece of software to give it additional features or capabilities or to customize it for some purpose.

modem: *Mo*dulator/*Dem*odulator. The interface box or board that translates your computer's signals into sound so they can be sent over the telephone. A modem on the other end "demodulates" the sound, converting it back into computer signals, before feeding the information to its host machine.

multi-tasking: The ability of a computer to run more than one program at a time. With special software, a computer's internal memory can be divided into two or more segments, all served by the same microprocessor. You can run a different program in each segment simultaneously, meaning that your computer can be serving as a bulletin board and answering callers while you use your word processing software to do something else.

nibble: Half a byte, or four bits.

null modem cable: A cable designed to connect two computers via the serial ports that are ordinarily connected to a modem. A null modem cable "fools" each system into thinking that it is actually talking to a modem instead of another computer. Offers a good way to overcome free-software disk-format problems if you can bring together two computers in the same room.

object code: A machine language program. Object code is produced by an assembler or a compiler operating on a source code program. A BASIC program consists of source code. A compiled BASIC program consists of object code.

online: In computer communications, "online" means "connected to a remote database." But the term also means "when you are using a program." Thus an "online help function" is help that is available while you are actually using your spreadsheet or word processor or some other program. The help information exists on the program disk, which usually must be "online" (inserted in a disk drive) for you to take advantage of it.

originate/answer: The two modes of operation for a modem. In any communications arrangement, one modem must be set to "originate" and the other must be set to "answer."

overhead: The amount of memory occupied by a program of any sort. If you have 128K of memory in your machine, and the program you want to use occupies 32K when it loads in, 32K is its overhead. Overhead is significant because the more memory occupied by a program, the less "room" there is for you to use when working with the program.

patch: A relatively small piece of computer programming added to a large program to customize or modify it in some way.

PD: Abbreviation for "public domain."

power down: To turn off your computer.

power up: To turn on your computer.

protocol file transfer: A procedure for accurately transferring files from one computer to another using some form of error-checking protocol. The best-known protocol is XMODEM, but many others exist. Both computers must use the same protocol.

public domain: Webster's says it best: "The realm embracing property rights that belong to the community at large, are unprotected by copyright or patent, and are subject to appropriation by anyone." In other words, free software. There is no law against selling public domain software, but those who try it will find that "the community at large" will enforce this prohibition.

RCPM: Remote CP/M system. Accessible by telephone, such systems serve as repositories for a vast array of public domain CP/M software. Anyone with a CP/M system running MODEM 7 or any other XMODEM-supporting program can dial up an RCPM system and download software at no charge.

ring-back: Technique used by some BBS SysOps to avoid installing a separate telephone line for their computer. To use a BBS with a ring-back specification, dial the number, let it ring once, hang up, then redial with your computer ready to communicate.

RS-232-C: A standard developed by The Electronics Industry Association (EIA) specifying what signals and voltages will be used to transmit data from a computer to a modem. The full standard covers some 25 pins on the RS-232-C plug interface found on a serial card, but most personal computers make use of only a handful of these. The *C* is often dropped from this term.

SASE: Self-Addressed, Stamped Envelope. What you should include whenever corresponding with a computer users group or other organization.

serial interface or serial card: A circuit board installed in a computer or word processor designed to convert the machine's internal parallel (eight-bits-at-a-time) communications into serial communications (one-bit-at-a-time). The card includes an RS-232-C interface plug to accept the cable that connects your machine with your modem.

SIG: Special Interest Group.

source code: See "object code."

string: A word or sentence or any other continuous "string of characters." In a computer program, a string is information that the computer is supposed to treat as text. A string is thus usually set off from regular program instructions by single or double quotation marks. For example, if you were to boot a program and see the sentence "Welcome to Tommy's Holiday Camp," you would know these words exist within the program as a character string, preceded by a programming instruction that tells the computer to "display the following text on the screen."

support: An elastic term that means "designed to work with" as "This program supports the Hayes Smartmodem"; or "includes" as "Our program offers XMODEM support"; or "aid, comfort, and assistance," as "You're on your own with public domain software since it is not formally supported by anyone."

SysOp: Prounounced "sis-op." The system operator. The individual who operates and maintains a computer bulletin board system.

system: Your computer and all of its associated equipment. Also, the operating system software your computer uses. Thus when you "go out to the system," you leave a program and return to DOS.

terminal program: Communications software.

third party: The manufacturer of your computer is the party of the first part and you're the party of the second part. A third party supplier is a company offering equipment or software designed to work with the products you bought from somebody else.

UART: Acronym for *Universal Asynchronous Receiver/Transmitter*. Pronounced "you-art." This is the microchip responsible for converting parallel signals into serial signals and vice versa. It is the heart of a serial interface card.

upload: To send information over the telphone lines to another computer directly from your floppy disk or cassette tape player, as opposed to typing at your keyboard.

user supported: Refers to software that is offered with the suggestion that you make a voluntary contribution to its author. Abbreviated "U/S," this term means the same thing as Freeware™ (discussed in Chapter 11).

volume: A rather inexact measure of quantities of free software. A single volume is one standard disk full of programs. The size and capacity of a "standard" disk varies with the computer and the accepted conventions of its associated community of users. Many sources have discarded the term altogether and simply refer to individual disk numbers instead of volume numbers.

winchester: A hard disk system. So called because "Winchester" was the code word IBM used when it developed the first hard disk drive.

X-ON/X-OFF: These are start/stop signals issued by two communicating computers to make sure that each is ready to send or receive at the proper time. This protocol is usually built into the communications software, and in most cases you won't be aware that the signals are being sent and received. However, you can generate each signal yourself to stop or start an onscreen scroll when accessing most databases. X-ON is generated by entering a <CONTROL>-<Q>, and X-OFF by entering a <CONTROL>-<S>.

Index

About the Author

Alfred Glossbrenner is president of FireCrystal Communications, a worldwide producer of computer documentation, films, and corporate communications for industry and science. Based in Bucks County, Pennsylvania, FireCrystal and Mr. Glossbrenner make extensive use of personal computers, word processors, and a wide range of online electronic databases to pursue their goal of making today's high technology accessible, understandable, and above all, useful to everyone. *How to Get Free Software* is Mr. Glossbrenner's tenth book.

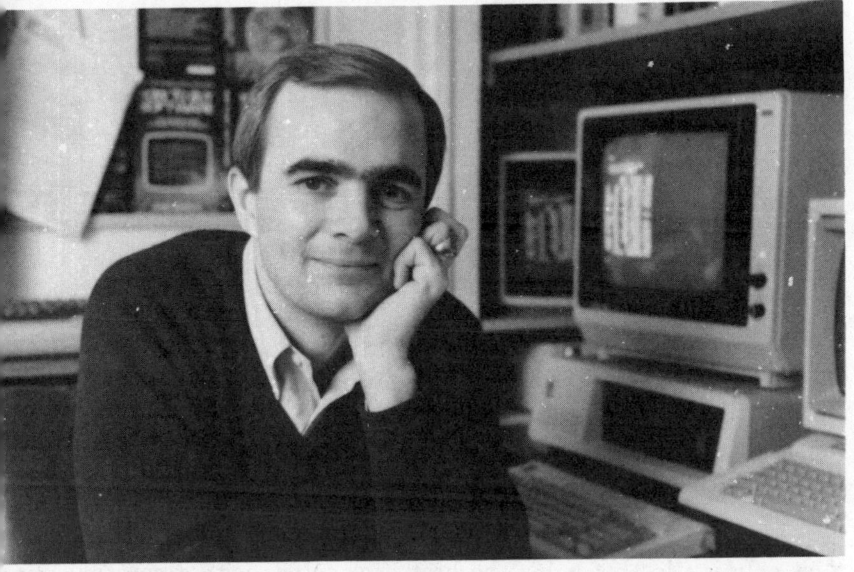

J. T. Miller

The author welcomes comments and suggestions about this book. They should be mailed to Alfred Glossbrenner, c/o St. Martin's Press, 175 Fifth Avenue, New York, NY 10010. Reader comments can also be sent to the author, via communicating computer, at the following electronic addresses:

Source: TCS772
CIS: 70065,745

. . . At Bookstores Everywhere

648 pages, Appendices, Glossary, Software Buyer's Quick Reference Checklists, Index. $14.95 paperback.

A Main Selection of the Small Computer Book Club.

A Book-of-the-Month Club/Science Alternate Selection.

"*How to Buy Software* is truly awesome. I'm sure it will set the standard for some time to come. The whole concept and execution is just what is needed in the field."

—Tom Beeston
co-author of *Hooking In*

"Something for everyone from novice to veteran. The novice should read from cover to cover to gain an understanding of how both the hardware and software operate and interface."

—Lee A. Hillard
MICOM Software

"Quite simply, excellent. *How to Buy Software* belongs in every computer owner's library."

—Jim Cambron, publisher,
The On-Line Computer Telephone Directory